# DEPONENCY AND MORPHOLOGICAL MISMATCHES

PROCEEDINGS OF THE BRITISH ACADEMY · 145

# DEPONENCY AND MORPHOLOGICAL MISMATCHES

Edited by
MATTHEW BAERMAN,
GREVILLE G. CORBETT, DUNSTAN BROWN,
AND ANDREW HIPPISLEY

*Published for* THE BRITISH ACADEMY
*by* OXFORD UNIVERSITY PRESS

*Oxford University Press, Great Clarendon Street, Oxford* OX2 6DP

*Oxford New York*

*Auckland Cape Town Dar es Salaam Hong Kong Karachi
Kuala Lumpur Madrid Melbourne Mexico City Nairobi
New Delhi Singapore Taipei Tokyo Toronto*

*With offices in
Argentina Austria Brazil Chile Czech Republic France Greece
Guatemala Hungary Italy Japan Poland Portugal Singapore
South Korea Switzerland Thailand Turkey Ukraine Vietnam*

*Published in the United States
by Oxford University Press Inc., New York*

*British Library Cataloguing in Publication Data
Data available*

*Library of Congress Cataloging in Publication Data
Data available*

*Typeset by
J&L Composition, Filey, North Yorkshire
Printed in Great Britain
on acid-free paper by
The Cromwell Press Limited
Trowbridge, Wilts*

*ISBN 978–0–19–726410–2
ISSN 0068–1202*

# Contents

Notes on Contributors                                                          vii

Editors' Preface                                                                ix

List of Abbreviations                                                          xiii

1. Morphological Typology of Deponency                                           1
   MATTHEW BAERMAN

2. Deponency, Syncretism, and What Lies Between                                 21
   GREVILLE G. CORBETT

3. Extending Deponency: Implications for Morphological
   Mismatches                                                                   45
   ANDREW SPENCER

4. A Non-Canonical Pattern of Deponency and Its Implications                    71
   GREGORY T. STUMP

5. Deponency in the Diachrony of Greek                                          97
   NIKOLAOS LAVIDAS AND DIMITRA PAPANGELI

6. Deponency in Latin                                                          127
   ZHENG XU, MARK ARONOFF, AND FRANK ANSHEN

7. Declarative Deponency: A Network Morphology Account
   of Morphological Mismatches                                                 145
   ANDREW HIPPISLEY

8. The Limits of Deponency: A Chukotko-centric Perspective                     175
   JONATHAN DAVID BOBALJIK

9. Slouching Towards Deponency: A Family of Mismatches
   in the Bantu Verb Stem                                                      203
   JEFFREY GOOD

10. Spanish Pseudoplurals: Phonological Cues in the Acquisition
    of a Syntax-Morphology Mismatch                                            231
    RICARDO BERMÚDEZ-OTERO

11.  Pseudo-Argument Affixes in Iwaidja and Ilgar: A Case of
     Deponent Subject and Object Agreement                        271
     NICHOLAS EVANS

12.  How Safe Are Our Analyses?                                   297
     P. H. MATTHEWS

Subject Index                                                     317
Language Index                                                    319
Author Index                                                      321

# Notes on Contributors

**Frank Anshen**'s (State University of New York, Stony Brook) most recent research has involved constructing and validating a model of lexical storage and retrieval of morphologically complex words.

**Mark Aronoff**'s (State University of New York, Stony Brook) research touches on almost all aspects of morphology and its relations to phonology, syntax, semantics, and psycholinguistics. From 1995 to 2001, he served as Editor of *Language*, the Journal of the Linguistic Society of America.

**Matthew Baerman** is a research fellow in the Surrey Morphology Group, University of Surrey. His work focuses on the typology and diachrony of inflectional morphology.

**Ricardo Bermúdez-Otero** is Lecturer in Linguistics and English Language at the University of Manchester. His main area of interest is phonology, with particular attention to the morphology–phonology interface and to phonological change. He is the author of the forthcoming *Stratal Optimality Theory* (Oxford University Press).

**Jonathan David Bobaljik** is an Associate Professor of Linguistics at the University of Connecticut, Storrs. His research interests include morphology and syntax, with an areal focus on Arctic languages. Since 1993, he has conducted fieldwork on the Chukotko-Kamchatkan language Itelmen.

**Greville G. Corbett** (University of Surrey) is a member of the Surrey Morphology Group, and works on morphology, syntax, and typology. He recently published *Agreement* with Cambridge University Press, and is currently working on the typology of morphosyntactic features.

**Nicholas Evans** teaches linguistics at the University of Melbourne and is a specialist in Australian Aboriginal languages (having published grammars of Kayardild (1995, Mouton de Gruyter) and Bininj Gun-wok (2003, Pacific Linguistics) and linguistic typology.

**Jeff Good** is Assistant Professor of Linguistics at the University at Buffalo. He has done research on Benue-Congo languages, Saramaccan creole, and Chechen.

**Andrew Hippisley** is assistant professor in syntax at the University of Kentucky. He is co-author of the morphological framework Network Morphology, and his research is primarily in computational modelling of the lexicon using defaults. He has also worked on basic colour terms in Slavonic.

**Nikolaos Lavidas** (MA, Ph.D. in Linguistics, University of Athens) has published articles on Diachronic Syntax, Argument Structure and the Lexicon, and Morphosyntax.

**Peter Matthews** is Emeritus Professor of Linguistics at Cambridge University, and author of many books on linguistics, including *Morphology, and Grammatical Theory in the United States from Bloomfield to Chomsky*.

**Dimitra Papangeli**: MA University College London, Ph.D. Utrecht University, visiting post-doc École Normale Supérieure (Netherlands Organisation for Scientific Research grant), post-doc University of Athens, currently occupied at the Academy of Athens, Greece.

**Andrew Spencer**'s (University of Essex) main research interests are in general morphological theory, morphological and lexical representations, and the morphology-syntax interface. He is the author of *Morphological Theory* (1991, Blackwell) and co-editor of *Handbook of Morphology* (1998, Blackwell).

**Gregory Stump** (Ph.D. 1981, Ohio State) is a professor of linguistics at the University of Kentucky. He is the author of *Inflectional Morphology* (Cambridge University Press, 2001) and of numerous articles on inflectional systems; in his work, he has argued extensively that inflectional paradigms must play a central role in grammatical theory and in morphological typology.

**Zheng Xu** is a Ph.D. candidate in the Department of Linguistics, Stony Brook University. He received his BA degree in English from Fudan University, Shanghai, in 2000. His research interests include morphology, phonology, historical linguistics, and Chinese linguistics.

# Editors' Preface

## 1. Introduction

THIS VOLUME IS A COLLECTION OF PAPERS on deponency from a cross-linguistic perspective, probably the first of its kind. Since deponency is not usually treated as a question for general linguistics, some words are in order about what we mean by the term. Briefly, deponency is a notion first applied to Latin, describing a particular kind of mismatch between morphosyntactic values and morphological form. The deponent verbs of Latin are largely passive in their morphology, but from the point of view of syntax and semantics are treated as active verbs. Consider first the normal verb *amant/amantur* in (1).

(1)  qu-ae       ex    se      nat-os      ita   **am-ant**    ad  quoddam
     which-N.PL  from  self.ABL born-ACC.PL thus  love-3PL     to  certain.ACC.SG
     tempus      et    ab      e-is        ita   **am-antur**
     time.ACC.SG and   from    them-ABL.PL thus  love-3PL.PASSIVE

     'which [animals] thus love their offspring for a certain time and thus are loved by them.' (Cicero, *De amicitia*, chapter VIII)

Contrast this with the deponent verb *hortantur* in (2).

(2)  me=que       **hort-antur**          ut    magn-o         anim-o
     me.ACC=and   exhort-3PL.PASSIVE      that  great-ABL.SG   spirit-ABL.SG
                  (=ACTIVE)
     sim
     be.1SG.SBJV

     'and they exhort me to be of good courage.' (Cicero, *Epistulae ad Atticum*, book 11, letter 6)[1]

In (1) the verb 'love' illustrates the regular alternation between the active form *amant* and the passive form *amantur*. In (2), the verb 'exhort', *hortantur,* has the same ending as the passive *amantur*, but is a transitive active verb. The alternation in (1) is productive, available to any transitive verb, while deponent verbs such as *hortor* are lexically specified. Thus, while passive morphology has a clear function for the majority of verbs, in some cases it has the opposite function. While traditionally seen as a problem peculiar to Latin

---

[1] This example was found using the Perseus Lookup Tool via <http://www.perseus.tufts.edu>.

—and, by extension, to other older Indo-European languages—the idea that morphological forms can give the 'wrong' signal about their function can be applied to other languages, and has broad implications for the study of morphology and its relationship to syntax. This recognition prompted the Surrey Morphology Group's research into *extended* deponency, made possible by a grant from the Economic and Social Research Council (United Kingdom), under grant number RES-000-23-0375.

This project in turn led to the conference from which the papers in the present volume have been drawn. The British Academy generously provided additional support, which among other things provided for bursaries for postgraduate students. We extend our thanks to the staff of the Academy, and in particular to Angela Pusey and Joanne Blore for making the conference the success that it was, and also to Lisa Mack for help in the preparation of the papers.

## 2. Overview of the Volume

The first chapter by Baerman offers a definition of deponency, extending it along several parameters to embrace a wide range of morphological mismatches. In the next chapter Corbett explores the boundaries between deponency and syncretism, which turn out to be surprisingly fluid, yielding phenomena that are difficult to classify with the analytical framework that we normally work with. Spencer, in the third chapter, concentrates on categorical mismatches, where a word has the morphological characteristics of one word class but the syntactic characteristics of another. The next three chapters deal with the older Indo-European languages. In his chapter Stump shows that Sanskrit deponent paradigms suggest a distinction between form- and property-deponency, and require us to introduce the notion of the context-dependent morphome. Lavidas and Papangeli trace the development of deponents in Greek. Verbs, or in some cases only parts of their paradigms, enter and exit the class of deponents across the various stages of Greek. Significantly, there is no apparent semantic motivation to these fluctuations. Xu, Aronoff, and Anshen show that Latin deponents, as a lexical class, can partially be described in terms of their semantic properties, though their morphological realization remains uninformative. The two chapters which follow the classical languages pick up the thread of formal analytical work already found in the chapter by Stump. Hippisley's paper is a study of the implications of deponency for formal morphological representation, providing a detailed implemented analysis of a variety of deponent paradigms in the default inheritance-based framework of Network Morphology, and Bobaljik's formal analysis looks beyond lexically specified deponency to environments where apparently spurious morphological marking is induced by a certain syntactic configuration. The subsequent papers extend the scope to other morphosyntactic features and to other languages. Patterns of deponency within a single language family are the topic of Good's paper, with a focus that is more typological than diachronic. He looks at the morphology of diathesis alternations in Bantu languages (e.g. causative and applicative, in addition to passive), pointing out instances where the morphological form is at odds with the argument structure. Bermúdez-Otero's paper examines nominal morphology in Spanish, where some words are morphologically but not morphosyntactically plural: he argues that this phenomenon arises during acquisition through the interaction of weighted parsing preferences grounded on morphological and phonological properties of the Spanish lexicon. In the penultimate chapter Evans, a consultant on the extended deponency project, looks at pronominal affixation in Iwaidja, a non Pama-Nyungan language of Australia. In this language, some verbs mark verbal arguments which are not syntactically present. The diachronic origins of these deponent paradigms are traced through comparison with related languages of the Iwaidjan family. Finally, Matthews looks back on some of the key issues, in particular pointing out some inherent difficulties in the analysis of deponency.

# Abbreviations

| | |
|---|---|
| (X) | the feature value 'x' is inherent to the lexeme, and has no overt expression (e.g. French *plage* would be glossed as 'beach(f)') |
| [X] | the feature value 'x' has no overt morphological expression (e.g. English *dog* would be glossed as 'dog[sg]') |
| X > Y | in a transitive verb, 'x' is the subject and 'y' is the object |
| 1, 2, 3 | first, second, third person (but see below) |
| 1. . . 12 | noun class (Bantu) |
| I. . . IV | noun class (Daghestanian) |
| . . . | indicates that there is fixed vegetable-class prefix, followed where appropriate by pronominal affix material, then the verb stem, which is shown after the ellipsis (Ilgar and Iwaidja) |
| A | transitive subject |
| AVL | ablative |
| ABS | absolutive |
| ACC | accusative |
| ALL | allative |
| ANTIP | antipassive |
| AOR | aorist |
| APPL | applicative |
| AUG | augment |
| C | common class |
| CAUS | causative |
| DAT | dative |
| DEM | demonstrative |
| DIM | diminutive |
| DIR | direct |
| DU | dual |
| ERG | ergative |
| EXCL | exclusive |
| F | feminine |
| FUT | future |
| FV | final vowel |
| GEN | genitive |

| HON | honorific |
|---|---|
| IMPRF | imperfect |
| INCL | inclusive |
| IND | indicative |
| INF | infinitive |
| INS | instrumental |
| IPFV | imperfective |
| IPV | imperative |
| IRR | irrealis |
| ITER | iterative |
| LOC | locative |
| M | masculine |
| MEDIOPASS | mediopassive |
| MID | middle |
| MIS | miscellaneous class |
| N | neuter |
| N- | non- (e.g. npst for non-past) |
| NMZ | nominalizer |
| NOM | nominative |
| OBJ | object |
| OBL | oblique |
| OPT | optative |
| PART | partitive |
| PASS | passive |
| PCL(S) | particle(s) |
| PFV | perfective |
| PL | plural |
| PLUPRF | pluperfect |
| PREP | prepositional |
| PRF | perfect |
| PROG | progressive |
| PRS | present |
| PST | past |
| PTCP | participle |
| PURP | purposive |
| Q | question word |
| RECP | reciprocal |
| REFL | reflexive |
| RESTRIC | restricted |
| S | intransitive subject |
| SBJ | subject |
| SBJV | subjunctive |

| | |
|---|---|
| SF | stem formative |
| SG | singular |
| TRANS | transitive |
| UNRESTRIC | unrestricted |
| V | vegetable class |
| VDEN | verbal denizen case |
| VOC | vocative |
| WIT | witnessed |

# 1

# Morphological Typology of Deponency*

## 1. Introduction

'DEPONENCY' IS A CONVENIENT TERM for morphological mismatches, but it is
also a term without an accepted definition. Traditionally, the term applies
only to a set of verbs in Latin; any further use of the term involves some kind
of metaphorical extension of its salient features. However, Latin deponents
have a number of peculiar properties, the full range of which one seldom
finds elsewhere. Below we offer a definition which picks out the features of
Latin deponents that are of primary theoretical interest, distinguishing the
defining characteristics of deponency from the contingent characteristics
which may vary across individual examples.

An abbreviated synopsis of the paradigm of a Latin deponent is given in
(1), contrasted with the corresponding forms of a normal verb. In a normal
verb, the opposition of active and passive has three different treatments
within the paradigm (i) the finite values and the infinitives have both active
and passive forms (1a), (ii) the perfect participle has a passive form but no
active (1b), and (iii) the other participles, as well as the supine and gerund,
have active forms but no passive (1c). Deponent verbs have passive forms
wherever they are available, but with active value.[1]

---

* The work presented here was funded by the ESRC under grant number RES-000–23–0375.
Their support is gratefully acknowledged

[1] The one exception to this is the future infinitive where, uniquely, a periphrastic active form is
contrasted with a periphrastic passive form, e.g. active *rēctūrus esse* 'to be about to rule' versus
passive *rēctum īrī* 'to be about to be ruled'. Deponent verbs use the active form here, not the
passive, thus *secūtūrus esse* 'to be about to follow' rather than *secūtum īrī*; see Hippisley (this
volume).

*Proceedings of the British Academy* **145**, 1–19. © The British Academy 2007.

(1)   Latin verbs, normal and deponent

|     |         | normal verb 'rule' | | deponent verb 'follow' | |
| --- | --- | --- | --- | --- | --- |
|     |         | active | passive | active | passive |
| a.  | PRS IND | reg-it | reg-itur | sequ-itur | —— |
|     | PRS INF | reg-ere | reg-ī | sequī | —— |
|     | PRF IND | rēx-it | rēct-us est | secūt-us est | —— |
| b.  | PTCP PRF | —— | rēct-us | secūt-us | —— |
| c.  | SUPINE | rēct-um | —— | secūt-um | —— |
|     | PTCP PRS | reg-ēn-s | —— | sequ-ēn-s | —— |

In (1) a definition of deponency in Latin is offered. We pick out six key points
for elaboration, which are numbered to match the following sections.

(2)   Deponency in Latin

> Deponency is **a mismatch between form and function** (§2). Given that there is **a
> formal morphological opposition** (§3) between **active and passive** (§4) that is the
> **normal realization** of the corresponding functional opposition (§5), deponents
> are **a lexically-specified set** (§6) of verbs whose passive forms function as actives.
> **The normal function is no longer available** (§7).

We take the salient feature of deponent verbs in Latin to be the first point:
there is an apparent mismatch between morphological form and grammatical
function. The other points define parameters of potential typological
variation.[2] Below we expand on these points.

# 2. A Mismatch Between Form and Function

By form we mean an inflected word form, by function we mean some identifiable grammatical role or set of roles. A mismatch occurs where the word
form is used in some function incompatible with its normal function.

In principle, a mismatch can be identified syntagmatically or paradigmatically. **Syntagmatically**, a mismatch can be identified by comparing the mor-

---

[2] Other authors have extended the term according to different criteria. For example, Kemmer
(1993: 22 and 251, fn. 19) treats deponency as a kind of defectiveness, defining deponents as
verbs which have overt marking for middle voice, but lack a morphologically unmarked non-
middle counterpart. (This interpretation assumes that the Latin morphological passive has two
functions, passive and middle, and that deponents are functionally equivalent to the latter.) A
form-function mismatch is not part of her definition, as she assumes that deponents are inherently middle, and so the middle/passive morphology is in fact justified. However, at a purely morphological level, this seems to be a mischaracterization of the Latin paradigm. Deponents
contain a mixture of (middle-) passive and active forms; if they were truly *media tantum*, we
should expect to find only the (middle-) passive forms. The deponents of Modern Greek, on the
other hand, DO conform to this expectation.

phosyntactic values needed to describe a word form with the syntactic values needed to describe its role in the text. In the example given in the foreword to this volume, the form *hortantur* 'they exhort' is morphologically passive, but when used in a sentence it functions as an active.[3] **Paradigmatically**, a mismatch can be identified by comparing the inflected forms of a lexeme. For example, alongside passive forms, deponent verbs have a number of active forms (the supine, future infinitive, present and future participle, and the gerund) so that in terms of the paradigm as a whole, there is an opposition of passive and active forms in the deponent paradigm. However, there is no corresponding opposition of voice, e.g. *hortor* 'I urge (someone)', *hortans* 'urging (someone)'. With a normal transitive verb, on the other hand, the opposition of active and passive morphology is invariably associated with an opposition of voice, e.g. *amor* 'I am loved (by someone)', *amans* 'loving (someone)'. That is, deponent verbs display a mixture of passive and active forms, but without the corresponding voice opposition. Thus, even within the confines of the paradigm of a single lexeme, one can conclude that something is amiss.

---

[3] The *syntactic* diagnostics for voice distinctions in Latin are not absolute, but there are clues. Passives involve object promotion (or the equivalent thereof) and so are intransitive, the exception being a small number of constructions involving two accusative objects, e.g. *aliquem sententiam rogo* 'ask somebody his opinion' yields a passive which still has *sententiam* 'opinion' as the accusative object:

> qu-i          utinam        omn-es        ante    me   sententi-am        rog-arentur
> who-NOM.PL would.that all-NOM.PL before me opinion-ACC.SG ask-3PL.IMPRF.SBJV.PASS
> 'Would that all of them were asked their opinion before me.'
> (Cicero, *Fifth Philippic*)

Passives allow expression of the agent by a prepositional phrase, but active intransitives do not. Finally, a phenomenon we can call 'voice attraction' was in force for a certain period in the history of Latin. During the Classical period (Hofmann and Szantyr 1965: 288), the auxiliary verbs *coepi* 'begin' and *desino* 'cease' match the voice of the main verb. However, the correspondence is not based directly on morphological voice: only true passives and impersonal passives (Kühner 1955: 677) induce passive morphology on the auxiliary:

> veter-es       oration-es        a      plerisque     leg-i           sunt        desitae
> old-NOM.PL speeches-NOM.PL by most.ABL.PL read-INF.PRS.PASS are.3PL ceased.NOM.PL
> 'The old speeches were no longer read by most people.' [literally 'were ceased to be read']
> (Cicero, *Brutus* 32, 123, cited by Ernout and Thomas 1953: 208)

Deponents, however, induce active morphology:

> qu-em          cum    egredient-em           insequ-i         coep-issem
> who-ACC.SG when go.out.PTCP.PRS-ACC.SG follow-INF.PRS.PASS begin-1SG.PLUPRF.SBJV.
> 'when I began to press upon [literally, 'follow'] him, as he was departing'
> (Cicero, *Oratio de Haruspicum responso* 1, in Yonge's translation)

However, it should be noted that 'middle' passives (i.e. passives with a reflexive sense and the like) behave like deponents in this respect.

## 3. A Formal Morphological Opposition

The term 'morphological opposition' implies that we are looking at word forms. Of course, what is construed as a word form may vary with the observer, e.g. there are approaches which would treat certain combinations of otherwise independent words as single forms with respect to morphological rules. In practice this is limited to instances where there is direct evidence for a morphological paradigm in the conventional sense, i.e. where periphrastic forms make up only part of the paradigm, as with the Latin periphrastic perfect.

Of course, this does not mean that we do not recognize the possibility of mismatches where the exponent is a bona fide syntactic construction rather than a morphological form: e.g. does the use of expletive subjects represent a mismatch between semantics and syntax? The limitation of our investigation to morphology is a heuristic matter: it may turn out that there are interesting parallels between morphological and syntactic mismatches (conversely, there may be some revealing differences).

## 4. Active and Passive

Latin deponents involve a voice opposition, and prior extensions of the term 'deponent' have tended to focus on features involved in voice- and valency-changing operations. However, if what interests us is specifically the form-function mismatch as such, there is no reason to limit it to this area of grammar. Potentially, any grammatical category may be involved, provided the criteria above are met. The papers found within this volume explore a range of different features, both verbal and nominal. Further, categorical features, i.e. word class membership, can be seen in the same light: if two word classes in a language are morphologically distinct, a mismatch can be identified if its syntactic behaviour is that of one word class while its morphological characteristics are those of another (see Spencer, this volume).

In order to speak sensibly about mismatches, the grammatical category involved should have some observable correlates. These are most obvious in the case of syntactic relations, e.g. verb valency or agreement: thus, if a formally intransitive verb form takes a direct object, or a formally plural noun takes singular agreement, something is evidently amiss. Some arguably semantic categories also provide sufficient evidence, e.g. tense, where there may be no direct syntactic correlate, but the structure of the surrounding context may provide good clues about what to expect. In all these cases there are overt indicators in the surrounding text.

Naturally, not all grammatical categories are associated with anything overt that can be identified. This is particularly true of semantic categories. For examples, some authors have spoken of mismatches between alienable and inalienable possession markers (e.g. Noonan 1992: 82 on Lango; Schütz 1985: 463 on Fijian). However, the relevance of this distinction is confined to the lexical item that manifests it, so there is nothing in the text one can point to as a diagnostic. This is not to say that construing such examples as mismatches is invalid, simply that the confidence with which one could make such an assertion is low, and the chances of convincing the sceptical are slim. Nevertheless, paradigmatic irregularities allow us to identify mismatches even with such less-than-obvious categories. One example comes from Keres, which has both stative and non-stative intransitive verbs, which differ inflectionally (the latter taking object affixes for their sole argument).

(3)    Person prefixes in Keres, non-modal forms (Miller 1965: 100)

|   | stative | non-stative |
|---|---------|-------------|
| 1 | sgu-    | s-          |
| 2 | gəz̧-   | ş-         |
| 3 | gj-     | g- *or* s-  |

The distinction between the two classes is semantic, and there are no obvious syntactic correlates that one can point to.[4] The verb 'to be lying down' displays the peculiarity that it inflects as a stative with its singular/dual stem and as a non-stative with its plural stem.

(4)    sədîučai            skúikai
       s-jûučai            sgu-Ji'ikaiD
       1-lie.down.SG/DU    1-lie.down.PL
       'I am lying down'   'we are lying down'    (Miller 1965: 64)

Here we can speak of a mismatch, without having to specify exactly what the function of the category is. That is, whatever the function of the stative ~ non-stative opposition, number is not a parameter which should have any effect on it, judging by the behaviour of the rest of the system.


# 5. Normal Realization

Deponent verbs in Latin, though a sizeable class (e.g. 291 are found in the works of Cicero; Flobert 1975: 588), are nevertheless exceptional: the association of passive morphology with passive voice otherwise obtains for

---

[4] Statives may be derived or underived. Derived statives fall into three classes: (i) so-called passives with the prefix *qjaʔa-*; (ii) inchoatives with the suffix *-duN*, and (iii) a small set of verbs with the suffix *-ńú* indicating characteristic behaviour (of a person).

the vast majority of verbs. Therefore there is some justification for distinguishing between normal and exceptional behaviour, with deponents being
exceptional. However, it is possible to imagine a situation where there was no
obvious basis for distinguishing between normal and exceptional behaviour.
One example involves transitivity marking in Ngiyambaa. Ngiyambaa has
three conjugation classes: the L-, R- and Y-conjugations:

(5)    Ngiyambaa conjugation classes (Donaldson 1980: 158)

|       | L-conjugation | R-conjugation | Y-conjugation |
|-------|---------------|---------------|---------------|
| IPV   | -: ~ -ya:     | -ra:          | -DHa ~ -ga    |
| PST   | -(i)yi        | -yi           | -NHi          |
| PRS   | -ṯa ~ -ya     | -na           | -NHa          |
| IRR   | -laga         | -raga         | -yaga         |
| PURP  | -li           | -ri           | -giri         |

Transitive verbs of the L- and R- conjugations regularly form intransitive
counterparts by switching to the Y-conjugation:

(6)    a. transitive (R-conjugation)              b. intransitive (Y-conjugation)

       ŋadhu=nu:      dhu-raga   mura-gu     ŋindu       dhuri-yaga  mura-gu
       I.NOM=you.OBL  spear-IRR  spear-INS   you.NOM     spear-IRR   spear-INS
       'I will spear you with a spear.'        'You will get speared by a spear.'
                                                             (Donaldson 1980: 169)

(7)    a. transitive (L-conjugation)

       winar-u        bura:y       ŋulu       ga:nb-iyi    biduṯa:-dhu
       woman-ERG      child.ABS    face.ABS   wipe-PST     cloth-INS
       'A woman wiped a child's face with a cloth.'

       b. intransitive (Y-conjugation)
       bura:y         ŋulu         ga:nba-nhi
       child.ABS      face.ABS     wipe-PST
       'A child wiped (its) face.'        (Donaldson 1980: 170)

This alternation obtains for the class of bound verb roots which form compound verbs (Donaldson 1980: 155); there are twenty-one of these, and this
is a highly productive means of verb formation (Donaldson 1980: 152).

    However, among the free verb roots, there is only a weak correlation
between conjugation class membership and transitivity:

(8)    Transitivity in Ngiyambaa free verbal roots (Donaldson 1980: 154)[5]

| conjugation class | number of roots | % transitive |
|-------------------|-----------------|--------------|
| L                 | 240             | 69           |
| R                 | 2               | 100          |
| Y                 | 126             | 44           |

[5] Donaldson (1980) in fact breaks down the figures for the individual subclasses of the two larger
conjugations:

That is, a substantial portion of verbs (around 40%) have the 'wrong' valence, so that one has little basis for deciding what is normal behaviour. However, the term 'normal' is perhaps a misnomer, albeit a convenient one. What is crucial is that the behaviour be attributed to a morphological rule, which is contingent on a given analysis. For example, if the alternations in (6)–(7) are treated as rule-based, then we can apply the label 'deponent' to intransitive L-conjugation and transitive Y-conjugation verbs. On the other hand, we might say that 'a' and 'b' in (6)–(7) simply constitute a pair of lexemes, unrelated to each other by any synchronic rule, then we have no reason to speak of deponency (e.g. the existence of the English pair *sit* ~ *set* does not warrant our calling *fret* deponent because it is not a causative).

# 6. A Lexically Specified Set

In Latin, deponency is a characteristic of individual lexical items. The mismatch is identifiable by comparing the behaviour of the majority of verbs, which use passive morphology for the passive function, with a smaller, lexically-specified set of verbs, which use the same morphology for the active function. But one can also identify paradigm-internal anomalies which are not lexically restricted, i.e. where the syntactic and morphological profile of the paradigm do not line up.

### 6.1. Paradigmatic deponency

One such example comes from Yurok, which employs morphologically passive forms in its transitive verb paradigm (Robins 1958; Blevins forthcoming). In order to appreciate this, first consider the passive paradigm (9b). It is identical to the regular intransitive paradigm (9a) with the addition of the passive suffix -*ey* (-*i* in the 3SG).

(9)  Yurok intransitive verb paradigm 'meet' (Robins 1958: 47)

|      | a. active | b. passive |
|------|-----------|------------|
| 1SG  | nekcen-ek' | nekcen-ey-(e)k' |
| 2SG  | nekcen-e'm | nekcen-ey-e'm |
| 3SG  | nekce<'>n | nekcen-i-' |
| 1PL  | nekcen-oh | nekcen-ey-oh |

| conjugation class | number of roots | % transitive |
|-------------------|-----------------|--------------|
| L1 | 200 | 70 |
| L2 | 40 | 66 |
| Y1 | 110 | 40 |
| Y2 | 16 | 63 |

|     | a. active   | b. passive        |
|-----|-------------|-------------------|
| 2PL | nekcen-u'   | nekcen-ey-u'      |
| 3PL | nekcen-ehl  | nekcen-ey-(e)hl   |

The transitive paradigm is given in Table 1. Its forms are heterogeneous: some are dedicated transitive forms, while others are taken from the active intransitive (9a) or the passive paradigm (9b). What concerns us here are the passive forms, found for the values 2/3>1PL, 3>2PL and, optionally, 3PL>1SG and 3>3PL. In each case, the passive verb form agrees with the logical object. (On forms with a 1PL object, whose interpretation involves further complexities, see below.)

Robins (1958: 69) suggests that these passive forms are 'used in syntactic structures appropriate to an active verb'. In fact, the evidence is somewhat mixed; nevertheless, there are two arguments in favour of Robins's assertion.

First, the behaviour of nominal arguments with these verb forms is closer to that found with the other transitive verb forms. With transitive verbs (10), where the subject is third person, a 1SG or 2SG object pronoun takes a distinct object form (*nekac* '1SG' and *kelac* '2SG', versus the default forms *nek* and *ke'l*); the subject pronoun takes the default form. In normal passive constructions (11), a 1SG or 2SG (logical) object is in the default form, and the agent, if overtly expressed, is typically marked by the preposition *mehl*.

(10)   Transitive construction (Robins 1958: 21)

       yo'     nekac       ki      newoh-pe'n
       3SG     1SG.OBJ     FUT     see-3SG>1SG
       'He will see me.'

(11)   Passive construction (Robins 1958: 50)

       nek    kic    teykelewom-oy-ek'    mehl    leyes
       I      PRF    bite-PASS-1SG        by      snake
       'I have been bitten by a snake.'

Where one of the morphologically passive transitive forms is used, both object and subject behave as they do with transitive verbs: a 1SG or 2SG object appears in a distinct object form, while an overtly expressed agent is unmarked.

(12)   Passive form in transitive construction (Robins 1958: 77)

       'no-too'mar     kelac        nimi    k'enroks-ey-e'm
       1-friend        2SG .OBJ     not     trust-PASS-2SG
       'My friends don't trust you.'

Second, the form for a 1PL object has characteristics of the passive, though with further complications which lead to its being distinct from the real passive, at least in some cases (Robins 1958: 71). One difference involves conjugation class. Any Yurok verb falls into one of two conjugation classes,

**Table 1.** Yurok transitive verb paradigm 'meet' (Blevins forthcoming)

|  |  | object | | | | | |
|---|---|---|---|---|---|---|---|
|  |  | 1SG | 1PL | 2SG | 2PL | 3SG | 3PL |
| subject | 1SG |  |  | nekcen-icek' | nekcen-ic'o' | nekcen-esek' | nekcen-es'o' |
|  | 1PL |  |  | nekcen-icoh | nekcen-ic'o' | nekcen-esoh | 1PL ACTIVE |
|  | 2SG | nekcen-a' | nekcen-oy, nekcen-oy-oh, nekcen-oy-og-oh | 2SG PASSIVE | 2SG PASSIVE | nekcen-ese'm | 2SG ACTIVE |
|  | 2PL | nekcen-a' | nekcen-oy, nekcen-oy-oh, nekcen-oy-og-oh | 2SG PASSIVE | 2SG PASSIVE | nekcen-ese'm | 2SG ACTIVE |
|  | 3SG | nekcen-e'n, nekcen-epe'n | nekcen-oy, nekcen-oy-oh, nekcen-oy-og-oh | 2SG PASSIVE | 2SG PASSIVE | 3SG ACTIVE | 3SG ACTIVE, 3PL PASSIVE |
|  | 3PL | nekcen-epaahl, 1SG PASSIVE |  | 2SG PASSIVE | 2SG PASSIVE | 3PL ACTIVE | 3PL ACTIVE, 3PL PASSIVE |

*Note that some of the cells have alternative forms*

the e-class and o-class. Among other things, they differ in the way their passive stems are formed: e-class verbs suffix *-ey*, the o-class suffixes *-oy*. All o-class verbs (naturally), and most e-class verbs form their 1PL object form with the passive suffix proper to the o-class; thus the passive stem of the e-class verb 'meet' is *nekceney-*, but its 1PL object stem is *neckenoy-*. Thus, the 1PL object stem is identifiable as a passive stem, but for e-class verbs it is not equivalent to the lexeme's own passive stem. The other difference involves the inflectional endings. The 1PL passive has the ending *-oh*, while the 1PL object form has three possible endings: (i) zero, (ii) *-oh*, like the passive, or (iii) a doubled version of the passive ending, namely *-oh-oh* → *-ogoh* (Blevins forthcoming). Thus, the 1PL object form may be a dedicated transitive form, but still contains all the morphological components of the passive. This shows that one cannot simply say that a syntactic alternation to passive occurs in this context.

### 6.2. Lexical-paradigmatic deponency (semi-deponency)

The two types of deponency that we have described—lexically conditioned in the case of Latin, and paradigmatically conditioned in the case of Yurok—are not mutually exclusive. That is, paradigmatically conditioned deponency could itself be lexically conditioned. This is precisely what happens in the class of verbs known in Latin as semi-deponents, which are deponent only for part of their paradigm, e.g. present tense *audeo* 'I dare' has the form of an active, but perfect *ausus sum* 'I have dared' has the form of a passive.

In many of the examples of semi-deponency that we have found, the deponent portion of the paradigm coincides with the locus of a stem alternation. Thus in Latin, semi-deponents are deponent for their perfect values, which coincide with a distinct stem (the perfect passive or supine stem). A particularly striking example of the interdependence of stems and semi-deponency comes from Takelma, an extinct isolate once spoken in Oregon. In this language, transitive verbs are morphologically distinct from intransitives. In (13), intransitive and transitive suffixes of the aorist and future are compared. The transitive forms illustrated are construed as having a third person object. First and second person objects are indicated by further suffixes.

(13)   Takelma subject-marking suffixes (Sapir 1922: 164, 170)

|      | aorist | | future | |
|------|--------------|--------------|------------------|------------------|
|      | intransitive[†] | transitive | intransitive | transitive |
| 1SG | -tʰeʔ, -teʔ | -(à)ʔn | -tʰeː, -teː | -(à)n |
| 1PL | -(pʰ)ikʰ | -(á)nakʰ | -(pʰ)ikam | -(a)nakàm |
| 2SG | -tʰam, -tam | -(á)tʰ | -tʰaʔ, -taʔ | -(a)taʔ |
| 2PL | -tʰapʰ, -tapʰ | -(á)tʰpʰ | -tʰapaʔ, -tapaʔ | -(à)tʰpaʔ |
| 3   | -Ø, -tʰ | -Ø | -tʰaː, -taː | -(á)nkʰ |

† Takelma has two classes of intransitives (I and II); Sapir characterizes the difference as follows: 'the main characteristic of Class II intransitives . . . is that they denote conditions and processes, while Class I intransitives are in great part verbs of action.' (p. 164). The suffixes here are class II, which is the only one which participates in semi-deponency.

There are a number of different types of semi-deponent verbs, which are intransitive (they take neither overt objects nor object markers), but take transitive subject markers for part of the paradigm. Consequently, these forms look like transitive forms with a third person object. In the first type (14), there is an anomalous stem augment -*n* in the first person singular and plural, and these forms are inflected as transitives; the other forms as intransitive.

(14)  Takelma semi-deponent verb, type 1 (aorist): 'work'

| 1SG | hekwêhak^hw-n-a?n |
|-----|------------------|
| 1PL | hekwêhak^hw-n-anák^h |
| 2SG | hekwêhak^hw-tam |
| 2PL | hekgwêhak^hw-tap^h |
| 3   | hekwêhak^hw |

(Sapir 1922: 182)

A second type displays the stem augment only in the aorist, but not in the other tenses; consequently, it is deponent only in the first person in the aorist:[6]

(15)  Takelma semi-deponent verb, type 2: 'be lean in one's rump' (Sapir 1922: 183)

|      | aorist | future |
|------|--------|--------|
| 1SG  | ti:-k'alâs-n-a?n | ti:-k'âlsi-te: |

A third type inflects as a transitive in all persons of the aorist, as an intransitive elsewhere:

(16)  Takelma semi-deponent verb, type 3: 'listen' (Sapir 1922: 183)

|      | aorist | future |
|------|--------|--------|
| 1SG  | ta:-skek'iy-à?n | ta:-skêk'i-t^he: |

Note that, unlike types 1 and 2, the deponent forms of type 3 lack a stem augment. Nevertheless, the aorist is a locus for stem alternations. For regular verbs, the aorist stem is typically distinct, characterized by a morphologically heterogeneous set of devices (including reduplication). Curiously, the

---

[6] Sapir states that only the first person forms display this behaviour; unfortunately, he does not provide examples of other forms.

semi-deponent verbs of this class that Sapir cites do *not* in fact have an observable stem alternation in the aorist. In effect, the stem alternation is manifested by deponency itself.

The fourth type is of particular interest. Some intransitive verbs are suppletive for plural subjects, whereby the singular stem inflects as an intransitive, and the plural stem as a transitive. For at least one verb, 'be seated', this suppletion is optional. Where the stem is non-suppletive, intransitive conjugation is maintained in the plural:

(17)   Takelma semi-deponent verb, type 4: be seated (Sapir 1922: 94–5)

| 1SG | šu?wilǐ:-tʰeʔ |
|---|---|
| 1SG | **xali:ya-nâkʰ** |
|  | šu?wilǐ:pʰ-ikʰ |

*suppletive plural*

*non-suppletive plural*

These examples of semi-deponency suggest that stems can be viewed as having the same properties as lexemes: just as a given lexeme can specify for idiosyncratic behaviour, so can individual stems of individual lexemes. This impression is strengthened when we consider a fifth pattern, which bridges the gap between stem-based and lexeme-based deponency, namely use of a deponent auxiliary. This occurs in the future: alongside a synthetic future form, there is a periphrastic future involving an auxiliary (*kulukʷ-* 'intend, desire') which is always inflected as a transitive, regardless of the transitivity of the main verb. For example, in (17), the auxiliary takes the 2SG transitive aorist ending, even though the main verb 'die' is intransitive.[7]

(18)   lohòkʰ        ti       kulukw-átʰ
       die          Q       intend-2SG[>3]
       'Do you intend to die?'

This phenomenon is especially interesting in the way it interacts with what Sapir calls the passive, but which is really an indefinite subject construction (which Sapir himself points out). Morphologically, the 'passive' involves a distinct suffix (*-an* in the examples below), which can be taken as standing in for the subject, plus object markers where applicable. In principle, the passive can only be formed from transitive verbs. However, Sapir (1922: 185) points out that '[i]nasmuch as all active periphrastic futures are transitive in form, passive futures [. . .] can be formed from all verbs, whether transitive or

---

[7] Sapir supposes that, morphologically, the verb stem in the periphrastic future can be interpreted as a verbal noun (*thus do:m gulugw-àn* 'I shall kill him' ≈ 'killing (him), I will it'), which may account for the transitive morphology, at least etymologically.

intransitive' and gives examples such as *hoita kulukw-àn* 'it will be danced' or *wê:kiau kulukw-ân* 'it will be shined' (= 'it was going to be daylight'). Significantly, this sort of impersonal construction with intransitives is only possible in the periphrastic future.[8]

On the other hand, there is at least one example of semi-deponency in which stems do not play a determining role, namely Latin *fio* 'become, be done', which mixes active and passive inflection. The verb is peculiar in a number of respects, not the least that it functions as the passive of the present stem forms of *facio* 'make, do'. However, what concerns us here is not this,[9] but the fact that its mixture of active and passive forms does not correlate with a stem alternation. As with any Latin verb, the present, imperfect and future are all formed from the same stem, but the present infinitive, and only the present infinitive, inflects as a passive, while the other forms inflect as actives.

(19)   Latin *fio* 'become, be done'

|  | active morphology | passive morphology |
|---|---|---|
| PRS IND | fi-t | |
| IMPRF IND | fī-ēbat | |
| FUT IND | fī-et | |
| PRS SBSJV | fī-at | |
| IMPRF SBJV | fi-eret | |
| IPV PRS | fī | |
| IPV FUT | fī-tō | |
| INF PRS | | fi-erī |

The alternation between active and passive morphology in *fio* must be described in terms of the morphosyntactic values, since it does not correlate with a stem alternation.

---

[8] Another example of auxiliary-based semi-deponency comes from Ika, a Chibchan language of Columbia, where the future auxiliary has subjects treated morphologically as objects (Frank 1990). Similarly, Bickel and Nichols (2001) describe certain 'super-light' verbs in Belhare (Kiryanti, Tibeto-Burman) and Chechen (Nakh-Dagestanian), typically modals, which are lexically specified to inflect as intransitives or transitives, regardless of the transitivity of the main verb.

[9] Because of the odd status of *fio*, somewhere between passive and active, it is not clear which morphology should be expected (indeed, the question probably makes little sense). Either way, the switch in morphology is not correlated with any switch in its syntactic or semantic behaviour.

## 7. The Normal Function is No Longer Available

The passive forms of Latin deponent verbs have not merely adopted a new voice value, they have abandoned their expected voice value. This means that there is a gap in the paradigm of any deponent verb that might require a passive form. Schematically, the defectiveness of the deponent paradigm is represented in (20), where *exponent A* is used for category Y, whose normal exponent is *exponent B*, and no exponent is available to express category X.

(20)   Deponency + defectiveness

|  | normal paradigm | deponent paradigm |
|---|---|---|
| category X | exponent A | ————— |
| category Y | exponent B | exponent A |

Though this is normally taken as a defining feature of deponency, it is possible to imagine a paradigm which has all the requisite characteristics, but where this gap is filled. There are three logical possibilities: polarity, heteroclisis, and syncretism.

### 7.1. Polarity

Polarity involves a mirror-image mismatch. In Hetzron's (1967: 184) formulation, polarity occurs 'when there exist two grammatical categories (*signifiés*) X and Y, and two corresponding exponents (*signifiants*) A and B, then value X can sometimes be assumed by A, while B denotes Y; and sometimes X is expressed by B, and then it is necessarily A that represents Y'. Schematically:

(21)   Polarity

|  | normal paradigm | deponent paradigm |
|---|---|---|
| category X | exponent A | **exponent B** |
| category Y | exponent B | exponent A |

Note that the first part of Hetzron's definition (up to 'expressed by *B*') defines a mismatch. The corollary mismatch makes it polarity. The most familiar example, treated by Hetzron, comes from Semitic. In Common Semitic, as reflected in Classical Arabic and in Hebrew, the normal morphological opposition between masculine and feminine agreement morphology, as found on adjectives, is switched with the numerals 3–10, which also mark gender. To show this is not just an isolated phenomenon, we illustrate polarity below with an example from the Uto-Aztecan language Tübatulabal, described by Voegelin (1935).

Every verb in Tübatulabal has two stems: telic and atelic. The telic (perfective) is 'used for an action (e.g. "to take a bite") or condition (e.g. "it got green") performed or arrived at in an instant (perfective without tense commitment), and for this reason the action or condition is generally, though not necessarily, felt to be completed at the time of talking' (Voegelin 1935: 94). The atelic (imperfective) is 'sometimes used when an action requires some duration for its performance ("to eat"), but frequently the atelic is quite vague in respect to aspectual meaning'. The difference between the two aspectual stems has a number of inflectional ramifications, in particular: (i) atelic stems are bound forms, telic stems may occur unsuffixed, and (ii) a number of suffixes are specific to either the atelic or telic stem.

The stem alternation is effected by reduplication. For the vast majority of verbal lexemes, the atelic is the basic stem and the telic the reduplicated stem. Reduplication targets the vowel of the initial syllable, accompanied by phonologically regular alternations of voicing and nasal harmony.

(22)  Typical aspectual stem alternations in Tübatulabal (Voegelin 1935: 95, 102)

| atelic | telic | |
|---|---|---|
| ela- | eʔela | 'jump' |
| tɨk- | itɨk | 'eat' |
| tana- | andana | 'get down' |
| pa:abɨ- | a:ba:abɨ | 'be tired' |
| yuʔudz- | uyuʔuts | 'throw' |

However, there is a small group of verbs (around 30) for which it is the telic stem which is morphologically basic, and the atelic is formed from it by reduplication.

(23)  Reversed aspectual stems in Tübatulabal (Voegelin 1935: 95–6)

| atelic | telic | | atelic | telic | |
|---|---|---|---|---|---|
| a:dza:ya:w- | tsa:ya:u | 'yell' | i:cɨy- | cɨ:i | 'rock a cradle' |
| apatsa:h- | patsa:h | 'shell nuts' | ɪndɪŋwa- | tɪŋwa | 'summon' |
| anaŋ- | naŋ | 'cry' | ɪcib- | ci:p | 'whittle' |
| anab- | nap | 'throw' | i:cilu:b- | cilu:p | 'split wood' |
| a:na:yuw- | na:yuw̱ | 'be tired' | i:ciug- | ciuk | 'comb' |
| aʔay- | ai | 'pick up' | ôtôlo:h- | tôlo:h | 'groan' |
| a:ya:n- | ya:n | 'sing' | ôcôlo:ŋ- | côlo:ŋ | 'snore' |
| acag- | ca:k | 'roast' | ô:yôm- | yô:m | 'copulate' |
| andaŋ- | taŋ | 'kick' | ʊkʊc- | ku:c | 'grow' |
| aha:idž- | ha:itc | 'chew' | ʊwuba- | wuba | 'whip' |
| ɨmbɨŋw- | pɨŋw̱ | 'roll string on thigh' | ʊyugʊʔ- | yugʊʔ | 'cut' |
| ɨmɨl:d- | mɨl:t | 'scold' | ʊndʊmu:ga- | tʊmu:ga | 'dream' |
| ɨtsɨxk- | tsɨxk | 'prick' | ʊndʊma:w- | tʊma:u | 'fail' |
| ɨhɨ:b- | hɨ:p | 'massage' | ʊtʊc- | tu:c | 'grind' |
| ɨhɨ:d- | hɨ:t | 'pluck feathers' | ʊnʊŋ- | nʊŋ | 'pound' |

Voegelin observes that there are no obvious shared semantic features that would justify regarding them as inherently telic. Instead, it must be lexically specified for these items that the normal morphological relationship is reversed.

### 7.2. Heteroclisis

Heteroclisis is the mixture of different inflection classes within a single paradigm. For example, the Latin *balneum* 'bath' declines as a second declension noun in the singular and a first declension noun in the plural.

(24)   Latin heteroclitic noun 'bath'

|  | second declension | | first declension | |
|---|---|---|---|---|
|  | SINGULAR | PLURAL | SINGULAR | PLURAL |
| NOM | balne -um | -a | -a | balne -ae |
| ACC | balne -um | -a | -am | balne -ās |
| GEN | balne -ī | -ōrum | -ae | balne -ārum |
| DAT | balne -ō | -īs | -ae | balne -īs |
| ABL | balne -ō | -īs | -ā | balne -īs |

Deponency can interact with heteroclisis to yield a non-defective paradigm: in place of the missing forms, the expected forms of another inflection class are found, as schematically represented in (25), where the deponent forms belong to inflection class 1, and the normal forms belong to inflection class 2.

(25)   Deponency + heteroclisis

|  | normal paradigm, class 1 | normal paradigm, class 2 | deponent paradigm |
|---|---|---|---|
| category X | exponent $A_1$ | exponent $A_2$ | **exponent $A_2$** |
| category Y | exponent $B_1$ | exponent $B_2$ | exponent $A_1$ |

As a concrete illustration of this we can take Gothic. As in other Germanic languages, Gothic has two conjugation classes, strong and weak. Strong verbs form their preterite (past tense) through ablaut, with a distinction between the vowel of the singular and dual/plural. Weak verbs form their preterite through a dental suffix (-*t*, -*d* or -*s*). In addition, the person-number endings of strong and weak verbs are at least partly different.

The so-called preterite-present verbs have present tense forms which inflect as the preterite of strong verb, displaying the characteristic singular ~ dual/plural vowel ablaut, and the distinctive preterite person-number endings. They have preterites as well, but these are formed according to the regular pattern for weak verbs. At (26), a portion of the relevant paradigms is given, showing indicative forms.

(26)   Gothic verb types (Birkmann 1987: 94)

|  |  | strong verb 'grip' | weak verb 'have' | preterite present 'know' |
|---|---|---|---|---|
| present indicative | 1SG | greip-a | hab-a | wait |
|  | 2SG | greip-is | haba-is | wais-t |
|  | 3SG | greip-iþ | haba-iþ | wait |
|  | 1PL | greip-am | hab-am | wit-um |
|  | 2PL | greip-iþ | haba-iþ | wit-uþ |
|  | 3PL | greip-and | hab-and | wit-un |
|  | 1DU | greip-os | hab-os | wit-u |
|  | 2DU | greip-ats | hab-ats | wit-uts |
| preterite indicative | 1SG | graip | habai-da | wis-sa† |
|  | 2SG | graip-t | habai-des | wis-seis |
|  | 3SG | graip | habai-da | wis-sa |
|  | 1PL | grip-um | habai-dedum | wis-sedum |
|  | 2PL | grip-uþ | habai-deduþ | wis-seduþ |
|  | 3PL | grip-un | habai-dedun | wis-sedun |
|  | 1DU | grip-u |  |  |
|  | 2DU | grip-uts |  |  |

† The weak preterite has a dental stop as its first element. In early Germanic, a sequence of two dental stops yielded two dental fricatives, hence the sequence -*ss*- in 'know'.

Thus, the finite paradigm of preterite presents consists entirely of preterite forms, but from two different conjugation classes: the strong preterite forms serve for the present, and hence can be characterized as deponent, while the weak preterite forms serve for the preterite.

### 7.3. Syncretism

Finally, it is possible to imagine that a particular exponent retains its normal function under deponency alongside the irregular function, resulting in syncretism. This is schematically represented in (27).

(27)   Deponency + syncretism

|  | normal paradigm | deponent paradigm |
|---|---|---|
| category X | exponent A | **exponent A** |
| category Y | exponent B | exponent A |

One such example comes from the Nakh-Dagestanian language Tsez, described by Corbett (this volume). The nouns *xex-bi* 'children' and *ɣˤana-bi* 'woman' always decline as plurals, but can be used as singulars as well, as evidenced by agreement:

(28)   Singular and plural use of *xexbi* 'child' (Comrie 2001: 381–3)

       *singular*                        *plural*

howda xex-bi     Ø-ik'i-s      howziri xex-bi     b-ik'i-s
this child-PL.ABS  I-go-PST.WIT  these child-PL.ABS  I.PL-go-PST.WIT
'This child went.'                'These children went.'

In their use as a singulars, the plural nouns *xex-bi* and *ɣʕana-bi* are deponent. However, in contrast to the other patterns discussed above, this does not preempt their use as ordinary plural forms.

# 8. Conclusion

The theoretical interest of deponent verbs in Latin is clear: morphological forms are not simply a blind reflection of the categories they represent. Instead, morphology may operate at cross-purposes with morphosyntax, without apparently hindering the functioning of the system of correspondences. But the language-specific peculiarities of Latin deponents have prevented any general acknowledgement of their broader significance; few languages have phenomena which match in all the particulars. However, as the papers in this volume show, morphological mismatches can be found in many different languages, affecting a wide range of grammatical categories. By teasing apart the definition of deponency in Latin, I hope to have shown how broadly the notion can be applied, and to have provided a typological framework for discussing them.

# References

Bickel, Balthasar, and Johanna Nichols. 2001. Syntactic ergativity in light verb complements. *Proceedings of the 27th Annual Meeting of the Berkeley Linguistics Society*. Berkeley: University of California.

Birkmann, Thomas. 1987. *Präteritopräsentia*. Tübingen: Max Niemeyer.

Blevins, Juliette. Forthcoming. Periphrastic agreement in Yurok. *Periphrasis and paradigms*, ed. by Farrell Ackerman, James P. Blevins, and Gregory T. Stump. Stanford: CSLI Publications.

Comrie, Bernard. 2001. How independent is Tsezic morphology? *CLS 37: The Panels: 2001: Proceedings from the Parasessions of the 37th Meeting of the Chicago Linguistic Society* [volume 37, 2], ed. by Mary Andronis, Christopher Ball, Heidi Elston and Sylvain Neuvel, 367–383. Chicago: Chicago Linguistic Society.

Donaldson, Tamsin. 1980. *Ngiyambaa: the language of the Wangaaybuwan*. Cambridge: Cambridge University Press.

Ernout, Alfred and François Thomas. 1953. *Syntaxe latine*, 2nd edn. Paris: Klincksieck.

Flobert, Pierre. 1975. *Les verbes déponents latins des origines à Charlemagne*. Paris: Société d'Édition 'Les Belles Lettres'.

Frank, Paul. 1990. *Ika syntax* (Studies in the Languages of Colombia 1). Dallas: Summer Institute of Linguistics.

Hetzron, Robert 1967. Agaw numerals and incongruence in Semitic. *Journal of Semitic Studies* 12.169–93.

Hofmann, Johann Baptist, and Anton Szantyr. 1965. *Lateinische Syntax und Stilistik* (Handbuch der Altertumswissenschaft 2, 2, 2). Munich: C. H. Beck.

Kemmer, Suzanne. 1993. *The middle voice*. Amsterdam/Philadelphia: John Benjamins.

Kühner, Raphael. 1955. *Ausführliche Grammatik der lateinischen Sprache* (part 2, 1, rev. by Andreas Thierfelder). Hamburg: Hahn.

Miller, Wick R. 1965. *Acoma grammar and texts*. Berkeley and Los Angeles: University of California Press.

Noonan, Michael. 1992. *A grammar of Lango*. Berlin: Mouton de Gruyter.

Robins, R. H. 1958. *The Yurok language*. Berkeley: University of California Press.

Sapir, Edward. 1922. The Takelma language of south-western Oregon. *Handbook of American Indian languages*, vol. 2, ed. by Franz Boas, 1–296. Washington, DC: Government Printing Office.

Schütz, Albert J. 1985. *The Fijian language*. Honolulu: University of Hawaii Press.

Voegelin, Charles F. 1935. *Tübatulabal grammar*. Berkeley: University of California Press.

# 2

# Deponency, Syncretism, and What Lies Between*

GREVILLE G. CORBETT

## 1. Introduction

IN ATTEMPTING TO DEFINE THE NOTION 'possible human language', linguists must be able to define what is a possible word. Part of that enterprise is establishing the possible phenomena within inflectional morphology. This paper contributes to that goal by giving a schema of these phenomena. As such it is part of a more general canonical approach to typology. Thus one aim of the paper is 'intellectual housekeeping', putting order into the description of inflectional morphology. This will allow us to analyse the diversity of inflectional morphology by confronting it with an elegant order.

Within the overall schema, our focus is naturally on deponency; we shall look in particular at how it is to be differentiated from syncretism, since the two show important similarities. Establishing the differences sheds light on both phenomena; it also allows us to recognize related phenomena that have not been given due attention, in part because there were no terms for them. We begin by clarifying our assumptions (§2), then laying out the canonical approach to inflectional morphology (§3), and the types of phenomena which can be described in terms of various relaxations of canonicity (§4). We then concentrate on deponency, syncretism, and related phenomena of interest (§5). Finally we investigate how deponency interacts with other morphological phenomena (§6).

* The support of the ESRC under grants RES-000-23-0375 and RES-051-27-0122 is gratefully acknowledged. I also wish all those who have offered data, ideas and helpful comments, especially Matthew Baerman, Marina Chumakina, Bernard Comrie, Andrew Hippisley, and Gregory Stump, and the participants at the Workshop on Deponency.

# 2. Assumptions

We start from the point where the features and their values are already established for the language in question, in other words, analysis of the 'syntactic'
part of morphosyntax is well advanced.[1] Underlying our work is the approach
to morphology termed 'inferential-realizational' morphology, as defined and
discussed in Stump (2001: 1–30). This covers the family of theories known as
'Word and Paradigm' theories (as in Matthews 1972). The specific variant in
mind is Network Morphology (for which see Corbett and Fraser 1993; Evans,
Brown, and Corbett 2002; Baerman, Brown, and Corbett 2005; and references
there). Though this is the general orientation, the essentials of the typology
could be restated to accommodate other assumptions. We shall present paradigms in tabular form, since this is often helpful, but we do not assume that
geometry has any relevance for inflectional morphology. The reader should
also bear in mind that throughout the discussion there is an implied 'all
other things being equal'. For instance, when discussing whether inflectional
markers are the same in particular paradigm cells we assume, unless otherwise
stated, that the stem remains the same.

# 3. Canonicity

We consider canonicity in general, and then see how it applies specifically to
inflectional morphology.

## 3.1. The canonical approach in typology

In the canonical approach we take definitions to their logical end point. This
enables us to construct theoretical spaces of possibilities. It is only at this point
that we investigate how this space is populated with real instances. The canonical instances are the clearest, the indisputable ones (those closely matching
the canon), in a sense they are the 'best' examples. Such instances are unlikely
to be frequent. On the contrary they are likely to be either rare or even non-
existent. To take a comparison from a quite different domain: 'there are so
many more ways of being disorderly than there are of being orderly, so that
disarray wins hands down'.[2] This expected dearth of canonical instances is not
a problem, since the convergence of criteria fixes a canonical point from which

---

[1] This is not to minimize the problems; this task can involve complex analytical decisions (see
Comrie 1986; Zaliznjak 1973 [2002] for examples).
[2] The source is: John Polkinghorne, *Quantum theory: a very short introduction*, Oxford: Oxford
University Press, 2002, p. 50. The quote continues: 'Just think of your desk, if you do not intervene
from time to time to tidy it up.'

the phenomena actually found can be calibrated.[3] There can subsequently be illuminating investigation of frequency distributions.

The canonical approach has been applied in syntactic typology, in particular in investigating agreement (Corbett 2003, 2006), where the theoretical space is defined in terms of twenty criteria. The criteria are used in accounts of Miraña by Seifart (2005: 156–74) and of Gujarati by Suthar (2006: 178–98). A preliminary discussion of canonicity can be found in Corbett (2005). The canonical approach is applied to inflectional morphology, and specifically to suppletion, in Corbett (2007). That paper shows how the notion can be applied recursively. Suppletion is a highly non-canonical phenomenon in inflectional morphology; having defined it, we can in turn establish canonical and less canonical instances of suppletion. A further application to inflectional morphology is in the investigation of 'higher order exceptionality', that is to say, of instances which involve the interaction of exceptional phenomena (Corbett forthcoming).

### 3.2. Canonical inflection

As pointed out in section 2, we begin from the point where the features and their values have been established. Once that is done, the feature values should 'multiply out', so that all possible cells in a paradigm exist. For example, if a language has five cases and three numbers in its nominal system, a noun paradigm should have fifteen cells. (This matches Spencer's notion of 'exhaustivity' 2003: 252.) In addition, to be fully canonical, a paradigm should be 'consistent', according to the following criteria:

(1)    Canonical inflection: the criteria

|  | comparison across *cells* of a lexeme (level one) | comparison across *lexemes* (level two) |
|---|---|---|
| composition/structure (of the inflected *word*) | same | same |
| lexical material (≈shape of *stem*) | same | different |
| inflectional material (≈shape of *affix*) | different | same |
| outcome (≈shape of inflected *word*) | different | different |

We shall go through this schema step by step. There are two levels of comparison:

---

[3] Note that the criteria converge on the canonical point; there is no ranking of criteria, in contrast to an OT approach (compare McCarthy 2005).

*level one:* we begin with the abstract paradigm gained by multiplying out the features and their values. We examine any one lexeme fitted within this paradigm. The centre column of (1) applies to a comparison cell with cell, within a single paradigm. Let us take in turn the criteria in the left column:

1.  We look at the *composition and structure* of the cells; suppose the first consists of a stem and a prefix: for the given lexeme to have a canonical paradigm, every other cell must be the 'same' in this regard. Finding a suffix, or a clitic, or any different means of exponence would reveal non-canonicity.
2.  In terms of the *lexical material* in the cell, absolute identity is required (the stem should remain the same).
3.  On the other hand, the *inflectional material* 'should' be different in every cell.

The outcome for a canonical lexeme (last row) is that every cell in its paradigm will realize the required morphosyntactic specification in a way distinct from that of every other cell.

*level two:* here we compare lexemes with lexemes within the given language (right column). We use the same criteria as before:

1.  A canonical system requires that the composition and structure of each cell remains the same, comparing across lexemes.
2.  The lexical information must be different (we are, after all, comparing different lexemes).
3.  In the canonical situation, the inflectional material is identical. That is, if our first lexeme marks genitive singular in *q-u-*, so does every other.

The interesting overall outcome is that every cell of every lexeme is distinct. In other words, the realization of every morphosyntactic specification is different.[4] We illustrate this with a hypothetical example:

(2)    Illustration of canonical inflection (hypothetical)

| DOG-a | DOG-i | | CAT-a | CAT-i |
|-------|-------|---|-------|-------|
| DOG-e | DOG-o | | CAT-e | CAT-o |

Such canonical inflection would make perfect sense in functional terms. Every morphosyntactic distinction is drawn unambiguously, for the smallest amount of phonological material.[5] Furthermore, the system is so simple that Item and Arrangement morphology would be able to account for it.

---

[4] Canonicity is not to be compared with the various paradigm-organizing principles which have been proposed in the literature. It is rather a yardstick against which typological variation can be measured.

[5] The inflections *a, e, i, o* indicate only that the realizations are distinct. They are not intended as actual inflections. We do not in this paper go down into the canonicity of particular inflections. At that level it might be claimed that, for instance, cumulative exponence of two features (which would be found if *a, e, i, o* were actual affixes) would not be fully canonical.

## 4. Deviations from Canonical Inflection

We now turn to real language, using the notion of canonicity as a way of calibrating the phenomena of inflectional morphology. The overall typology would take us too far from our main concern. We shall therefore sketch it briefly, and look at just a four illustrative phenomena, before focusing on deponency and syncretism.

### 4.1. Comparison across the cells of a lexeme (level one comparison)

We look at the deviations from canonicity first in terms of cells of a lexeme, then in terms of lexemes. Note that in general, where we actually find 'same' in place of canonical 'different' this will give a non-functional outcome. If we find 'different' in place of canonical 'same' this will lead to increased complexity and/or redundancy.

(3)    Deviations established by comparison across the *cells* of a lexeme

|  | canonical behaviour | deviant behaviour | types of deviation |
|---|---|---|---|
| composition/structure (of the inflected *word*) | same | different | fused exponence periphrasis |
| lexical material (≈shape of *stem*) | same | different | alternations suppletion |
| inflectional material (≈shape of *affix*) | different | same | syncretism uninflectability |

We start with *composition/structure*, where in canonical instances we find identity. For instance, if we find an inflectional prefix in one cell of the paradigm, canonicity would require this same structure in all cells. We might instead find fused exponence, the situation where the structure found in other cells is not available: the morphosyntactic distinctions are realized but not according the pattern of the remaining paradigm. A second type of deviation is periphrasis, the use of an analytic form when the paradigm pattern is of synthetic forms.

Let us move on to *lexical material*. In the canonical situation we again find identity across the cells of a particular lexeme. However, we may find various types of alternations, predictable to a greater or lesser extent. The least canonical situation is that in which the lexical material is completely different, which is what we find in suppletion:

(4)    Illustration of suppletion (hypothetical)

| DOG-a | DOG-i |
|---|---|
| DOG-e | CAT-o |

Here is a genuine example from Polish:

(5)  Suppletion in Polish *być* 'be' (present tense)

| PERSON | SINGULAR | PLURAL |
|--------|----------|--------|
| 1 | jest-em | jest-eśmy |
| 2 | jest-eś | jest-eście |
| 3 | jest | s-ą |

Suppletion is an interesting part of the typology of possible words, and fourteen criteria have been established to determine canonical suppletion, which is one of the extremes of non-canonicity (Corbett 2007).

Finally within the comparison across the cells of a single lexeme we should examine *inflectional material*. In the canonical situation, the inflectional material is different in every cell of the lexeme. The major deviation here is syncretism, which we may represent as follows:

(6)  Illustration of syncretism (hypothetical)

| DOG-a | **DOG-i** |
|-------|-----------|
| DOG-e | **DOG-i** |

With this lexical item there is the expectation of four forms, which would represent the canonical situation, but in fact only three distinct forms are found. The basis for the expectation may differ, as may the means used for modelling the syncretism. The key point is that two morphosyntactic descriptions share a single realization. Here is a Russian example:

(7)  Examples of syncretism in the Russian noun *komnata* 'room'

| | SINGULAR | PLURAL |
|--------------|----------|--------|
| NOMINATIVE | komnata | **komnaty** |
| ACCUSATIVE | komnatu | **komnaty** |
| GENITIVE | komnaty | komnat |
| DATIVE | **komnate** | komnatam |
| INSTRUMENTAL | komnatoj | komnatami |
| LOCATIVE | **komnate** | komnatax |

Russian gives good evidence for two numbers and (at least) six cases. We can therefore expect twelve distinct forms. This noun shows syncretism of the dative and locative singular (though these cases are distinguished by the same noun in the plural), and of the nominative and accusative in the plural (distinguished in the singular).[6] For discussion of the significant of syncretism, with extensive examples, see Baerman, Brown, and Corbett (2005).

The ultimate failure to distinguish cells by inflectional material is uninflectability. Once we have established that there is an inflectional paradigm to

---

[6] This noun is a fully regular member of an inflectional class with many thousands of nouns.

which a particular item would be expected to conform, then uninflectability stands out as non-canonical. It is also an end point in that it could be seen as the extreme case of syncretism.

## 4.2. Comparison across the lexemes (level two comparison)

We now move on to deviations from canonicity which emerge when we compare lexemes with each other cell by cell. The canonical situation, and types of deviation are as follows:

(8)     Deviations established by comparison across *lexemes*

|  | canonical behaviour | deviant behaviour | types of deviation |
|---|---|---|---|
| composition/structure (of the inflected *word*) | same | different | defectiveness overdifferentiation anti-periphrasis |
| lexical material (≈shape of *stem*) | different | same | homonymy |
| inflectional material (≈shape of *affix*) | same | different | inflectional classes heteroclisis deponency |

Again we shall discuss these briefly, looking in more detail at just two.

In terms of composition/structure, there are different types of deviation, of which defectiveness is particularly interesting:

(9)     Illustration of defectiveness (hypothetical)

| DOG-a | DOG-i | CAT-a | CAT-i | PIG-a | PIG-i |
|---|---|---|---|---|---|
| DOG-e | DOG-o | CAT-e | CAT-o | PIG-e | |

We can recognize the last item as defective by comparison: the other lexemes set up the expectation of the cells which should be realized. This is evident in Matthews's definition of defective: '(Lexical item) whose paradigm is incomplete in comparison with others of the major class that it belongs to.' Matthews (1997: 89). Here is an example of a defective Russian noun. We noted earlier that Russian nouns have at least twelve paradigm cells. For many speakers the noun *mečta* 'dream' lacks a realization for one cell, the genitive plural:

(10)     The defective Russian noun *mečta* 'dream'

| | *mečta* 'dream' | | compare: *mačta* 'mast' | |
|---|---|---|---|---|
| | SINGULAR | PLURAL | SINGULAR | PLURAL |
| NOMINATIVE | mečta | mečty | mačta | mačty |
| ACCUSATIVE | mečtu | mečty | mačtu | mačty |
| GENITIVE | mečty | *** | mačty | mačt |

|              | *mečta* 'dream' |         | compare: *mačta* 'mast' |         |
|--------------|-----------------|---------|-------------------------|---------|
|              | SINGULAR        | PLURAL  | SINGULAR                | PLURAL  |
| DATIVE       | mečte           | mečtam  | mačte                   | mačtam  |
| INSTRUMENTAL | mečtoj          | mečtami | mačtoj                  | mačtami |
| LOCATIVE     | mečte           | mečtax  | mačte                   | mačtax  |

Note that there is no phonological problem with the expected genitive plural *\*mečt* since *mačta* 'mast' has the genitive plural *mačt* (Mel′čuk 1993: 360–1, 1996: 176–7). Equally there is no semantic motivation for the gap. For further discussion of defectiveness see Corbett (2000: 174–6), Baerman and Corbett (2006) and references there.

In contrast, overdifferentiation is shown by a lexeme which, in comparison with others, has additional cells. Thus in the Dravidian language Kolami, there are two genders, basically male human and other. However, the lower numerals '2', '3', and '4' have an additional form for female human (Emeneau 1955: 56). As compared with all the other agreement targets these three lexemes are overdifferentiated.

Finally within this type we find 'anti-periphrasis', the situation where there is a synthetic form in a particular cell contrary to a pattern found in the majority of lexemes. This term is from Haspelmath (2000), who provides an example from Maltese.

The question of *lexical material* is relatively straightforward. Naturally we expect lexemes to be phonologically distinct. However, we find non-canonical instances like English *bank*. Such instances may be completely indistinguishable, as with *bank*, or there may be differences elsewhere in the system. Thus Russian *byk* 'bull' and *byk* 'pier of bridge' have different accusative case forms since the first is animate and the second is not.

Finally in this section we turn to deviations in terms of inflectional material. In the canonical situation, if we compare across lexemes, cell by cell, we find the same inflectional material. If one lexeme realizes the genitive plural in *-dh-a,* all do. Of course we find the well-known inflectional classes, where sets of formatives realize the morphosyntactic specifications. Futhermore, there may be small numbers of lexemes, heteroclites, which take some of their forms from one inflectional class and others from another. We shall now concentrate on deponency. Compared with our other hypothetical illustrations, this is the most complex:

(11)   Illustration of deponency (hypothetical)

Feature value:   a         b         a         b         a

| DOG-a | DOG-i | CAT-a | CAT-i | PIG-i |
|-------|-------|-------|-------|-------|
| DOG-e | DOG-o | CAT-e | CAT-o | PIG-o |

It is worth noting that deponency can be identified only by comparison with the majority of lexemes. If all items were like PIG in our example there would be nothing to indicate any non-canonicity. The point is that we have forms whose function is apparently clear from the majority of lexemes but whose function is different for a minority of lexemes. The best instances of deponency are found in Latin. Here is part of the paradigm of a regular verb, representing a large number of lexemes.

(12)   Partial paradigm of a regular Latin verb

*amāre* 'love'

|  | active | passive |
|---|---|---|
| 1 SG | amō | amor |
| 2 SG | amās | amāris |
| 3 SG | amat | amātur |
| 1 PL | amāmus | amāmur |
| 2 PL | amātis | amāmini |
| 3 PL | amant | amantur |

Here the passive forms are clearly distinguished from the active. Compare now a deponent verb:

(13)   Partial paradigm of a deponent Latin verb

*mīror* 'admire'

|  | active | passive (virtual) |
|---|---|---|
| 1 SG | mīror | ~~mīror~~ |
| 2 SG | mīrāris | ~~mīrāris~~ |
| 3 SG | mīrātur | ~~mīrātur~~ |
| 1 PL | mīrāmur | ~~mīrāmur~~ |
| 2 PL | mīrāmini | ~~mīrāmini~~ |
| 3 PL | mīrantur | ~~mīrantur~~ |

We have labelled the right column 'virtual'. These are cells which would be realized in this way, if they existed. They are struck through because they do not. (Similarly, English *health* may be said to have the virtual plural ~~healths~~: that is what the plural would be, if it existed.) The actual forms are active in use, but they have the appearance of passive forms (by comparison with the majority). This mismatch is of course deponency.[7] While the term has been traditionally reserved for verbs and for voice (and even restricted to Latin and Greek by some scholars), we use '(extended) deponency' as a term for all similar mismatches, extending to other parts of speech, grammatical

---

[7] For earlier discussion and references see Embick (2000), Sadler and Spencer (2001), and Stump (2002).

features, and languages (see Baerman, this volume). We return to deponency in section 5.

## 4.3. Types of deviation

We now present the different types of deviation together for comparison:

(14)   Both types of deviation (levels one and two comparison)

|  | canonical situation | | types of deviation | |
|---|---|---|---|---|
|  | cells (level one) | lexemes (level two) | cells (level one) | lexemes (level two) |
| composition/structure (of the inflected *word*) | same | same | fused exponence periphrasis | defectiveness overdifferentiation anti-periphrasis |
| lexical material (≈shape of *stem*) | same | different | alternations suppletion | homonymy |
| inflectional material (≈shape of *affix*) | different | same | **syncretism** uninflectability | inflectional classes heteroclisis **deponency** |

While all the deviations are non-canonical, we can apply the notion of canonicity to these phenomena too. This will prove helpful particularly when we consider more unusual phenomena. One approach to the degree of canonicity is to consider what part of the paradigm in question is involved. We might consider a single cell (or a set not representing a morphosyntactic pattern), a set of cells forming a natural class (a 'slab'), or all the cells.

For all the phenomena defined in terms of composition or structure, it is sufficient for a single cell to be involved. Indeed we might argue that such instances are the canonical ones. The general requirement (within and across lexemes) is identity. Therefore a single cell behaving in a way out of line with all others is a clear deviation. This is particularly evident with defectiveness: a single missing cell (as in (10)) is striking. A lexeme lacking, say, all the singular can still be defective, but less canonically so. A lexeme lacking all cells would be of rather uncertain status. The general point here is that all of these deviations represent a formal distinction with no apparent functional motivation. If a slab of cells is involved, then the formal distinction may be seen as realizing the function associated with those forms (e.g. plural number) and so the mismatch is less clear and the deviation less canonical.

For deviations involving lexical material or inflectional material the picture is different according to whether we consider the phenomena found by comparing across cells or across lexemes. For alternations and suppletion, the canonical situation is for individual cells (or morphological patterns of cells) to be involved. Once we have a slab involved, then that may introduce some functional validity to the phenomena. And if all cells are involved, then the phenomenon disappears. For syncretism again the canonical situation is for one cell to be involved (syncretic on another). As more cells are involved, the contrast with the rest of the paradigm is reduced. Uninflectability can be seen as the special case of all cells being syncretic with each other.

Turning now to those phenomena established by comparison across lexemes. For homonymy, which goes against the expectation of lexical material being different, the canonical situation is for all cells to be involved. The fewer cells involved, the more like normal lexemes we have. For inflectional classes, the more cells involved the more clearly we have distinct classes. Each additional cell gives more evidence that the 'same' requirement is not met. The same is true of heteroclisis in the sense that the more cells from each contributing class, the clearer it is that we have heteroclisis and not simply a lexeme with some odd forms. And finally for deponency, the more cells that are involved (up to and including all) the clearer the failure to meet the identity requirement and the more canonical the instance of deponency.

## 5.  Extremes Which Have No Name: Syncretism or Deponency?

It is now time to analyse some interesting data on lexemes exhibiting behaviour for which there is currently no name, but clearly falling in the area of syncretism and deponency. We shall approach the data by first examining the characteristics of syncretism and deponency. Both phenomena are of course non-canonical. However, since that is true of both, we may look for canonical instances of syncretism and of deponency. The notion of canonical deponency is discussed also by Stump (this volume).

### 5.1.  Canonical syncretism and canonical deponency

At an abstract level, both phenomena involve relations between cells in a paradigm. In the case of syncretism, there are some instances where we can see that one cell 'takes over' the form of another (those where there is a good reason for appealing to a rule of referral; see Evans, Brown, and Corbett (2001: 215), and Baerman, Brown, and Corbett (2005: 175–7)). In our example above (7), nominative and accusative plural are syncretic. Closer inspection of the nominal system reveals an asymmetrical relationship here, in that there are nouns which are otherwise similar, which would have the same nominative plural, but for which the accusative plural would be syncretic with the genitive (these are animate nouns). In instances like these the source cell retains its original function. That is, the nominative plural form is taken over by the accusative plural, but it is available for the nominative plural too. Contrast that with instances of deponency, as in (13). Here the passive is taken over to be used as the active, but it is not also available as the passive. This is our first criterion for contrast:

(15)   Comparison of syncretism and deponency [criterion 1][8]

| | Syncretism | Deponency |
|---|---|---|
| [1] | Syncretic form retains 'original' function. | Deponent form does not retain 'original' function. |

Recall the distinction between real and virtual forms. How will this affect the two phenomena? Consider first syncretism. This normally affects real forms. Thus in the *komnata* 'room' example (7), *komnaty* is the real nominative plural but since, as just discussed, using it as the accusative also does not prevent it being used as nominative plural, this means that the paradigm remains complete.

There is a possible instance of syncretism involving a virtual form, from the Daghestanian language Tsez. Consider the forms of the ergative singular, in these partial paradigms:

(16)   The ergative in Tsez (Bernard Comrie, personal communication)

| | 'fish' | 'apricot' | 'water' |
|---|---|---|---|
| ABSOLUTIVE | besuro | kukum | ɬi |
| GENITIVE 1 | besuro-s | kukum-yo-s | ɬ-ā-s |
| INESSIVE | **besur-ā** | **kukum-y-ā** | none, alternative local case used |
| ERGATIVE | **besur-ā** | kukum-yo / **kukum-y-ā** | ɬ-ā / ɬiy-ā |

Notes:  (i)   ɬ is a voiceless lateral fricative.
          (ii)  a vowel is dropped before a following vowel.

*Besuro* 'fish' is a regular noun. In regular nouns, the inessive and ergative are identical. There is some evidence that the ergative refers to the inessive. In the simple instances, the inessive is in -*ā*, as is the ergative. However, some nouns have the ergative in -*o*, as with *kukum* 'apricot'. These are a large and increasing minority; there is no obvious semantic motivation for the particular nouns involved (some are phonologically determined). The inessive is not affected. However, many of them have as an alternative the expected ergative in -*ā*, as with our example *kukum* 'apricot'. Thus it appears that the ergative refers to the inessive, rather than the reverse, because the doublets do not appear in the inessive.

---

[8] For those who think in terms of processes, syncretism may be thought of as 'copy and paste' while deponency is 'cut and paste'.

Many nouns (including those denoting humans) have no inessive; thus *ti* 'water' does not, perhaps for semantic reasons. It does have an ergative, and this can be equivalent to what would be the inessive. The situation is muddied somewhat by the existence of an alternative ergative, a dialectal or perhaps idiolectal variant. Such forms appear to exist in order to avoid deforming very short stems. Thus nouns like *ti* 'water' have an ergative syncretic with the inessive (as other nouns) but with an inessive form which is virtual. This takes us to the edge of what could be called 'syncretism'. Note that referring to a virtual form does not reduce the paradigm: this retains all the forms it otherwise had.

As a consequence of the first point (retaining or not retaining the original function), the difference between real and virtual has a greater effect on items showing deponency than on those showing syncretism. Suppose we have a Latin verb which is transitive; its passive is therefore real. Suppose too that the verb is deponent. The passive is taken over as the active, and as a result the verb is defective (the passive forms were needed for the passive). If on the other hand we have an intransitive verb, the passive forms are virtual (the verb does not need a passive). If the verb is deponent, the passive forms are used for the active and the verb's paradigm is complete.

(17)  Comparison of syncretism and deponency [criterion 2]

|  | Syncretism | Deponency |
|---|---|---|
| [2] | If (as usually is the case) the form is from the 'real' paradigm, then the paradigm remains complete. | If the form is from the real paradigm, then the paradigm will be defective. |
| [2.1] | If (as exceptionally in the Tsez ergative) the form is from the 'virtual' paradigm, then the paradigm is not thereby reduced. | If the form is from virtual paradigm, then the paradigm will be complete. |

Next we should consider the extent of the two phenomena within a paradigm. In canonical syncretism, two single cells are involved, one as source and the other as goal. Thus in (7) the accusative plural is syncretic with the nominative plural. To specify such a syncretism needs reference to more than one feature (in this instance, case and number). However, we also find instances where syncretism extends further, as in Slovene nouns:

(18)  Syncretism in Slovene *grad* 'castle'

|  | SINGULAR | DUAL | PLURAL |
|---|---|---|---|
| NOM | grad | gradova | gradovi |
| ACC | grad | gradova | gradove |
| GEN | grada/gradu | **gradov** | **gradov** |
| DAT | gradu | gradovoma | gradovom |
| INST | gradom | gradovoma | gradovi |
| LOC | gradu | **gradovih** | **gradovih** |

The forms in bold show that the genitive dual and genitive plural are syncretic; the locative dual and locative plural are similarly syncretic (and these syncretisms are both general for nouns). We could of course treat each as separate. But this appears to be missing a generalization. They fit together as part of a more general pattern (particularly given that the remaining four dual forms are realized by only two distinct forms, since there are two more syncretisms within the dual). Within Network Morphology the dual-plural syncretism of Slovene is treated as a 'generalized referral' (Evans, Brown, and Corbett 2001: 216, and Baerman, Brown, and Corbett 2005: 186–204). The analysis would be that the dual (as a whole) is syncretic with the plural; this is overridden by the nominative dual (and the accusative is syncretic with that) and by the dative (and the instrumental is syncretic with that).

The main point is that we have an instance of syncretism which applies to more than one cell as source and goal. This would be the canonical situation with deponency, and thus syncretism and deponency contrast at this point, as discussed in section 4.3 above. However, the source and goal for deponency can be reduced. This is the situation we find with semi-deponents, where for instance a verb is deponent in one aspect. This requires a more specific feature specification and so a reduced number of cells is involved:

(19)   Comparison of syncretism and deponency [criterion 3]

|  | Syncretism | Deponency |
|---|---|---|
| [3] | Refers to single cell as source and as goal (so refers to more than one feature). | Takes 'slab' as source and goal (refers to a single feature). |
| [3.1] | May refer to more than one cell, as in Slovene GEN and LOC DUAL syncretic with GEN and LOC PL. | If there is reference to more than one feature this can give rise to a semi-deponent. |

Thus the canonical instance of syncretism involves fewer cells, while canonical deponency involved all cells of a lexeme.

Let us now move on to compare the domain of the two phenomena, that is the lexemes to which they apply. Syncretism may apply to larger or smaller numbers of lexemes; put another way, it may be stated at different points on the inheritance hierarchy (Baerman, Brown, and Corbett 2005: 206–17). The higher it is (the more lexemes are involved) the more canonical. This fits also with Matthews's (1997: 367) definition of syncretism: 'The relation between words which have different *morphosyntactic features but are identical in form. . . . Used especially when the identity is regular across all paradigms.' For deponency, by contrast, the canonical situation is for the lexemes involved to have to be listed. Thus we have the following contrast:

·

(20)   Comparison of syncretism and deponency [criterion 4]

|  | Syncretism | Deponency |
|---|---|---|
| [4] | Generalizes across lexemes (so, given [3] and [4]: few cells, many items). | Generalizes across cells (so, given [3] and [4]: few items, many cells). |

For convenience we bring together the points of comparison here:

(21)   Comparison of syncretism and deponency (overview)

|  | Syncretism | Deponency |
|---|---|---|
| [1] | Syncretic form retains 'original' function. | Deponent form does not retain 'original' function. |
| [2] | If (as usually is the case) the form is from the 'real' paradigm, then the paradigm remains complete. | If the form is from the real paradigm, then the paradigm will be defective. |
| [2.1] | If (as exceptionally in the Tsez ergative) the form is from the 'virtual' paradigm, then the paradigm is not thereby reduced. | If the form is from virtual paradigm, then the paradigm will be complete. |
| [3] | Refers to single cell as source and as goal (so refers to more than one feature). | Takes 'slab' as source and goal (refers to a single feature). |
| [3.1] | May refer to more than one cell, as in Slovene GEN and LOC DUAL syncretic with GEN and LOC PL. | If there is reference to more than one feature this can give rise to a semi-deponent. |
| [4] | Generalizes across lexemes (so, given [3] and [4]: few cells, many items). | Generalizes across cells (so, given [3] and [4]: few items, many cells). |

Why do these properties cluster in this way? Recall that syncretism and deponency share the fact that there is a reuse of forms within a paradigm (including the possibility of using virtual forms). They differ in that syncretism involves cells being the 'same' against a background of 'different'. For syncretism, having two forms the same, against a system of otherwise full differentiation, is the clearest, canonical case. For deponency, we are dealing with forms with the 'wrong' function, which is seen against the background of other lexemes. Here the more cells involved, the clearer and more canonical the case.

Thus canonical syncretism and deponency are as far apart as possible, with syncretism being identifiable within lexeme, and deponency only by comparison with other lexemes.

### 5.2. Between syncretism and deponency: Tsez *xexbi* 'child(ren)'

An interesting example is from the Nakh-Daghestanian language Tsez (Bernard Comrie, personal communication). It is *xexbi* 'child(ren)'; this noun is plural in form (the *-bi* is a regular plural marker) and it has a full plural paradigm of case forms (thus the genitive is *xex-za-s*). It may denote one or more children, and takes the appropriate agreements, singular for one and plural for more than one. The noun *γ⁽anabi* 'woman/women' behaves similarly.

Consider first a regular noun in Tsez:

(22)   Regular Tsez noun *besuro* 'fish' (Bernard Comrie, personal communication)

|  | SINGULAR | PLURAL |
|---|---|---|
| ABSOLUTIVE | besuro | besuro-bi |
| GENITIVE 1 | besuro-s | besuro-za-s |
| INESSIVE/ERGATIVE | besur-ā | besuro-z-ā |
| . | . | . |
| . | . | . |
| . | . | . |

Note: a vowel is dropped before a following vowel.

It is against that background that we should consider *xexbi* 'child(ren)':

(23)   Paradigm of Tsez *xexbi* 'child(ren)'

|  | SINGULAR | PLURAL |
|---|---|---|
| ABSOLUTIVE | xex-bi | xex-bi |
| GENITIVE 1 | xex-za-s | xex-za-s |
| INESSIVE/ERGATIVE | xex-z-ā | xex-z-ā |
| . | . | . |
| . | . | . |
| . | . | . |

According to this paradigm, *xexbi* 'child(ren)' is both singular and plural. Before discussing the significance of these forms, we need to demonstrate that this surprising situation is indeed right. For this we need agreement evidence, and agreement involves four genders as well as two numbers. Assignment to these genders is by a combination of semantic and formal criteria. The main semantic rules are: male humans are assigned to gender I; female humans (also some inanimates) to gender II; animals (and some inanimates) to gender III; and the residue is in gender IV (Polinsky and Comrie 1999: 110). The agreement forms for Tsez verbs are as follows:

(24)   Gender and number agreement forms in Tsez

|  | SINGULAR | PLURAL |
|---|---|---|
| I | Ø- | b- |
| II | y- |  |
| III | b- | r- |
| IV | r- |  |

The syncretisms in this system are somewhat unhelpful for our purposes. There is in addition the demonstrative, which distinguishes singular and plural, and Comrie takes advantage of this to provide clear diagnostic frames. Examples (25)–(27) show the forms for singular nouns (gender III and gender I) and for the plural of gender I.

Tsez (Comrie 2001: 381–3)

(25) howdu            k'et'u            b-ik'i-s.
     this.II/III/IV.SG.ABS   cat(III)[SG.ABS]   III-go-PST.WIT
     'This cat went.'

(26) howda            uži            Ø-ik'i-s.
     this.I.SG.ABS        boy(I)[SG.ABS]    I-go-PST.WIT
     'This boy went.'

(27) howziri        uži-bi            b-ik'i-s.
     this.PL.ABS      boy(I)-PL.ABS      I.PL-go-PST.WIT
     'These boys went.'

While the verb agreements are the same in (25) and (27), the different forms of the demonstrative distinguish the two situations. Given these diagnostic environments we can now turn to *xexbi* 'child(ren)'.

The first example is exactly as we might expect:

(28) howziri        xex-bi            b-ik'i-s.
     this.PL.ABS      child-PL.ABS        I.PL-go-PST.WIT
     'These children went.'

Here more than one child is referred to and the agreements are plural. Now consider what happens for one child. There are two possibilities here. Traditional usage is as follows:

(29) traditional usage (gender III in the singular)

     howdu            xex-bi            b-ik'i-s.
     this.II/III/IV.SG.ABS   child-PL.ABS        III-go-PST.WIT
     'This child went.'

Here the combination of agreements makes it clear that we have gender III singular agreement. The noun itself is unchanged. Younger usage has gender I:

(30) younger speaker's version (gender I in the singular)

     howda            xex-bi            Ø-ik'i-s.
     this.I.SG.ABS        child-PL.ABS        I-go-PST.WIT
     'This child went.'

Here again one child is referred to, and the agreements are singular. The agreements are singular or plural as appropriate, but the forms of the noun stay the same, irrespective of number. Tsez has a substantial paradigm of cases (Comrie and Polinsky 1998), and *xexbi* 'child(ren)' has just one number form for each of them.

Having elucidated the behaviour of *xexbi* 'child(ren)', we can now ask how it measures up to the criteria we established earlier.

(31)   Tsez *xexbi* 'child(ren)' evaluated for syncretism and deponency

|   | Syncretism | Deponency | Tsez *xexbi* 'child(ren)' |
|---|---|---|---|
| 1. | Syncretic form retains 'original' function. | Deponent form does not retain 'original' function. | Retains original function (*syncretic*). |
| 2. | If (as usually is the case) the form is from the 'real' paradigm, then the paradigm remains complete. | If the form is from the real paradigm, then the paradigm will be defective. | From real paradigm, remaining complete (*syncretic*). |
| 3. | Refers to single cell as source and as goal (so refers to more than one feature). | Takes 'slab' as source and goal (refers to a single feature). | Takes slab (*deponent*). |
| 4. | Generalizes across exemes (so, given [3] and [4]: few cells, many items). | Generalizes across cells (so, given [3] and [4]: few items, many cells). | Few items (two in fact), many cells (*deponent*). |

Note: the special factors 2.1 and 3.1 of (21) above do not apply and so are omitted

In terms of our first criterion, *xexbi* 'child(ren)' retains its original function. *Xexbi*, and all the other forms, can certainly be used as plurals. Thus, though these forms, when used as singulars, are taken from the real paradigm, the paradigm remains complete. All the cells are filled. In terms of these first two criteria, it seems rather that we are dealing with syncretism. However, when we look at the cells involved, we see that a whole slab (the entire plural) is involved. Moreover, in terms of domain, only two nouns behave this way. These two factors therefore point in the other direction, suggesting that we are dealing with deponency. One may choose to give more weight to one or other factor. It is clear, however, that *xexbi* 'child(ren)' represents neither canonical syncretism nor canonical deponency. It falls between these two, and is rather far from either canonical type. It is a very unusual lexeme.

# 6.  Interactions Involving Deponency

It is possible for deponency to interact with other non-canonical phenomena, giving rise to lexemes which are even less canonical.

## 6.1. Deponency interacting with suppletion and overdifferentiation

Our first example (32) shows a complex interaction:

(32)  Serbian *dete* 'child' and *žena* 'woman, wife'

| NOMINATIVE | dete | deca | žena |
|---|---|---|---|
| VOCATIVE | dete | deco | ženo |
| ACCUSATIVE | dete | decu | ženu |
| GENITIVE | deteta | dece | žene |
| DATIVE | detetu | deci | ženi |
| INSTRUMENTAL | detetom | decom | ženom |
| LOCATIVE | detetu | deci | ženi |
| | SINGULAR | | SINGULAR |

Consider the forms in the unlabelled column (*deca* and so on). Viewed against the rest of the inflectional system they look odd. First there is a problem with the stem (*dec-* instead of *detet-*). Even leaving aside the augment, *t ~ c* is is not a possible alternation in modern Serbian, and so we must recognize the stems as being suppletive. Not fully suppletive of course, but partially suppletive (or as showing a completely irregular alternation, if preferred). Second, and rather worse, are the inflections. They are apparently completely out of place as plurals; the plural inflections look rather different from these.[9] A comparison with the singular forms of *žena* 'woman, wife', a regular noun of a different inflectional class from *dete*, shows what is going on. We have a set of inflections which have an established function (marking singular) in the morphological system here being used in a minority of instances for the opposite function. That is, an instance of extended deponency. And third, a noun in the plural in Serbian normally distinguishes three case forms (nominative-vocative-accusative versus genitive versus dative-instrumental locative) though one large group has four forms (there is a unique form for the accusative). *Deca* 'children' has six forms and so is overdifferentiated. Thus we find deponency interacting both with partial suppletion and with overdifferentiation.[10] More generally, if interactions involving three of the phenomena investigated are possible, the space of possible words is potentially very large.

## 6.2. Examples from Archi

There are other examples from Archi which, like Tsez, is a Daghestanian language. For these we should start with the typical paradigm structure of a noun. The main distinctions are between singular and plural and, crosscutting

---

[9] Agreements are complex and interesting; see Corbett (1983: 76–86) and Wechsler and Zlatić (2000: 816–21).

[10] Such items are characterized as showing 'higher order exceptionality' in Corbett (forthcoming b).

that distinction, between absolute and ergative. The ergative stems also function as the oblique stems (in the singular and in the plural), on which the
remaining eight grammatical cases are built. In addition there are twenty-eight
spatial cases (Kibrik 1998: 468–73). The basic schema is as follows:

(33)   Schema for Archi noun paradigms (simplest instances)

|  | SINGULAR | PLURAL |
|---|---|---|
| ABSOLUTIVE | bare stem | stem + plural marker |
| ERGATIVE | stem + oblique singular marker | stem + plural marker + oblique plural marker |
| DATIVE | stem + oblique singular marker + dative inflection | stem + plural marker + oblique plural marker + dative inflection |
| . | . | . |
| . | . | . |
| . | . | . |

Here is an example:

(34)   Partial paradigm of the Archi noun *aʕnš* 'apple' (Kibrik 1998: 471)

|  | SINGULAR | PLURAL |
|---|---|---|
| ABSOLUTIVE | aʕnš | aʕnš-um |
| ERGATIVE | aʕnš-li | aʕnš-um-čaj |
| DATIVE | aʕnš-li-s | aʕnš-um-če-s |
| . | . | . |
| . | . | . |
| . | . | . |

There are various alternations, as here with -*čaj* and -*če*. There are different
irregular possibilities, detailed in Kibrik and Kodzasov (1990: 283–4), but the
regular markers are as follows:

(35)   Regular markers for Archi nouns (Kibrik 1998: 468)

|  | SINGULAR | PLURAL |
|---|---|---|
| ABSOLUTIVE | bare stem | -mul (after consonant) -ɩ̄u (after vowel) |
| ERGATIVE | -li | -(č)aj |

The case markers added further are regular.

Given this essential information, we can now consider three interesting
Archi nouns (Marina Chumakina, personal communication). The first two
show limited deponency, in that a form with a function clearly established
from the main noun lexicon has the 'wrong' function in two items:

(36)   Archi *c'aj* 'female goat' (Marina Chumakina, personal communication)

|  | SINGULAR | PLURAL |
|---|---|---|
| ABSOLUTIVE | c'aj | c'ohor |
| ERGATIVE | c'ej-ɨaj | c'ohor-čaj |

In this item the marker *-ɨaj*, an allomorph of *-čaj*, which is the regular ergative plural marker, is used for the ergative singular.

The following item is similar:

(37)   Archi *haˁtəra* 'river' (Marina Chumakina, personal communication)

|  | SINGULAR | PLURAL |
|---|---|---|
| ABSOLUTIVE | haˁtəra | haˁtər-mul |
| ERGATIVE | haˁtər-čaj | haˁtər-mul-čaj |

Here the marker *-čaj*, the regular ergative plural marker, is used for the ergative singular.

Examples (36) and (37) represent interesting if minor instances of deponency. The main reason for considering Archi is, however, this item:

(38)   Archi *χˁon* 'cow' (Marina Chumakina, personal communication)

|  | SINGULAR | PLURAL |
|---|---|---|
| ABSOLUTIVE | χˁon | būc'i |
| ERGATIVE | χˁini | būc'i-li |

This item is suppletive. On top of that it is deponent in that the form *būc'i-li* is clearly marked with the regular singular ergative marker *-li,* yet it is ergative plural. Thus besides the minor instances of deponency, Archi also provides an example of an interaction of deponency and suppletion.

# 7. Conclusion

We have brought the phenomena of inflection, especially deponency, into a coherent scheme. We adopted a canonical approach, which has previously been applied more widely in syntax. Our approach reveals that there are types of lexeme (like Tsez *xexbi* 'child(ren)') whose interest and importance had not previously been fully recognized. We also noted instances like Serbian *deca* 'children', which are more than merely exceptional; they involve an interaction of deponency with other phenomena, and so represent a higher order of exceptionality. Such extremes of inflection are of interest not only to morphologists and typologists but also to psycholinguists.

# References

Baerman, Matthew, Dunstan Brown, and Greville G. Corbett. 2005. *The syntax-morphology interface: a study of syncretism.* Cambridge: Cambridge University Press.

Baerman, Matthew, and Greville G. Corbett. 2006. Three types of defective paradigm. Paper read at the Linguistic Society of America, Annual Meeting, Albuquerque.

Comrie, Bernard. 1986. On delimiting cases. *Case in Slavic*, ed. by Richard D. Brecht and James Levine, 86–106. Columbus, OH.: Slavica.

—— 2001. How independent is Tsezic morphology? *CLS 37: The Panels: 2001: Proceedings from the Parasessions of the 37th Meeting of the Chicago Linguistic Society* [volume 37, 2], ed. by Mary Andronis, Christopher Ball, Heidi Elston, and Sylvain Neuvel, 367–83. Chicago: Chicago Linguistic Society.

Comrie, Bernard, and Maria Polinsky. 1998. The great Daghestanian case hoax. *Case, typology and grammar*, ed. by Anna Siewierska and Jae Jung Song, 95–114. Amsterdam: John Benjamins.

Corbett, Greville G. 1983. *Hierarchies, targets and controllers: agreement patterns in Slavic.* London: Croom Helm.

—— 2000. *Number.* Cambridge: Cambridge University Press.

—— 2003. Agreement: Canonical instances and the extent of the phenomenon. *Topics in morphology: Selected papers from the Third Mediterranean Morphology Meeting (Barcelona, 20–22 September 2001)*, ed. by Geert Booij, Janet DeCesaris, Angela Ralli, and Sergio Scalise, 109–28. Barcelona: Universitat Pompeu Fabra.

—— 2005. The canonical approach in typology. *Linguistic diversity and language theories* (Studies in Language Companion Series 72), ed. by Zygmunt Frajzyngier, Adam Hodges, and David S. Rood, 25–49. Amsterdam: Benjamins.

—— 2006. *Agreement.* Cambridge: Cambridge University Press.

—— 2007. Canonical typology, suppletion and possible words. *Language* 83.8–42.

—— forthcoming Higher order irregularity. *Expecting the unexpected: exceptions in grammar*, ed. by Horst J. Simon and Heike Wiese. Berlin: Mouton de Gruyter.

Corbett, Greville G., and Norman M. Fraser. 1993. Network Morphology: A DATR account of Russian inflectional morphology. *Journal of Linguistics* 29.113–42. [Reprinted 2003 in *Morphology: Critical concepts in linguistics*, VI: *Morphology: its place in the wider context*, ed. by Francis X. Katamba, 364–96 London, Routledge.]

Embick, David. 2000. Features, syntax and categories in the Latin perfect. *Linguistic Inquiry* 31.185–230.

Emeneau, Murray B. 1955. *Kolami: A Dravidian language* (University of California Publications in Linguistics, vol. 12). Berkeley and Los Angeles: University of California Press.

Evans, Nicholas, Dunstan Brown, and Greville G. Corbett. 2001. Dalabon pronominal prefixes and the typology of syncretism: a Network Morphology analysis. *Yearbook of Morphology 2000*, ed. by Geert Booij and Jaap van Marle, 187–231. Dordrecht: Kluwer.

—— 2002. The semantics of gender in Mayali: partially parallel systems and formal implementation. *Language* 78.111–55.

Haspelmath, Martin. 2000. Periphrasis. *Morphologie: ein internationales Handbuch zur Flexion und Wortbildung* = *Morphology: an international handbook on inflection and word-formation*, vol. 1, ed. by Geert Booij, Christian Lehmann, and Joachim Mugdan, 654–64. Berlin: de Gruyter.

Kibrik Aleksandr E. 1998. Archi (Caucasian-Daghestanian). *The handbook of morphology*, ed. by Andrew Spencer and Arnold M. Zwicky, 455–76. Oxford: Blackwell.

Kibrik, Aleksandr E., and Sandro V. Kodzasov. 1990. *Sopostavitel'noe izučenie dagestanskix jazykov: Imja, fonetika*. Moscow: Izdatel'stvo Moskovskogo universiteta.

McCarthy, John. 2005. Optimal paradigms. *Paradigms in phonological theory*, ed. by Laura Downing, Tracy Alan Hall, and Renate Raffelsiefen, 170–210. Oxford: Oxford University Press.

Matthews, P. H. 1972. *Inflectional morphology: A theoretical study based on aspects of Latin verb conjugation*. Cambridge: Cambridge University Press.

—— 1997. *The concise Oxford dictionary of linguistics*. Oxford: Oxford University Press.

Mel'čuk, Igor. 1993. *Cours de morphologie générale (théorique et descriptive)*. I: *Introduction et Première partie: Le mot*. Montréal: Les Presses de l'Université de Montréal.

—— 1996. *Cours de morphologie générale (théorique et descriptive)*. III: Troisième partie: *Moyens morphologiques*; Quatrième partie: *Syntactiques morphologiques*. Montréal: Les Presses de l'Université de Montréal.

Polinsky, Maria, and Bernard Comrie. 1999. Agreement in Tsez. *Agreement* (Special issue of *Folia Linguistica* XXXIII/2), ed. by Greville G. Corbett, 109–30. Berlin: Mouton de Gruyter.

Sadler, Louisa, and Andrew Spencer. 2001. Syntax as an exponent of morphological features. *Yearbook of Morphology 2000*, ed. by Geert Booij and Jaap van Marle, 71–96. Dordrecht: Kluwer.

Seifart, Frank. 2005. *The structure and use of shape-based noun classes in* Miraña (*North West Amazon*). Ph.D. thesis, Radboud University, Nijmegen.

Spencer, Andrew. 2003. Periphrastic paradigms in Bulgarian. *Syntactic structures and morphological information* (Interface Explorations 7), ed. by Uwe Junghanns and Luka Szucsich , 249–82. Berlin: Mouton de Gruyter.

Stump, Gregorgy T. 2001. *Inflectional morphology: a theory of paradigm structure*. Cambridge: Cambridge University Press.

—— 2002. Morphological and syntactic paradigms: arguments for a theory of paradigm linkage. *Yearbook of Morphology 2001*, ed. by Geert Booij and Jaap van Marle, 147–80. Dordrecht: Kluwer.

Suthar, Babubhai Kohyabhai. 2006. *Agreement in Gujarati*. Ph.D. Dissertation, University of Pennsylvania.

Wechsler, Stephen, and Larisa Zlatić. 2000. A theory of agreement and its application to Serbo-Croation. *Language* 76.799–832.

Zaliznjak, Andrej A. 1973 [2002]. O ponimanii termina 'padež' v lingvističeskix opisanijax. In: Andrej A. Zaliznjak *Russkoe imennoe slovoizmenenie*. Moscow: Jazyki slavjanskoj kul'tury. 613–47. [originally in *Problemy grammatičeskogo modelirovanija*, ed. by Andrej A. Zaliznjak, 53–87. Moscow: Nauka].

# 3

# Extending Deponency:
# Implications for Morphological
# Mismatches*

ANDREW SPENCER

## 1. Introduction

IN THIS CHAPTER I DISCUSS A NUMBER OF TYPES of mismatch that don't fit neatly into more traditional schemas. The bulk of these are mismatches which occur when a word of one morpholexical category (say, a noun) inflects as though it were a member of a different morpholexical category (say, adjective). Mismatches of this sort have not been extensively discussed in the literature, which tends to concentrate on within-class mismatches. For instance, 'classical' deponency, syncretism, and heteroclisis all involve 'borrowing' parts of the paradigm of a single lexeme (deponency, syncretism) or a related lexeme in the same inflectional subclass (heteroclisis). The morphology is all from the same major lexical class. However, we also find mismatches in which:

- verbs inflect like adjectives/nouns
- nouns inflect like adjectives/verbs
- adjectives inflect like nouns/verbs.

Any typology of mismatches has to take such cases into account.

Even less familiar are mismatches in which only a part of the word exhibits the mismatch, as when a verb inflects like a verb except for one of its affixed forms, which inflects like an adjective.

I begin by providing a rough preliminary typology of mismatches, based on four properties (this is heavily influenced by the work of Corbett, this volume,

* I am grateful to the editors of this volume for very helpful comments on an earlier draft and to Marina Zaretskaya for discussion of some of the Russian examples.

*Proceedings of the British Academy* 145, 45–70. © The British Academy 2007.

though with slightly different emphasis). I sketch a few instances of within-class mismatches (including some that are less often discussed in this context, such as German honorific personal pronouns). The next subsection introduces some of the between-category mismatches, such as Russian nouns which inflect like adjectives or the Russian past tense, which inflects like an adjective. Section 3 discusses a number of complications in the Hindi verb system, including the future tense forms which combine the canonical morphology of a finite verb form with the canonical morphology of an attributive adjective in one word form. The rest of that section discusses similar instances from the literature on 'Suffixaufnahme', for instance, the Romani 'genitive', which behaves like a genitive case form of a noun in some respects, but like an attributive adjective in other respects (and which behaves like a non-genitive case form when it itself is modified). Section 4 briefly (and inconclusively) raises the question of how morphological mismatches might be reflected in syntactic behaviour (that is, whether there are syntactic mismatches paralleling the morphology) and section 5 summarizes the mismatches and attempts to clarify their relation to each other. The final section presents brief conclusions.

# 2. Morphological Mismatches

## 2.1. General characterization

Where we encounter 'unexpected' morphology amongst the inflected forms of a word this can be distributed in various ways, as enumerated in (1):

(1)   Unexpected morphology occurs
    1.   Domain ('Dom')
         (i)   within lexical classes ('within')
         (ii)  between lexical classes ('between')

    2.   Paradigm coverage ('Para')
         (i)   in some easily definable 'slab' of the paradigm (the whole paradigm being a limiting case) ('slab')
         (ii)  in an isolated cell or cells of the lexeme's paradigm ('cell')

    3.   Generality ('Gen')
         (i)   for isolated lexical exceptions ('exc')
         (ii)  for an (independently definable?) subclass ('subcl')
         (iii) for the whole lexical class ('class')

    4.   Defectivity (in the case of 1(i), within-class mismatches) ('Def')
         (i)   with defectivity in the rest of paradigm ('yes')
         (ii)  without defectivity in the rest of paradigm ('no')

Most discussion of deponency, syncretism and so on devotes little attention to between-class mismatches, and concentrates on within-class mismatches. The second property requires a little explanation. The idea is that some mismatches, such as syncretism, canonically relate just isolated cells in the paradigm, while other mismatches, such as deponency and heteroclisis tend to relate whole sections of a paradigm, or in the case of deponency, sometimes the entire set of inflected forms of the lexeme. It is, however, only when we consider between-class mismatches, such as when a noun inflects entirely like an adjective, that we regularly see entire paradigms participating in the mismatch. It should be recognized, however, that there is some arbitrariness in deciding whether a given portion of a paradigm is a 'slab' or not, especially for paradigms which are in any case small. The third and fourth criteria are relatively clear, though again, there is room for arbitrariness in deciding whether a 'subclass' should be considered a bona fide 'class' all on its own. Finally, note that defectivity is only definable where we have within-class mismatches (see §5 for further discussion).

To see how these mismatch types relate to standard mismatches I provide mismatch codings for syncretism, deponency, and heteroclisis in (2), basing myself on the canonical characterizations provided in Corbett (this volume):

(2)    Mismatch coding for

    syncretism:   Dom(within), Para(cell), Gen(class), Def(no)
    deponency:   Dom(within), Para(slab), Gen(exc, subcl), Def(yes)
    heteroclisis:  Dom(within), Para(slab), Gen(exc, subcl), Def(no)

In canonical syncretism only part of the paradigm is involved (canonically only two cells), the syncretism is exceptionless and doesn't give rise to defective paradigms. In canonical deponency the whole paradigm of the lexeme is involved, only exceptional lexemes or small lexical classes are affected, and the resulting paradigm is defective. In heteroclisis, a slab of the paradigm is typically involved, only exceptional lexemes or small lexical classes are affected, but the resulting paradigm is not defective, in the sense that the heteroclitic lexeme makes all the grammatical contrasts available to a canonical lexeme.

## 2.2. Intraclass mismatches

These are the mismatches which occur within a given word class and hence come under Dom(within) in (1). Classical deponency in Latin verbs is an instance of an intraclass mismatch, in that the unexpected forms are still verb forms. A non-standard example of such deponency (which isn't generally described as deponency in standard handbooks of Latin) is found with verbs in which the present tense is expressed by preterite (perfect) forms. An example of this is found with the verb *odi* 'I hate', imperfect *oderam* 'I used to hate', imperfective future *odero* 'I shall hate'. These endings are those of the standard perfective aspect (cf. *video* 'I see', *videbam* 'I used to see', *videbo* 'I shall see' vs *vidi* 'I saw', *videram* 'I had seen', *videro* 'I shall have seen').

This mismatch only affects part of the paradigm (some forms are regular), but it does affect an easily definable 'slab'. It only affects particular lexemes (not the whole class of verbs or even an identifiable subclass) and it induces defectivity, because there is no way of expressing the perfective meanings normally associated with the perfective forms. This gives the 'mismatch coding' in (3):

(3)    Mismatch coding for *odi* 'I hate':
       Dom(within), Para(slab), Gen(exc), Def(yes)

The Chukchee 'spurious antipassive' (see Spencer 2000; Bobaljik, this volume) superficially resembles Latin (classical) deponency. Transitive verbs show subject and object agreement. However, 'inverse' portions of the active paradigm, in which 2nd person acts on 1st person, use one or other of the two antipassive paradigms. The 2nd person acting on 1SG forms use the antipassive prefixed with *ine-*, while the 2nd person acting on 1PL forms use the antipassive suffixed with *-tku*. This is found in all parts of the verb paradigm except for two sets of de-participial tense forms, that is eight tense-aspect-mood subparadigms and there are no lexical exceptions. It is a moot point whether this mismatch affects a 'slab' or not, because only four person/number/argument cells are involved, but I have chosen to represent this as affecting a slab, on the grounds that the combination of features isn't entirely arbitrary, and exactly the same feature combination is relevant to the whole conjugational system. This makes the mismatch look like deponency. However, if this is deponency then we should think of this as a particularly striking form of 'extended deponency', because it affects all transitive verbs, not just a lexically or morphologically defined subclass. The mismatch coding is therefore that shown in (4):

(4)    Mismatch coding for Chukchee 'spurious antipassive':
       Dom(within), Para(slab), Gen(class), Def(yes?)

It's possible that the cells of the antipassive paradigms to which the transitive cells are referred do not have any syntactic antipassive role. That is, it is likely that one cannot have a syntactic antipassive with the interpretation, roughly, 'you see (with respect to me)', in which case we have defectivity. Syntactic antipassives generally require the direct object of the active form to be 3rd person.

Chukchee declension furnishes a different type of mismatch. Chukchee nouns fall into two inflectional classes broadly corresponding to proper names and close kin (Class II) and others (Class I). Nouns inflect for eight or nine cases (depending on one's analysis of 'case'). Class I nouns (i.e. non-personal nouns) have distinct singular and plural forms only in the absolutive case. This makes Chukchee Class I nouns superficially similar to Tzez *xexbi* (Corbett, this volume) except that a definable subclass is involved rather than a lexical exception, not all of the relevant subparadigm is affected (because absolutive case marked nouns do distinguish number), and there is no clear sense in which the singular forms are using the 'wrong' morphology (because there is no identifiable plural marker for Class I nouns).

(5)   Mismatch coding for:

| | |
|---|---|
| Chukchee Class I nouns: | Dom(within), Para(slab), Gen(subcl), Def(no) |
| *xexbi*: | Dom(within), Para(slab), Gen(exc), Def(no) |

Heteroclitic lexemes are those which inflect according to one inflectional class in some parts of the paradigm and according to a different inflectional class for other parts of the paradigm. Typically, heteroclisis is ascribed to a small set of exceptional lexemes, whose behaviour can't be predicted from other properties. Otherwise, we would tend to speak of a separate inflectional subclass rather than heteroclites. In classical heteroclisis, the unexpected inflectional markers are associated with the expected feature specifications. That is, suppose a noun declines as a 1st declension lexeme in the singular and a 2nd declension lexeme in the oblique cases of the plural, then the 2nd declension oblique case endings have exactly the same function they would have with a genuine 2nd declension noun. This is not the only logical possibility, however. In principle, we could encounter a kind of heteroclisis in which the mismatched cells not only belong to an unexpected class, but had unexpected meanings or functions, too.

An example of this might be German honorific pronouns (and similar honorific systems in many other languages), as shown in (6):

(6)   German honorific pronouns:

Sie (nominative, accusative), Ihnen (dative)
Ihr (possessive pronoun)
meaning     'HON, 2nd SG' or 'HON, 2PL'
form          '3PL(plain)'

The plain 3rd person plural pronominal forms (including the possessive pronoun) function as honorific forms with both singular and plural reference. The familiar, non-honorific forms of the 2nd person, however, distinguish number (*du* 'you.SG' vs *ihr* 'you.PL'). In this respect the declension of the honorific pronouns is distinct from the homophonous 3PL plain pronouns, because the 3rd person pronouns are unambiguously plural, whereas the honorific forms syncretize singular and plural (by using the plural forms to express the singular property).

The mismatch codings are given in (7):

(7)   Dom(within), Para(slab), Gen(subcl)

Chukchee common nouns denoting humans such as 'friend' illustrate an interesting variation on the theme of heteroclisis. They are able to decline either as Class I nouns (non-human) with no number distinction in non-absolutive case forms, or as Class II nouns, with a singular-plural contrast for all cases.

### 2.3. Interclass mismatches

In this type of mismatch a lexeme takes inflections proper to (the corresponding part of) the paradigm of a different lexical class altogether. A clear example of this is provided by certain types of Russian noun which inflect as though they were adjectives. In (8) I compare the noun *stolovaja* 'dining room' with the feminine forms of the adjective *gotovyj* 'ready' and the ordinary feminine noun *lampa* 'lamp':

(8)   Russian adjectival nouns: *stolovaja* 'dining room' (F) compared with an adjective
      and a noun

|          | 'dining room' (F) | 'ready.F' | 'lamp' (F) |
|----------|-------------------|-----------|------------|
| Singular |                   |           |            |
| NOM      | stolov-aja        | gotov-aja | lamp-a     |
| ACC      | stolov-uju        | gotov-uju | lamp-u     |
| GEN      | stolov-oj         | gotov-oj  | lamp-i     |
| DAT      | stolov-oj         | gotov-oj  | lamp-e     |
| INS      | stolov-oj         | gotov-oj  | lamp-oj    |
| PREP     | stolov-oj         | gotov-oj  | lamp-e     |
| Plural   |                   |           |            |
| NOM      | stolov-ye         | gotov-ye  | lamp-y     |
| ACC      | stolov-ye         | gotov-ye  | lamp-y     |
| GEN      | stolov-yx         | gotov-yx  | lamp       |
| DAT      | stolov-ym         | gotov-ym  | lamp-am    |
| INS      | stolov-ymi        | gotov-ymi | lamp-ami   |
| PREP     | stolov-yx         | gotov-yx  | lamp-ax    |

The lexeme *stolovaja* is a noun in its syntax and semantics but an adjective in form. In this case the entire paradigm of the noun is taken over from the adjectival declension. Historically, this kind of mismatch typically arises when a word of one class is derived from a word in a different class, without changing the morphology. In Spencer (2005: 104, 117) I refer to this as 'morphologically inert derivation'.

We can also have a situation in which such a mismatch only occurs for part of the paradigm. Russian provides another case in point. In (9) we see the present and past tense forms of a regular verb (I give the present tense forms in 'morphophonemic' transcription so that the underlying pattern is clearer):

(9)   Partial paradigm interclass mismatch: Russian past tense

*delat'* 'make'

| Present tense | SINGULAR | PLURAL |
|---|---|---|
| 1 | delaj-u | delaj-om |
| 2 | delaj-oš | delaj-ote |
| 3 | delaj-ot | delaj-ut |

| Past tense | | SINGULAR | | PLURAL |
|---|---|---|---|---|
| | masculine | feminine | neuter | |
| | delal | delala | delalo | delali |
| predicative | mal | mala | malo | maly |

predicative
adjective form
*mal* 'short'

The present tense forms inflect in the way expected of Indo-European verbs, while the past tense forms inflect just like a so-called 'short form' adjective, a class which is used predicatively. Historically, this situation arose when a perfect tense series formed with the *l*-participle (e.g. *dela-l*) and the auxiliary verb 'be' was reinterpreted as a past tense form, and the auxiliary was lost. Similar situations often arise (see below on Hindi) either with adjectival forms (participles) or nominal forms ('verbal nouns' in many languages). The results are somewhat similar to the morphologically inert derivation illustrated in de-adjectival nouns in Russian and many languages, but the perspective is slightly different because what we find is that one part of an otherwise well-behaved paradigm acquires mismatched morphology, often in a relatively small sub-paradigm. In Spencer (2005: 104, 125) I refer to this type of mismatch as a 'morphological shift'.[1]

Again, Russian provides even more complex instances of partial paradigm mismatches (see Spencer 2002, Corbett 2004 for further discussion). Russian has a large number of possessive adjectives derived from names kin terms, or animal names. Such adjectives share the inflections of standard adjectives but some of their inflected forms are similar to those of common nouns. In the examples (10–11) I have given the noun-like endings in boldface. The symbol Ø indicates that there is no ending. Alternations such as *-ogo/-ego*, *-oj/-ej* are the result of regular morphophonemic processes or are spelling conventions.

---

[1] Baerman, Brown, and Corbett (2005: 32) claim that Russian present tense verbs express gender, but are uninflected for gender, in the same way that an indeclinable noun such as *sheep* can express plural number without being inflected for number. The reason is that predicative adjectives used after copular verbs such as *javljat'sja* 'be, appear' agree in gender with the subject. But this is a fact about adjectives in predicate position and nothing to do with verbs. Notice that Baerman et al's analysis would commit them to the implausible claim that an infinitive form such as *byt'* 'to be' expresses gender (without being inflected for gender) on the basis of examples such as *Nataša xočet byt' bogatoj* 'Natasha wants to-be rich.F'. I therefore reject the idea that present tense verb forms in Russian express gender in any way.

(10)  a.  Standard adjective declension (ignoring neuter singular) *gotovyj* 'ready'

|      | masculine | feminine | plural |
|------|-----------|----------|--------|
| NOM | gotov-yj | gotov-aja | gotov-ye |
| ACC | (NOM/GEN) | gotov-uju | (NOM/GEN) |
| GEN | gotov-ogo | gotov-oj | gotov-yx |
| DAT | gotov-omu | gotov-oj | gotov-ym |
| INS | gotov-ym | gotov-oj | gotov-ymi |
| PREP | gotov-om | gotov-oj | gotov-ym |

   b.  Possessive adjectives, others: *volčij* 'wolf's'

|      | masculine | feminine | plural |
|------|-----------|----------|--------|
| NOM | volč(i)j-Ø† | volčj-**a** | volčj-**i** |
| ACC | (NOM/GEN) | volčj-**u** | (NOM/GEN) |
| GEN | volčj-ego | volčj-ej | volčj-ix |
| DAT | volčj-emu | volčj-ej | volčj-im |
| INS | volčj-im | volčj-ej | volčj-imi |
| PREP | volčj-em | volčj-ej | volčj-ix |

   †The /i/ of *volč(i)j* in this paradigm is epenthetic

   c.  Russian possessive adjectives, names/kin: *Ivanov* 'Ivan's', *mamin* 'Mama's'[2]

|      | masculine | feminine | plural |
|------|-----------|----------|--------|
| NOM | mamin-**Ø** | mamin-**a** | mamin-**y** |
| ACC | (NOM/GEN) | mamin-**u** | (NOM/GEN) |
| GEN | mamin-**a** (mamin-ogo) | mamin-oj | mamin-yx |
| DAT | mamin-**u** (mamin-omu) | mamin-oj | mamin-ym |
| INS | mamin-ym | mamin-oj | mamin-ymi |
| PREP | mamin-om | mamin-oj | mamin-yx |

In (11) we see the paradigm for some typical surnames. Surnames are some-times purely adjectival (e.g. *Dostoevskij*, *Tolstoj*), declining exactly like *gotovyj* in which case they are equivalent morpholexically to nouns such as *stolovaja*, but in many cases they decline differently and the declension overlaps with that of the personal possessive adjectives in (10c):

(11)  Partial paradigm interclass mismatch: Russian surnames, *Čexov(a)*, *Puškin(a)*

|      | masculine | feminine | plural |
|------|-----------|----------|--------|
| NOM | Čexov-**Ø** | Čexov-**a** | Čexov-**y** |
| ACC | Čexov-**a** | Čexov-**u** | Čexov-yx |
| GEN | Čexov-**a** | Čexov-oj | Čexov-yx |
| DAT | Čexov-**u** | Čexov-oj | Čexov-ym |

---

[2] My informant permits the purely adjective endings *-ogo/omu* for adjectives in *-in*, though these are not really possible for adjectives in *-ov*. Generally, the *-in* adjectives are more productive and common than *-ov* adjectives, which tend to occur in fixed expressions only.

|      | masculine | feminine | plural |
|------|-----------|----------|--------|
| INS  | Čexov-ym  | Čexov-oj | Čexov-ymi |
| PREP | Čexov-e   | Čexov-oj | Čexov-yx |

The example *Ivanov* forms a minimal pair in this regard. In addition to meaning 'pertaining to Ivan', it is also a (very common) surname. As a surname it declines like *Čexov* and not as its homophonous possessive adjective in (10a) and thus the two usages differ in the masculine prepositional singular: *o gospodine Ivanove* 'about Mr Ivanov' but *ob Ivanovom detstve* 'about Ivan's childhood'.

The declensions can be characterized as a simple pattern of default inheritance, summarized in (12):

(12)  Possessive adjective (non-human) e.g. *volčij* 'wolf's' = adjective except for nominative/accusative feminine singular, nominative/accusative (inanimate) plural.

Possessive adjective (human) in *-ov/in* = possessive adjective (non-human) except for accusative/genitive masculine singular

Surname = possessive adjective (human) except for prepositional masculine singular.

The mismatch in inflectional patterning of the surnames doesn't affect the whole paradigm. The accusative/genitive and the prepositional cases in the masculine singular paradigm are like those of a noun while the other cells are those of a human possessive adjective. In this respect surnames are like Russian past tenses rather than like *stolovaja*-nouns. On the other hand, by no means all adjectival surnames have this declensional pattern, so we have to speak of a subclass of lexemes.

As a final example of mismatches in Russian nouns I shall cite a phenomenon which is very widespread, namely the use of converted adjectives (especially, but not exclusively, participle forms) with human referents. For example, present active or perfective passive participles are productively converted to nouns (modulo semantics/pragmatics): *učit'sja* 'study' *učaščijsja* 'student' (present participle); *ranit'* 'injure' *ranenyj* 'injured person' (passive participle), as are adjectives such as *bol'noj* 'sick', adjective, giving *bol'noj* '(doctor's) patient', noun. The resulting nouns decline exactly like adjectives, and thus are different from surnames. However, this affects a well-defined subclass of nominals, namely those converted from adjectives and so this is a different type of lexeme from the *stolovaja* type. The pattern of mismatches for surnames and deadjectival nouns is compared with that of *stolovaja* in (13):

(13)  *stolovaja* 'dining room':  Dom(between), Para(slab), Gen(exc)
      *Čexov* 'Chekhov':          Dom(between), Para(cell?), Gen(subcl)
      *Ivanov* 'Ivan's':          Dom(between), Para(slab), Gen(subcl)

(I discuss the surnames in more detail in §5).

So as to allay any suspicion that such mismatches are peculiar to Russian, consider the Japanese verb. Japanese verbs inflect for various categories, including tense (past/non-past), status (plain vs polite) and polarity (positive/ negative). The polite non-past negative forms are synthetic while the polite past negative forms are periphrastic. However, the plain negative forms in both tenses inflect (almost) entirely like adjectives. In (14) we see a number of forms for a typical adjective *takai* 'high' and the corresponding forms of the plain negative form, *tabenai*, of the verb *taberu* 'eat'. These can be compared to the other forms of *taberu* in (15). The *-i* ending of *takai* and *tabenai* is characteristic of inflecting adjectives in their citation form.

(14) Partial paradigm interclass mismatch (unrestricted)—Negative plain verb forms *tabenai* 'not eat' compared with adjective *takai* 'high':

|              | 'not eat'       | 'high'        |
|--------------|-----------------|---------------|
| present      | *tabenai*       | *takai*       |
| adverbial    | *tabe-na-ku*    | *taka-ku*     |
| gerund       | *tabe-na-ku-te* | *taka-ku-te*  |
| past         | *tabe-na-katta* | *taka-katta*  |
| conditional1 | *tabe-na-kattara* | *taka-kattara* |
| conditional2 | *tabe-na-kereba* | *taka-kereba* |

(15) Japanese conjugation: *taberu* 'eat'

|              | plain positive | polite positive | polite negative     |
|--------------|----------------|-----------------|---------------------|
| present      | *taberu*       | *tabemasu*      | *tabemasen*         |
| adverbial    | (no form)      | (no form)       | (no form)           |
| gerund       | *tabe-te*      | (no form)       | (no form)           |
| past         | *tabe-ta*      | *tabe-masi-ta*  | *tabe-masen desita* |
| conditional1 | *tabe-tara*    | (no form)       | (no form)           |
| conditional2 | *tabe-reba*    | (no form)       | (no form)           |

The part of the verb paradigm that exhibits this mismatch is clearly delineated: it is all and only those forms expressing the {[Status: Plain], [Polarity: Negative]} property set that show the mismatch. In that respect we can say that the mismatch applies uniformly across a well-defined subparadigm. Indeed, if we had found that all verbs inflect like adjectives for the whole of their paradigm we would not bother setting up a distinct morphological class of verb (or adjective). Exactly the same situation holds of the Russian past tense. The mismatch coding for both systems is therefore that given in (16):

(16) Russian past tense, Japanese plain negative:

Dom(between), Para(slab), Gen(class)

# 3. More Complex Cases

Thus far we have seen instances in which the word form occupying a cell in an inflectional paradigm is similar to a word form of a different lexeme, inflectional class or lexical class. Thus, Russian *stolovaja* looks like an adjective, even though it's a noun and Japanese *tabenai* looks like an adjective, even though it's a verb. In this subsection I consider more complex instances in which the morphosyntactic mismatch occurs within the word form itself, so that part of the word form has the shape of a verb while another part of that same word form has the shape of an adjective. As far as I know such mismatches have not been discussed extensively in the literature on morphological form mismatches. A particularly striking example is found in Hindi.

## 3.1. Hindi-Urdu conjugation

The first complication with this language is that most verbs inflect like adjectives for most of their conjugation. Indeed, there is only one verb which has verb inflections in its present indicative form, *honaa* 'be' and no verb has verb inflections in its past tense forms. Rather, the past tense forms are effectively adjectival. This is illustrated in (17):

(17)   Conjugation of Hindi *honaa* 'be'

Present indicative

|   | SG | PL |
|---|-----|-----|
| 1 | hũũ | hãi |
| 2 | hai | ho |
| 3 | hai | hãi |

Past tense

| | masculine | | feminine | |
|---|-----|-----|-----|-----|
| | SG | PL | SG | PL |
| | thaa | the | thii | thĩĩ |

Compare the past tense forms with those of the inflecting adjective *acchaa* 'good' (adjectives don't inflect for tense, so these forms are tenseless):

(18)   Declension of Hindi adjective *acchaa* 'good' (direct and oblique cases)

| | masculine | | feminine | |
|---|-----|-----|-----|-----|
| | SG | PL | SG | PL |
| Direct: | acchaa | acche | acchii | acchii |
| Oblique: | acche | acche | acchii | acchiyõ |

The direct case forms are used for predicative agreement with a subject, as well as in attributive modification.

The simple perfective past tense (already seen in ( 17) for the verb 'be') is participial in original, but, like the Russian past tense, it is formed without an auxiliary verb. Like the Russian verb forms, the Hindi past tense forms are very slightly different from those of a pure adjective, in that the feminine plural ending is nasalized in the verb forms but not in direct case form of the adjective:

(19)  Hindi simple perfective past

| masculine | feminine | |
|-----------|----------|---|
| likhaa | likhii | 'I wrote' |
| likhe | likhĩĩ | 'they wrote' |

On the one hand this is a minor deviation from adjectival morphology, in that the forms still inflect for adjectival properties, gender/number, and not verbal properties, person/number. However, the unexpected nasalization (like the unexpected palatalization in Russian past tense forms) effectively serves as a curious partial exponent of the category 'verb' within an adjective-like morphological paradigm. In this respect the forms contrast with the true participial bases, *likh-* and *likht-,* which behave exactly like adjectives. This is clearly visible in (20). This shows the past perfect (pluperfect), which is formed by combining the past tense of 'be' with the same participial form which is used to form the past tense.

(20)  likh-ii          th-ĩĩ
      write-F.PL    be.PST-F.PL
      'They(feminine) had written'

Here it can be seen that the auxiliary *thĩĩ* has nasalization but not the participle *likhii*:

*Interim summary*

Only the verb 'be' actually conjugates in the traditional Indo-European manner, that is for person/number, and then only in the present tense. All other verb forms, including the simple past and the past of 'be' inflect like adjectives.

So far, however, we have only seen examples of the indicative mood. Hindi verbs also have a set of subjunctive or irrealis mood forms, illustrated for 'write' and 'be' in (21a, b):

(21)  Hindi subjunctive

| | a. | 'write' | | b. | 'be' | |
|---|---|---|---|---|---|---|
| | | SG | PL | | SG | PL |
| 1 | | likhũũ | likhẽ | | hũũgaa | hõge |
| 2 | | likhe | likho | | hogaa | hoge |
| 3 | | likhe | likhẽ | | hogaa | hõge |

The Hindi future form is based on the subjunctive, but in an interesting fashion. It is formed by taking the subjunctive as a base to which is suffixed an adjectival ending -*gaa*:

(22)   Hindi future
      'write'

|   | masculine | | feminine | |
|---|---|---|---|---|
|   | SG | PL | SG | PL |
| 1 | likhũũgaa | likhẽge | likhũũgii | likhẽgii |
| 2 | likhegaa | likhoge | likhegii | likhogii |
| 3 | likhegaa | likhẽge | likhegii | likhẽgii |

      'be'

|   | masculine | | feminine | |
|---|---|---|---|---|
|   | SG | PL | SG | PL |
| 1 | hũũgaa | hõge | hũũgii | hõgii |
| 2 | hogaa | hoge | hogii | hogii |
| 3 | hogaa | hõge | hogii | hõgii |

Thus, the future form combines the verbal and the adjectival mode of inflection in a single word form.

The relevant aspects of the Hindi verb system are summarized in (23):

(23)   (a)   Most Hindi verb forms are adjectival, only 'be' (present tense) and the subjunctive are genuinely verbal.
      (b)   The future is a verb-adjective hybrid.

In classical deponency a lexically restricted set of items lack part A of their paradigm, and use part B to mean part A. Hindi verbs don't fit into this scheme very well. Thus, the verb 'to be' is a lexically restricted (indeed unique) item, but for its present tense it maintains those verbal features of its paradigm which have been lost in all other verbs and replaced by adjectival features. The obvious descriptive solution is to say that the verb 'be' is irregular in maintaining vestigial person/number agreements and that the verb system is now essentially adjectival. However, this fails to account for two things. First, there are the subjunctive forms of all verbs, which also maintain the 'vestigial' person/number morphology (not to mention the hybrid future forms). But more importantly, most of the non-past tense finite clause types in Hindi involve a verb form inflected for person/number. This is because most of the periphrastic constructions require the auxiliary verb 'be', and that verb has person/number inflection in the non-past (though not in the past tense). Looked at from this perspective person-number marking plays a rather important role in Hindi morphosyntax. It is therefore at best misleading to relegate it to some kind of vestigial form.

The kind of mismatch seen in the Hindi future is not just a matter of paradigm organization, it is a matter of the linear organization of the word form. For this reason we can think of it as a syntagmatic morphological mismatch. Such mismatches have not, as far as I know, been discussed widely in the literature on morphological typology.[3]

## 3.2. Other examples

Hybrid morphology of the kind found in the Hindi future is not unique, even though such clear cases are not common. In the nominal domain we might mention a phenomenon often designated as Suffixaufnahme. In many languages with a case system the genitive case form can agree with its head in the manner of an adjective. This most famously happens in Australian languages, of course, though there the agreement tends to be limited to case marking, which in some ways is better seen as part of an independent pattern of multiple case marking (see Dench and Evans, 1988, for a very informative survey of multiple case marking in Australian languages).

Clearer instances of hybrid morphology occur in those Indo-Aryan languages which have developed a new morphological case system from the old postpositions. In a language such as Hindi a declinable noun distinguishes singular/plural number and direct, oblique and vocative case. The direct case is used as a nominative, while the oblique case is almost always found as the complement of a clitic postposition (the oblique can be used on its own as a kind of directional locative with place names). These six case/number forms are frequently referred to as 'Layer I' inflections. The clitic postpositions are often referred to as 'Layer II' elements. Declinable attributive adjectives agree with their noun heads for case/number (that is, in terms of the Layer I properties). However, no agreement process is sensitive to whether or not a noun is the complement of a postposition. Thus, the postpositions, or Layer II elements, have no important case-like properties.

One of the Layer II postpositions, *kaa*, even has adjectival properties. This postposition is the canonical way of expressing the possessive construction (sometimes misleadingly referred to as the 'genitive case'). Like the other

---

[3] The Hindi future is similar in some respects to what Evans and Nordlinger (ms) refer to as a case of extreme morphological shift, that of verbal case in Kayardild (see also Evans 1995: 163–84). One of the set of case markers in this language, verbal case, turns the noun, morphologically speaking, into a verb. The resulting noun has to agree with the main verb in tense/mood/polarity, and has to be nominalized before taking further case markers. An example of the verbal denizen case is shown in (i)

(i)   ngijin-mirdi-n-da          dul-wirdi-n-da              jardi-y
      my-VDEN-NMLZ-NOM       place-VDEN-NMLZ-NOM       mob-NOM
      'the people staying at my place'

postpositions it selects the oblique Layer I case form of its noun complement. The postposition then shows adjectival agreement with the possessum (possessed noun). This is illustrated in (24) (adapted from Snell and Weightman 1989: 62):

(24)  acchaa laRkaa 'good boy', acche laRke 'good boys'
      acchii laRkii 'good girl', acchii laRkiyãã, 'good girls'

  a.  acche              laRke           kaa            kamraa
      good.M.OBL.SG      boy.OBL.SG      KAA.M.DIR.SG   room(M).DIR.SG
      'the good boy's room'

  b.  acche              laRke           kii            kursii
      good.M.OBL.SG      boy.OBL.SG      KAA.F.DIR.SG   chair(F).DIR.SG
      'the good boy's chair'

  c.  acchii             laRkii          ke             kamre
      good.F.OBL.SG      girl.OBL.SG     KAA.M.DIR.PL   room(M).DIR.PL
      'the good girl's rooms'

  d.  acchiyõ            laRkiyõ         kaa            kamraa
      good.F.OBL.PL      girl.OBL.PL     KAA.M.DIR.SG   room(M).DIR.SG
      'the good girls' room'

  e.  laRke              kii             kursiyõ        par
      boy.OBL.SG         KAA.F.OBL.PL    chair(F).OBL.PL on
      'on the boy's chairs'

  f.  laRkiyõ            ke              kamre          mẽ
      girl.OBL.PL        KAA.M.OBL.SG    room(M).OBL.SG in
      'in the girls' room'

As is clear from these examples the features of the possessor noun are irrelevant to the inflection of the *kaa* postposition. The possessor phrase is therefore adjectival in its agreement properties. Compare the examples in (24) with those in (25) in which the possessor phrase is replaced with an adjective:

(25) a./d. acchaa             kamraa
           good.M.DIR.SG      room(M).DIR.SG
           'the good room'

  b.  acchii             kursii
      good.F.DIR.SG      chair(F).DIR.SG
      'the good chair'

  c.  acche              kamre
      good.M.DIR.PL      room(M).DIR.PL
      'the good rooms'

  e.  acchii             kursiyõ         par
      good.F.OBL.PL      chair(F).OBL.PL on
      'on the good chairs'

  f.  acche              kamre          mẽ
      good.M.OBL.SG      room(M).OBL.SG in
      'in the good room'

In some languages of this group the postpositions have become morphologized as suffixes, making them look more like true case endings. However, in most languages these new inflections still lack the agreement morphosyntax of cases, in the sense that they fail to trigger agreement on declinable attributive modifiers. Thus, there is still a difference between the old Layer I morphology (that is, number morphology and the direct/oblique forms) and the now affixal Layer II morphology.

In most dialects of Romani, the innovated case suffixes (formerly Layer II postpositions) are attached, as expected, to the (Layer I) oblique stem form of the noun. The examples in (26) are taken from a grammar of the North Russian dialect (Ventcel' 1964):

(26)  'man, Gypsy'

|          | SG       | PL        |
|----------|----------|-----------|
| direct   | rom      | roma      |
| oblique  | romes-   | roman-    |

'Gypsy woman'

|          | SG       | PL        |
|----------|----------|-----------|
| direct   | romny    | romn'a    |
| oblique  | romn'a-  | romnen-   |

| romes-kiro gad       | 'Gypsy's shirt'         |
|----------------------|-------------------------|
| romes-kiri stady     | 'Gypsy's hat'           |
| romes-kire tyraha    | 'Gypsy's boots'         |
| romnen-giro khelyben | 'Gypsy women's dances'  |
| romnen-giri gily     | 'Gypsy women's songs'   |
| romnen-gire id'a     | 'Gypsy women's clothes' |

However, when an adjective modifies a case-marked noun it completely ignores the new case endings and agrees along the Layer I direct-oblique dimension, just as in Hindi. The interesting situation arises with the innovated genitive forms. These behave like attributive adjectives, again as in Hindi. However, any attributive modifier which modifies such a 'genitive' case noun will agree with the oblique stem form of the noun. This is equally true for 'genitives' modifying 'genitives' in iterated possessive constructions (examples from Šebková & Žlnayová 2001: 254; Matras 2002: 90; see also Koptjevskaja-Tamm, 2000, for detailed discussion):

(27)  a.  la            čora          da-ker-o                  čhavo
          the.F.OBL     poor.OBL      mother-GEN-M.SG.NOM       son.SG.NOM
          'the poor woman's son'

b. le          bare                   lavuteris-ker-o              čhavo
   the.M.OBL   well-known.M.OBL       musician-GEN-M.SG.NOM        son.SG.NOM
   'the well-known musician's son'

c. le          rakles-k-e             dade(s)-sa
   the.M.OBL   boy-GEN-M.OBL          father-INS
   'with the boy's father'

Similar constructions, in which a genitive case marked noun has the agreement properties of an adjective, have been reported in certain Daghestan languages (Boguslavskaja 1995; Kibrik 1995) and in Central Cushitic (Hetzron 1995). The type of morphosyntactic mismatch involved is rather similar to that reported with possessive adjectives in Upper Sorbian (Corbett 1987, 1995).

The reason examples such as the Romani 'genitive' are of importance for a typology of morphological, cross-paradigm mismatches is that on the one hand such a word form has the morphological properties of an adjective, but on the other hand it is clearly an inflected form of a noun (without, however, being a derivational form, such as a relational adjective; see Payne, 1995: 293f., for further arguments for why it would be a mistake to treat such cases as straightforward noun-to-adjective derivation). This makes the 'agreeing genitive' look like the *stolovaja* nouns of Russian. But the 'genitives' (along with other case-suffixed forms) become a part of a two-term direct/oblique case system when they are modified. The question therefore arises as to where in the set of paradigmatic oppositions such word forms belong.

It should be admitted here that the analysis of Indo-Aryan presented here is not uncontroversial. Recent theoretical discussion of these languages has almost universally taken it for granted that the postpositions themselves are cases (or case markers) and that the direct/oblique distinction is something to do with stem formation. Thus, Mohanan (1994: 61) speaks of 'stem forms' rather than 'case forms' in describing the direct/oblique distinction. Masica (1991: 239), too, points out that some descriptions regard the oblique form as an 'Oblique Base' rather than a case 'since it has no casal function', that is, it cannot be used on its own to signal argument structure relationships (though this is not entirely true, at least for Hindi and Romani). He then adds in a footnote 'The historically-minded conversely sometimes prefer to treat it as the *only* "case", very general in function, with specifying postpositions added (1991: 474, fn. 17, emphasis original).' This is essentially the analysis I am proposing here. The jibe at the 'historically-minded' is aimed at those who stress the fact that the oblique forms generally reflect earlier inflectional cases in Sanskrit. However, Masica soon afterwards finds himself in a quandary when dealing with the morphosyntax of adjectives (p. 250), for he is obliged to describe that as agreement with Layer I case (*sic*), even though he has no way of describing such a notion, and even though he seems to have accepted that it is the Layer II elements that are case markers. It is easy to find recurrence of such incoherence in the recent literature on Indo-Aryan.

It is therefore important to note that the problem of assigning a noun to a case form is not restricted to languages in which a 'genitive' or possessive construction acquires the morphosyntax of an attributive adjective. A type of mismatch exactly homologous to that of Indo-Aryan is seen with the 'four last cases' of Estonian. Estonian nouns are generally considered to have fourteen case forms, for each of the singular and plural numbers. Adjectives agree with their head nouns in case and number. In (28) we see this for a simple phrase (adapted from Uuspõld and Valmet 2001: 192), formed from *noor* 'young' and *inimeme* 'person':

(28)   Paradigm for *noor inimeme* 'young person'

|  | SG | | PL | |
|---|---|---|---|---|
| NOMINATIVE | noor | inimeme | noore-d | inimese-d |
| GENITIVE | noore | inimese | noor-te | inimes-te |
| ILLATIVE | noore-sse | inimese-sse | noor-te-sse | inimess-te-sse |
| ALLATIVE | noore-le | inimese-le | noor-te-le | inimes-te-le |
| <...> | | | | |
| TERMINATIVE | noore | inimese-ni | noor-te | inimes-te-ni |
| ESSIVE | noore | inimese-na | noor-te | inimes-te-na |
| ABESSIVE | noore | inimese-ta | noor-te | inimes-te-ta |
| COMITATIVE | noore | inimese-ga | noor-te | inimes-te-ga |

As can be seen from these data, the 'four last cases', the terminative, essive, abessive, and comitative cases behave exactly like the innovated case forms of Romani that have been based on the genitive. However, the genitive case doesn't itself behave like an attributive modifier. What is important about these examples is that the genitive case form, both of the noun and adjective, is unequivocally part of the case paradigm and not some special extra-paradigmatic form. When an adjective modifies a noun in one of the last four cases that adjective really is therefore in the genitive case, despite the mismatch with the case of its noun head. We might say that the agreement system, considered in the abstract, lacks specific expression for the last four cases, and instead uses 'the wrong case', genitive. This is therefore an abstract kind of deponency (but without defectivity, because the agreement system is still able to express agreement for genitive case).

# 4. What is (Mis)matched with What?

When morphological forms play a crucial role in syntax, for instance, agreement or case government, then we often find that a morphological mismatch will be associated with a corresponding syntactic mismatch. A clear example of this is found with verb forms that are formally adjectival, such as the Russian past tense. A verb in the past tense still has argument structure and the basic syntax of a verb but it shares its agreement morphosyntax with predicative adjectives, in the sense that the past tense verb inflects for gender/number and not person/number. Somewhat more complex examples are found when nominalized verb forms take (say) genitive-marked arguments instead of nominative/accusative or ergative/absolutive. Such forms will often be used to realize subordinate clauses but grammatical change can lead to them being given tense/aspect marking and reanalysed as finite forms, while the argument marking remains that of a nominal. Such constructions can in principle complicate the analysis because it isn't always clear whether we have a stable syntactic category with unusual, mismatched morphology (presumably the case with the Russian past) , or whether we actually wish to say that the syntactic category of a word is dependent on relatively low-level details such as whether it's marked for tense.

A relatively subtle version of this problem is found with Russian adjectival nouns of the *stolovaja* type, or converted adjectives and participles. When qualified by numerals (ending in) the paucal numerals for *two*, *three*, or *four* nouns appear in a form which is formally identical to the genitive singular. Qualifying adjectives also appear in the genitive, but in plural number, as seen in (29):

(29)  dva      bol'š-ix        tarakan-a
      two      large-GEN.PL    cockroach-GEN.SG
      'two large cockroaches'

When qualified by paucal numerals adjectival nouns behave like adjectives, not nouns:

(30)  dva      bol'š-ix        nasekom-ix      (*nasekom-ogo)
      two      large-GEN.PL    insect-GEN.PL   (insect-GEN.SG)
      'two large insects'

Here, the fact that the word is morphologically an adjective overrides the fact that it is syntactically a noun. A similar situation is found with deadjectival nouns in German of the type *Angestellte(r)* 'employee' F(M). This noun is derived from the passive participle of a verb (*anstellen*) and it declines exactly like an adjective. Adjectives in German have two sets of inflections, exhibiting a 'strong/weak' declension distinction. The weak declension is used when the noun phrase is definite and the strong declension is used otherwise. Deadjectival nouns, whilst showing most of the syntax of nouns, are also subject to this strong/weak declensional distinction. Thus we see the strong declension in *ein Angestellter* 'a (male) employee' and the weak declension in the definite phrase *der Angestellte* 'the employee'. Another intriguing property exhibited by nouns denoting people derived from adjectives is that of inflection for gender (see Spencer 2002). For example, in

Russian a noun derived from an adjective denoting a human must indicate the sex of the referent by means of the gender agreement morphology of the original adjective. Thus, the adjective *bol'noj* 'sick' gives rise to the homophonous noun *bol'noj* 'patient'. This is the masculine gender form and it can be used only for male referents or when the sex of the referent is unknown, otherwise the feminine gender form, *bol'naja* '(female) patient', has to be used. No non-adjectival noun in the language has this property of obligatorily realizing sex/gender.

# 5. Summary

In Table 1 I summarize the way the examples discussed fit into my partial typology of mismatches. Ignoring defectivity, most if not all scenarios seem to occur (the annotation '??' under Type indicates that I have not found any relevant examples; 'mismatches' affecting the whole paradigm of all members of a lexical class wouldn't be noticeable, so two types are logically impossible):

We are now in a position to ask how these various mismatches relate to the classical notion of deponency, syncretism, and other types of mismatches. Following Corbett (this volume) I take canonical syncretism to be a situation in which the form associated with one cell in the paradigm is identified with that of a different cell, for all lexemes of the appropriate inflectional class, without defectivity. Deponency is found when a slab of a paradigm of a lexically restricted set of lexemes is associated with the forms from a different

**Table 1.** Classification of mismatches

| Domain | Paradigm coverage | Generality | Defectivity | Type |
|--------|-------------------|------------|-------------|------|
| within | slab | exceptions | yes | (true) deponency |
| within | cell | exceptions | yes | semi-deponency |
| within | cell | class | no | syncretism |
| within | cell | exceptions/ sublcass | no | heteroclisis |
| within | slab | subclass | | <Chukchee Cl I plural?> |
| within | cell | subclass | no | Chukchee Cl I plural |
| within | slab | class | | <impossible> |
| within | cell | class | yes? | Chukchee spurious antipassive |
| between | slab | sublcass | | *stolovaja*-nouns |
| between | cell | sublcass | | ?? |
| between | slab | subclass | | Russian converted participles |
| between | cell | subclass | | Russian surnames |
| between | slab | sublcass | | <impossible> |
| between | cell | class | | Japanese plain negative; Russian past tense |

slab, with defectivity. Heteroclisis is found when a slab of a paradigm of a definable subset set of lexemes is associated with the forms from a different slab, without defectivity. In terms of the typology under consideration syncretism and deponency are characterized as in (31):

(31)   Canonical codings for

      syncretism:    Dom(within), Para(cell), Gen(class), Def(no)
      deponency:    Dom(within), Para(slab), Gen(exc), Def(yes)
      heteroclisis:   Dom(within), Para(slab), Gen(subcl), Def(no)

I begin with a consideration of the within-class mismatches. The Chukchee 'spurious antipassive' has nearly all the properties of canonical syncretism:

(32)   Chukchee 'spurious antipassive':

Dom(within), Para(slab), Gen(class), Def(yes?)

The only uncertainty is with the status of the 'virtual paradigm' forms of the antipassive which are referred to in the active conjugation. If the corresponding antipassive forms turn out not to exist (in some sense of 'exist') then the paradigm is defective and this is a property of deponency. In (33) we see repeated the coding for Chukchee Class I nouns compared with Tzez *xexbi*:

(33)   Chukchee Class I nouns:   Dom(within), Para(slab), Gen(subcl), Def(no)
      *xexbi*:                 Dom(within), Para(slab), Gen(exc), Def(no)

The Chukchee mismatch covers an open-ended subclass of lexemes while the Tzez mismatch affects exactly two lexemes. Chukchee class I nouns neutralize number marking in all but one case form, while the neutralization is found in all forms of *xexbi*. Thus, 'slab' means 'whole paradigm' for Tzez and 'almost whole paradigm' for Chukchee. However, the coding hides an important difference between the two cases. In Tzez *xexbi* the singular paradigm has forms which are clearly plural when compared to other lexemes. For the Chukchee nouns we can't say this. Rather, we have pure neutralization of a distinction and the forms themselves are strictly speaking neutral with respect to number, unlike Class II nouns, which have a separate plural marker. The Chukchee situation therefore can't be considered to be a kind of mirror-image of the Tzez except as a first approximation. This shows how important it is to understand the full set of contrasts and the full nature of the paradigmatic structures being compared. In fact, the Chukchee situation is fairly common in inflectional systems. Thus, in Russian, adjectives fail to distinguish gender in the plural and there is no sense in which one can say that the plural forms are 'basically' in one gender and that the other two gender forms are referred to that basic gender. A more complex situation is found with Latin 3rd declension adjectives. These adjectives neutralize gender throughout the singular and plural except that they distinguish the nominative/accusative forms of the neuter gender (e.g. *atrox* 'fierce, NOM SG, N ACC SG', *atrocem* 'ACC SG M/F' *atrocia* 'N NOM/ACC PL'). Some adjectives distinguish masculine/ feminine from neuter in the nominative singular: *levis* 'light, M/F NOM SG', *leve* 'N NOM/ACC SG'. Others also distinguish masculine from feminine in the nominative singular.: *acer* 'keen, M NOM SG', *acris* 'F NOM SG', *acre* 'N NOM SG'. Again, what we see here is a failure, with some items, to mark all the distinctions formally, that is, we see syncretism, not the appropriation of the 'wrong' morphology, which we think of as deponency. If Latin adjectives all bore independent markers indicating gender, and if, say, masculine/feminine forms of 3rd declension adjectives bore the neuter gender marker, then we would have a situation comparable to that of *xexbi*.

These within-class mismatches are relatively familiar from recent theoretical discussion. However, the central concern of this chapter is with instances in which lexemes borrow morphology from the 'wrong' word class, the between-class mismatches.

The picture for the various Russian nouns with adjectival morphology is summarized in (13) repeated here as (34):

(34)  *stolovaja* 'dining room':     Dom(between), Para(slab), Gen(exc)
      *Čexov* 'Chekhov':             Dom(between), Para(cell?), Gen(subcl)
      *Ivanov* 'Ivan's':             Dom(between), Para(slab), Gen(subcl)

How do such mismatches fit in with the more familiar typologies? The *stolovaja* type involve the whole paradigm and affect only exceptional lexemes. This makes them look like deponents. Are they defective? This is a difficult question, since it depends on specific examples. In the most common instances of the noun-inflected-like-adjective mismatch, the noun is clearly derived from the adjective. Thus, de-adjectival and de-participial nouns such as *bol'noj* 'patient' or *učaščijsja* 'student' generally retain fairly transparently related sources, to the extent that it requires a certain amount of detailed argumentation to prove that they really are nouns and not adjectives. Thus, these words are not defective. Similarly, the noun *stolovaja* itself is derived from a relational adjective *stolovyj* 'pertaining to a table'. That adjective still exists, so we can maintain that there is at least a formal derivational relationship between the noun and its source adjective. On the other hand, there are *stolovaja*-type words which do not correspond to any adjective, such as *nasekomoe* 'insect'. So is *this* an instance of defectivity? This question is difficult to answer, because even when there is transparent lexical relatedness the mismatched lexeme and its morphological source are not members of the same lexemic paradigm (in other words, the lexeme *bol'noj* 'patient' is not a form of the lexeme *bol'noj* 'sick', any more than the English verb *to hammer* is a form of the noun *hammer*). This means that the property of defectivity cannot be applied easily to any of the between-class mismatches. It is for this reason that I have not included a specification for the 'Def' property in the between-class mismatches.[4]

The surnames derived from possessive adjectives occupy an intermediate position and a rather complex one. A name such as *Čexov* declines essentially as though it were a possessive adjective (though such an adjective usually doesn't exist). The problem here is to decide what is matched with what. From the perspective of a noun *Čexov* is exceptional for most of its feminine and plural forms and for one of its masculine forms. From the perspective of a possessive adjective it is exceptional just in its masculine prepositional singular form, in which it behaves like a noun, not like an adjective. In effect, this form is a stipulated default from the noun paradigm. It seems to me that such cases defy any straightforward typology, the principal problem being that we are dealing with a between-class mismatch.

We next turn to instances such as the Russian past tense and the Japanese plain negative. The mismatch coding for these latter is repeated as (35):

(35)   Russian past tense, Japanese plain negative:

   Dom(between), Para(slab), Gen(class)

This case neatly illustrates the need for factoring the causes of mismatches. These 'morphological shifts' don't fit into any standard picture of mismatches. They are not syncretisms because they involve the 'wrong' morphology rather than just identifying the contents of one cell in a paradigm with the contents of another cell. Indeed, it's far from clear that we could ever talk of syncretism where cross-categorial borrowing of this sort occurs. On the other hand, this is not deponency, because it's entirely regular and it doesn't involve defectivity (to the extent such a notion is coherent for between-class mismatches). The mismatch most closely resembles heteroclisis, though if we are to think of this as heteroclisis it would be best to call it something like 'cross-categorial heteroclisis': rather than inflecting as though part of the paradigm belonged to a different inflectional class, the word inflects as though part of its paradigm belonged to a different word class altogether. However, since this affects every verb lexeme in the language it can hardly be counted as genuine heteroclisis.

We have so far examined the easier cases. When we look at phenomena such as the Hindi conjugation system we find that our attempts at typologizing become rather complicated. This is because different parts of a word form may behave differently with respect to the various criteria. I therefore leave it

---

[4] Terminological note: *stolovaja*-type nouns are sometimes referred to as 'deponent', in that they use the 'wrong' morphology and are exceptional. However, it's not clear that this is ever an appropriate use of the term for such words. Personal nouns converted from adjectives are not exceptional (Spencer 2002) and defectivity is difficult to define for between class mismatches, so such cases lack most of the properties of deponents.

to others to decide exactly how such morphology fits into the grand scheme of things. It is worth noting that such phenomena are widespread, though they needn't involve cross-categorial mismatches. If we look at a Spanish verb form such as *cantaría* 'I would sing' we see a word form illustrating the imperfect tense of a 2nd/3rd conjugation verb, except that *cantar* is a 1st conjugation verb and the form is conditional not imperfect (and although the form clearly 'contains' the infinitive form *cantar*, it's finite). Syntagmatic mismatches of this sort, whether between-category or within-category have not been subjected to detailed study from the point of view of canonicity, so this may be a fruitful avenue for future exploration.

## 6. Conclusions: Is Anything (Im)possible?

One of the virtues of a conceptually well-grounded typology is that it can help us distinguish that which is possible from that which is impossible (or at least highly unlikely). What combination of mismatches is impossible? I would say that no logical possibility can be ruled out. What determines whether a mismatch arises or not is general the accidents of historical change. Put crudely, if there is a feasible grammaticalization path for a mismatch then it's possible. I would be very surprised if it were possible to put universal constraints on such mismatches whether of an a prioristic nature or even in terms of psycholinguistic processing and learning. So I would claim that my typology (and others like it) cannot in general be expected to place limits on what might be found.

Can such a typology help us to understand the statistical prevalence of various types of mismatch? As Corbett has stressed (e.g. this volume) just because a certain combination of properties is 'canonical' doesn't mean that it's common, or even necessarily attested. Can such a typology help us to understand traditional notions such as syncretism and deponency? I have had a certain amount of difficulty in applying these terms to a number of the mismatches I have discussed, particularly where between-class mismatches are concerned. In part this is because traditional grammars of classical languages failed to draw specific attention to these phenomena and therefore generally failed to name them. But in part it's because the traditional labels for mismatches only tell some of the story. What is more important is to factor out the contributing properties and find a clear way of assigning each of those properties to a given instance. It will then be possible for us to examine existing descriptions in greater detail to find out whether the more traditional labels are useful or whether they should be replaced entirely with a full set of descriptors for each type of mismatch. My suspicion is that the old labels have outlived their usefulness, especially when we consider the cross-categorial mismatches and the syntagmatic mismatches discussed in this chapter.

# References

Baerman, Matthew, Dunstan Brown, and Greville G. Corbett. 2005. *The syntax-morphology interface: a study of syncretism*. Cambridge: Cambridge University Press.
Bobaljik, Jonathan. (this volume) The limits of deponency: a Chukotko-centric perspective.
Boguslavskaja, Ol'ga. 1995. Genitives and adjectives as attributes in Daghestanian. In Plank, 230–39. Oxford: Oxford University Press.
Corbett, Greville G. 1987. The morphology-syntax interface. *Language* 63.299–345.
—— 1995. Slavonic's closest approach to suffix copying: The possessive adjective. In Plank, 265–82.
—— 2004. The Russian adjective: a pervasive yet elusive category. *Adjective classes: a cross-linguistic typology*, ed. by R. M. W. Dixon and Alexandra Y. Aikhenvald, 199–222. Oxford: Oxford University Press.
—— (this volume). Deponency, syncretism, and what lies between.
Dench, Alan, and Nicholas Evans. 1988. Multiple case-marking in Australian languages. *Australian Journal of Linguistics* 8.1–47.
Evans, Nicholas. 1995. *A grammar of Kayardild*. Berlin: Mouton de Gruyter.
Evans, Nicholas, and Rachel Nordlinger (ms). Extreme morphological shift: verbal case in Kayardild, Unpublished paper, University of Melbourne.
Hetzron, Robert. 1995. Genitival agreement in Awngi: variation on an Afroasiatic theme. In Plank, 325–35.
Kibrik, Aleksandr. 1995. Direct-oblique agreement of attributes in Daghestanian. In Plank, 216–29.
Koptjevskaja-Tamm, Maria. 2000. Romani genitives in cross-linguistic persepctive. *Grammatical relations in Romani: the noun phrase*, ed. by Viktor Elšík and Yaron Matras, 123–49. Amsterdam: Benjamins.
Masica, Colin P. 1991. *The Indo-Aryan languages*. Cambridge: Cambridge University Press.
Matras, Yaron. 2002. *Romani: a linguistic introduction*. Cambridge: Cambridge University Press.
Mohanan, Tara. 1994. *Argument structure in Hindi*. Stanford: CSLI Publications.
Payne, John. 1995. Inflecting postpositions in Indic and Kashmiri. In Plank, 283–298.
Plank, Frans (ed.). 1995. *Double case: agreement by Suffixaufnahme*. Oxford: Oxford University Press
Šebková, Hana, and Edita Žlnayová. 2001. *Romaňi čhib*. Prague: Fortuna.
Snell, Rupert and Simon Weightman. 1989. *Teach yourself Hindi*. London: Hodder and Stoughton.
Spencer, Andrew. 2000. Agreement morphology in Chukotkan. *Morphological analysis in comparison*, ed. by Wolfgang Dressler, Oskar Pfeiffer, Markus Poechtrager, and John Rennison, 191–222. Amsterdam: Benjamins.

Spencer, Andrew. 2002. Gender as an inflectional category. *Journal of Linguistics* 38.279–312.

—— 2005. Towards a typology of 'mixed categories'. *Morphology and the web of grammar: essays in memory of Steven G. Lapointe*, ed. by C. Orhan Orgun and Peter Sells, 95–138. Stanford: CSLI Publications.

Uuspõld, Elen, and Aino Valmet. 2001. *Populjarnaja grammatika èstonskogo jazyka.* Tallinn: Valgus.

Ventcel', Tat'jana. 1964. *Cyganskij jazyk (severnorusskij dialekt).* Moscow: Nauka.

# 4

# A Non-Canonical Pattern of Deponency and Its Implications*

GREGORY T. STUMP

## 1. Canonical Deponency, Form-Deponency, and Property-Deponency

IN THIS PAPER, I PROPOSE A CONCEPTION of canonical deponency in language; I then demonstrate that instances of canonical deponency are susceptible to two very different analyses; I then examine a particular pattern of non-canonical deponency and its implications for choosing between the contrasting analyses to which canonical deponency is subject.

In its extended sense, deponency is the property of a word whose meaning is at odds with its inflectional exponence. Latin deponent verbs are the classic example of this phenomenon. An ordinary Latin verb such as LAUDĀRE 'to praise' has both active forms (such as *laudat* 's/he praises') and passive forms (such as *laudātur* 's/he is praised'). A deponent verb, however, has forms whose inflectional exponence makes them appear to be passive but which are nevertheless interpreted as active: *hortātur* 's/he urges'.

I will regard Latin deponent verbs as an instance of CANONICAL DEPONENCY. In particular, they exhibit three characteristics which, together, I assume to be definitive of canonical deponency; these are the characteristics of (i) contrariness of form and meaning, (ii) concurrent defectiveness, and (iii) lexical exceptionality.[1] Consider each of these characteristics in turn.

Suppose first that in some language, $\sigma_1$ and $\sigma_2$ are morphosyntactic property sets that are minimally contrastive in the sense that they differ with respect to the value of a single inflectional category. Suppose, in addition, that A and B are the respective meanings associated with the property sets $\sigma_1$

---

* I wish to thank the editors of this volume for helpful comments on this paper.
[1] Compare the conception of canonical deponency with that of Corbett (this volume).

*Proceedings of the British Academy* **145**, 71–95. © The British Academy 2007.

and $\sigma_2$ and that $x$ and $y$ are inflectional exponents associated with these respective property sets. This pattern of associations is schematized in Figure 1.

Let's assume, however, that in the inflection of certain lexemes, the inflectional marking $x$ appears in words expressing the meaning B and not the meaning A; in that case, those words exhibit a CONTRARINESS OF FORM AND MEANING relative to the pattern of associations in Figure 1. Thus, in Latin, *hortātur* exhibits a contrariness of form and meaning, since the *-ur* suffix— ordinarily an expression of passive voice—coincides with the active meaning of this word.

Consider now the characteristic of concurrent defectiveness. Suppose that in a language exhibiting the pattern of associations in Figure 1, a word $w$ has the inflectional marking $x$ but expresses the meaning B and not the meaning A; in that case, the paradigm containing $w$ exhibits CONCURRENT DEFECTIVE-NESS if it has no word expressing the content which the pattern of associations in Figure 1 predicts for $w$.[2] Thus, the paradigm of HORTĀRĪ 'urge' exhibits concurrent defectiveness because it lacks a form expressing the meaning 's/he is urged' that is predicted for *hortātur.*

A final property of canonical deponency is that of LEXICAL EXCEPTION-ALITY: in the canonical case, only a minority of the words in a given syntactic category are deponent; indeed, they usually constitute only a tiny part of that category's membership. Thus, *hortātur* contrasts with the large majority of Latin verbs, which exhibit no deponency at all.

If the properties of contrariness of form and meaning, concurrent defectiveness, and lexical exceptionality are seen as the definitive characteristics of canonical deponency, then Latin *hortātur* 's/he urges' is an instance of canonical deponency. In a theoretical context, instances of canonical deponency can be seen in either of two ways. On one hand, one might think of a depon-

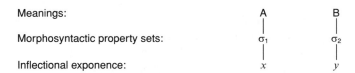

**Figure 1.** Two minimally contrastive morphosyntactic property sets and their associated meanings and inflectional exponents in a hypothetical language

---

[2] By this definition, concurrent defectiveness is a more restrictive notion than simple defectiveness. If a paradigm P exhibits concurrent defectiveness, then (a) there is some meaning M that ought to be expressed by a member of P but isn't (hence P exhibits simple defectiveness), and (b) P has some member $w$ exhibiting a contrariness of form and meaning such that $w$'s meaning is distinct from M even though the form of $w$ implies the meaning M.

ent form as having unexpected exponence for a semantically appropriate set of morphosyntactic properties. On that view, *hortātur* is a third-person singular present imperfective active indicative form; that is, its morphosyntactic properties are right for the meaning it expresses but its inflectional exponence is wrong for those properties. There is, however, another imaginable perspective: that a deponent form has the expected exponence for a semantically inappropriate set of morphosyntactic properties. On this view, *hortātur* is a third-person singular present imperfective passive indicative form, yet one whose meaning isn't passive; that is, its morphosyntactic properties are wrong for the meaning that it expresses, but its exponence is right insofar as it is appropriate to its morphosyntactic properties.

For clarity, let us say that a word possessing the wrong exponence for its morphosyntactic properties is FORM-DEPONENT and that a word possessing the wrong morphosyntactic properties for its meaning is PROPERTY-DEPONENT.[3] If one assumes that the cells in a lexeme's paradigm are pairings of that lexeme with particular morphosyntactic property sets,[4] then these two conceptions of deponency can be schematically represented as in (1).

(1)   a.   *Hortātur* as a form-deponent word:

  Meaning:    $\lambda e[$ Urging(e) & Agent $(x_{SUBJ}, e)]$

  Cell:    ⟨HORTĀRĪ, {3rd singular present imperfective <u>active</u> indicative}⟩
                                                                    ↑
  Realization:  *hortātur* ◄──────────────────────── (?!)

   b.   *Hortātur* as a property-deponent word:

  Meaning:    $\lambda e[$ Urging(e) & Agent $(x_{SUBJ}, e)] $ ◄──────── (?!)
                                                                            ↓
  Cell:    ⟨HORTĀRĪ, {3rd singular present imperfective <u>passive</u> indicative}⟩

  Realization:  *hortātur*

Whether an instance of deponency is seen as involving form-deponency or property-deponency is independent of its status as an instance of canonical deponency. For instance, *hortātur* clearly exhibits the characteristics of canonical deponency whether it is seen as form-deponent or property-deponent. If it is seen as form-deponent, then the contrariness of its form and meaning is mediated by a property set that is suited to its meaning but

---

[3] Thus, one might say that in the phrase *mon bel ami*, *bel* is form-deponent, since it takes the phonological shape of a feminine adjective even though it is masculine; similarly, one might say that in discourse (i), *who* is property-deponent, since it is grammatically singular but logically plural in reference.

  (i)   Q: Who is carrying the piano?
        A: Pat and Kim are.

[4] See Stump (2002, 2006) and Stewart and Stump (2007) for a development of this notion of paradigm.

not to its form; if it is seen as property-deponent, then the mediating property set is suited to its form but not to its meaning. Similarly, if *hortātur* is seen as form-deponent, then its paradigm exhibits concurrent defectiveness because it lacks a third-person singular present indicative passive cell; if it is seen as property-deponent, then its paradigm exhibits concurrent defectiveness because it lacks a third-person singular present indicative active cell.

One might suppose that syntactic considerations would favour the assumption that *hortātur* is form-deponent rather than property-deponent insofar as its syntax is that of an active verb. But in fact, there is no reason to assume that principles of syntactic combination are directly sensitive to the distinction between active voice and passive voice. A verb's combinatory properties are an effect of its semantics and of its properties of subcategorization and case-assignment, and these are specifiable independently of its voice. In the default case, the property 'passive' will, of course, be associated with particular configurations of properties relating to semantics, subcategorization, and case-assignment, but there is no syntactic obstacle to assuming that these default associations are overridden in the case of deponent verbs.

Thus, the question arises: are all instances of deponency instances of form-deponency, or are some deponents instances of property-deponency? If the latter is true, then some morphosyntactic properties must clearly be regarded as 'morphomic' (Aronoff 1994) in the sense that they receive a uniform morphological realization within a given category of inflectional paradigms but lack uniformity in their syntax or semantics. In what follows, I shall argue that this is in fact the case. This is a surprising conclusion in view of the commonplace assumption that morphosyntactic properties stand in a one-to-one relation with semantic operators.

Because instances of canonical deponency can generally be seen as involving either form-deponency or property-deponency, they shed no light on the foregoing question; but as I now show, certain instances of non-canonical deponency leave little doubt that at least some instances of deponency involve property-deponency.


# 2. The Sanskrit Middle Voice

As my main exemplar of the non-canonical pattern of deponency at issue here, I shall examine the characteristics of the Sanskrit middle voice. Additional instances of this pattern will, however, be discussed in section 4.

## 2.1. Active vs middle in Sanskrit

In its most straightforward uses, the Sanskrit middle voice stands in full semantic contrast to the active voice: according to Burrow (1973: 294), '[t]he middle is used when the subject is in some way or other specially implicated in the result of the action; when this is not so the active is used.' Thus, in the Sanskrit grammatical tradition, a verb in the active voice is termed a *parasmai padam* ('word for another'), while a verb in the middle voice is an *ātmane padam* ('word for oneself'). For example, the sentence 'he makes a mat' would be expressed as *kaṭam karoti* (where *karoti* is an active form of the verb KṚ 'make') if the reference is to a matmaker, who makes mats for others; but it would instead be expressed as *kaṭam kurute* (where *kurute* is a middle form of KṚ) if the reference is instead to someone who is making a mat for himself. Similar examples are given for the verbs PAC 'cook' and YAJ 'sacrifice' in (2).

(2)  a.  Active *pacati* 'he cooks' (said of a cook preparing food for others)
         Middle *pacate* 'he cooks' (said of one cooking for himself)

     b.  Active *yajati* 'he sacrifices' (said of a priest sacrificing on someone else's behalf)
         Middle *yajate* 'he sacrifices' (said of one sacrificing on his own behalf)[5]

Certain verbs—typically expressing movement or change of state—appear in the middle voice when used intransitively and in the active voice when used transitively (Burrow 1973: 294). For example, the root PŪ 'purify' inflects in the middle voice with the meaning 'become pure' and in the active voice with the meaning 'make pure', as in the examples in (3); compare, likewise, the uses of DṚH 'firm up', VṚDH 'increase' and VAH 'ride/carry' in (4). These cases are unlike the examples in (2) insofar as the subjects of the middle forms in (3) and (4) are non-agents; on the other hand, they are like the examples in (2) insofar as the use of the middle entails that the subject's referent is directly affected by the event described by the verb.

(3)  a.  ágne          dákṣaiḥ        punīhi                       naḥ       [*Ṛg-Veda* 9.67.26]
         Agni:VOC.SG   ability:INS.PL purify:2SG.IPV.ACT           us
         'O Agni, purify us with powers'

     b.  agne          dakṣaiḥ        punīmahe.            [*Maitrāyaṇī-Saṁhita* 3.11.10]
         Agni:VOC.SG   ability:INS.PL become.pure:1PL.PRS.IND.MID
         'O Agni, may we become pure with powers.'
                                          (Bloomfield and Edgerton 1930:32)

---

[5] According to Speijer (1886: 238), *yajate* can also be said of the one on whose behalf a priest conducts a sacrifice.

(4)    a.  Active *dṛṁhati* 'makes firm'
           Middle *dṛṁhate* 'becomes firm'
       b.  Active *vardhati* 'increases (tr.), makes bigger'
           Middle *vardhate* 'increases (intr.), becomes bigger'
       c.  Active *vahati* '(chariot) carries (man)'
           Middle *vahate* '(man) rides (in chariot)'

In each of the foregoing examples, the use of a middle form can be taken to imply *that the event designated by the verb has a direct influence on the subject's referent.*

The Sanskrit system of voice inflection is, however, complicated by the fact that in their non-passive subparadigms, most verbs inflect in only the active or only the middle, and do so without obvious regard to the presence or absence of any implied influence on their subject's referent. That is, Sanskrit verbs fall into three classes: ĀTMANEPADIN verbs, whose non-passive forms are always middle (e.g. ĀS 'sit', LABH 'receive', KṢAM 'endure', VAS 'wear (clothes)', SAC 'accompany', and many others); PARASMAIPADIN verbs, whose non-passive forms are always active (e.g. AD 'eat', KṢUDH 'be hungry', AS 'be', BHUJ 'bend', SARP 'creep', and many others); and UBHAYAPADIN verbs,[6] whose non-passive forms may (as in the cases above and many others) be middle or active.[7] Henceforth, I shall refer to the three classes of verbs as Ā-verbs, P-verbs, and U-verbs, respectively.

## 2.2. The distinction between U-verbs, P-verbs, and Ā-verbs is not semantically determined

One might have expected that the distinction between Ā-verbs, P-verbs, and U-verbs is semantically determined—for example, that an Ā-verb only shows up in the middle because it inherently describes the type of event that always influences its subject's referent, and that a P-verb always shows up in the active because it inherently describes the type of event that has no influence on its subject's referent. Indeed, some evidence seems to favour this assumption. There are, for instance, Ā-verbs that seem to have intrinsically middle meanings (an example being the verb ĀS 'sit'). Moreover, passive verb forms always exhibit middle inflections: for example, in the present system (i.e. in the various moods of the present as well as in the imperfect), passives generally come from the passive stem (the result of appending *-ya* to a special, usually weakened, form of the root) through the addition of a middle inflection,

---

[6] *Ubhayapadin* 'having words for both [oneself and another]' (< *ubhaya-* 'both' + *pada-* 'word').
[7] Verbs of all three sorts have passives, e.g. *labhyate* 'it is obtained' (from the ātmanepadin verb LABH), *bhajyate* 'it is broken' (from the parasmaipadin verb BHAÑJ), *pacyate* 'it is cooked' (from the ubhayapadin verb PAC).

as in (5). This use of middle inflections in the passive seems to follow from their semantics since they generally designate events that affect their subject's referent (as the event of cooking designated by *pácyate* in (5) affects the referent of its subject *váyaḥ*).

(5)  pác-ya-te              yávaḥ
     cook                   food:NOM.SG
     ROOT-PASS-3SG.IND.MID
     'The food is (being) cooked'                          [*Ṛg-Veda* 1.135.8 ]

Notwithstanding this ostensible evidence in favour of the assumption that the distinction between Ā-verbs, P-verbs, and U-verbs is semantically determined, there are at least four kinds of evidence against this assumption. First, it is not only personal passives that exhibit middle inflections: so do impersonal passives, as in (6). The use of the middle voice is, however, at odds with the semantics of impersonal passives: there's no sense in which the referent of its subject can be affected by the event that its describes, because its subject is non-referential.

(6)  yatheṣṭaṁ     gam-ya-tāṁ           tvayā.
     at.pleasure   go-PASS-3SG.IPV.MID   you:INS.SG
     'May it be gone by you at pleasure.'                   [*Mahābhārata* 1.68.80]
     (≈'Please leave at your pleasure.')

Second, an Ā-verb may be virtually synonymous with a P-verb. For instance, the verbs VIJ 'tremble', DHAV 'flow', APA-HĀ 'go away', TUŚ 'drip', MAN 'think' in (7a)–(11a) are all Ā-verbs, while the synonymous verbs TRAS 'tremble', ṚṢ 'flow', PARĀ-GĀ 'go away', ŚCUT 'drip', DHYĀ 'think' in (7b)–(11b) are all P-verbs.

(7)  a.  VIJ 'tremble' (Ā-verb)
         gauró              ná   kṣepnór          avije        jyāyāḥ
         *bos.gaurus*:NOM.SG  as   springing:ABL.SG  tremble:      bowstring:
                                                    1SG.IMPF.MID  GEN.SG
         'I trembled as a wild ox (trembles) at the springing of a bowstring.'
                                                              [*Ṛg-Veda* 10.51.6]

     b.  TRAS 'tremble' (P-verb)
         yásya     trásanti         śávasaḥ       sañcákṣi          śátravo    bhiyā́.
         who:      tremble:         prowess:      observation:      enemy:     fear:
         GEN.SG    3PL.PRS.IND.ACT   ABL.SG        LOC.SG            NOM.PL     INS.SG
         'in observation of whom his enemies tremble through fear of his prowess.'
                                                              [*Ṛg-Veda* 6.14.4]

(8)  a.  DHAV 'flow' (Ā-verb)
         ā́pa              iva    sadhryàñco         dhavadhve.
         water:NOM.PL      like   converging:NOM.PL   flow:2PL.PRS.IND.MID
         'You flow like converging waters.'                   [*Ṛg-Veda* 5.60.3]

b.   R̥Ṣ 'flow' (P-verb)

|  | etá́ | arṣanty | alalābhávantīr | r̥tá́ | varī́r |
|--|------|---------|----------------|------|--------|
|  | these: | flow: | sounding.cheerfully: | holy.one: | river: |
|  | NOM.PL | 3PL.PRS.IND.ACT | NOM.PL | VOC.PL | NOM.PL |

'These rivers flow murmuring, O Holy Ones'              [R̥g-Veda 4.18.6]

(9)  a.  APA-HĀ 'go away' (Ā-verb)

|  | ápéd | u | hāsate | támaḥ. |
|--|------|---|--------|--------|
|  | = ápa (PREVERB) | EMPHATIC PCL | go.away: | darkness:NOM.SG |
|  | + íd (AFFIRMATIVE PCL) |  | 3SG.AOR.SBJV.MID |  |

'and then the darkness departs.'                       [R̥g-Veda 10.127.3]

b.  PARĀ-GĀ 'go away' (P-verb)

|  | kám | svid | árdhaṁ | párāgāt. |
|--|-----|------|--------|----------|
|  | what:ACC.SG | INTERROGATIVE PCL | place:ACC.SG | went:3SG.AOR.ACT |

'Where did she go?'                                    [R̥g-Veda 1.164.17]

(10)  a.  TUŚ 'drip' (Ā-verb)

|  | índur | índrāya | tośate | ní | tośate | śrīṇánn | ugró | riṇánn apáḥ. |
|--|-------|---------|--------|----|--------|---------|------|-------------|
|  | Indu: | Indra: | drip: | down | id. | mixing: | powerful: | flowing: water: |
|  | NOM.SG | DAT.SG | 3SG.PRS. |  |  | NOM.SG | NOM.SG | NOM.SG ACC.PL |
|  |  |  | IND.MID |  |  |  |  |  |

'Indu [a drop of Soma] drips for Indra, drips down, mixing, powerful, flowing to the waters.'              [R̥g-Veda 9.109.22]

b.  ŚCUT 'drip' (P-verb)

|  | ghr̥távantaḥ | pāvaka | te | stoká́ | ścotanti | médasaḥ |
|--|-------------|--------|-----|-------|----------|---------|
|  | full.of.fat: | purifier: | you: | drops: | drip: | marrow: |
|  | NOM.PL | VOC.SG | DAT.SG | NOM.PL | 3PL.PRS.IND.ACT | GEN.SG |

'The drops of marrow charged with fat drip, purifier, to you'

[R̥g-Veda 3.21.2]

(11)  a.  MAN 'think' (Ā-verb)

|  | tam | evaitad | rasaṃ | syandamānam | manyante. |
|--|-----|---------|-------|-------------|-----------|
|  | that: | = eva 'very' | sap: | flowing: | think: |
|  | ACC.SG | + etad 'here' ACC.SG | PRS.MID.PPLE.ACC.SG | 3PL.PRS.IND.MID |  |

'They believe that very sap to be flowing here.'

[Śatapatha-Brāhmaṇa 3.9.2.[1]]

b.  DHYĀ 'think' (P-verb)

|  | prajāpatir | agnirūpāṇy | abhyadhyāyat. |
|--|-----------|-----------|--------------|
|  | Prajāpati: | Agni-forms: | think: |
|  | NOM.SG | ACC.PL | 3SG.IMPF.ACT |

'Prajāpati thought about Agni's forms.'

[Śatapatha-Brāhmaṇa 6.2.1.[1]]

Third, a verb's membership in the class of Ā-verbs or P-verbs is in some cases exactly the opposite of what one would expect from its meaning. In (12), the verb GARH 'rebuke' is an Ā-verb, though it's not clear that instances of rebuking in any way affect the rebuker; by the same token, the verb SNĀ 'bathe oneself' in (13) in a P-verb, despite the fact that bathing oneself is an activity that affects the bather.

(12)  GARH 'rebuke' (Ā-verb!)

| kathā́ | ha | tád | váruṇāya | tvám | agne | kathā́ | divé | garhase. |
|-------|----|-----|----------|------|------|-------|------|----------|
| why | EMPHATIC | then | Varuṇa: | you: | Agni: | why | heaven: | rebuke: |
| | PCL | | DAT.SG | NOM.SG | VOC.SG | | DAT.SG | 2SG.PRS. |
| | | | | | | | | IND.MID |

'Why, Agni, do you reproach (us) to Varuṇa, why to the heaven?'

[*Ṛg-Veda* 4.3.5]

(13)  SNĀ 'bathe oneself' (P-verb!)

| kṣīréṇa | snātaḥ | kúyavasya | yóṣe. |
|---------|--------|-----------|-------|
| water:INS.SG | bathe:3DU.PRS.IND.ACT | Kuyava:GEN.SG | wife:NOM.DU |

'The two wives of Kuyava bathe with the water.'      [*Ṛg-Veda* 1.104.3]

Finally, one can find verbs that regularly inflect as Ā-verbs in one tense but as P-verbs in another. The verb VṚT 'turn, roll' inflects as an Ā-verb in the present tense, as in (14); in the perfect tense, however, it instead inflects as a P-verb, as in (15). There's no plausible sense in which this alternation can be seen as an effect of the distinction between verbs designating events that affect their subject's referent and verbs designating non-affecting events.

(14)

| suvṛ́d-rátho | vartate | dákṣiṇāyāḥ. |
|--------------|---------|-------------|
| well.turning-chariot:NOM.SG | rolls:3SG.PRS.IND.MID | (donation to the officiating priest):GEN.SG |

'The well-running chariot of the *dakṣiṇā* rolls.'      [*Ṛg-Veda* 10.107.11]

(15)

| vām | ékaḥ | pavír | ā́ vavarta. |
|-----|------|-------|-----------|
| you:GEN.DU | one:NOM.SG | tire (= chariot, by metonymy):NOM.SG | turn.around: 3SG.PRF.ACT |

'The one chariot of you two went round.'      [*Ṛg-Veda* 5.62.2]

It's therefore clear that there is no simple semantic explanation for the classification of verbs as Ā-verbs, P-verbs, and U-verbs.

The existence of Ā-verbs and P-verbs in Sanskrit can be seen as one manifestation of a general collapse in the significance of the active/middle distinction in the history of early Indic. Later stages of Indic exhibit this trend to an even greater degree: thus, contexts that invariably call for middle inflections in Sanskrit sometimes exhibit active inflections in Pāli; for instance, the Sanskrit passive *pacyate* 'is cooked' (whose termination *-te* is a middle inflection) corresponds to the Pāli passive *paccati* (whose termination *-ti* is historically active). Even the earliest forms of Sanskrit give evidence of an incipient bleaching of the active/middle distinction; for instance, the choice between an active form and its middle counterpart sometimes appears to be motivated by metrical considerations. The Vedic verse in (16), for example, contains the active form *huvema* 'may we invoke'; in verse (17) from the Atharva-Veda, however, it is supplanted by the middle form *havāmahe* 'we invoke', whose substitution brings the stanza into full conformity with the dodecasyllabic Jagatī metre which it otherwise exhibits (Bloomfield and Edgerton 1930: 45).

(16) prātáḥ    sómam  utá   rudráṁ   huvema.                    [*Rg-Veda* 7.41.1;
    at.dawn  Soma:  and   Rudra:    invoke:              *Vājasaneyi-Saṁhitā* 34.34;
               ACC.SG         ACC.SG   1PL.OPT.ACT   *Taittirīya-Brāhmaṇa* 2.8.9.7;
    'At dawn may we invoke Soma and Rudra.'   *Āpastamba-Mantra-Pāṭha* 1.14.1]

(17) prātaḥ somam uta rudraṁ      havāmahe.                     [*Atharva-Veda* 3.16.1]
                                invoke:
                                1PL.PRS.IND.MID
    'At dawn we invoke Soma and Rudra.'

The fundamental problem posed by Ā-verbs and P-verbs is that although the forms in their paradigms carry the morphology of the middle and active voices (respectively), verbs of both types are compatible with subjects whose referents are either affected or unaffected. In sections 2.3 and 2.4, I discuss the implications of this problem for a semantic analysis of the active and middle voices in Sanskrit.

### 2.3. The semantics and pragmatics of voice in U-verbs and P-verbs

Apparently, Ā-verbs and P-verbs are both deponent; that is, verbs of both types seem to have 'set aside' the meanings that are customarily associated with their voice inflections. I shall argue here, however, that a closer examination of the semantics of active voice casts doubt on the assumption that P-verbs are genuinely deponent.

I shall assume here that in the semantics of a U-verb, the property 'middle' denotes the operator (18), where 'Affects' is a relation between events and individuals and $x_{SUBJ}$ is a variable to be bound by the referent of the verb's subject; thus, operator (18) entails that the event designated by a middle verb form is one that affects the referent of its subject.

(18)   Middle voice operator: $\lambda P \lambda e[\text{Affects}(e, x_{SUBJ}) \& P\{e\}]$

Figure 2 shows how (18) might enter into the composition of a middle verb form's denotation. Pairing (a) in Figure 2 is the third-person singular present indicative middle cell of the paradigm of PAC 'cook'. Three of the elements in this cell are semantically significant: the lexeme PAC itself, the present-tense property, and the middle-voice property. The lexeme PAC itself denotes the set (d) of cookings by the referent of its subject; the present-tense property denotes a present-tense operator (b); and the middle-voice property denotes the middle-voice operator (c) (= (18)). The composition of

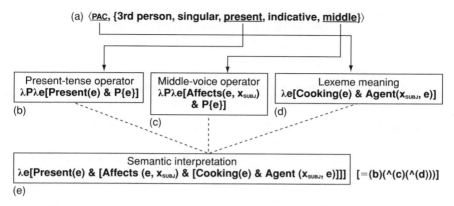

**Figure 2.** The semantic interpretation of the cell realized by Sanskrit *pacate* 's/he cooks (middle voice)'

these three denotations produces the semantic interpretation in (e) for the cell in (a): (e) is the set of present cookings by the referent of the verb's subject that affect that referent.

Given this conception of the morphosyntactic property 'middle' in the semantics of U-verbs, Ā-verbs must clearly be seen as deponent. But the question then also arises whether the contrasting property 'active' should be seen as denoting the contrasting operator (19) in the semantics of U-verbs; by (19), a U-verb's active forms would denote events that do not affect the referent of their subject. If 'active' has this interpretation in the semantics of U-verbs, then P-verbs, like Ā-verbs, must be seen as deponent.

(19)   Hypothetical active voice operator: $\lambda P \lambda e[\neg \text{Affects}(e, x_{SUBJ}) \ \& \ P\{e\}]$

But there is evidence against the assumption that 'active' entails non-affectedness in the semantics of U-verbs. Note first that a U-verb in the middle voice may have a reflexive or reciprocal interpretation. In (20a), the verb BRŪ 'speak, call' is in the active voice, because the subject's referent is not affected by the event of speaking. In (20b), on the other hand, the subject's referent is to call himself by a particular name, and would in that sense be affected by the event of calling; the verb BRŪ is therefore in the middle voice, accounting for the sentence's reflexive interpretation. In the same way, the verb BR in (20c) is in the middle voice in accordance with this sentence's intended reciprocal interpretation.

(20)   a.   índra          brávīmi            te       vácaḥ.
             Indra:VOC.SG   speak:1SG.PRS.IND.ACT   thy     speech:ACC.SG
             'Indra, I speak your praise.'                    [Ṛg-Veda 1.84.19]

b.  satyakāma        eva       jābālo        bravīthāḥ
    Satyakāma:NOM.SG  indeed    Jābāla:NOM.SG  call:2SG.OPT.MID
    'Indeed, you might call yourself Satyakāma Jābāla'
                                        [*Chāndogya Upaniṣad* 4.4.2]

c.  bruvāte            mithunáni      nā́ma.
    speak:3DU.PRS.IND.MID  paired:ACC.PL   name:ACC.PL[8]
    'The two of them speak paired names to each other.'     [*Ṛg-Veda* 3.54.7]

Thus, the middle voice is appropriately used to describe reflexive or reciprocal events. But in the presence of an overt reflexive or reciprocal pronoun,
U-verbs don't invariably exhibit the middle voice, as the active voice of the U-
verbs in (21) reveals; indeed, Pāṇini's rule 1.3.77 allows either the middle or
the active of a U-verb in the presence of an overt reflexive pronoun (as in
(21a)), and rule 1.3.16 actually excludes the use of a U-verb's middle voice in
the presence of a reciprocal pronoun (as in (21b)).

(21)  a.  tebyaḥ         prajāpatir       ātmānam     pradadau.
          them:DAT.PL    Prajāpati:NOM.SG  self:ACC.SG  give:3SG.PRF.ACT
          'Prajāpati gave himself to them.'       [*Śatapatha-Brāhmaṇa* 5.1.1.[2]]

      b.  anyó          anyám          ánu gṛbhṇáty      enoḥ
          other:NOM.SG  other:ACC.SG   welcome:3SG.PRS.IND.ACT  that:GEN.DU
          'Each of those two welcomes the other'       [*Ṛg-Veda* 7.103.4]

This avoidance of the middle voice in instances such as those in (21) should
presumably be seen as the effect of an economy principle disfavouring the
redundant expression of voice. Be that as it may, it is in any event clear that
the property 'active' doesn't denote the active-voice operator in (19); otherwise, (21a,b) would be overt contradictions. Instead, the property 'active' is
semantically empty, denoting an identity function in the interpretation of
U-verbs. Nevertheless, the use of an active form of a U-verb conversationally
implicates that its more informative middle counterpart is inappropriate;[9]
that is, it conversationally implicates that the event being described doesn't
affect the subject's referent, since otherwise, the middle voice would be used.
But this implicature is cancellable in the presence of a reflexive or reciprocal
pronoun, as in the examples in (21).

Once the property 'active' is recognized to be semantically empty in the
interpretation of U-verbs, it becomes clear that P-verbs aren't genuinely
deponent. Although P-verbs are always active in their inflection, they can be
used to describe events that either affect or fail to affect the referent of their
subject because the property 'active' simply denotes an identity function. And

---

[8] This looks like a singular form, but it's plural; see Whitney (1889: §425d).
[9] Here I am using the notion of conversational implicature in the technical sense introduced by
Grice (1975).

because a P-verb lacks middle forms, its active forms (unlike those of a U-verb) naturally fail to give rise to the conversational implicature that their subject's referent is unaffected by the event they describe.

But what of Ā-verbs? They appear to have middle forms without the middle semantics proposed earlier in (18) for the middle forms of U-verbs. That is, they appear to be deponent: middle forms that have set aside their middle interpretation for use in describing events that may or may not have an effect on their subject's referent. This is in fact what I will conclude in the following section: that Sanskrit Ā-verbs are indeed deponents.

## 2.4. Sanskrit Ā-verbs as deponents

Although active voice can be regarded as having the same semantic value in U-verbs and P-verbs, middle voice seems not to have the same value in U-verbs and Ā-verbs: while the property 'middle' denotes the operator (18) in the interpretation of a U-verb, it seems to be semantically empty in the interpretation of an Ā-verb. Thus, because Ā-verbs apparently have middle forms without middle semantics, they must seemingly be construed as deponents. One might question this conclusion, however, since on the face of it, there are two alternative ways of accounting for the fact that the referent of an Ā-verb's subject can be either affected or unaffected by the event that it describes; but as I show here, closer scrutiny of the Sanskrit evidence excludes these alternative accounts.

### 2.4.1. 'Active' and 'middle' are not simply inflection classes

One way of avoiding the conclusion that Ā-verbs are deponent would be to assume that 'active' and 'middle' aren't morphosyntactic properties in Sanskrit, and that the active/middle distinction is merely an inflection-class distinction. On this view, the traditional Ā-verbs and P-verbs would be basic members of the 'middle' and 'active' conjugations (respectively), and the traditional U-verbs would reflect the existence of a rule allowing verbs possessing a middle interpretation to be derived by transfer from the 'active' conjugation to the 'middle' conjugation; thus, middle voice would in effect constitute a derivational category rather than a morphosyntactic property.[10] In this analysis, middle semantics would be associated not with the 'middle' conjugation, but with the rule transferring verbs from the 'active' to the 'middle' conjugation; accordingly, Ā-verbs wouldn't be expected to exhibit middle

---

[10] The rule deriving middle verbs in this approach would, in fact, be similar in character to the rule that derives causative verbs in Sanskrit, since morphologically, causativization simply involves a transfer from one conjugation to another—to the tenth conjugation in the present system, to the reduplicating conjugation in the aorist system, and so on (Stump 2005a).

semantics, and therefore wouldn't have to be seen as deponent. While such an approach to the active/middle distinction might seem to resolve the apparent inconsistency in the semantics of Ā-verbs, it must be rejected for two reasons.

Consider first the properties of perfects in Sanskrit. The default perfect formation in Sanskrit is a synthetic one. A periphrastic perfect formation is instead, however, used in certain instances: it is the usual perfect formation for derived verbal lexemes (including intensive, desiderative, causative, and denominal derivatives) as well as for most verbs whose roots are vowel-initial heavy syllables or are polysyllabic; a small number of verbs possessing synthetic perfect forms also allow the periphrastic perfect formation. (See Whitney 1889: §1071.) The periphrastic perfect formation involves a main verb appearing in a nominalized form in *-ām* accompanied by the finite synthetic perfect form of an auxiliary verb. The key observation here is that in the periphrastic perfect, P-verbs take the active form of the auxiliary verb, while Ā-verbs take the middle form; this is illustrated in (22) and (23). In (22), the Ā-verb ĪKṢ 'see, see in one's mind, think' takes the middle form of the auxiliary verb KṚ 'do', while in (23), the P-verb VID 'perceive, understand' takes the active form of KṚ. If 'active' and 'middle' were conjugation classes, then in the periphrastic perfect, the auxiliary would have to be seen as agreeing with respect to a P-verb or Ā-verb's conjugation class. This would be unprecedented: conjugation class membership is not a locus of agreement relations in language.

(22)  Periphrastic perfect of the Ā-verb ĪKṢ 'see, see in one's mind, think':

| īkṣāṃ | cakra | ime | ha | me | prajā | na | vimathnīrann | iti. |
|---|---|---|---|---|---|---|---|---|
| see: | do: | this: | indeed | my | creature: | not | destroy: | DIRECT |
| NMLZ. | 3SG.PRF. | NOM.PL | | | ACC.PL | | 3PL.PRS. | DISCOURSE |
| ACC.SG | MID | | | | | | OPT.MID | PCL |

'he thought "I hope these ones will not destroy my creatures."'
[*Śatapatha-Brāhmaṇa* 2.5.2.[26]]

(23)  Periphrastic perfect of the P-verb VID 'perceive, understand':

| śamyur | ha vai | bārhaspatyo | 'ñjasā | yajñasya | saṃsthāṃ | vidāṃ | cakāra |
|---|---|---|---|---|---|---|---|
| Śamyu: | EMPHATIC | Bārhaspatya: | truly | sacrifice: | consummation: | perceive: | do: |
| NOM.SG | PCLS | NOM.SG | | GEN.SG | ACC.SG | NMLZ. | 3SG.PRF. |
| | | | | | | ACC.SG | ACT |

'Śamyu Bārhaspatya truly perceived the consummation of the sacrifice'
[*Śatapatha-Brāhmaṇa* 1.9.1.[24]]

A second kind of evidence against the assumption that 'active' and 'middle' are inflection classes in Sanskrit is the fact that although the addition of a preverb generally doesn't change a verb root's inflection class membership, the addition of a preverb can change the status of a verb as a P-verb, U-verb, or Ā-verb, as the examples in (24) (all specifically licensed by Pāṇini) show.

(24)  a.   VIŚ 'enter' (P-verb) → NI-VIŚ 'enter in' (Ā-verb)          [*Aṣṭādhyāyī* 1.3.17]

    b.   KRĪ 'buy' (U- verb) → PARI-KRĪ, AVA-KRĪ 'buy', VI-KRĪ 'sell' (Ā-verbs)

                                                             [*Aṣṭādhyāyī* 1.3.18]

    c.   MṚṢ 'endure' (U-verb) → PARI-MṚṢ 'endure patiently' (P-verb)

                                                             [*Aṣṭādhyāyī* 1.3.82]

It is clear from these kinds of evidence that 'active' and 'middle' must be seen as morphosyntactic properties in Sanskrit.

### 2.4.2. *Ā-verb paradigms are not instances of voice syncretism*

A second possible approach to avoiding the conclusion that Ā-verbs are deponent would be to assume that their paradigms are instances of voice syncretism—that Ā-verbs have a full paradigm of active and middle forms, but that the active forms all happen to be syncretized with their middle counterparts. (Likewise, one might assume that P-verbs have a full paradigm of active and middle forms, and that their middle forms are syncretized with their active counterparts.) But the assumption that Ā-verbs and P-verbs have full voice paradigms is also disconfirmed by their behaviour in the periphrastic perfect. In the periphrastic perfect, the auxiliary verb is in general capable of expressing voice distinctions by means of overt morphology. One would therefore expect that although Ā-verbs and P-verbs don't express voice distinctions in their own synthetic inflection, even they should exhibit overt voice distinctions in the periphrastic perfect thanks to the presence of an auxiliary verb whose synthetic morphology expresses such distinctions. But again, an Ā-verb's auxiliary is always in the middle voice, and that of a P-verb, in the active voice. For this reason, the idea that we simply have massive voice syncretism in the inflection of Ā-verbs and P-verbs isn't a reasonable assumption.

### 2.4.3. *Ā-verbs are non-canonical deponents*

In view of the foregoing considerations, we must conclude that Ā-verbs truly are deponent; they've 'laid aside' their specifically middle meaning in favour of use with subjects that are either affected or unaffected by the events that they describe.

Are they canonical deponents? The answer is clearly no. To see this, consider again the three definitive properties of canonical deponency presented in section 1 above, beginning with the contrariness of form and meaning.

As was seen in section 1, Latin *hortātur* 's/he urges' exhibits a contrariness of form and meaning: despite its form, it is interpreted as active and not passive. While Sanskrit Ā-verbs exhibit a clear mismatch between form and meaning, they don't participate in the same sort of contrariness as *hortātur*. The forms of a Latin deponent verb can't be used with both agent subjects and patient subjects: they must have agent subjects (even though their morphology suggests that they should have patient subjects). By contrast, a Sanskrit Ā-verb's middle forms can be used with subjects whose referents are either affected or unaffected (even though their morphology suggests that they should only go with affected subjects). In view of this difference, a Sanskrit Ā-verb might be said to exhibit INDISCRIMINATE deponency, while a Latin deponent verb instead exhibits CONTRARY deponency; this distinction is illustrated in Figure 3. Contrary deponency involves the use of an inflectional exponent $x$ to express a meaning B that is contrary to the meaning A that $x$ would ordinarily be used to express in a non-deponent form. But indiscriminate deponency involves the use of an inflectional exponent $x$ in a way that fails to express anything at all—that is, rather than express the meaning A that it might ordinarily be used to express in the inflection of non-deponent forms, $x$ is used in a way that is semantically empty; its use is therefore compatible with either its usual meaning A or the contrary meaning B.[11]

Consider now the property of concurrent defectiveness. While the paradigms of Ā-verbs can certainly be regarded as defective (since they lack forms with active morphology), they don't exhibit concurrent defectiveness, which (according to the definition in §1 above) presupposes the contrariness of form and meaning.

Thus, Sanskrit Ā-verbs exhibit neither the contrariness of form and meaning nor the concurrent defectiveness of canonical deponents. But what of the third property of canonical deponents, that of lexical exceptionality? In fact, Ā-verbs are not very exceptional. Making a precise count of the number of Ā-verbs would be difficult, since (a) the most authoritative sources— the traditional root-inventories known as *dhātupāṭhas*—differ both in the number of verb roots they recognize and in their classification of specific roots as U-verbs, P-verbs, or Ā-verbs; moreover, (b) the class membership of a preverb+root compound may (as observed in (24) above) differ from that of the root upon which it is based. Even so, the *dhātupāṭhas* do give at least

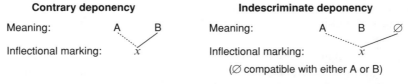

(Dotted line represents the semantic association usual for $x$ in non-deponent forms; solid line represents $x$'s semantic association in deponent forms)

**Figure 3.**   Two types of deponency

---

[11] Compare the notion of indiscriminate deponency to the instance of syncretic deponency in Tsez discussed by Corbett (this volume).

a rough picture of the relative size of the classes of U-verbs, P-verbs, or Ā-verbs. As a representative case, consider the classification of verb roots in the *Kavikalpadruma*[12] (the *dhātupāṭha* of the thirteenth-century grammarian Vopadeva): among the 2,430 listed roots, 68.7% are classified as P-verbs, 23.4% as Ā-verbs, and 7.9% as U-verbs. That is, roots belonging to the class of Ā-verbs are roughly three times more common than those belonging to the class of U-verbs; on the other hand, they are only about a third as common as those belonging to the class of P-verbs.

In summary, Sanskrit Ā-verbs aren't like canonical deponents: of the three definitive properties of canonical deponents, they clearly fail to exhibit the first two (those of form/meaning contrariness and concurrent defectiveness) and they don't exhibit the third (that of lexical exceptionality) at all convincingly. Granted, then, that Sanskrit Ā-verbs are deponents of a decidedly non-canonical sort, another issue remains: are they instances of form-deponency or property-deponency?

## 3. Ā-Verbs as Instances of Property-Deponency

As we saw in section 1, instances of canonical deponency can be seen as involving either form-deponency or property-deponency. But as non-canonical deponents, Sanskrit Ā-verbs do not afford the same analytic choice: as I show, they are clearly instances of property-deponency.

Thus, consider the two different possibilities for the representation of an Ā-verb presented in (25). In (25a), the Ā-verb GARH 'rebuke' is presented as a form-deponent verb, whose inflectional exponence is at odds with its morphosyntactic property set. In (25b), it is instead presented as a property-deponent verb, whose meaning is at odds with its morphosyntactic property set. Are both of these possible analyses?

(25)  a.  *Garhate* as a form-deponent word:

　　　Meaning:　　　'rebukes'
　　　Cell:　　　　　⟨ GARH, {3rd singular present indicative **active**}⟩
　　　　　　　　　　　　　　　　　　　　　　　　　　　　　　　↑
　　　Realization:　　*garhate* ◄―――――――――― (?!)

　　　b.  *Garhate* as a property-deponent word:

　　　Meaning:　　　'rebukes' ◄―――――――――――(?!)
　　　　　　　　　　　　　　　　　　　　　　　　　↓
　　　Cell:　　　　　⟨ GARH, {3rd singular present indicative **middle**}⟩
　　　Realization:　　*garhate*

---

[12] For present purposes, Vopadeva's *dhātupāṭhas* may be regarded as representative. The statistics cited here are based on the summary of Vopadeva's root classifications in Palsule (1955). For discussion of the relations between the different *dhātupāṭhas*, see Palsule (1961).

On first consideration, the assumption that Ā-verbs are form-deponent would seem to be more plausible: insofar as the morphosyntactic property 'active' is semantically empty (§2.3), this assumption would, to all appearances, better account for the fact that Ā-verbs are compatible with subjects whose referents are either affected or unaffected by the event that they describe. But in fact, only the assumption that Ā-verbs are property-deponent is consistent with two key characteristics of such verbs. We have already seen the first of these characteristics, namely the fact that in the periphrastic perfect, Ā-verbs require the accompanying auxiliary verb to exhibit middle rather than active inflections (§2.4.1). In view of this fact, Ā-verbs must be assumed to carry the morphosyntactic specification 'middle', as in (25b).

The second key characteristic of Ā-verbs is their behaviour with respect to a general pattern of syncretism in Sanskrit. In Sanskrit, special passive forms exist in the present system and in the third-person singular of the aorist; but generally outside of those contexts—and sometimes within them—a verb's passive forms are simply syncretized with their corresponding middle forms. Thus, consider the Ā-verb JṜ 'invoke, sing hymns of praise, glorify'. In (26), its present middle participial form *járamāṇaḥ* (sandhi variant *járamāṇo*) is a predicate of the one doing the glorifying; in (27), by contrast, this same form serves instead a predicate of the one being glorified. As this example shows, the forms of the Ā-verb JṜ function as middle forms with respect to the principle by which passive forms are syncretic with their middle counterparts. If *járamāṇaḥ* were instead regarded as an active form in (26) (in accordance with the assumption that Ā-verbs are form-deponent), then it would be surprising indeed to see *járamāṇaḥ* serving as a passive form in (27), since there is no independently motivated principle of syncretism relating passive forms to active forms in Sanskrit.

(26)  ...   aśvínā           huve             járamāṇo          arkaíḥ
            Aśvin:ACC.DU     call:1SG.PRS.    glorify:PRS.MID.  song.of.praise:
                             IND.MID          PPLE.NOM.SG       INS.PL
            'Glorifying with songs of praise I call the Aśvins . . .'   [*Ṛg-Veda* 6.62.1]

(27)  járamāṇaḥ        sám idhyase       devébhyo         havyavāhana
      glorify:PRS.      kindle:2SG.PRS.   god:DAT.PL       oblation.bearer:
      MID.PPLE.NOM.SG   IND.PASS                           VOC.SG
      'Glorified (by hymns) you are kindled, O oblation-bearer for the gods . . .'
                                                           [*Ṛg-Veda* 10.118.5]

Here, then, we have a basis for choosing between form-deponency and property-deponency, and the evidence shows that Sanskrit Ā-verbs are indeed property-deponent: they unquestionably possess the morphosyntactic property 'middle' (as their behaviour in the periphrastic perfect and passive constructions shows), yet this property does not entail that they have middle semantics.

This is a very interesting conclusion, since it means that some morphosyntactic properties depend for their semantic content upon the kind of
paradigm in which they appear. In Sanskrit, the property 'middle' denotes the
middle-voice operator in (18) in those paradigms in which it is in full contrast
with the property 'active' (that is, in the paradigms of U-verbs); but in the
paradigms of Ā-verbs, in which 'middle' fails to contrast with 'active', it simply denotes an identity function. In other words, 'middle' is what might be
called a PARADIGM-DEPENDENT MORPHOME: a morphosyntactic property
whose semantic content in a given paradigm depends on whether or not it
fully contrasts (in that paradigm) with some other property belonging to the
same inflectional category. Thus, the semantics of the active and the middle
in Sanskrit might be represented schematically as in Figure 4: the active-voice
property uniformly denotes an identity function, but whether the middle-
voice property denotes the middle-voice operator in (18) depends upon the
type of paradigm in which it appears.

In the semantic analysis of middle voice schematized in Figure 4, the
interpretation of the property 'middle' in a given paradigm depends upon
whether it fully contrasts with the property 'active' in that paradigm. The
intended notion of full contrast in this analysis is as follows: 'middle' fully
contrasts with 'active' in a given paradigm P if and only if for every cell containing the property set {X active} in P there is a corresponding cell containing the property set {X middle}. Thus, 'middle' is not in full contrast with

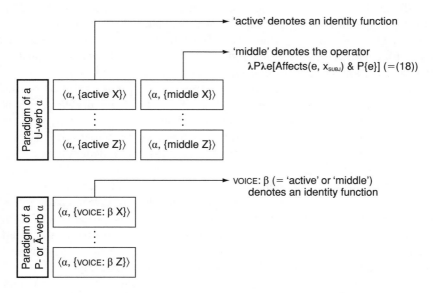

**Figure 4.**   The semantics of the morphosyntactic properties 'active' and 'middle' in Sanskrit

'active' in the paradigm of a verb exhibiting only the active voice in some tenses but only the middle voice in others (e.g. the verb vṛt 'turn, roll'; cf. again (14), (15)); accordingly, 'middle' is interpreted as an identity function in the paradigm of such a verb.

Moreover, 'middle' is interpreted as an identity function in a paradigm in which middle cells have active counterparts in some tenses but not others. Pāṇini (*Aṣṭādhyāyī* 1.3.91–3) identifies a number of verbs possessing paradigms of this sort. These include: (i) Ā-verbs that optionally exhibit the active voice in the aorist tense, e.g. DYUT 'shine' (3sg aor. ind. act. *adyutat* / mid. *adyotiṣṭa*); (ii) Ā-verbs that optionally exhibit the active voice in the synthetic future and conditional tenses and in their desiderative derivative, e.g. SYAND 'flow, run, hasten' (3sg fut. act. *syantsyati* / mid. *syantsyate*); and (iii) the Ā-verb KḶP 'be fit for', which optionally exhibits the active voice in the synthetic and periphrastic future and conditional tenses and in its desiderative derivative (3sg fut. act. *kalpsyati* / mid. *kalpsyate*). None of the verbs of types (i)–(iii) has a paradigm in which 'middle' stands in full contrast to 'active'; accordingly, 'middle' is interpreted as an identity function in their paradigms.

Finally, note that the semantics proposed here for the property 'middle' doesn't absolutely necessitate a different interpretation even if 'middle' does stand in full contrast with 'active'. As was observed in (21a) above, a U-verb describing a self-directed action needn't exhibit a middle inflection (i.e. may instead exhibit an active inflection) if there is another word in the same clause expressing this reflexivity. For this reason, a U-verb that inherently denotes a self-directed action also allows the free alternation of active and middle inflection. Pāṇini (*Aṣṭādhyāyī* 1.3.90) identifies denominal verbs in -*ya*, as a class of U-verbs exhibiting this sort of free variation, e.g. LOHITĀYA 'become red' (from LOHITA 'red'): 3sg prs. ind. act. *lohitāyati* / mid. *lohitayate*. Just as the conversational implicature ordinarily associated with the use of the active voice is cancelled by the reflexive pronoun in (21a), it is cancelled by the inherent semantics of the verb itself in the case of *lohitāyati*, which is therefore effectively synonymous with its middle counterpart *lohitayate*.

The account of Sanskrit non-canonical deponency schematized in Figure 4 raises an interesting possibility for canonical instances of deponency such as that of Latin *hortātur* 's/he urges': perhaps these, too, should be seen as instances of property-deponency. That is, one could assume that *hortātur* carries the property 'passive' but that this property fails to receive a passive interpretation in this word because it fails to contrast with the property 'active' in the paradigm of HORTĀRĪ. This assumption would be contrary to the usual view that forms such as *hortātur* are 'really' active, but it's not clear how one could prove that they aren't in fact property-deponent. One might object that Latin deponents can't actually be passive because Latin syntax doesn't treat deponents as passive. But as noted above (§1), it's not clear that Latin syntax is ever directly sensitive to a verb's voice property (as opposed to its argument structure, subcategorization restrictions, and case-assignment properties). That is, it may well be that the property 'passive' has no syntactic function at all in Latin—that its functions are instead purely morphological and semantic: in the morphological domain, a verb form's inflectional realization is sensitive to it, as is a paradigm-dependent rule of interpretation in the semantic domain.

This analysis recalls the claim by Kiparsky (2005) that Latin syntax is insensitive to the property 'passive'; but the analysis suggested here for Latin is crucially different from Kiparsky's analysis. Kiparsky treats 'passive' as a conjugation-class feature in Latin, essentially rejecting the assumption that the so-called deponent verbs are in fact truly deponent. By contrast, the analysis proposed here for Latin deponents (and advocated for Sanskrit Ā-verbs) treats the Latin property 'passive' and the Sanskrit property 'middle' as morphosyntactic properties whose semantics depend on the kind of paradigm in which they appear. Kiparsky's Latin analysis cannot be successfully extended to cover the Sanskrit facts, since as I have shown (§2.4.1), the Sanskrit middle cannot simply be reduced to an inflection class.

# 4. Two More Examples of Paradigm-Dependent Morphomes

I wish to emphasize that the postulation of paradigm-dependent morphomes such as the Sanskrit middle (and perhaps the Latin passive) is motivated in other languages as well. To demonstrate this, I shall present a pair of examples of paradigm-dependent morphomes in non-Indo-European languages.

## 4.1. The property 'reflexive' in Sora verb inflection

As a first example, consider the inflection of verbs in Sora, an Austro-Asiatic language of India. In Sora, the verb ᴋᴜŋ 'shave' inflects differently according to whether it is to be interpreted reflexively or non-reflexively; for instance, 'I shave myself' is realized as *kuŋtenay* whereas 'I shave someone else' is realized as *kuŋtay*. Many verbs in Sora exhibit this same kind of contrast, possessing one set of inflected forms for reflexive interpretations and a different set for non-reflexive interpretations. The inflection of many verbs, however, always follows the reflexive pattern despite the fact that they don't have a specifically reflexive interpretation; and there is a different set of verbs that always follows the non-reflexive pattern. The examples in Table 1 illustrate.

This three-way contrast among Sora verbs is comparable to the contrast between U-, P- and Ā-verbs in Sanskrit. The Sora verb ᴋᴜŋ 'shave' is similar to a Sanskrit U-verb: it exhibits both reflexive and non-reflexive morphology

**Table 1.** Partial paradigms of three Sora verbs (cf. Ramamurti 1931: 128f., Biligiri 1965: 232ff.)

| Lexeme: | | | BER 'speak' | KUŊ 'shave' | GU 'call' | |
|---|---|---|---|---|---|---|
| Inflection: | | | Reflexive | Non-reflexive | | |
| Non-past | Singular | 1 | ber-te-n-ay | kuŋ-te-n-ay | kuŋ-t-ay | gu-t-ay |
| Affirmative | | 2 | ber-te-n | kuŋ-te-n | kuŋ-t-ɛ | gu-t-ɛ |
| | | 3 | ber-te-n | kuŋ-te-n | kuŋ-t-ɛ | gu-t-ɛ |
| | Plural | 1 incl | ber-te-n-be | kuŋ-te-n-be | kuŋ-tə-be | gu-tə-be |
| | | 1 excl | ə-ber-te-n-ay | ə-kuŋ-te-n-ay | ə-kuŋ-t-ay | ə-gu-t-ay |
| | | 2 | ə-ber-te-n | ə-kuŋ-te-n | ə-kuŋ-t-ɛ | ə-gu-t-ɛ |
| | | 3 | ber-te-n-ji | kuŋ-te-n-ji | kuŋ-t-ɛ-ji | gu-t-ɛ-ji |
| Past | Singular | 1 | ber-re-n-ay | kuŋ-le-n-ay | kuŋ-l-ay | gu-l-ay |
| Affirmative | | 2 | ber-re-n | kuŋ-le-n | kuŋ-l-ɛ | gu-l-ɛ |
| | | 3 | ber-re-n | kuŋ-le-n | kuŋ-l-ɛ | gu-l-ɛ |
| | Plural | 1 incl | ber-re-n-be | kuŋ-le-n-be | kuŋ-lə-be | gu-lə-be |
| | | 1 excl | ə-ber-re-n-ay | ə-kuŋ-le-n-ay | ə-kuŋ-l-ay | ə-gu-l-ay |
| | | 2 | ə-ber-re-n | ə-kuŋ-le-n | ə-kuŋ-l-ɛ | ə-gu-l-ɛ |
| | | 3 | ber-re-n-ji | kuŋ-le-n-ji | kuŋ-l-ɛ-ji | gu-l-ɛ-ji |
| Similar lexemes: | | | ÑA 'walk', | SO 'hide', | ÑI 'buy', | |
| | | | DER 'believe', | BɨB 'drown', | JUM 'eat', | |
| | | | DAKU 'stay' | ABUMA 'bathe' | GɨJ 'see' | |

and this morphological distinction corresponds to a clear-cut semantic distinction in its interpretation. On the other hand, BER 'speak' is more like an Ā-verb in Sanskrit: it follows only one of the inflectional patterns exhibited by KUŊ, but in the case of BER, this inflectional pattern doesn't carry any direct association with the semantics that that pattern has in the case of KUŊ. And if BER is comparable to a Sanskrit Ā-verb, then GU 'call' is comparable to a P-verb, following the second of the two contrasting inflectional patterns combined in the paradigm of KUŊ.

Thus, just as the property 'middle' functions as a paradigm-dependent morphome in Sanskrit, so, likewise, does the property 'reflexive' in Sora: though it is realized in both the paradigm of KUŊ 'shave' and that of BER 'speak', it is semantically significant in only the former of these paradigms.

### 4.2. The property 'definite object' in Muna verb inflection

As a second example, consider now the inflection of verbs in Muna (Austronesian; Indonesia). In Muna, most transitive verbs can inflect in either of two different ways according to whether they have a definite or an indefinite object. Examples of this inflectional sensitivity to the definiteness of the object (cited from van den Berg 1989: 60f.) are given in (28)–(30): in each of the (a) examples, the object is indefinite, so the verb assumes an indefinite-object form; in each of the (b) examples, by contrast, the object is definite, so the verb instead assumes a definite-object form.

(28) a. ne-aso                kalei.           'She is selling bananas.'
        3SG.REALIS-sell    bananas

    b. no-aso-e.                                 'She is selling them.'
        3SG.REALIS-sell-it

(29) a. ne-ala-mo             kapulu.          'He took a machete.'
        3SG.REALIS-take-PFV  machete

    b. no-ala-mo             kapulu-no.    'He took his machete.'
        3SG.REALIS-take-PFV  machete-his

(30) a. ne-pongko-mo         se-ghulu        ghule.  'He killed a snake.'
        3SG.REALIS-kill-PFV  one-CLASSIFIER  snake

    b. no-pongko-mo         ghule            amaitu. 'He killed the snake.'
        3SG.REALIS-kill-PFV  snake           that

Many verbs, however, including some transitives, follow only the definite-object or the indefinite-object pattern (or yet a third pattern, the 'ao-class' pattern), and when they do so, their semantics carries no implication about object definiteness (and indeed, they may lack an object). There is a tendency for dynamic intransitives (e.g. KALA 'go') to follow the definite-object pattern and for stative intransitives (e.g. LODO 'sleep') to follow the ao-class pattern. Sample paradigms are given in Table 2.

Muna PONGKO 'kill' is similar to a Sanskrit U-verb, possessing a choice of morphological patterns which directly corresponds to a choice in its semantic interpretation. Muna KALA 'go', by contrast, is more like an Ā-verb, following only one of the morphological patterns available to PONGKO: notwithstanding the semantic significance of this pattern in the interpretation of PONGKO's forms, it has no comparable significance in the interpretation of KALA. Thus, the property 'definite-object' in Muna might be regarded as a paradigm-dependent morphome comparable to the Sanskrit middle

**Table 2.** Realis paradigms of four Muna verbs (van den Berg 1989: 53)

| | Lexeme: | KALA 'go' | PONGKO 'kill' | | LATE 'live' | LODO 'sleep' |
|---|---|---|---|---|---|---|
| | Inflection: | Definite object ('a-class') | Indefinite object | ('ae-class') | | ('ao-class') |
| Singular | 1 | a-kala | a-pongko | ae-pongko | ae-late | ao-lodo |
| | 2 | o-kala | o-pongko | ome-pongko | ome-late | omo-lodo |
| | 2 polite | to-kala | to-pongko | te-pongko | te-late | to-lodo |
| | 3 | no-kala | no-pongko | ne-pongko | ne-late | no-lodo |
| Dual | 1 incl | do-kala | do-pongko | de-pongko | de-late | do-lodo |
| Plural | 1 incl | do-kala-amu | do-pongko-amu | de-pongko-emu | de-late-emu | do-lodo-omu |
| | 1 excl | ta-kala | ta-pongko | tae-pongko | tae-late | tao-lodo |
| | 2 | o-kala-amu | o-pongko-amu | ome-pongko-emu | ome-late-emu | omo-lodo-omu |
| | 2 polite | to-kala-amu | to-pongko-amu | te-pongko-emu | te-late-emu | to-lodo-omu |
| | 3 | do-kala | do-pongko | de-pongko | de-late | do-lodo |

voice: its interpretation within a given paradigm depends on whether it
contrasts with the property 'indefinite-object' in that paradigm.

# 5. Conclusion

I conclude from the facts examined here that Sanskrit Ā-verbs are deponent
verbs of a non-canonical type, and that their properties reveal that at least
some instances of deponency must be seen as involving property-deponency
rather than form-deponency. I have argued that in Sanskrit, the property-
deponency of Ā-verbs follows from the status of the middle voice as a
paradigm-dependent morphome; as I have shown, similar paradigm-
dependent morphomes exist in other languages as well.

Further research will doubtless uncover other, comparable instances of
paradigm-dependent morphomes and will facilitate a more detailed understanding of their properties. But their chief significance is already clear: they
demonstrate that a given morphosyntactic property cannot necessarily be
assumed to express the same semantic content in all of its instances; instead,
the semantics of a given morphosyntactic property must be assumed to be at
least potentially sensitive to its paradigmatic context.

# References

Aronoff, Mark, 1994. *Morphology by itself: stems and inflectional classes*. Cambridge,
     Mass., and London: MIT Press.
Arya, Ravi Prakash, and K. L. Joshi (eds.). 2001. *R̥gveda Saṃhitā* [2nd rev. edn].
     Delhi: Parimal Publications.
Van Den Berg, René. 1989. *A grammar of the Muna language*. Dordrecht and
     Providence: Foris.
Biligiri, Hemmige Shriniwasarangachar. 1965. The Sora verb: a restricted study. *Indo-
     Pacific studies,* Part II: *Descriptive linguistics [Lingua* 15], ed. by G. B. Milner and
     Eugénie J. A. Henderson, 231–50. Amsterdam: North-Holland.
Bloomfield, Maurice. 1906. *A Vedic concordance*. Cambridge, Mass.: Harvard
     University Press.
Bloomfield, Maurice, and Franklin Edgerton. 1930. *Vedic variants,* Volume I: *The
     verb*. Philadelphia: Linguistic Society of America and University of Pennsylvania.
Burrow, T. 1973. *The Sanskrit language* [3rd rev. edn]. London: Faber and Faber.
Grice, H. P. 1975. Logic and conversation. *The logic of grammar*, ed. by Donald
     Davidson and Gilbert Harman, 64–75. Encino, California.: Dickenson.
Katre, Sumitra Mangesh. 1987. *Aṣṭādhyāyī of Pāṇini*. Austin: University of Texas
     Press.

Kiparsky, Paul. 2005. Blocking and periphrasis in inflectional paradigms. *Yearbook of Morphology 2004*, ed. by Geert Booij and Jaap van Marle, 113–35. Dordrecht: Springer.

Palsule, Gajanan Balkrishna. 1955. *A concordance of Sanskrit Dhātupāṭhas*. Poona: Deccan College Postgraduate and Research Institute.

—— 1961. *The Sanskrit Dhātupāṭhas: a critical study*. Poona: University of Poona.

Ramamurti, G. V. 1931. *A manual of the Soːra: (or Savara) language*, Madras: Government Press.

Speijer, J. S. 1886. *Sanskrit syntax* [1980 reprint]. Delhi: Motilal Banarsidass.

Stewart, Thomas, and Gregory Stump. 2007. Paradigm Function Morphology and the morphology/syntax interface'. *Handbook of linguistic interfaces*, ed. by Gillian Ramchand and Charles Reiss, 383–421. Oxford University Press.

Stump, Gregory T. 1991, A paradigm-based theory of morphosemantic mismatches, *Language* 67. 675–725.

—— 2001. *Inflectional morphology*. Cambridge University Press.

—— 2002. Morphological and syntactic paradigms: arguments for a theory of paradigm linkage. *Yearbook of Morphology 2001*, ed. by Geert Booij and Jaap van Marle, 147–80. Dordrecht: Kluwer.

—— 2005a. Delineating the boundary between inflection-class marking and derivational marking: The case of Sanskrit *-aya*. *Morphology and its demarcations*, ed. by Wolfgang U. Dressler, Dieter Kastovsky, Oskar E. Pfeiffer, and Franz Rainer, 293–309. Amsterdam: John Benjamins.

—— 2005b. Referrals and morphomes in Sora verb inflection. *Yearbook of Morphology 2005*, ed. by Geert Booij and Jaap van Marle, 227–51. Dordrecht: Springer.

—— 2006. Heteroclisis and paradigm linkage. *Language* 82. 279–322.

Whitney, William Dwight. 1889. *Sanskrit grammar* [2nd edition]. Cambridge, Mass.: Harvard University Press.

# 5

# Deponency in the Diachrony of Greek*

NIKOLAOS LAVIDAS AND DIMITRA PAPANGELI

## 1. Introduction

DEPONENT VERBS HAVE ATTRACTED GREAT INTEREST in the traditional grammar of Greek and Latin, usually from a descriptive perspective that sheds little theoretical light on their marginal characteristics. Deponent verbs are specified in the Greek language as an idiosyncratic group that requires exceptional syntactic structure or else appears in surprising morphology. These verbs may appear in middle or passive morphological form and take an object in the accusative, hence they behave as a transitive construction; or they may have only an active morphological form and lack middle/passive morphology.

In this paper, we investigate deponent verbs that bear the middle/passive morphology of the Greek language and take an object in the accusative case. The diachronic overview of the data seeks to provide innovative information regarding the class of deponent verbs and the role of the suffix in these examples. Our ultimate goal is to determine whether there exist any systematic factors from the areas of syntax and semantics that influence the presence of deponent verbs throughout the history of the Greek language. We conclude,

* We should like to thank the Surrey Morphology Group and the British Academy for the stimulating conference they organized. The discussions during the conference helped us elaborate on many issues. We would like to thank all the participants for their questions and comments: G. Corbett, D. Adger, R. Kempson, N. Vincent, D. Kalluli among others. Lastly, we should like to thank D. Theophanopoulou-Kontou for providing us with valuable insights and our colleagues at the University of Athens for raising interesting issues during an informal presentation of this paper.

Lavidas's research was initially supported by the Greek State Scholarship Foundation (IKY) and, at the present time, by the A. Onassis Foundation. Papangeli carried out the research at the École Normale Supérieure, Department of Cognitive Sciences, with the Talent grant, from the Netherlands Organization for Scientific Research (NWO) and currently is a postdoctoral researcher at the University of Athens, with a grant from the Greek State Scholarship Foundation (IKY). Our sources of funding are gratefully acknowledged here.

after an extensive overview of the data, that deponent verbs require an independent theoretical explanation, optimally drawn from the properties of
morphology. Specifically, we examine the behaviour of deponents in the
three main periods of the Greek language: firstly, we look into the data from
Classical Greek, secondly, we turn to examples from the Hellenistic and
Roman Koine period, and, lastly, we discuss the cases of Medieval and
Modern Greek.

## 2. The Data

Our discussion of the Greek data starts from the period of Classical Greek
with numerous examples from different kinds of texts. As we shall see in more
detail, deponent verbs exist already from this stage, giving the impression
that deponency is a well-established phenomenon in this first period. The
diachronic change of verbs is demonstrated from the evolution of deponents in
Hellenistic, in Roman Koine and, especially, in Medieval Greek, when the language displays many parallel forms, such as deponent and non-deponent verbs
with identical semantic interpretation. In Modern Greek, we reach the final,
synchronic stage, where some deponent verbs originate already from the
Classical period, and, at the same time, new deponents appear in the language.[1]

    In this paper, we use the term *deponents* for the verbs that have no active
transitive form, but bear stably middle/passive morphology.[2] We concentrate

---

[1] The term *Ancient Greek* (*c*.800–300 BC) refers to the stage of the Greek language corresponding
to Classical Antiquity, which applies to two periods of Greek history: Archaic and Classical
Greece. As the Greeks colonized the regions from Asia Minor to Egypt and to the Middle East,
the Greek language began to evolve into multiple dialects: these dialects were combined together,
to form the international language of that era, namely the *Hellenistic Koine Greek*. This stage is
also known as *Postclassical Greek* or even *New Testament Greek*. With the term *Medieval Greek*
we refer to the data from the 6th–15th cent. AD, and we distinguish two subperiods, following the
standard analyses: Early Medieval or Byzantine (6th–11th cent.) and Late Medieval (12th–15th
cent.). The examples from the Late Byzantine/ Early Modern Greek (16th cent.) are used here to
present some tendencies we observe in the language. *Modern Greek* had started taking shape well
into the Middle Ages but for reasons of convenience linguists place its starting point at the Fall
of Constantinople in 1453 AD (Jannaris 1968; Horrocks 1997; Theophanopoulou-Kontou 2000).
We are not concerned here with issues that regard the exact start and end points of the periods
of the Greek language or with the subperiods. However, we give great importance to the
distinction of different stages, in order to have a clear picture of the data.

[2] Interestingly, there is another group of verbs that resembles the group of deponents, namely the
unaccusatives. To be more accurate, the presence of the middle/passive suffix on some unaccusative verbs of Modern Greek is expected. However, the existence of unaccusatives with an
active morphological form raises a number of questions. Unaccusatives without a suffix could be
viewed as deponents that display an unexpected syntactic pattern, that is, they cannot take any
object in the accusative case, like their ordinary counterparts. However, deponents have no other
variant, such as an active or a passive form, which is the case with unaccusatives; hence many

more on *transitive deponents*, i.e. middle/passive transitive verbs (a verb is considered to be transitive only if it contains an accusative case marked object). In these examples, middle/passive morphology, regularly used for reflexive and passive structures, behaves like its active counterpart.[3]

## 2.1. Ancient Greek

Ancient Greek displays the same pattern as Modern Greek. In particular, transitive constructions appear with active verbs (*ze:t-o:*.PRS.1SG.ACT 'I search'— example 1a) and passive constructions (1b) appear with middle/ passive morphology (*ze:t-oumai*.PRS.1SG.MEDIOPASS 'I am searched'), as shown in the Appendix (at the end of the paper). Middle and passive are morphologically distinct only in the future (middle ze:te:-somai, passive ze:te:-the:somai 'I shall be searched') and past (middle eze:te:-same:n, passive eze:te:-the:n 'I was searched') tenses. Therefore, we use the combined label 'middle/passive' throughout the paper without any theoretical implications. As we will see in more detail, the middle/passive distinction disappears very early from the language, giving rise to the use of a single suffix for multiple semantic readings, such as passive, reflexive, and reciprocal.

(1a)  te:n            orthe:n          ze:tousi
      the.ACC.SG      truth.ACC.SG     search.PRS.3PL.ACT
      'They are searching for the truth.'           (Plato, *Politicus* 302e, 4)

(1b)  ho            kybos          ou    ze:teitai                       autois
      the.NOM.SG    cube.NOM.SG    not   search.PRS.3SG.MEDIOPASS        they.DAT.PL
      'The cube is not being searched by them.'     (Plato, *Spuria* 388e, 10)

There are three voices in Ancient Greek: active (suffix *-o:*), middle and passive (suffix *-mai*). The middle and passive voice morphology are distinguishable only in the future (middle suffix *-somai*, passive suffix *-the:somai*) and in the past tense (middle suffix *-same:n*, passive suffix *-the:n*). For the other tenses, there is no morphological distinction between middle and passive voice endings (cf. Ancient Greek in the Appendix). Already in Ancient Greek, both middle and passive suffixes are used with reflexive, reciprocal, anticausative, or passive readings. A transitive verb could bear active or middle/passive morphology; with the middle/passive morphology the transitive verb denotes

---

attempts to account for unaccusatives in a syntactic way (Pesetsky 1995; Reinhart 1997, 2000, 2003; and Alexiadou and Anagnostopoulou 2003 for Greek), but not for deponents, which are always mentioned in traditional grammars as exceptions from the general rules of the language.
[3] See Baerman (this volume) for Latin, and Corbett (this volume) who define deponency as a deviation between the ways one would gloss some inflected form in isolation versus its function in some given context, where it would appear to require a different gloss.

also the involvement of the subject in the action (and the direct influence of the event on the subject):[4]

(2)  hoi astoi          aleura      te kai  alphita
     the townspeople.NOM.PL  wheat.ACC  and   barley-flour.ACC
     epoieun
     make.PST.3PL.ACT
     'The townspeople were cooking dinner with wheat and barley-flour (for the Persian king).'  (Herodotus, *Historiae* 7, 119)

(3)  apo     olyreo:n   poieuntai                    sitia
     from    spelt      makePRS.3PL.MEDIOPASS        bread.ACC.PL
     hoi  Aigyptioi
     the  Egyptians.NOM.PL
     'The Egyptians make bread from spelt (for themselves).'  (Herodotus, *Historiae* 2, 36)

Deponent verbs, namely verbs which bear only the middle/passive morphology and can take an object in the accusative (transitives), appear already from the period of Ancient Greek. (The alternative of an active type with a different meaning is not attested, similarly to the non-deponent transitive verbs we observed in examples 2 and 3.) Two types of Ancient Greek deponents are distinguished:

(i)   Deponents with middle morphology in past and in future tense, which are traditionally called *media tantum*. For example:

      Middle past    →   apekri-*same:n*     'I answered'
      Middle future  →   apokri-*somai*      'I will answer'

      The class of middle deponent verbs that are at the centre of our interest takes an object in the accusative case, as illustrated in example (4):

(4)  tous      tote parontas      aitiasontai              symboulous
     the.ACC.PL  then present.ACC.PL  accuse.FUT.3PL.MID     adviser.ACC.PL
     'They will accuse all those advisers who were then present.'  (Plato, *Gorgias* 519a, 5)

      A detailed list of this type of deponent verbs, with middle morphology, is spelled out in Table 1 on the basis of texts from this period, grammars, and relevant monographs.[5]

[4] The same is observed for Sanskrit (Stump, this volume): active voice *pacati* 'he prepares food for others' vs middle voice *pacate* 'he cooks for himself'. Detailed analyses of these transitive constructions are also found in Cohen 1930 (for Arabic), Vendryes 1948 (for French, Latin and Greek) and Humbert 1954 (for Greek). There is an issue here of distinguishing passive constructions from middle constructions, which we leave aside, and we take the above examples as instances of middles, along the lines of the relevant literature.

[5] The data in this paper are a result of an exhaustive search of the corpus of Classical, Hellenistic, and Byzantine texts of the *Thesaurus Linguae Graecae* (TLG), in electronic corpora of papyri

**Table 1.**  Middle transitive deponent verbs in Ancient Greek

| | | | | | | | |
|---|---|---|---|---|---|---|---|
| apokrinomai | 'I answer' | memphomai | 'I blame' | iaomai | 'I heal' |
| makhomai | 'I fight' | aitiaomai | 'I accuse' | akrooamai | 'I listen' |
| kharizomai | 'I gratify' | lymainomai | 'I injure' | araomai | 'I beseech' |
| do:reomai | 'I present' | mimeomai | 'I imitate' | aspazomai | 'I greet' |
| dekhomai | 'I receive' | akeomai | 'I heal' | biazomai | 'I force' |
| pheidomai | 'I spare' | he:geomai | 'I lead' | parakeleuomai | 'I urge' |
| stokhazomai | 'I aim' | theaomai | 'I look' | paramytheomai | 'I console' |
| logizomai | 'I reflect' | masaomai | 'I chew' | pragmateuomai | 'I deal' |
| hepomai | 'I follow' | osphrainomai | 'I smell' | prokalizomai | 'I challenge' |
| eukhomai | 'I wish' | palamaomai | 'I handle' | prooimiazomai | 'I preface' |
| rhyomai | 'I deliver' | hypokrinomai | 'I feign' | o:neomai | 'I buy' |
| ergazomai | 'I work' | kheiroomai | 'I subdue' | martyroomai | 'I attest' |
| hypiskhneomai | 'I promise' | khraomai | 'I use' | entellomai | 'I enjoin' |
| toksazomai | 'I shoot with a bow' | apergazomai | 'I prepare' | | |

Some of the verbs in Table 1 also display a passive reading, in the middle/passive form (5) or in the past passive form (6). In example (5), the verb bears the middle/passive suffix and takes a nominal element in dative case, characteristic for regular passive constructions, the dative of Ancient Greek being the equivalent of the by-phrase in Modern Greek and other languages. In (6), the verb bears the past passive suffix, while the agent is denoted by the Prepositional Phrase *hypo* ('by') + genitive:[6]

(5)  panta            apeirgastai                      to:i        Theo:i
     all.NOM.PL      prepare.PRF.3SG.MEDIOPASS          the.DAT.SG  God.DAT.SG
     'Everything is prepared from God.'   (Plato, *Leges* 710d)

(6)  e:tiathe:n                     mentoi hypo tino:n prodounai tas naus
     was.accused.PST.3SG.PASS       however by   some  betray.INF  the ships
     'However, he was accused by some of betraying the ships.'   (Xenophon, *Hellenica* 2, 1, 32)

Apart from the deponent verbs that take an object in the accusative case, we also distinguish a group of verbs with the middle suffix that appear with no object (intransitives). See Table 2.

and inscriptions (UPZ, Cair, Oxyrhynchus etc.), in critical editions of Byzantine and post-Byzantine literature and administrative texts, and in dictionaries and grammars from all the periods of the Greek language, which, due to space restrictions, are not mentioned in detail.
[6] According to Corbett's analysis (this volume), we could note that the behaviour of the Ancient Greek deponent verbs falls between *syncretism* and *deponency* with regard to the use of the same middle/passive type also in passive structures. The characteristic of syncretism regards the observation that Ancient Greek deponent forms, which are deponents because they are used for transitive structures as there exists no active type, retain also their original function and they are used for passive structures as well.

**Table 2.**  Middle intransitive deponent verbs in Ancient Greek

| | | | | | |
|---|---|---|---|---|---|
| aisthanomai | 'I feel' | knyzaomai | 'I whine' | oio:nizomai | 'I augur from' |
| hallomai | 'I leap' | gignomai | 'I become' | lo:baomai | 'I outrage' |
| ble:khaomai | 'I bleat' | hikneomai | 'I arrive' | khasmaomai | 'I yawn' |
| me:kaomai | 'I bleat' | hiptamai | 'I flee' | metapempomai | 'I send for' |
| bro:maomai | 'I stink' | kalamaomai | 'I glean' | ne:khomai | 'I swim' |
| ogkaomai | 'I bray' | osmaomai | 'I smell' | phtheggomai | 'I speak' |
| odyromai | 'I wail' | o:ryomai | 'I howl' | petomai | 'I fly' |
| oikhomai | 'I am gone' | orkheomai | 'I skip' | prophasizomai | 'I pretend' |
| olophyromai | 'I lament over' | parre:siazomai | 'I speak freely' | | |

(ii)  Having examined the behaviour of deponent verbs with a middle suffix, we next turn to examples of verbs with passive morphology. Ancient Greek displays deponent verbs with passive morphology in the past and future tense, traditionally called *passiva tantum*:

Passive past    →    e-sebas-*the:n*        'I respected'
Passive future    →    sebas-*the:somai*      'I will respect'

Passive deponent verbs usually appear with an object in the accusative (transitives), as illustrated in (7) and in Table 3 below:

(7)    dokei kai emoi        ho        Tisaphernis        to
       seems and me.DAT.SG   the.NOM.SG   Tisafernis.NOM.SG   the.ACC.SG

       auto                     boule:the:nai
       same.ACC.SG              want.PST.INF.PASS
       'It seems also to me that Tisafernis wanted the same.'    (Thucydides, *Historiae* 8, 56, 3)

However, there are also examples of deponent verbs with a passive suffix that appear without an object in accusative (intransitives); hence the label intransitive deponents (Table 4).

Some of these verbs also appear with the middle suffix in the past tense, as an alternate to their regular passive suffix. This is especially attested in the Postclassical period of Greek. A list of such examples is presented in Table 5.

**Table 3.**  Passive transitive deponent verbs in Ancient Greek

| | | | | | |
|---|---|---|---|---|---|
| sebomai | 'I respect' | arneomai | 'I refuse' | hestiaomai | 'I sup' |
| boulomai | 'I wish' | dianoeomai | 'I meditate' | mimne:skomai | 'I recollect' |
| deomai | 'I need' | enantioomai | 'I oppose' | oiomai | 'I deem, I think' |
| epistamai | 'I know' | enthymeomai | 'I consider' | fobeomai | 'I fear' |
| hagamai | 'I admire' | epimelomai | 'I care' | me:sattomai | 'I loathe' |
| aideomai | 'I revere' | hypotopeomai | 'I surmise' | he:domai | 'I rejoice' |

**Table 4.**   Passive intransitive deponent verbs in Ancient Greek

| planaomai | 'I ramble' | dynamai | 'I can' | dialegomai | 'I converse' |
|---|---|---|---|---|---|
| mainomai | 'I am mad' | eulabeomai | 'I beware' | metamelomai | 'I repent' |
| he:ttaomai | 'I am overcome' | kremamai | 'I hang' | pronoeomai | 'I provide' |
| diaitaomai | 'I live' | amillaomai | 'I emulate' | hormaomai | 'I start' |
| fantazomai | 'I appear' | akhthomai | 'I am unwilling' | | |
| orgizomai | 'I get angry' | poreuomai | 'I wander' | | |

**Table 5.**   Deponent verbs with middle or passive morphology in Ancient and Postclassical Greek

| agamai | / e:gasame:n | 'I admire' | mimne:skomai / emne:same:n | 'I recollect' |
|---|---|---|---|---|
| he:domai | / he:de:same:n | 'I rejoice' | arneomai | / e:rne:same:n | 'I refuse' |
| amillaomai | / e:mille:same:n | 'I emulate' | dialegomai | / dieleksame:n | 'I converse' |
| planaomai | / eplane:same:n | 'I ramble' | dynamai | / edyne:same:n | 'I can' |
| pronoeomai | / prounoe:same:n | 'I provide' | hormaomai | / horme:same:n | 'I start' |
| dianoeomai | / dienoe:same:n | 'I meditate' | oiomai | / oie:same:n | 'I deem, I think' |

The overview of the data in the period of Ancient Greek leads us to a number of conclusions regarding the nature and the behaviour of deponent verbs in the early stages of the language.

Firstly, we observe that an active transitive verb and a deponent transitive verb could have an identical meaning and appear in the same contexts, for example, in Ancient Greek the transitive verb *thiggano:* and the deponent verb *haptomai* are used in the same contexts with the reading 'I touch'.[7]

(8a)  ti            to:n          houto:  diakeimeno:n  en  to:i  polemo:i  oude
      any.ACC.SG    the.GEN.PL    so      part.GEN.PL   in  the   war       not

      haptontai
      touch.PRS.3PL.MEDIOPASS
      'They do not touch any of the parts that are in the war.'    (Plato, *Symposium*
      221, b, 8)

(8b)  parthenon                 me:   thiggano:
      young.woman.ACC.SG        not   touch.PRS.1SG.ACT
      'I do not touch any young women.'    (Euripides, *Electra* 51)

This is a first indication that deponent verbs are *not linked with any particular semantic reading*. It is difficult to assume that the passive suffix of the deponent verbs has any specific semantic function, given its appearance on a par with a transitive verb that does not bear a passive suffix and has exactly the same reading as the deponent verb.

---

[7] Stump (this volume) observes that the same occurs in Sanskrit: a verb whose non-passive forms are always in middle voice may be synonymous with a verb whose non-passive forms are always active.

Another example is provided from the comparative perspective of dialectology. From a cross-dialectical perspective, the active verb *katalambano:* from the Attic Classical period, and the deponent verb *katalambanomai* from the Ionic Classical language, are used in the same contexts with the reading 'I occupy'. Once again, the deponent verb and the active verb have identical interpretation, which necessarily rules out any particular semantic function of the middle/passive morphology of deponents.

The argument builds further on the observation that deponents in Ancient Greek include verbs of any semantic type: transitives, unaccusatives, unergatives, and psych-verbs. This is compatible with Aronoff et al. (this volume), who suggest that deponents are due to rules of morphology rather than semantics, and, more in particular, they are derived from adjectives, and Kiparsky (2005), according to which deponents in Latin consist of verbs of every semantic reading.[8] The issue of the semantic properties of deponent verbs is left aside for now. We shall discuss this in more detail in the last part of our paper. At this stage, we concentrate on further details of the data and on general remarks on the morphological status of deponents in the Greek language.

Having established two types of deponents in Ancient Greek, namely deponents with passive morphology and deponents with middle morphology, we next turn to a third group of deponents: the verbs that bear stably active morphology (they never appear with middle/passive voice). These verbs are also called deponents in traditional grammar and are characterized as *activa tantum*. The notion refers precisely to their property of never appearing in passive syntax:

> *klyo:* 'I listen to'   *herpo:* 'I creep'   *tremo:* 'I quail'
> *ethelo:* 'I want'   *zo:* 'I live'

(9)   o:         pai         Pe:leo:s,    klyeis            tade
       the.VOC.SG  child.VOC.SG  Pileus.GEN  listen.to.PRS.2SG.ACT  this.ACC.PL
       'Child of Peleus, do you listen to these.'   (Euripides, *Iphigenia Aulidensis*, 896)

---

[8] A different view, however, is put forth by Zombolou (2004), who distinguishes the following semantic categories of deponent verbs in Modern Greek that could, in principle, be applicable to the verbs from Ancient Greek as well:

| | (Modern Greek) | – Ancient Greek |
|---|---|---|
| **1.** Transitive meaning (+ accusative / + PP) | (*agonizomai* 'I fight') | – *enantioomai* 'I oppose' |
| **2.** Experiencer | (*fovamai* 'I fear') | – *phobeomai* 'I fear' |
| **3.** Passive-like | (*ipositizomai* 'I eat less than enough') | |
| **4.** Spontaneous event | (*ginomai* 'I become') | – *phantazomai* 'I appear' |
| **5.** Stative | (*paravriskomai* 'I attend') | – *epimelomai* 'I attend to' |
| **6.** Reflexive / reciprocal | (*sinagonizomai* 'I compete') | – *dialegomai* 'I converse' |

Interestingly, some of these verbs have middle future tense (cf. Schwyzer and Debrunner 1950; Jannaris 1968; Horrocks 1997). We distinguish two groups of examples, the verbs that take an object in the accusative case, also in future tense, where they bear middle morphology, and the verbs that appear without any object. The former, namely the verbs that take middle morphology in future tense and an object in the accusative, are called deponents according to the way the notion is defined in this volume: the verbs in the middle paradigm should not take an accusative object. The verbs in Table 6 bear middle morphology (or both middle and active) in the future tense, although they take only active morphology in the other tenses.[9]

To conclude, in this class of verbs with middle morphology in the future, a paradigmatic levelling is observed in the Postclassical period of the Greek language. This raises the theoretical issue of the extent to which regularity is imposed by the grammarians of this period or takes place as a natural result of the evolution of language. We leave this issue open for further discussion.

In the next section, we look into deponents from the Hellenistic and Roman Koine period of Greek and we provide a first attempt to understand the continuity of such examples in the history of the Greek language.

## 2.2. Hellenistic and Roman Koine Greek

One of the most interesting characteristics of the Hellenistic and Roman Koine Greek is that the middle reading (the meaning of the involvement of the subject) with transitive verbs (cf. (2) and (3) above) is lost (Lavidas 2003, 2005). We notice that the active and middle/passive transitive interchange without any difference in meaning since the Koine period:

(10)   *timo:men ton myrion—timo:metha ton myrion*   (Mayser 1926: 112)
       both active and middle/passive with the meaning 'we count them ten thousands'

The distinction between middle and passive suffix in past and future tense, that had started to disappear already from Ancient Greek, disappears completely in the Hellenistic Koine (resulting in an interchange between middle and passive morphology for both middle and passive reading). Neither this change nor the loss of the middle reading (involvement of the subject) had implications for deponent verbs. Conversely, a number of *'novel' deponent*

---

[9] Sanskrit shows a similar behaviour (Stump, this volume): some verbs inflect as middle in one tense but as active in another: middle *vartate* ('rolls') vs active *â vavarta* ('went around'). The proposed analysis, according to which this is due to the initial desiderative meaning of the future (Vendryes 1948), fails to explain the limitation of the non-active future in some verbs, and the occurences of past-tense non-active types of verbs, which are active in the other tenses. Partially deponent verbs are attested also in Latin (Aronoff 1994): *devortor* 'turn in' and *revortor* 'turn back' are deponents only in the present, but not in the perfect stem; *fido* 'trust', *audeo* 'dare', *gaudeo* 'be happy', *soleo* 'be used' are deponents only in the perfect.

**Table 6.** Active verbs with middle (or both active and middle) future in Ancient and Postclassical Greek

| Active Present | | Middle Future | Active Future |
|---|---|---|---|
| Transitives: | | | |
| aid-o: | 'I sing' | aisom-ai | ais-o: |
| akou-o: | 'I hear' | akouso-mai | akous-o: (Postclassical Greek) |
| apanta-o: | 'I meet' | apante:so-mai | |
| apolau-o: | 'I enjoy' | apolauso-mai | apolaus-o: (Postclassical Greek) |
| harpaz-o: | 'I snatch' | harpaso-mai | |
| dio:k-o: | 'I persue' | dio:kso-mai | dio:ks-o: |
| epaine-o: | 'I praise' | epaineso-mai | |
| thaumaz-o: | 'admire' | thaumaso-mai | thaumas-o: |
| klept-o: | 'I steal' | klepso-mai | kleps-o: |
| sko:pt-o: | 'I mock' | sko:pso-mai | |
| tikt-o: | 'I bear' | tekso-mai | teks-o: |
| tro:g-o: | 'I eat' | tro:kso-mai | |
| Intransitives: | | | |
| badiz-o: | 'I step' | badiou-mai | |
| boa-o: | 'I cry' | boe:so-mai | boe:s-o: (Postclassical Greek) |
| gela-o: | 'I laugh' | gelaso-mai | gelas-o: (Postclassical Greek) |
| oimo:z-o | 'I lament' | oimo:kso-mai | oimo:ks-o: (Postclassical Greek) |
| pe:dao: | 'I leap' | pe:de:somai | |
| pleo: | 'I swim' | pleusomai | pleuso: |
| pneo: | 'I blow' | pneusomai | |
| rheo: | 'I flow' | rhye:somai | |
| sigao: | 'I keep silent' | sio:pe:somai | sio:pe:so: |
| tygkhano: | 'I chance' | teuksomai | |
| pheugo: | 'I flee' | pheuksomai | |
| phthano: | 'I anticipate' | phthe:somai | phthaso: |
| spoudazo: | 'I make haste' | spoudasomai | |

*verbs* are attested in the Hellenistic Koine period of Greek (Mayser 1970), as illustrated in the Table 7. This is a first indication that deponents are not semantically determined (as the middle transitive constructions that were lost), and that they preserve their 'deponent' character throughout the history of the Greek language (in contrast to the transitive middle constructions).

(11) te:s        philoksenias      me:      epilanthanesthe
     the.GEN.SG    hospitality.GEN.SG  not    forget.PRS.INF.MEDIOPASS
    'Do not forget the hospitality.' (Novum Testamentum, *Epistula Pauli ad Hebraeos* 13, 2, 2)

Having established the existence of deponent verbs in the Hellenistic Koine period, as well as in the Classical period of Greek, we next turn to the data from Medieval and Modern Greek. This will reveal further aspects of the phenomenon of deponency and will allow for a systematic comparison between the synchronic and the diachronic characteristics of the data.

**Table 7.**   Deponents that are attested for the first time in texts of the Hellenistic Koine period

| | | | |
|---|---|---|---|
| enaraomai | 'I adjure by' | eksidiazomai | 'I win over' |
| ekkarpizomai | 'I reap, I enjoy' | ananeomai | 'I mount up' |
| drassomai | 'I grasp with the hand' | diomologeomai | 'I agree mutually' |
| sphragizomai | 'I close or I enclose with a seal' | theoreomai | 'I look at, I view' |
| deksiooomai | 'I canvass, I greet with the right hand, I welcome' | | |
| epilanthanomai | 'I let a thing escape, I forget' | | |

## 2.3. Medieval and Modern Greek

In Medieval Greek, we observe a number of *novel deponents*, that is verbs that display a deponent character for the first time in the language. (See Table 8).[10]

(12)  tin              aftu    empistevete                       filakin
      the.ACC.SG       his     trust.PRS.3SG.MEDIOPASS           guard.ACC.SG
      'He trusts him with his guard.' (Constantinus VII Porphyrogenitus, *De legationibus* 580, 16)

There are also a number of *novel deponents* that appeared for the first time in Modern Greek (Holton, Mackridge, and Philippaki-Warburton 1997 and Clairis and Babiniotis 2005). A distinction is made between transitive deponents that take an object in the accusative and intransitive deponents (often with a Prepositional Phrase as a complement):

(13)  i        egkios               ligureftike                 pagoto
      the      pregnant.NOM.SG      desire.PST.3SG.MEDIOPASS     ice cream.ACC.SG
      'The pregnant woman desired an ice cream.'

The examples in Tables 8 and 9 are taken from Zombolou (2004: 216–17), who provides a detailed analysis of deponent and other types of verbs, on the basis of semantic properties, that we discuss in the last section, but we do not endorse completely for reasons that are explained there.

Zombolou argues for the existence of regular patterns that underlie the behaviour of deponents. The diachronic overview of the data, though, does not comply with such an approach. We turn to this issue in the next section.

---

[10] We have faced many difficulties transcribing the historical data from the different periods of Greek. In this paper, we are following general phonological rules and we are giving the transcription of the Ancient Greek close to the Erasmian conventions. Of course, major phonological changes had systematic effects on the pronunciation in different periods: for the present purposes, it is crucial to mention the following: (1) the long [o:] in the ending of the active voice, has changed after the Hellenistic period to a short [o] (as every long vowel in the language), (2) the diphthong [ai] in the ending of the middle/passive voice [-mai] is pronounced after the Hellenistic period and until today as [-e]. As our analysis is not a phonological one, we will not discuss any further the phonological changes.

**Table 8.**  Deponents that are attested in texts of Medieval Greek for the first time

Transitives

| | | | |
|---|---|---|---|
| exthrevome | 'I hate' | onirevome | 'I dream' |
| empistevome | 'I trust' | limpizome | 'I desire' |
| erotevome | 'I fall in love with' | oramatizome | 'I dream' |

Intransitives

| | | | |
|---|---|---|---|
| katapianome | 'I undertake' | paraponume | 'I complain' |
| krimatizome | 'I sin' | ksenitevome | 'I emigrate' |
| sovarevome | 'I get serious' | logikevome | 'I see reason' |
| seliniazome | 'I have epilepsy' | simposume | 'I add up to' |
| astievome | 'I joke' | | |

**Table 9.**  Deponents that are attested in Modern Greek for the first time

Transitives

| | | | |
|---|---|---|---|
| tsigkounevome | 'I stint' | ekmistirevome | 'I confide in' |
| oregome | 'I lust for' | ligurevome | 'I desire' |
| psixoponume | 'I pity' | psiliazome | 'I suspect' |
| kapsurevome | 'I fall in love with' | osmizome | 'I smell' |

Intransitives

| | | | |
|---|---|---|---|
| | | androkratume | 'it is ruled by men' |
| niazome | 'I care for' | ginekokratume | 'it is ruled by women' |
| orgizome | 'I get angry' | griponome | 'I go down with flue' |
| ksekardizomai | 'I fall about' | tavliazome | 'I fall down because of tiredness' |
| idikevome | 'I specialize' | ipositizome | 'I am underfed' |
| arxontopianome | 'I have genteel pretensions' | enilikionome | 'I become adult' |
| karavotsakizome | 'I am tossed about' | kselarigkiazome | 'I talk myself hoarse' |
| gkremotsakizome | 'I tumble' | komatizome | 'I am part-spirited' |
| kordonome | 'I am like bowstring' | megalopianome | 'I strike a pose' |
| ksexinome | 'I pour out' | sindikalizome | 'I am trustee with' |
| ksekumpizome | 'I clear out' | | |

# 3.  Changes in Deponents

*Not all deponents display stable behaviour* through the different stages of Greek. In many cases, the deponent verbs have changed to actives, and, in other cases, they have attracted other verbs from the class of actives.

The diachronic changes are discussed in more detail below, with special reference to the different periods of the language: Ancient, Hellenistic and Roman Koine, Medieval and Modern Greek. We believe that the diachronic overview of the data may reveal new insights regarding the synchronic analysis of deponents.

### 3.1. Deponents in Ancient Greek → actives in Postclassical / Modern Greek

Different types of historical changes are observed in Greek, indicating the complex character of deponent verbs. We concentrate here on deponents, which lost the middle/passive morphology and became actives in later stages of the language: in Postclassical, in Medieval, or in Modern Greek. This is shown in detail in Table 10, where we distinguish deponent transitive from intransitive verbs.

Many of these verbs retain their semantic interpretation, after changing morphological form, that is, after switching from deponents to non-deponents. However, there exist some verbs that change their meaning when they lose their deponent character, for example:

| Ancient Greek | Postclassical / Medieval | Modern Greek |
|---|---|---|
| *peiro:-mai* 'I try' | *piraz-o* 'I tease' | *piraz-o* 'I tease' |

Looking into the evolution of these deponents, we note the *presence of both* active and middle/passive types in their development to non-deponents. This is illustrated below with three examples; the first example being the verb *ekse:geomai* 'explain':

(i)   *ekse:geomai*.MEDIOPASS. 'I tell at length, I relate in full, I set forth, I explain'

**Ancient Greek**

The verb appears with a middle/passive suffix and takes an object in the accusative:

(14a) kai    ta          epeita     hos    epoleme:the:
      and    the.ACC     rest.ACC   how    fight.PST.3SG.MEDIOPASS

      ekse:ge:somai
      explain.FUT.1SG.MEDIOPASS
      'And the other facts how the war was waged I shall tell at length.'   (Thucydides, *Historiae* 5, 26, 6)

**Medieval Greek**

In Medieval Greek, the verb appears with the active suffix and, of course, still takes an object in the accusative (active transitive):

(14b) ke    kata         tin    sinithian   su     s' emas        na    to
      and   according    the    habit       your   to we.ACC      to    it.ACC

      eksigisis
      explain.SBJV.2SG.ACT
      'And according to your habit, explain that to us.'   (Sumakis Mixail, *Pastor fidos* E' [1015])

**Table 10.**  Ancient Greek deponents that change morphology

| Ancient Greek | | Postclassical / Medieval | Modern Greek |
|---|---|---|---|
| Transitives: | | | |
| ekse:geo-mai | 'I interpret' | eksigeo-me | eksig-o |
| kharizo-mai | 'I present with' | xariz-o | xariz-o |
| do:reo-mai | 'I present with' | dore-o | doriz-o |
| ktao-mai | 'I acquire' | kt-o | apokt-o |
| biazo-mai | 'I force' | viaz-o | viaz-o |
| Intransitives: | | | |
| bro:mao-mai | 'I stink' | vrama-o | vroma-o |
| masao-mai | 'I chew' | masa-o | masa-o |
| aitiao-mai | 'I accuse' | aitia-o | – (no existing form) |
| akeo-mai | 'I heal' | ake-o | – |
| metapempo-mai | 'I send for' | metapemp-o | – |
| entello-mai | 'I enjoin' | entel-o | – |
| parre:siazo-mai | 'I speak freely' | parisiaz-o | – |
| kheirou-mai | 'I subdue' | xiro-o | – |

However, in this period, the verb may also appear with middle/passive morphology, thus retaining its deponent character (middle/passive transitive):

(14c)  o        thios        Zonaras        eksigite                                taftin
       the   holy.NOM   Zonaras.NOM   explain.PRS.3SG.MEDIOPASS   this.ACC

       tin              enian              kataleptos
       the.ACC   meaning.ACC   comprehensible
       'Holy Zonaras explains this concept so that it is comprehensible.'  (*Historia politica et patriarchica Constantinopoleos* 195.15)

**Modern Greek**
In Modern Greek, only one option is available, namely the verb with active morphology (active transitive):

(14d)  o        daskalos        eksigise                        to              mathima
       the   teacher.NOM   explain.PST.3AG.ACT.   the.ACC   lesson.ACC
       'The teacher explained what the lesson is about.'

To sum up, the verb *ekse:geomai* 'I explain' starts out as deponent in Ancient Greek and displays a dual behaviour in Medieval Greek, namely appearing both as deponent and as regular active verb. Modern Greek makes use of only one form, namely the active form of the verb. We thus have a clear change from deponent to non-deponent verb.

However, in the following sections, we notice that the type of change appearing in the history of Greek is not stable. For example, the verb *memphomai* 'I accuse' behaves like a deponent verb in all periods of

Greek, except for Medieval Greek, where the middle/passive and the active form appear simultaneously.

(ii)   *memphomai.*MEDIOPASS. 'I accuse'

### Ancient Greek

The verb *memphomai* 'I accuse' behaves as a transitive deponent verb in the Ancient period of Greek: it takes the middle/passive suffix and an object in the accusative case.

(15a)  memphomai                          tina              pros    tous    philous
       accuse.PRS.1SG.MEDIOPASS           one.ACC           from    the     friends
       'I accuse one of the friends.'     (Xenophon, *Oeconomicus* 11, 23)

### Medieval Greek

In Medieval Greek, the verb appears either without the middle/passive suffix, like any ordinary transitive verb that takes an object in the accusative, or it retains its deponent character. The transitive example is given below:

(15b)  mi   mempsis                  anthropon         tina
       not  accuse.SBJV.3SG.ACT      human.ACC         somebody.ACC
       'Do not accuse any human being.'   (Spaneas, R 283)

The active verb is also attested with a complement in the genitive case:

(15c)  na mempsi             parafta    tis      lolis      tu       kefalis
       to accuse.SBJV.3SG.ACT  directly  the.GEN  mad.GEN    his.GEN  head.GEN
       'to accuse directly his madness'   (Georgilas, *Thanatikon tis Rodu* 437)

The deponent alternate of the verb is shown by the appearance of the middle/passive suffix together with an accusative object:

(15d)  ke   mempsete                   me         o         igumenos
       and  accuse.PRS.3SG.MEDIOPASS   me.ACC     the.NOM   abbot.NOM
       'And the abbot accuses me.'   (Prodromos, III 216)

### Modern Greek

In Modern Greek, the verb appears only as deponent, as shown in the following construction:

(15e)  memfome                     osus       me         adikisan
       accuse.PRS.1SG.MEDIOPASS    all.ACC    me.ACC     unjust.ACT.PST.3PL
       'I accuse all that did me wrong.'

We are presenting here a number of detailed examples, as an attempt to better understand how deponent verbs have evolved in the Greek language and whether there are any systematic linguistic factors that play a crucial role in this phenomenon.

Next, we look into the verb *arneomai* 'I deny, I disown', in order to build further on the history of deponency. This verb also displays two morphological forms in the intermediate stage of Greek, that is, in Medieval Greek.

(iii)   *arneomai*.MEDIOPASS. 'I deny, I disown'

**Ancient Greek**
The verb is deponent in Classical Greek, taking the middle/passive suffix and an accusative object:

(16a) ekeinoi        arnountai                        ta            meme:nymena
      those.NOM      refuse.PRS.3PL.MEDIOPASS         the.ACC       charges.ACC
      'those refuse the charges'   (Lysias, *In Andocidem*, 14, 1)

**Medieval Greek**
In Medieval Greek, the verb displays a dual behaviour: it either appears as an active transitive construction (16b) or as deponent verb (16c), giving rise to an interesting phenomenon, namely the availability of two different forms for the same semantic function:

(16b) i     fili          ton            arnusin
      the   friends.NOM   him.ACC        reject.PRS.3PL.ACT
      'The friends reject him.'   (Saxlikis, *Afigisis Paraksenos* 465)

(16c) aksodon              arniontusan
      inexpensive.ACC      refuse.PST.3PL.MEDIOPASS
      'They were refusing inexpensive things.'   (*Xronikon turkon sultanon* 86, 27)

**Modern Greek**
Interestingly, the verb retains its deponent character in Modern Greek, where the active alternate is no longer attested:

(16d) arnithike / *arnise            tin            protasi
      refuse.PST.3SG.MEDIOPASS       the.ACC        proposal.ACC
      'He refused the proposal.'

In the next section, we discuss verbs that appear as actives in Ancient Greek and change into deponents in later stages of the language. This complies with our general claim that deponency displays no systematic change through the history of the language, but the verbs seem to vary morphologically either way (from deponent to non-deponent or from non-deponent to deponent).

### 3.2. Actives in Ancient Greek → deponents in Postclassical/Modern Greek

A detailed list of verbs that start out as actives and become deponents is given in Table 11, with special reference to verbs that appear in transitive constructions and verbs that appear as intransitives.

**Table 11.**  Active transitive verbs of Ancient Greek that occur as deponents in Postclassical or Modern Greek

| Ancient Greek | | Postclassical / Medieval | Modern Greek |
|---|---|---|---|
| Transitives: | | | |
| epikheire-o: | 'I attempt' | epixirizo-**me** | epixir-**o** |
| sikkhain-o: | 'I loathe' | sikxeno-me | sixeno-me |
| ekhthair-o: | 'I hate' | exthero-me / exther-o | exthrevo-me |
| empisteu-o: | 'I trust' | empistevo-me | empistevo-me |
| ekdike-o: | 'I avenge' | ekdiku-me | |
| Intransitives: | | | |
| khair-o: | 'I rejoice' | xero-me | xero-me |
| hypere:phane-o: | 'I am proud' | iperifanevo-me | perifanevo-me |
| dysareste-o: | 'I am displeased' | | disarestu-me |

## Ancient Greek

(17a) ou     gar           ekhthairo                 se
        not   because   hate.PRS.1SG.ACT      you.ACC.SG
        'because I do not hate you'   (Euripides, *Alcestis* 179)

## Hellenistic and Roman Koine

(17b) pasan monarkhian.ACC.SG   to      ison      ekhthairein
        every  monarchy                 the     same     hate.PRS.3SG.ACT
        'He hates every monarchy the same.'   (Polybius, *Historiae* 21, 22, 8)

## Modern Greek

(17c) exthrevete                         olus           tus            gitones           tu
        hate.PRS.3SG.MEDIOPASS   all.ACC.PL   the.ACC.PL   neighbours   his
        'He hates all his neighbours.'

There are also some Ancient Greek verbs that change their semantic interpretation, depending on whether they appear with or without the middle/passive morphology.

(i)     *apokrino:*.ACT

### Ancient Greek

The verb *apokrino:* 'I set apart, I distinguish, I choose' is active in Ancient Greek:

(18a) apokrinein                dynatous       gignesthai      tous         aksious
        distinguish.INF.ACT   fair.ACC[11]   become.INF   the.ACC   deserving.ACC
        'become fair to distinguish those who deserve ...'   (Plato, *Leges* 751d)

---

[11] The subject of the Ancient Greek infinitive is usually in accusative case.

It also appears in passive structures:

(18b) antipalon      es      hen      onoma      apokekre:sthai
      rival.ACC.SG   to      one      name       be called.PRF.INF.MEDIOPASS
      'The rival was brought under one name.'    (Thucydides, *Historiae* 1, 3)

(ii)   *apokrinomai*.MEDIOPASS.

**Ancient Greek**
The verb in Ancient Greek bears the middle/passive morphology and takes an accusative object. Interestingly, it also has a different semantic interpretation 'I give answer to, I reply to a question' (i.e. it has become, in effect, a different lexeme):

(19a) haplos    hyme:n      apokrinomai              haper       poie:so:
      simply    you.DAT     reply.PRS.1SG.MEDIOPASS  what.ACC    do.FUT.1SG
      'I am simply answering to you what exactly I am going to do'   (Xenophon, *Hellenica* 4, 1, 37)

(19b) kai   peiro:           apokrinesthai          to          ero:to:menon
      and   try.PRS.1SG      reply.INF.MEDIOPASS    the.ACC     question.ACC
      'And I am trying to answer the question.'   (Plato, *Crito* 49a, 1)

**Medieval Greek**
In Medieval Greek, only the deponent alternate of the verb is available, with the same reading as in the Classical period of Greek (*apokrinomai*. MEDIOPASS 'give an answer'):

(19c) os ikusa      tin      ksenodoxisa, palin  apekrinome                    tin
      as hear.1SG    the      hotelkeeper  again  reply.PRS.1SG.MEDIOPASS       she.ACC
      'As I heard the housekeeper, I answered to her again.'   (Livistros 3125)

**Modern Greek**
The situation is identical also in Modern Greek, where the verb is deponent and retains its semantic reading from the previous stages of the language:

(19d) apokrinome                        ston     Jani      /    tu         Jani
      answer.PRS.1SG.MEDIOPASS          to       Jani.ACC       the.GEN    Jani.GEN
      'I am answering to Janis.'

## 3.3. Deponents through the history of Greek

Despite the changes from deponents to non-deponents or from non-deponents to deponents, there exists also a group of verbs that start out as deponents, in earlier stages of the Greek language, such as Ancient Greek, and remain deponents also in Modern Greek. We illustrate this with two examples below.

(i)   *makhomai*.MEDIOPASS. 'I fight'

The verb *makhomai* 'I fight' is deponent through all the different stages of the Greek language.

**Ancient Greek**
The verb is middle/passive transitive in Ancient Greek, usually taking a PP complement (or else appearing without any complement, like an intransitive):

(20a) kai     pros      eme       makhetai
      and     against   me        fight.PRS.3SG.MEDIOPASS
      'He fights against me as well.'  (Plato, *Theages* 123a, 8)

**Medieval Greek**
In Medieval Greek, the verb displays the same behaviour as in Ancient Greek, that is, the verb is deponent taking the middle/passive morphology and a complement either in the accusative (20b) or in the genitive case (20c):

(20b) na maxete                        tus          Fragkus
      to fight.PRS.3SG.MEDIOPASS     the.ACC      Franks.ACC
      'to fight against the Franks'   (Chronicle of Morea H 1216)

(20c) emaxomin                  kata       nou
      fight.PST.1SG.MEDIOPASS   against    he.GEN
      'I was fighting against him.'   (Livistros 2190)

**Modern Greek**
The deponent nature of the verb is attested in Modern Greek:

(20d) maxete                       tin adikia          / kata       tis       adikias
      fight.PRS.3SG.MEDIOPAS      the injustice.ACC   / against    the       injustice.GEN
      'S/he fights injustice.'

(ii)   *dekhomai*.MEDIOPASS. 'I accept'
The verb *dekhomai* 'I accept' starts out as deponent in Ancient Greek, and remains deponent in Medieval and Modern Greek.

**Ancient Greek**
In Ancient Greek, the verb takes the middle/passive morphology and an object in the accusative case:

(21a) hoi     edekhonto                  ton        phoron
      they    accept.PST.3PL.MEDIOPASS   the.ACC    tax.ACC
      'They accepted the tax.'   (Thucydides, *Historiae* 1, 96)

**Medieval Greek**

The verb remains middle/passive transitive in Medieval Greek.

(21b) ta sentukia    opu mas    estiles        edexthikame                         ta
the settles.ACC that we.ACC send.PST.2SG accept.PST.1PL.MEDIOPASS they.ACC
'The settles that you sent us we accepted them.'   (*Diigisis Aleksandru* V 41)

The verb is also attested in passive structures, as illustrated below:

(21c) kinonos             martiron           uk     edexthi
participant.NOM    testimonies.GEN   not    accept.PST.3SG.MEDIOPASS
'He was not accepted as a participant of the testimonies.' (Armenopulos
Eksavivlos A' 6.50)

**Modern Greek**

In Modern Greek, the verb is deponent:

(21d) dexome                      tin           apopsi              tu
accept.PRS.1SG.MEDIOPASS   the.ACC   opinion.ACC   his
'I accept his opinion.'

Having established the different kinds of change, we first summarize our
data, and then we discuss the possible theoretical analyses.

*Summary of the data*

We have seen that there is *no systematic* change in the history of deponents:

(a) Deponent verbs of the Medieval period may lack an active alternate
also in Modern Greek (for example the verb: *maxo-me, *max-o* 'I
fight'), showing that the passive morphology often remains on the
verb and that deponents do not necessarily evolve into active forms.

(b) In some cases, though, the verbs develop an active alternate resulting in two options: (a) either the ancient deponents lose the middle/
passive morphology and become actives (for example: *ekse:geo-mai*
→ *eksig-o*) in a later stage of the language: in Postclassical, in
Medieval, or in Modern Greek (note also that the presence of both
active and middle/passive types in a specific period is possible), or
some verbs start out as actives and become deponents (for example:
*ekhair-o* → *exthrevo-me*). Once again, the data lack any systematic
pattern: an initially deponent verb may have an active variant with
identical interpretation that is used in parallel or, even, instead of
the deponent.

The diachronic changes that are attested in the Greek language with respect
to deponent verbs are illustrated in Table 12.

**Table 12.**  Summary of diachronic changes

|  | Classical Period | Hellenistic Period | Medieval Period | Modern Period |
|---|---|---|---|---|
| deponents in Ancient Greek → actives in Postclassical/ Modern Greek | *ekse:geo-mai* (mediopassive) 'I interpret' | *ekse:geo-mai* (mediopassive) | *eksig-o* (active) | *eksig-o* (active) |
| actives in Ancient Greek → deponents in Postclassical/ Modern Greek | *empisteu-o:* (active) 'I trust' | *empisteuo-mai* (mediopassive) | *empistevo-me* (mediopassive) | *empistevo-me* (mediopassive) |
| deponents through the history of Greek | *makho-mai* (mediopassive) 'I fight' | *makho-mai* (mediopassive) | *maxo-me* (mediopassive) | *max-ome* (mediopassive) |
| change to active morphological form with change in the meaning | *peiro:-mai* (mediopassive) 'I try' | *peiraz-o:* (active) 'I tease' | *piraz-o* (active) 'I tease' | *piraz-o* (active) 'I tease' |

An immediate question is raised: can we view deponents as a lexically specified class of verbs, given the observed changes in the Greek language? In order to answer this question, we need to look into the theoretical implications of our data. This is discussed in the following section.

# 4.  Theoretical Issues

In this section, we provide an extensive discussion of different theoretical approaches to deponent verbs, seeking to account for the historical changes that we have observed in the Greek language. The overview of the theoretical analyses is given on the basis of the prevailing features of each framework, that is, semantic, syntactic, or morphological characteristics. Noting that all semantic and syntactic approaches require regularities that are absent from deponent verbs, at least when discussed throughout the different stages of the language, we conclude that only a morphological analysis could in principle explain the appearance of deponents in the language. Abstracting away from the exact morphological framework that could better explain the data, we view morphology as a module with its own regularities that differ from the syntactic and the semantic properties of the grammar. Similarly to Draeger (1878), Meillet (1966), and Baldi (1976) for Latin, we argue that the systematic semantic and syntactic factors, which could in principle explain this class of verbs and the attested changes in Greek, seem, at least at first sight, incompatible with the data.[12]

(a)  *semantic approach*

According to the semantic approaches, there exist specific semantic readings that are associated with the groups of deponent verbs across languages. In other words, there is some specific semantic function that characterizes the unexpected presence of middle/passive morphology together with an object in the accusative case.

Kemmer (1993, 1994) analyses the middle morphology as a *unified* semantic concept expressing *the limited differentiation of participants in the situation described.*[13] However, this generalization cannot capture the idiosyncratic properties of deponent verbs: deponent like other (non-deponent) transitives take nominative subjects and accusative objects. In addition, some deponents may also appear in passive syntax, which complicates further the parallelism between morpho-syntactic structure and semantic interpretation.

Similarly, Zombolou (1997, 2004) provides an attempt to *unify* the Modern Greek middle/passive morphology, which occurs in passives, reflexives, reciprocals, middles, deponents, under the claim that the middle/passive voice in Greek refers to *a state which denotes the end result.* Modern Greek deponents lack, not only the active morphology of the verb, but also the *causative meaning* associated with this active morphology (the corresponding active of earlier periods had the meaning of causative accomplishments).

The deponents for Kemmer and Zombolou are a natural by-product of middle (non-active, i.e. mainly reflexive and passive) systems. Since non-active voice is semantically motivated, the non-active can be extended to verbs of the appropriate semantic class regardless of whether a corresponding transitive verb exists or not. The hypothesis[14]

---

[12] According to the *traditional analysis*, Duhoux (1992) attributes deponency to a tendency of the Indo-European proto-language to mark voice and diathesis on the verbal stems. For a discussion of the Indo-European 'medium' cf. also Gonda (1960).

[13] According to this opinion, deponents fall cross-linguistically into these specific semantically defined verb classes that are unified under the notion of the limited differentiation of participants: grooming or body care, non-translational motion, change in body posture, indirect middle, natural reciprocal events, translational motion, emotion middle, speech actions, cognition middle, spontaneous events.

[14] Kemmer and Zombolou do not comment on true historical data; Kemmer makes a general diachronic hypothesis based on the analysis of cross-linguistic synchronic data. For example, Kemmer hypothesizes (but without any direct historical evidence for it) that the Latin deponent *loquor* could be explained as having descended from an old verb of naturally reciprocal type, possibly meaning 'converse'; the Latin verb at some point lost the sense of mutuality and began to occur with singular subjects with the meaning 'speak'.

that transitive non-active verbs arise diachronically when the non-active marker has been grammaticalized to the point where it no longer denotes a referential entity, but only marks middle semantics (the limited differentiation of participants) is not confirmed by the Greek diachronic data. Contrary to this opinion, the diachronic data do not display any systematic change in the meaning, when the active morphology is lost.

Manney (2000) assumes that the *semantic classes* of the Modern Greek verbs are of great importance. However, the deponent verbs belong to many semantic classes: some verbs are attested with experiencer subject, others depict mental attitude or focused thinking, some depict the intentional and focused actions of an agent, while there exist also stative deponent verbs. As becomes clear from the data, deponent verbs of Modern Greek belong to so many different semantic classes, that it is difficult to analyse deponency on the basis of the semantic clusters of verbs.[15]

*(b)   syntactic approach*

In a syntactic analysis, the presence of the middle/passive suffix can be associated with some syntactic properties of the verb, such as the lack of (accusative) case.

Building on the account of Reinhart (1997, 2000, 2003) and Reinhart and Siloni (2003, 2005) for reflexives and other verbal alternations, Papangeli (2003, 2004, 2005) argues that the variation on verbal morphology in Greek systematically reflects the elimination of the accusative case, while other elements in other languages, such as the Romance clitics, reflect the elimination of a number of cases: accusative, dative, or nominative, in all instances of verbal alternations (reflexives, reciprocals, impersonals, passives).[16] The possibility of verbal morphology to reflect the elimination of the accusative case is supported by the diachronic data of impersonals in Lavidas and Papangeli (forthcoming). The morpho-syntactic relation of the middle/passive morphology and the accusative case is also mentioned in the Greek literature for distinct instances of verbal variants (passives or reflexives, for example cf. Tsimpli 1989, Rivero 1990).

Moreover, deponents fail to comply with any other syntactic analysis of the Greek verbs, such as Alexiadou and Anagnostopoulou's proposal

---

[15] We leave aside issues of pragmatics, raised, for example, in Ter Meulen (2000) for reflexive verbs, that could be relevant also here.

[16] The relevance of case and morphology seems quite obvious for passives, already put forth by Chomsky (1981), Burzio (1981) and often appears in the literature for reflexives (Everaert 1986; Sportiche 1998; Reinhart and Siloni 2005, among others), with special interest on the effects that the different analyses have on the comparative perspective of the cross-linguistic data.

(1999, 2003) for unaccusatives, according to which the suffix is associated with different types of eventuality ('result' or 'become'), which builds on Kratzer's (1993) suggestions on voice and argument structure. The class of deponents embodies a challenge for this type of analysis given the presence of the accusative argument together with the middle/passive morphology, irrespectively of the kind of eventuality that is denoted. In general, deponents are mentioned as instances of exceptional constructions, for example in Theophanopoulou (1981, 1999, 2001), who discusses the relation of the semantic diatheses of Greek verbs with their morpho-syntactic realization.

*(c)  morphological approach*
The main claim of any morphological approach is based on the assumption that there is a separate level, outside the module of syntax that is responsible for the voice morphology of verbs. Both the lexicalist and the paradigmatic analyses of morphology have supported this idea. Lexicalist approaches (Lieber 1980; Kiparsky 1982; Di Sciullo and Williams 1987) suggest that a process of affixation in a pre-syntactic lexicon determines the syntactic behaviour of a verbal form. The formation of a passive verb is directly related to affixation with passive morphemes, which produces the passive syntax. However, deponent verbs have passive morphology (affixation) and they take an object in the accusative, lacking the passive syntax that is predicted by this analysis.

Within the paradigmatic analyses, Aronoff (1994) suggests that a level mediating syntax and morphology (syntactic structures can be related to morphology in an arbitrary way) could account for the apparent mismatch. Furthermore, according to Börjars, Vincent, and Chapman (1996) there is a space outside syntactic structure, which contains entries in cells that are correlated with morphosyntactic feature combinations.

We take here the morphological approach to allow for a non-systematic view of the data, in the sense that the *feature specification* that accounts for deponent verbs is realized in a random way and possibly relies on the idiosyncratic properties of each verb. A certain set of transitive deponents verbs could be treated as being *inherently specified for a feature* responsible for their inflectional properties (labelled as [pass] by Embick 2000, within the general view of Distributed Morphology).[17]

According to this approach,[18] the features that embody the idiosyncratic properties of particular Roots are not present in the syntactic

---

[17] Halle and Marantz (1993), Marantz (1997).
[18] Grimshaw's (1982) approach is also similar to this analysis. According to Grimshaw, the 'constraint equation', which is used to specify that non-active morphology must appear in the

derivation (they are present independently of the syntax of passive formation): they are required for morphological reasons, but they have no syntactic status; they are arbitrary properties of the Roots. The feature [pass] is related to deponents; syntactically, the verbs of this type are not different from their active, non-deponent counterparts. Consequently, certain verbs possess this feature for reasons that have nothing to do with passive syntax or related semantics: (i) the elimination of the (accusative) case implies the feature [pass] but the converse is not true, (ii) they do not form a natural class of verbs, as they do not appear in passive form for systematic syntactic or semantic reasons.

# 5. Concluding Remarks

We have provided an overview of deponent verbs through the history of the Greek language, showing that 'deponency' can be viewed only as a morphological phenomenon: the diachronic change of deponents does not comply with any systematic syntactic or semantic account. This was illustrated in detail in section 2, where the data from Classical, Postclassical, Hellenistic Koine, Medieval and Modern Greek displayed idiosyncratic behaviour.

Our data revealed a group of deponent verbs, which appear already from the Classical stage and remain consistently deponent through all the periods of the language. However, there are also deponent verbs that become actives at later stages. Lastly, we saw active verbs that gain a deponent character in Medieval or Modern Greek (novel deponent verbs).

This leaves aside any syntactic explanation, such as issues of case, that could in principle account for the presence of the middle/passive morphology in Greek deponent verbs. In addition, this rules out any semantic explanation, such as the different types of semantic interpretation that could, in principle, be associated with deponent verbs, concluding that it is impossible to link the presence of the suffix with any systematic semantic reading.

We thus believe that the diachronic data of Greek accord with the idea that deponency is a morphological phenomenon; or else, deponency requires the existence of morphology in the design of grammar.

---

surface realization for all verbs that have undergone the lexical rules to derive non-active constructions, is placed directly in the lexical entry for the verb. The effect of this equation is that deponent verbs are required to appear with the non-active form in all their occurrences.

# Appendix

An example of the different forms of the middle/passive morphology is listed below: the verb *pau-o:* 'to stop, to interrupt' is declined in Ancient Greek and the verb *pleno* 'to wash' is declined in Modern Greek. The paradigm changes form depending on aspect, tense, number, and person (Joseph and Smirniotopoulos 1993).

## Ancient Greek

### *Present/Imperfective*

| Person | active | middle / passive |
|---|---|---|
| 1 singular | pau-o: | pau-omai |
| 2 singular | pau-eis | pau-e:i |
| 3 singular | pau-ei | pau-etai |
| 1 plural | pau-omen | pau-ometha |
| 2 plural | pau-ete | pau-esthe |
| 3 plural | pau-ousi | pau-ontai |

### *Present/Perfective*

| Person | active | middle | passive |
|---|---|---|---|
| 1 singular | pau-so: | pau-somai | pau-the:somai |
| 2 singular | pau-seis | pau-se:i | pau-the:se:i |
| 3 singular | pau-sei | pau-setai | pau-the:setai |
| 1 plural | pau-somen | pau-sometha | pau-the:sometha |
| 2 plural | pau-sete | pau-sesthe | pau-the:sesthe |
| plural | pau-sousi | pau-sontai | pau-the:sontai |

### *Past/Imperfective*

| Person | active | middle / passive |
|---|---|---|
| 1 singular | epau-on | epau-ome:n |
| 2 singular | epau-es | epau-ou |
| 3 singular | epau-e | epau-eto |
| 1 plural | epau-omen | epau-ometha |
| 2 plural | epau-ete | epau-esthe |
| 3 plural | epau-on | epau-onto |

### *Past/Perfective*

| Person | active | middle | passive |
|---|---|---|---|
| 1 singular | epau-sa | epau-same:n | epau-the:n |
| 2 singular | epau-sas | epau-so | epau-the:s |
| 3 singular | epau-se | epau-sato | epau-the: |
| 1 plural | epau-samen | epau-sametha | epau-the:men |
| 2 plural | epau-sate | epau-sasthe | epau-the:te |
| 3 plural | epau-san | epau-santo | epau-the:san |

## Modern Greek

### Present/Imperfective

| Person | Active | middle / passive |
|---|---|---|
| 1 singular | plen-o | plen-ome |
| 2 singular | plen-is | plen-ese |
| 3 singular | plen-i | plen-ete |
| 1 plural | plen-ume | plen-omaste |
| 2 plural | plen-ete | plen-este |
| 3 plural | plen-un | plen-onte |

### Present/Perfective

| Person | Active | middle / passive |
|---|---|---|
| 1 singular | plin-o | pli-tho |
| 2 singular | plin-is | pli-this |
| 3 singular | plin-i | pli-thi |
| 1 plural | plin-ume | pli-thume |
| 2 plural | plin-ete | pli-thite |
| 3 plural | plin-un | pli-thun |

### Past/Imperfective

| Person | active | middle / passive |
|---|---|---|
| 1 singular | eplen-a | plen-omun |
| 2 singular | eplen-es | plen-osun |
| 3 singular | eplen-e | plen-otan |
| 1 plural | plen-ame | plen-omaste |
| 2 plural | plen-ate | plen-osaste |
| 3 plural | eplen-an | plen-ontan |

### Past/Perfective

| Person | active | middle / passive |
|---|---|---|
| 1 singular | eplin-a | pli-thika |
| 2 singular | eplin-es | pli-thikes |
| 3 singular | eplin-e | pli-thike |
| 1 plural | plin-ame | pli-thikame |
| 2 plural | plin-ate | pli-thikate |
| 3 plural | eplin-an | pli-thikan |

# References

Alexiadou, Artemis, and Elena Anagnostopoulou. 1999. Non-active morphology and the direction of transitivity alternations. *North East Linguistic Society* 29.27–40.
—— 2003. Voice morphology in the causative-inchoative alternation: evidence for a non-unified structural analysis of unaccusatives. *The unaccusativity puzzle: explorations of the syntax-lexicon interface*, ed. by Artemis Alexiadou, Elena Anagnostopoulou, and Martin Everaert, 114–36. Oxford: Oxford University Press.

Aronoff, Mark. 1994. *Morphology by itself: stems and inflectional classes*. Cambridge, Mass.: MIT Press.

Baldi, Phillip. 1976. Remarks on the Latin r-form verbs. *Zeitschrift für vergleichende Sprachforschung* 90.222–57.

Baerman, Matthew. This volume. *Morphological typology of deponency*.

Börjars, Kersti, Nigel Vincent, and Carol Chapman. 1996. Paradigms, periphrases and pronominal inflection: a feature-based account. *Yearbook of Morphology 1996*, ed. by Geert Booij, and Jaap van Marle, 155–80. Dordrecht: Kluwer Academic Publishers.

Burzio, Luigi. 1981. *Intransitive verbs and Italian auxiliaries*. Cambridge, Mass.: MIT dissertation.

Chomsky, Noam. 1981. *Lectures on government and binding*. Dordrecht: Foris.

Clairis, Christos, and Giorgos Babiniotis. 2005. *Grammar of Modern Greek*. Athens: Ellinika Grammata [in Greek].

Cohen, Marcel. 1930. Verbes déponents internes (ou verbes adhérents) en sémitique. *Mémoires de la Société Linguistique* 23.225–48.

Corbett, Greville G. This volume. *Deponency, syncretism, and what lies between*.

Di Sciullo, Anna-Maria, and Edwin Williams. 1987. *On the definition of word*. Cambridge, Mass.: MIT Press.

Draeger, Anton. 1878. *Historische Syntax der lateinischen Sprache*. Leipzig: B. G. Teubner.

Duhoux, Yves. 1992. *Le verbe grec ancien: éléments de morphologie et de syntaxe historiques*. Louvain-la-Neuve: Peeters.

Embick, David. 2000. Features, syntax and categories in the Latin perfect. *Linguistic Inquiry* 31.185–230.

Everaert, Martin. 1986. *The syntax of reflexivization*. Utrecht: Utrecht Institute of Linguistics, OTS dissertation.

Gonda, Jan. 1960. Reflections on the Indo-european medium I. *Lingua* 9.30–67.
—— 1960. Reflections on the Indo-european medium II. *Lingua* 9.175–93.

Grimshaw, Jane. 1982. On the lexical representation of Romance reflexive clitics. *The mental representation of grammatical relations*, ed. by Joan Bresnan, 87–148. Cambridge, Mass.: MIT Press.

Jannaris, Antonius N. 1968. *An historical Greek grammar chiefly of the Attic dialect*. Hildescheim: Georg Olms.

Joseph, Brian, and Jane Smirniotopoulos. 1993. The morphosyntax of the Modern Greek verbs as morphology and not syntax. *Linguistic Inquiry* 24.388–98.

Halle, Morris, and Alec Marantz. 1993. Distributed morphology and the pieces of inflection. *The view from building 20*, ed. by Kenneth Hale and Samuel Jay Keyser, 111–76. Cambridge, Mass.: MIT Press.

Holton, David, Peter Mackridge, and Irene Philippaki-Warburton. 1997. *Greek: a comprehensive grammar of the modern language.* London: Routledge.

Horrocks, Geoffrey. 1997. *Greek: a history of the language and its speakers.* London: Longman.

Humbert, Jean. 1954. *Syntaxe grecque.* Paris: Klincksieck.

Kemmer, Suzanne. 1993. *The middle voice.* Amsterdam: John Benjamins.

—— 1994. Middle voice, transitivity and the elaboration of events. *Voice: form and function*, ed. by Barbara Fox and Paul J. Hopper, 179–230. Amsterdam: John Benjamins.

Kiparsky, Paul. 1982. Lexical morphology and phonology. *Linguistics in the morning calm*, ed. by Yang In-Seok, 3–91. Seoul: Hanshin.

—— 2005. Blocking and periphrasis in inflectional paradigms. *Yearbook of Morphology 2004*, ed. by Geert Booij and Jaap van Marle, 113–36. Dordrecht: Kluwer.

Kratzer, Angelika. 1993. *The event argument and the semantics of voice.* Cambridge, Mass.: MIT Press.

Lavidas, Nikolaos. 2003. Transitivity alternations: diachronic and synchronic tendencies in Greek and French. *Studies in Greek Linguistics* 24.369–81 [in Greek].

—— 2005. *The diachrony of the Greek anticausative morphology.* Paper presented at the workshop on the morphosyntax of Greek, Linguistic Society of America Institute, MIT.

Lavidas, Nikolaos, and Dimitra Papangeli. Forthcoming. Impersonals in the diachrony of Greek. *Proceedings of the 7th International Conference of Greek Linguistics*, University of York.

Lieber, Rochelle. 1980. *On the organization of the lexicon.* Cambridge, Mass.: MIT dissertation.

Manney, Linda. 2000. *Middle voice in Modern Greek.* Amsterdam: Benjamins.

Marantz, Alec. 1997. No escape from syntax. Don't try morphological analysis in the privacy of your own lexicon. *Proceedings of the 21st Penn linguistics colloquium.* 201–25.

Mayser, Edwin. 1926. *Grammatik der griechischen Papyri aus der Ptolemaerzeit: mit Einschluss der gleichzeitingen Ostraka und der in Ägypten verfassten Inschriften, II.* Berlin: Walter de Gruyter.

—— 1970. *Grammatik der griechischen Papyri aus der Ptolemaerzeit: mit Einschluss der gleichzeitingen Ostraka und der in Ägypten verfassten Inschriften, III.* Berlin: Walter de Gruyter.

Meillet, Antoine. 1966. *Esquisse d'une histoire de la langue latine.* Paris: Klincksieck.

Papangeli, Dimitra. 2003a. Greek reflexives and the syntax/lexicon parameter. *Proceedings of the 31st Western Conference of Linguistics.*191–202.

—— 2003b. On impersonals. *UiL-OTS Yearbook. Utrecht Institute of Linguistics.* 37–45.

—— 2004. *The morphosyntax of argument realization.* The Netherlands: LOT Dissertation series 86.

—— 2005. *Morpho-syntactic restrictions on argument alternations: the role of the Greek suffix.* Paper presented at the workshop on the morphosyntax of Greek, Linguistic Society of America Institute, MIT.

Pesetsky, David. 1995. *Zero syntax.* Cambridge, Mass.: MIT Press.

Reinhart, Tanya. 1997. Syntactic effects of lexical operations: reflexives and unaccusatives. *OTS Working Papers in Linguistics.*

—— 2000. The theta system: syntactic realization of verbal concepts. *OTS Working Papers in Linguistics.*

—— 2003. The theta system: an overview. *Theoretical Linguistics* 28.229–90.

Reinhart, Tanya, and Tal Siloni. 2003. Against an unaccusative analysis of reflexives. *The unaccusativity puzzle: explorations of the syntax-lexicon interface,* ed. by Artemis Alexiadou, Elena Anagnostopoulou, and Martin Everaert, 159–80. Oxford: Oxford University Press.

—— and —— 2005. Thematic arity operations and parametric variations. *Linguistic Inquiry* 36, 3.389–436.

Rivero, Maria-Luisa. 1990. The location of nonactive voice in Albanian and Modern Greek. *Linguistic Inquiry* 21.135–46.

Schwyzer, Eduard, and Albert Debrunner. 1950. *Griechische Grammatik II: Syntax und syntaktische Stilistik.* München: C. H. Beck.

Sportiche, Dominique. 1998. *Partitions and atoms of the clause structure. Subjects, case and clitics.* London: Routledge.

Stump, Gregory T. This volume. *A non-canonical pattern of deponency and its implications.*

Ter Meulen, Alice. 2000. Optimal reflexivity in Dutch. *Journal of Semantics* 17.263–80.

Theophanopoulou-Kontou, Dimitra. 1981. The middle verbs of modern Greek. Some preliminary remarks on the system of voices. *Studies in Greek Linguistics* 2.51–78 [in Greek].

—— 1999. Middle intransitive verbs in modern Greek and the mediopassive morphology. *Proceedings of the 3rd International Conference of Greek Linguistics.* 114–22 [in Greek].

—— 2000. Locative adverbs and case in Greek. Diachronic perspective. *Glossologia* 11/12.1–40 [in Greek].

—— 2001. *The structure of 'VP' and the mediopassive morphology. The passives and anticausatives in modern Greek.* Paper presented at the workshop on Greek syntax and the minimalist seduction, University of Reading.

Tsimpli, Ianthi-Maria. 1989. On the properties of the passive affix in Modern Greek. *UCL Working Papers in Linguistics* 1.235–60.

Vendryes, Joseph. 1948. Une catégorie verbale: le mode de participation du sujet. *Mémoires de la Société Linguistique* 44.1–20.

Zheng, Xu, Mark Aronoff, and Frank Anshen. This volume. *Deponency in Latin.*

Zombolou, Katerina. 1997. Searching for the agent. . . . deponents vs. mediopassive: a different approach of the Modern Greek voice. *Studies in Greek Linguistics* 17.229–42 [in Greek].

—— 2004. *Verbal alternations in Greek: a semantic analysis.* Reading: University of Reading dissertation.

# 6

# Deponency in Latin*

## ZHENG XU, MARK ARONOFF, AND FRANK ANSHEN

## 1. Introduction

A *DEPONENT VERB* HAS A MORPHOLOGICALLY PASSIVE FORM but active meaning (Bennett 1907). Classical examples of deponent verbs come from Latin
and have been much discussed in the literature, going back to Roman
times. In Latin, an active verb in passive form and a deponent verb share the
same paradigm, but contrast in meaning with respect to voice:

(1)  Verb in passive form
     *amor*        'I am loved'        *amaːmur*      'we are loved'
     *amaːris*     'you are loved'     *amaːminiː*    'you are loved'
     *amaːtur*     'he is loved'       *amantur*      'they are loved'

(2)  Deponent verb
     *miːror*      'I admire'          *miːraːmur*    'we admire'
     *miːraːris*   'you admire'        *miːraːminiː*  'you admire'
     *miːraːtur*   'he admires'        *miːrantur*    'they admire

The specific question we attempt to tackle in this paper is why certain
Latin verbs are deponent. Compared to recent works on Latin deponent
verbs (Embick 2000; Sadler and Spencer 2001; Kiparsky 2005) which avoid
this question by simply assigning Latin deponents a syntactico-semantic or

* We owe thanks to many people who helped with this project. First is October Dow, who did
the original manual tagging of the deponent verbs in the *Oxford Latin Dictionary*. Richard
Larson spent a good deal of time discussing our semantic findings with us. Philip Baldi, Andrew
Carstairs-McCarthy, Alice Harris, Beth Levin, and Martin Maiden provided very quick feed-
back on an earlier draft of this work, for which we are grateful. This work was presented at Stony
Brook University and the Deponency Workshop in London, which generously supported the
attendance of the first author at the meeting. We thank all those who provided comments on
those occasions. Latin deponent verbs provide one of the oldest topics in the Western grammatical tradition and we are grateful to all those scholars who have devoted themselves to this rich
area of study over the last two millenia.

*Proceedings of the British Academy* **145**, 127–143. © The British Academy 2007.

conjugational class feature [Passive], we give a nearly all-inclusive description of Latin deponents and discuss the factors that determine their morphological and syntactico-semantic nature in more detail. We do not ask the most general question, which is why classical Latin had a deponent construction in the first place. Instead, we assume that the existence of the deponent in classical Latin was purely fortuitous, and then go on to ask what value the construction had, given its existence in the language.

Our interest is purely synchronic and our data comes only from the classical language. Readers interested in the history of the Latin deponent and in what Latin grammarians had to say about this class of verbs should consult Flobert 1975. Baldi (1977) provides a concise history of modern linguistic scholarship on Latin deponents.

We analyse Latin deponents from two perspectives. From a syntactico-semantic perspective, we categorize Latin deponents into syntactico-semantic classes, using the classification of Levin 1993, which was developed for English verbs, but which appears to be universal in scope. Levin provides a classification of a large number of English verbs, based on a variety of syntactico-semantic criteria. We find that Latin deponents can be defined negatively from a syntactico-semantic perspective: they tend not to fall into syntactico-semantic classes in which the object of a verb is *physically affected*. Additionally, we analyse the morphological characteristics of Latin deponents. We find that nearly half of Latin deponents are derived from either nouns or adjectives; these fall into several non-causative semantic categories. A majority of those deponent verbs that are not derived from nouns or adjectives contain *deponent roots*, which we define as roots whose verbs always take deponent forms. In these cases, we say that the deponent feature is a lexical property of the root and we have what we call a deponent root. In others, though, not all verbs in a given root are deponent, so that the root itself is not deponent and a lexeme or a stem may bear the deponent feature. In terms of percolation, if a root is marked as deponent, then the deponent feature will percolate down to all lexemes containing that root and all the stems of that lexeme. If a lexeme is deponent, then so will all its forms be deponent. Finally, if a stem is deponent, then only the forms in that stem will be deponent. We know of no cases of individual suppletive verb forms being deponent, though only the word ESSE 'to be' is suppletive at the individual verb form level in Latin.

Our method in this work is largely numerical, based on fairly exhaustive counts of Latin deponent verbs and their senses. Similarly for the conclusions that we extract from the data. Thus, we show that Latin deponent verbs and their senses exhibit a number of strong generalizations, both syntactico-semantic and morphological, none of which are by any means absolute.

# 2. Syntactico-Semantic Categorization of Latin Deponent Verbs

## 2.1. Methodology

We manually collected 543 deponent verbs and their relevant information from the *Oxford Latin Dictionary* (1983).[1] Our interest is not in the verbs alone, but just as much in the senses of these verbs, since a single verb may have more than one distinct sense, each of which may fall into a different semantic class. We are not always careful to distinguish the expressions 'deponent verbs' and 'senses of deponent verbs', but the latter notion is primary in our research. We started off, perforce, from verbs, simply because that is how the dictionary is arranged, not by senses. First, we tagged all verbs whose citation form ends in *-or* in the dictionary, from *abo:minor* to *ulciscor*. We then analysed each deponent verb sense through the following steps (a–g):

**a.** We checked the senses of each deponent verb and only considered the first definition for each sense listed in the dictionary. For example, *aborior* has two senses: 1) 'to pass away, disappear, be lost'; 2) 'to miscarry, be aborted.' We only considered the first definition for each sense, i.e. 'to pass away' and 'to miscarry' and ignored the other definitions, such as 'to disappear', 'to be lost', and 'to be aborted.'

**b.** We categorized each resulting sense of a deponent verb into one of the 49 verb classes (numbered 9 through 57) in Levin 1993. For example, we put *adveneror* 'to worship' in the class of *admire* verbs (labelled as 31.2 in Levin 1993).

**c.** If we could not find the English gloss of a Latin deponent verb in Levin 1993, we would look for its synonyms via the webpage http://www.rhymezone.com/, an online English synonym dictionary. For example, *abo:minor* has two senses: 1) 'to avert'; 2) 'to loathe.' We put *avert* in the class of *avoid* verbs, though *avert* is not listed in Levin 1993, because via the webpage we found *avoid*, the only synonym of *avert* that is listed in Levin 1993.

**d.** If we did not find any English synonym of a sense of a deponent verb in Levin 1993, we would just ignore the sense. For example, the second sense of *abu:tor* is 'to utilize'. We did not find it or its synonyms such as 'to use' in Levin 1993, so we ignored it.

---

[1] This dictionary 'treats classical Latin from its beginnings to the end of the second century AD' (p. v) and thus does not include the post-classical cases that are covered in Flobert's (1975) comprehensive treatment of all Latin deponent verbs.

e. We only considered the 'big class' and ignored subclass numbers. If several senses of a deponent verb fall into one big semantic class, we only counted one sense. For example, *praefor* has three senses: 1) 'to say'; 2) 'to recite'; 3) 'to speak'. They belong to the classes *say* verbs (37.7), verbs of transfer of a message (37.1), and *talk* verbs (37.5) respectively. They all belong to the big class of verbs of communication (37). We thus count for *praefor* only one sense that belongs to the class of verbs of communication. We did the same with the English verb senses in Levin 1993 against which we compared the Latin deponents. For example, the English verb *brush* has two senses that fall into the subclasses 41.2.1, '*floss* verbs' and 41.2.2, '*braid* verbs'. which we collapse into a single class, 41 'verbs of grooming and bodily care'.

f. For a family of deponent verbs sharing the same root that falls into a single sense class, only one token sense was counted. Unlike the English verbs in Levin 1993, there are many derivative Latin deponents that share one root and whose senses fall into one big verb class. For example, there are 15 deponents with the root *sequ-*, which have 41 senses listed in Levin 1993. Among the 41 senses, there are 16 senses which fall into the big class of verbs of motion. We counted the 16 senses as one sense which falls into the class of verbs of motion. By doing so, we could control for the influence of derivations that repeatedly create senses in one verb class so that we could make a more reasonable comparison between Latin deponents and English verbs. Note that steps (e) and (f) both lead to conservative numbers, because they greatly reduce the numbers of deponent senses. If we had omitted these steps, our results might have been even more robust, but perhaps misleadingly so.

g. By using the distribution of English verb senses in Levin 1993 as a reference, we compared the **ratio$_1$** of the number of senses of a syntactico-semantic class of Latin deponents divided by the number of senses of all Latin deponents to the **ratio$_2$** of the number of senses of a class of English verbs divided by the number of senses of all English verbs. This gives us an indirect measure of the distribution of the meanings of deponent verbs in Latin, compared to the distribution of 'normal' verbs. If, for a given class, we find that ratio$_1$ is larger than ratio$_2$, this may suggest that there is a relation between the meaning of a verb and its deponency.

## 2.2. Results

We obtained 1,215 senses from the *Oxford Latin Dictionary* through step (a) and reduced this number to 655 senses through steps (b–e).[2] We then obtained a net total of 394 senses through step (f). The results we obtained through analysing these senses in step (g) are given in Table 1.

**Table 1.**   Syntactico-semantic classes of Latin deponents and English verbs

| Verb class | Class name | Number of deponent senses | Ratio1 | Ratio2 | Ratio1/Ratio2 |
|---|---|---|---|---|---|
| 15 | Hold and Keep | 10 | 2.54% | 0.27% | 9.41 |
| 55 | Begin, Complete | 14 | 3.55% | 0.45% | 7.89 |
| 52 | Avoid | 5 | 1.27% | 0.20% | 6.35 |
| 14 | Learn | 3 | 0.76% | 0.17% | 4.47 |
| 34 | Assessment | 3 | 0.76% | 0.17% | 4.47 |
| 46 | Lodge | 4 | 1.02% | 0.27% | 3.78 |
| 36 | Social interaction | 26 | 6.60% | 1.89% | 3.49 |
| 12 | Push/Pull | 3 | 0.76% | 0.25% | 3.04 |
| 53 | Lingering and Rushing | 3 | 0.76% | 0.27% | 2.81 |
| 50 | Assuming a position | 5 | 1.27% | 0.47% | 2.70 |
| **20** | **Contact** | **3** | **0.76%** | **0.32%** | **2.38** |
| 48 | Appear, Disappear, Occur | 14 | 3.55% | 1.54% | 2.31 |
| 13 | Change of possession | 32 | 8.12% | 3.70% | 2.19 |
| 37 | Communication | 35 | 8.88% | 4.05% | 2.19 |
| **44** | **Destroy** | **3** | **0.76%** | **0.35%** | **2.17** |
| 32 | Desire | 4 | 1.02% | 0.50% | 2.04 |
| 33 | Judgement | 12 | 3.05% | 1.69% | 1.80 |
| **26** | **Creation and Transformation** | **21** | **5.33%** | **3.01%** | **1.77** |
| **35** | **Searching** | **12** | **3.05%** | **1.81%** | **1.69** |
| 31 | Psych-Verbs | 47 | 11.93% | 7.65% | 1.56 |
| 29 | Vs with predicative complements | 28 | 7.11% | 4.67% | 1.52 |
| 30 | Perception | 8 | 2.03% | 1.34% | 1.51 |
| **39** | **Ingesting** | **6** | **1.52%** | **1.29%** | **1.18** |
| 54 | Measure | 4 | 1.02% | 0.97% | 1.05 |
| 51 | Motion | 23 | 5.84% | 5.86% | 1.00 |
| 47 | Existence | 20 | 5.08% | 5.47% | 0.93 |
| 11 | Sending and Carrying | 3 | 0.76% | 1.39% | 0.55 |
| **10** | **Removing** | **13** | **3.30%** | **6.86%** | **0.48** |
| **18** | **Contact by impact** | **2** | **0.51%** | **1.59%** | **0.32** |
| 38 | Sounds made by animals | 2 | 0.51% | 1.66% | 0.31 |
| **17** | **Throwing** | **1** | **0.25%** | **0.87%** | **0.29** |

[2] We ignored 7 deponent verbs which were rarely used or whose meaning is dubious and 266 senses whose English glosses or their synonyms we could not find in Levin 1993.

| Verb class | Class name | Number of deponent senses | Ratio1 | Ratio2 | Ratio1/Ratio2 |
|---|---|---|---|---|---|
| 40 | **Verbs involving the body** | 5 | 1.27% | 4.77% | 0.27 |
| 21 | **Cutting** | 1 | 0.25% | 1.04% | 0.24 |
| 45 | **Change of state** | 8 | 2.03% | 8.82% | 0.23 |
| 22 | Combining and Attaching | 3 | 0.76% | 3.73% | 0.20 |
| 41 | **Grooming and Bodily care** | 1 | 0.25% | 1.39% | 0.18 |
| 25 | **Image creation verbs** | 1 | 0.25% | 1.47% | 0.17 |
| 23 | **Separating and Disassembling** | 1 | 0.25% | 1.57% | 0.16 |
| 9 | **Putting** | 4 | 1.02% | 8.94% | 0.11 |
| 43 | Emission | 1 | 0.25% | 4.20% | 0.06 |
| 16 | Concealment | 0 | 0.00% | 0.27% | 0 |
| 19 | **Poke** | 0 | **0.00%** | 0.15% | **0** |
| 24 | **Colouring** | 0 | **0.00%** | 0.32% | **0** |
| 27 | Engender | 0 | 0.00% | 0.17% | 0 |
| 28 | Calve | 0 | 0.00% | 0.25% | 0 |
| 42 | **Killing** | 0 | **0.00%** | 0.62% | **0** |
| 49 | Body-internal motion | 0 | 0.00% | 0.37% | 0 |
| 56 | Weekend Verbs† | 0 | 0.00% | 0.22% | 0 |
| 57 | Weather Verbs | 0 | 0.00% | 0.67% | 0 |
| Total | | 394 | 100% | 100% | |

† This class is named after the verb *to weekend* 'to spend the weekend'.

In Table 1, the leftmost column lists the numbers of verb classes used in Levin 1993. Corresponding to these numerical labels are the names of verb classes in Levin 1993; the adjacent column gives the names of theses classes. The third column lists the total number of deponent senses that belong to each verb class. The fourth column lists the ratio$_1$ of the number of senses of each class of Latin deponents divided by 394, the number of senses of all Latin deponents we calculated through steps (a–f). The fifth column lists the ratio$_2$ of the number of senses of each class of English verbs divided by 4,025, the number of senses of all English verbs in Levin 1993 analysed through step (e). The rightmost column lists the value of ratio$_1$ divided by ratio$_2$. The rows in Table 1 are arranged based on the values in the rightmost column in descending order. We have grouped the rows into three sets, those whose value in the last column is greater than 2, those whose value is less than 0.5, and those between 2 and 0.5.

The most noticeable generalization that falls out from Table 1 is that Latin deponents tend NOT to fall into classes of verbs whose objects are *physically affected*. An entity is considered physically affected only if a material influence upon it is followed by changes in size, shape, colour, or weight, or object-internal physical alternation in the entity itself. A row in Table 1 is bolded if its verb class contains a significant number of English verbs whose objects are physically affected.

If we draw a line between the class of judgement verbs and the *desire* verb class in which the percentage of Latin deponents is twice that of English verbs, there are 16 verb classes (from the *hold* and *keep* class to the *desire* class) above the line. In other words, Latin deponents tend more to fall into these classes compared to English verbs. For the most part, these classes do not involve affected objects, but two of the 16 classes (12.5%) contain a significant number of English verbs whose objects are physically affected.[3] They are the class of contact verbs and the *destroy* class. However, none of the deponent verbs in the class of contact verbs have physically affected objects, and only two deponent verbs in the *destroy* class seem to. There are 13 English verbs in the class of contact verbs in Levin 1993 and four of them, namely *pinch, prod, sting,* and *tickle* relate to physical affectedness. The three Latin deponent senses in this class are *osculor* 'to kiss', *palpor* 'to stroke', and *sa:vior* 'to kiss'. They do not relate to physical affectedness according to our definition. There are 14 English verbs in the *destroy* class and all of them involve physically affected objects. The three deponent senses in the *destroy* class are *nepo:tor* 'to waste', *populor* 'to ravage', and *spolor* 'to ravage'. We put *nepo:tor* 'to waste, squander', which does not relate to physical affectedness, in the *destroy* class only because it is the single place where *waste* is listed in Levin 1993. Thus, only two of the 167 deponent senses (1.2%) in the 16 classes that fall above 2 in Table 1 arguably involve affected objects.

There are 11 verb classes for which the value of ratio$_1$ divided by ratio$_2$ is between 2 and 0.5, which means that Latin deponent senses in these classes roughly have a distribution similar to that of English verbs. Three of the 11 classes (27.3%) contain a significant number of English verbs whose objects are physically affected. They are the class of verbs of creation and transformation, the class of verbs of searching, and the class of verbs of ingesting.

There are 121 English verbs in the class of verbs of creation and transformation in Levin 1993 and many of them (such as *cook, squeeze,* and *transform*) involve physically affected objects. There are 21 Latin deponent senses in this class but none of them involve physically affected objects. Four of them are intransitive only: *orior* 'to be born', *poe:tor* 'to write poetry',

[3] Among the 10 English verbs in the *push/pull* class, *press* is the only verb which can arguably take physically affected objects. Three Latin deponent senses fall into the *push/pull* class, viz. *obni:tor* 'to press' (intransitive only), *remo:lior* 'to push back', and *aspernor* 'to push away'. None of them take physically affected objects. Among the 76 English verbs in the class of verbs of social interaction, only a few verbs such as *fight* can arguably take physically affected objects. There are 26 Latin deponents in the class of verbs of social interaction. Most of them are intransitives. The 5 transitive deponents are *complector* 'to embrace', *contechnor* 'to plot', *continor* 'to meet', *nanciscor* 'to get (a person) attached to one in a particular relationship or connection', and *sector* 'to visit'. None of them relate to physical affectedness.

*supernascor* 'to develop on the surface', and *modulor* 'to make music (on an instrument)' (*modulor* can be transitive when it takes other meanings). Among the 21 senses, *perplexor* 'to twist' does not relate to physical affectedness because it is followed by an abstract noun meaning, for example, 'facts'. The verb *moderor* 'to arrange' does not relate to physical affectedness, either. The other 15 senses basically have the following meanings:

(3)　a.　'to perform' (e.g. *abu:tor*)　　　b.　'to design' (e.g. *architector*)
　　　c.　'to construct' (e.g. *confabricor*)　d.　'to invent' (e.g. *fa:bulor*)
　　　e.　'to develop' (e.g. *ex(s)equor*)　　f.　'to play (notes)' (e.g. *praemeditor*)
　　　g.　'to weave' (e.g. *ordior*)

All of the senses involve creation and are thus said to take *effected* objects instead of affected ones (the terms are standard in the lexical semantic literature). Notice there is a difference between effected objects and physically affected ones. 'effect' means 'to cause to come into being' rather than 'to exert a physical impact on an existing object and trigger some changes in it'.

There are 73 English verbs in the class of verbs of searching. Quite a few, such as *dig, mine, excavate, sift, burrow, scratch*, and *tunnel*, relate to physical affectedness. There are 12 deponent senses in this class and none of them involve physically affected objects. The 12 senses basically have the following meanings:

(4)　a.　'to seek' (e.g. *aucupor*)　　　b.　'to inspect' (e.g. *intueor*)
　　　c.　'to investigate' (e.g. *percontor*)　d.　'to explore' (e.g. *ruspor*)

There are 52 English verbs in the class of verbs of ingesting. Many of them, such as *eat, chew, gobble*, and *ingest*, involve physically affected objects. There are 6 deponent senses in this class. The major senses of *epulor* 'to dine' and *pa:bulor* 'to graze' are intransitive. The verb *impascor* 'to feed' can only be used intransitively. Three verbs take physically affected objects and they are *tuburcinor* 'to gobble', *u:tor* 'to consume', and *vescor* 'to devour' (*vescor* can only be intransitive when it means 'to eat' and its morphological properties are dubious).

Thus, three of the 184 deponent verbs (1.6%) of these 11 intermediate verb classes, i.e. *tuburcinor* 'to gobble', *u:tor* 'to consume', and *vescor* 'to devour', take physically affected objects.

Next, let us consider the 22 verb classes based on which the value of $ratio_1$ divided by $ratio_2$ is smaller than 0.5. These are the verb classes that Latin deponents tend not to fall into compared to English verbs. Thirteen of the 22 verb classes (59.1%) contain a significant number of English verbs that relate to physical affectedness. We shall show in detail that the number of Latin deponent verbs in each of these categories that relate to physical affectedness is very small compared to the number for English.

There are 276 English verbs in the class of verbs of removing and many of them, such as *erase*, *trim*, and *bone*, involve physically affected objects. There are 13 senses of deponents in this class and all of them are transitive verbs. Two of the deponents, i.e. *medeor* 'to cure' and *medicor* 'to cure' seem to relate to physical affectedness. The other deponents do not take physically affected objects. They basically have the following senses:

(5)  a.  'to steal' (e.g. *fu:ror*)           b.  'to omit' (e.g. *transgredior*)
     c.  'to discharge' (e.g. *e:iaculor*)     d.  'to remove' (e.g. *e:mo:lior*)
     e.  'to defraud' (e.g. *pecu:lor*)        f.  'to despoil' (e.g. *praedor*)
     g.  'to capture' (e.g. *potior*)          h.  'to exorcise' (e.g. *de:veneror*)

There are 64 English verbs in the class of verbs of contact by impact and many of them such as *hammer*, *bite*, and *scratch* can take physically affected objects. The two deponents, *admo:lior* 'to beat' and *iaculor* 'to strike (with a javelin or other missile)' relate to physical affectedness.

There are 35 English verbs in the class of verbs of throwing and quite a few, such as *bash*, *slam*, and *smash*, relate to physical affectedness. The only deponent sense in this class is *iaculor* 'to throw', which does not take a physically affected object.

There are 192 English verbs in the class of verbs involving the body and many of them, such as *suffocate*, *bruise*, *hurt*, and *injure*, can take physically affected objects. All of the 5 deponent senses in this class are intransitives:

(6)  a.  *a:versor* 'to recoil'   b.  *blandior* 'to smile'   c.  *conscreor* 'to hawk'
     d.  *morior* 'to faint'      e.  *pandiculor* 'to grimace'

There are 355 English verbs in the class of verbs of change of state and many of them, such as *break*, *crash*, *crease*, and *boil*, take physically affected objects. Seven of the 8 deponent senses in this class can only be intransitives:

(7)  a.  *aboriscor* 'to fade'    b.  *colla:bor* 'to give way'   c.  *de:fetiscor* 'to tire'
     d.  *e:nascor* 'to sprout'   e.  *li:quor* 'to melt'        f.  *morior* 'to wither'
     g.  *vagor* 'to vary'

The only deponent in this class that may be transitive is *de:grassor* '(w. acc.) to descend upon', but it is not clear whether the object of the transitive sense is physically affected.

There are 42 English verbs in the class of verbs of cutting and all of them relate to physical affectedness. The only deponent in this class is *manticulor* 'cut open', which takes physically affected objects.

There are 56 English verbs in the class of verbs of grooming and bodily care and many of them, such as *shave*, *comb*, and *clip*, which take *beard*, *hair*, and *nail* as their objects, relate to physical affectedness. The only deponent in this class is *meditor* 'to exercise oneself' which is intransitive.

There are 59 English verbs in the class of image creation verbs and quite a few of them (such as *engrave*, *mark*, and *paint*) can take physically affected objects. The only deponent in this class is *ima:ginor* 'to imagine' which does not relate to physical affectedness.

There are 63 English verbs in the class of verbs of separating and disassembling and quite a few of them such as *sever*, *break*, *hack*, and *saw* can take physically affected objects. The only deponent in this class is *redordior* 'to unravel' which relates to physical affectedness.

There are 360 English verbs in the class of verbs of putting and many of them such as *coil*, *infect*, and *poison* can take physically affected objects. None of the four deponents in this class relate to physical affectedness:

(8)    a.    *aucupor* 'to lay a trap for'
       b.    *reme:tior* 'to cover (a distance) in the reverse direction'
       c.    *obmo:lior* 'to put in the way as an obstruction'
       d.    *amplector* 'to move around, circle'

There are 6 English verbs in the class of *poke* verbs, 13 English verbs in the class of verbs of colouring, and 25 English verbs in the class of verbs of killing. All of them relate to physically affected objects. There is no deponent in these classes.

Thus, only 6 of the 43 senses (14.0%) belonging to the verb classes which deponents tend not to fall into can take physically affected objects. They are senses corresponding to the verbs *medeor* 'to cure', *medicor* 'to cure', *admo:lior* 'to beat', *iaculor* 'to strike (with a javelin or other missile)', *manticulor* 'to cut open', and *redordior* 'to unravel'.

To summarize briefly the above discussion, 12.5% of the verb classes where Latin deponents tend to fall compared to English contain a significant number of English verbs which relate to physical affectedness but only 1.2% of the deponents in these verb classes take physically affected objects; 27.3% of the verb classes where Latin deponents roughly have a distribution similar to that of English verbs contain a significant number of English verbs which relate to physical affectedness but only 1.6% of the deponents in these verb classes take physically affected objects; 59.1% of the verb classes where Latin deponents tend not to fall contain a significant number of English verbs which relate to physical affectedness and 14.0% of the deponents in these verb classes take physically affected objects. Table 2 shows that the less likely Latin deponents are to fall into a set of verb classes, the more we find among them classes of verbs whose objects are physically affected and more deponents that relate to physical affectedness.

Additionally, only 11 of the 394 deponents (2.8%) take physically affected objects. By contrast, English has a much higher rate of verbs which relate to physical affectedness. All of the verbs in the classes of *destroy* verbs, *poke*

**Table 2.**   The distribution of verb classes and deponents that relate to physical affectedness

| Ratio$_1$/Ratio$_2$ | > 2 | 0.5–2 | < 0.5 |
|---|---|---|---|
| Percentage (and number) of classes of English verbs (with physically affected objects) | 12.5% (2) | 27.3% (3) | 59.1% (13) |
| Percentage (and number) of deponents (with physically affected objects) | 1.2% (2) | 1.6% (3) | 14.0% (6) |

verbs, verbs of cutting, colouring, and killing, and a majority (66.0%) of the verbs in the class of verbs of change of state take physically affected objects. The verbs in these classes alone constitute over 8% of all the 4,025 English senses, around three times the 2.8% we have found for Latin deponents. The other 12 verb classes, each of which contains a significant number of English verbs that relate to physical affectedness, comprise verbs that constitute around one third of all the English senses. Assuming that even a small fraction of the approximately 1,300 senses in these classes relate to physical affectedness, it is clear that a much greater proportion of English verb senses than Latin deponent verb senses take physically affected objects.

# 3. Morphological Analyses of Latin Deponent Verbs

We also analyse the morphological structure of each Latin deponent verb. We find that nearly half of the 536 deponent verbs are derived from either nouns or adjectives and that these basically fall into several non-causative semantic categories. Additionally, a majority of the other half (those not derived from other lexical categories) contain *deponent roots* whose verbs always take deponent forms. For those deponent verbs not containing deponent roots, we show that in some the lexeme must be marked as deponent, while in a few, the famous semi-deponents, individual stems must be so marked.

## 3.1. Denominal and deadjectival deponents

There are 249 Latin deponents that are either denominal or deadjectival out of a total of 536 (46.5%). Their verbal stems are zero-derived from their nominal or adjectival stems. Consider the example in (9). Both the noun *architectus* 'a master builder' and the deponent *architector* share the same stem *architect-*. Both *-us* and *-or* are inflectional markers.

(9)     *architect-us* 'a master builder' → *architect-or* 'to construct'

The 249 denominal or deadjectival deponent verbs fall into five general non-causative semantic categories, which depend to a great extent on the syntax and semantics of their bases. If a deponent is derived from an adjective

$x$, it basically means 'to act or to be $x$'; if a deponent is derived from an animate noun $y$, it basically means 'to act like $y$'; if a deponent is derived from an inanimate noun $z$, it may fall into one of the three semantic categories: it may mean either 'to give or make (with a sense of creation) $z$', 'to use $z$', or 'to get $z$'. Some examples are given in (10).

(10)  a.  *fatu-us*    'silly'        →    *fatu-or*      'to play the fool'
       b.  *ancill-a*   'handmaid'  →    *ancill-or*    'to act like a handmaid'
       c.  *fa:bul-a*   'fable'        →    *fa:bul-or*    'to make up a fable'
       d.  *copi-a*     'supply'      →    *copi-or*      'to furnish oneself (with supplies)'
       e.  *aqu-a*      'water'       →    *aqu-or*       'to fetch water'

Table 3 gives the numbers of denominal or deadjectival deponents which fall into the five non-causative semantic categories. *Equor* 'to procure horses', which is derived from the animate noun *equus* 'horse', and *piscor* 'to get fish', which is derived from the animate noun *piscis* 'fish', are the only two exceptions to the semantic category 'to act like $y$'; instead, they fall into the category 'to get $z$', which is otherwise reserved for inanimate nouns. Disregarding the 19 deponent verbs whose meanings are unclear with respect to their nominal bases, our generalizations cover 224 deponent verbs (97.4% of the 230 deponents), with only 6 exceptions.[4]

**Table 3.**   Denominal and deadjectival deponent verbs

| Base | Semantic categories of deponents | Number of deponents |
|---|---|---|
| Adjective | 'to act or to be $x$' | 35 |
| Noun (+Animate) | 'to act like $y$' | 52 |
| Noun (−Animate) plus *equus* and *piscis* | 'to give or make $z$' (with a sense of creation) | 62 |
| | 'to use $z$' | 51 |
| | 'to get $z$' | 24 |

It is enlightening to compare this set of deponents to the set of Latin denominal or deadjectival verbs that are active in both form and meaning, a substantial majority of which have a causative sense. We went through every tenth page of the *Oxford Latin Dictionary* and obtained a sample of 65 Latin active verbs derived from adjectives or nouns.[5] Disregarding 4 verbs which are rarely used or whose morphological structure is unclear and 3 verbs whose semantic structure is unclear, we find that 42 of the 58 verbs (72.4%)

---

[4] The six exceptions are comprised of four denominal deponents including *libi:dinor* 'to gratify lust', *manticulor* 'to cut open (a bag or purse)', *nego:tior* 'to do business', and *reliquor* 'to be in arrears in respect of money owed', and two deadverbial deponents including *frustror* 'to delude' and *de:frustror* 'to foil or thwart completely'.

[5] The bases of two active verbs relate to prepositional phrases. They are *e:li:mino* 'to turn out of doors', from *ex limine* 'out the threshold' and *obvio:* 'to go against' from *ob via:* 'from the road'.

have a causative sense (11a, b). Eleven of the remaining 16 verbs (19.0%) fall into the semantic category 'to use' (11c). Two verbs (3.4%) fall into the semantic category 'to get' (11d). One has the sense of 'to become' (11e). One has the sense of 'to plant' (11f). One has the sense of 'to put in' (11g).

(11)  a.  *crispus*   'curly'                      →   *crispo:*   'to make wavy'
      b.  *lumen*     'light'                      →   *lumino:*   'to light up'
      c.  *regnum*    'office of king'             →   *regno:*    'to rule as a king'
      d.  *pilus*     'a hair'                     →   *pilo:*     'to grow hairy'
      e.  *sponsa*    'woman betrothed             →   *sponso:*   'to become engaged
                       in marriage'                              to marry'
      f.  *holus*     'vegetables'                 →   *holero:*   'to plant with vegetables'
      g.  *humus*     'earth'                      →   *humo:*     'to bury'

Thus, we conclude that Latin denominal or deadjectival verbs differ in form depending on whether they have a causative sense. Those with causative senses tend to be active, while those that fall into general non-causative semantic categories such as 'to act or to be $x$', 'to act like $y$', 'to give or make (with a sense of creation) $z$', 'to use $z$', and 'to get $z$' tend to assume deponent forms. This generalization is by no means absolute, since Latin denominal or deadjectival verbs which fall into the semantic categories 'to use $z$' and 'to get $z$' take either active or deponent forms.

### 3.2. Deponent roots

Once the denominal and deadjectival deponents are extracted, we are left with 287 verbs. We find that 52 *deponent roots* account for 244 of these verbs (85.0%). A verb with a deponent root always takes a deponent form.

We analysed the morphological structure of each of the 287 verbs and obtained 70 roots. We typed key letters of each of the 70 roots into the Perseus online Latin-English lexicon (www.perseus.tufts.edu), which then gave us a list of words with the letters. If the list does not contain any active form which has the root, then we say that the root is a deponent root. For example, we typed the key letters *sequ* and *sect* (a variant of *sequ*) of the root -*sequ*- into the online lexicon, which then gave us a list of words containing *sequ* and *sect*. Since no word with *sequ* or *sect* has an active form like *sequo:* or *secto:*, we conclude that -*sequ*- is a deponent root. Table 4 gives us a list of deponent roots each of which has four or more deponent verbs.[6]

---

[6] -*gredi*- is a variant of the deponent root -*gradi*-. A few prefixed verbs with -*gredi*- have rare active variants: *aggredio:*, *progredio:*, *supergredio:*. None of the deponents with -*min*- have active forms, while -*min*- is not deponent when it is associated with the meaning 'to drive' (e.g., *commino:* 'to drive together'). Active forms *mo:lio:* 'to build up' and *de:mo:lio:* 'to remove' coexist with their corresponding deponent forms, but *mo:lio:* and *de:mo:lio:* are rare variants. *Adorio:*

**Table 4.**   Latin deponent roots

| Latin deponent root | Number of verbs with each deponent root | Example verb | Gloss |
| --- | --- | --- | --- |
| *gradi* | 22 | *gradior* | 'to proceed' |
| *la:b* | 16 | *la:bor* | 'to glide' |
| *sequ* | 15 | *sequor* | 'to follow' |
| *min* | 11 | *comminor* | 'to threaten' |
| *loqu* | 10 | *loquor* | 'to talk' |
| *nasc* | 10 | *nascor* | 'to be born' |
| *mo:li* | 9 | *mo:lior* | 'to build up' |
| *mori* | 9 | *morior* | 'to die' |
| *ori* | 8 | *orior* | 'to rise' |
| *tue* | 8 | *tueor* | 'to look at' |
| *f(or)* | 7 | *affor* | 'to address' |
| *hor(t)* | 7 | *hortor* | 'to encourage' |
| *luct* | 7 | *luctor* | 'to wrestle' |
| *me:ti* | 7 | *me:tior* | 'to measure' |
| *fate* | 5 | *fateor* | 'to concede' |
| *prec* | 5 | *precor* | 'to ask for' |
| *quer* | 5 | *queror* | 'to regret' |
| *apisc* | 4 | *apiscor* | 'to grasp' |
| *fru* | 4 | *fruor* | 'to enjoy' |
| *fung* | 4 | *fungor* | 'to perform' |
| *medit* | 4 | *meditor* | 'to contemplate' |
| *spic* | 4 | *conspicor* | 'to see' |
| *u:t* | 4 | *u:tor* | 'to make use of' |

### 3.3. Roots whose verbs have both active and passive forms

The remaining 43 of the 287 deponent verbs (15.0%) have 18 roots whose verbs have both active and deponent forms. See Table 5. Each row in the third column of Table 5 gives a pair of deponent (left) and active (right) forms with the same root. These verbs fall into two sets. In one, a verb lexeme has both deponent and active uses.[7] These are treated at length in Flobert (1975). The remaining set is comprised of pairs where the bare root lexeme is active but a prefixed lexeme is deponent. These are bolded in the table. From them, we conclude that the deponent feature may sometimes reside in the lexeme rather than in the root. In the pair of verbs *frango:* and *refra:gor*, the first shows that the root itself is not deponent. We therefore must say that the lexeme

---

'to attack' coexists with its corresponding deponent form, but *adorio:* is rare. *-spic-* is a deponent root when it is not followed by the suffix *-i*, but not with the suffix. With *-i*, the verb is always irregular: *spicio:*, *spexi*, *spectum*. Without *-i*, the verb is always regular and deponent: *spicor*, *spicatum*. Minimal pairs like *conspicio:* and *conspicor*, both meaning 'to catch sight of', can be found.

[7] Not all the active forms are listed in the *Oxford Latin dictionary*, but they are all attested in the Perseus online Latin-English lexicon.

**Table 5.**  Roots whose verbs have both active and passive forms

| Roots whose verbs have both active and passive forms | Number of verbs with such a root | Example verb | Gloss |
|---|---|---|---|
| *vers* | 8 | *conversor/converso:* | 'to consort/to turn' |
| *plec* | 6 | *amplector/amplecto:* | 'to embrace' |
| *lice* | 4 | *liceor/liceo:* | 'to bid/to fetch' |
| *palp* | 3 | *palpor/palpo:* | 'to stroke' |
| *sent* | 3 | *assentior/assentio:* | 'to assent' |
| *veho* | 3 | ***praevehor/veho:*** | 'to travel/to carry' |
| *fra:g* | 2 | ***refra:gor/frango:*** | 'to resist/to break' |
| *scisco* | 2 | *sciscitor/sciscito:* | 'to inquire' |
| *spern* | 2 | ***aspernor/sperno:*** | 'to despise/to separate' |
| *volu:* | 2 | *convolu:tor/convolu:to:* | 'to whirl round' |
| *cer* | 1 | *certor/certo:* | 'to compete/to contend' |
| *facio* | 1 | *proficiscor/proficisco:* | 'to set out' |
| *li(:)qu* | 1 | *li:quor/liquo:* | 'to become/make liquid' |
| *pasc* | 1 | ***impascor/pasco:*** | 'to feed' |
| *pergo* | 1 | *expergiscor/expergisco:* | 'to wake up' |
| *scre* | 1 | ***conscreor/screo:*** | 'to hawk' |
| *tin* | 1 | *continuor/continuo:* | 'to encounter/connect' |
| *va:ric* | 1 | *praeva:ricor/praeva:rico:* | 'to straddle across anything' |

REFRA:GOR bears a deponent feature. We will show below that in some cases a single stem of a lexeme may be deponent. Thus, the deponency feature may be borne by a root, a stem, or a lexeme.

### 3.4. Semi-deponent verbs

A few Latin verbs have in the perfect tenses passive forms only, but with active meanings. They are usually called *semi-deponent* verbs. There are four basic semi-deponent verbs and others derived from them (*-us* is the first person masculine nominative marker; the equivalent form for a regular verb, e.g. *ama:tus sum* 'I have been loved', is passive):

(12)   a.   *audeo:, ausus sum*          'to dare'
       b.   *gaudeo:, ga:vi:sus sum*     'to rejoice'
       c.   *soleo:, solitus sum*        'to become accustomed to'
       d.   *fi:do:, fi:sus sum*         'to believe'
       e.   *confi:do:, confi:sus sum*   'to have confidence in'
       f.   *diffi:do:, diffi:sus sum*   'to distrust'

The deponent feature of these semi-deponent verbs is in their perfect stems: *aus-*, *ga:vi:s-*, *solit-*, and *fi:s-*. There is no deponent root in these semi-deponent verbs and no lexeme of these verbs is specified with the deponent feature, because otherwise all of their verb forms besides the perfects should take deponent forms.

# 4. Conclusion

We have shown that several factors play a role in predicting whether a verb in Latin may be deponent. Semantically, Latin deponent verbs tend not to take physically affected objects and a Latin verb derived from a noun or adjective tends to be deponent if its meaning is non-causative. Additionally, a Latin verb is deponent if the deponent conjugational class feature is inherent in its root, though in some cases we need to mark an individual stem or lexeme with a deponent feature.

We shall draw one broad conclusion on the function of the deponent in Latin. After all, that is the greatest puzzle: why should a language have such an anti-iconic phenomenon as the deponent? Why should the marker of passive be used to mark active and even transitive verbs? One possible response is that the deponent verbs are just leftovers from some past age and that the construction has no synchronic 'psychologically real' status. Given the strong generalizations that hold over deponent verbs and their senses, however, this conclusion is unwarranted. Rather, the deponent construction does seem to have a coherent synchronic function within classical Latin: it marks non-canonical active verbs. The canonical active verb is one that is high on Hopper and Thompson's (1980) scale of transitivity. They define transitivity globally as 'an activity [that] is "carried-over" or "transferred" from an agent to a patient.' (251). This global property is broken down into a number of parameters. Prominent among these are 'affectedness of O[bject]', whether the object is concrete, action vs non-action, and the number of participants. Causative verbs are also clearly high in transitivity.

Latin speakers had a choice at their disposal that speakers of other languages do not: they could inflect an active verb according to either the active system or the system that was used to express passive verbs. What we see is that they used the latter for active verbs only when these verbs were non-canonical. On a more general level, this is an unusual example of a very general principle sometimes called 'avoid synonymy' (Kiparsky 1982): when a language gives you two constructions, use them in such a way as to make them non-synonymous. Thus, because Latin speakers had at their disposal both the normal active inflectional system and the *r* system for forming active verbs, they had to find a way to differentiate the two semantically, which they did by using the latter only for non-canonical verb senses. In the end, of course, this solution proved cumbersome, and the deponent verbs disappeared, but when they did, they took the entire *r* system along with them, including any normal means of expressing the passive. To this day, no Romance language has a vibrant passive system, thus showing the power of morphology.

This observation leads to a caution about attempts to unify terminology. Other recent analyses of the Latin deponent (Embick 2000; Kiparsky 2005; Sadler and Spencer 2001) have used the term passive to cover both a syntactic phenomenon (true syntactic passives) and a morphological phenomenon (the -*or* conjugation system, which is used both for syntactic passives and for deponent verbs). By doing so, they disguise a truth that unites syntactic passives and deponents that we have uncovered here: both passives and deponents stand in semantic opposition to the class of canonical (transitive) verbs. In other words, what unifies all the verbs in the -*or* conjugation, both passive and deponent, is not syntax, but marked or non-canonical semantics.

We have not answered the most general question of why Latin had deponent verbs. Rather, we have argued that, since the language had such a construction, speakers had to find some Saussurean value for it within the system of the language and we have tried to explicate that value. Questions for future research remain. For example, do the above generalizations also hold cross-linguistically? Can the relation between Latin deponency and physical affectedness be deduced from any theoretical framework? We leave these for more ambitious folk.

# References

Baldi, Philip. 1977. Remarks on the Latin *R*-form verbs. *Zeitschrift für vergleichende Sprachforschung* 90.222–57.

Bennett, Charles. 1907. *New Latin grammar*. New York: Allyn and Bacon.

Embick, David. 2000. Features, syntax, and categories in the Latin perfect. *Linguistic Inquiry* 31.185–230.

Flobert, Pierre. 1975. *Les verbes déponents latins des origines à Charlemagne*. Paris: Belles Lettres.

Glare, P. G. W. 1983. *The Oxford Latin dictionary*. Oxford: Oxford University Press.

Hopper, Paul, and Sandra A. Thompson. 1980. Transitivity in grammar and discourse. *Language* 56.251–99.

Kiparsky, Paul. 1982. Word-formation and the lexicon. *Proceedings of the 1982 Mid-America Linguistics Conference*, ed. by Frances Ingemann. Lawrence, Kansas.

—— 2005. Blocking and periphrasis in inflectional paradigms. *Yearbook of Morphology* 2004.113–35.

Levin, Beth. 1993. *English verb classes and alternations: a preliminary investigation*. Chicago: University of Chicago Press.

Sadler, Louisa, and Andrew Spencer. 2001. Syntax as an exponent of morphological features. *Yearbook of Morphology 2000*, ed. by Geert Booij and Jaap van Marle 71–96. Dordrecht: Kluwer.

# 7

# Declarative Deponency:
# A Network Morphology Account of
# Morphological Mismatches

ANDREW HIPPISLEY

## 1. Introduction

IN THE FIRST CHAPTER WE WERE PRESENTED with a working definition of
deponency which is based on the facts of deponent verbs in Latin (Baerman,
this volume). The definition was then extended in various directions to show
that morphological mismatches in languages besides Latin can be thought of
as instances of 'extended' deponency. Implicit in the basic definition and
its extensions is the notion of defaults and overrides. Thus if we think of
Baerman's basic definition in terms of properties, the primary property is that
the *default* association between form and function is *overridden*. Once the
mismatch has been identified, another property is that all morphosyntactic
cells in the paradigm are involved in the mismatch in the same way. This
property can be viewed as a 'second order' default: having established the
exceptional phenomenon, we can state its typical behaviour. But this second
order default can also be overridden. For Greek there is no override: all cells
are involved in the mismatch (for Greek deponents see Lavidas and
Papangeli, this volume) However for Latin standard deponent verbs, a few
cells consistently override this default, i.e. they are the same cells for every
deponent verb (see Baerman's chapter, and discussion below). Again, we can
think of the consistency of the overrides in Latin as a third order default. We
can then characterize semi-deponents as items that override this default by
extending the set of morphosyntactic cells that do not participate in the mismatch. If these defaults concern the function, there is another (second order)
default which concerns the form, namely that the deponent form is identical
to the 'source' form. In Latin deponents the passive form used to realize
active morphosyntax is identical to the source passive morphology used to

*Proceedings of the British Academy* **145**, 145–173. © The British Academy 2007.

realize passive morphosyntax. Thinking about it this way then allows for the possibility of an override at this level. Mismatches in Archi nominal morphology provide an example of this. We might then expect the property of defectiveness discussed by Baerman to simply fall out from whether or not an item inherits this default: where it does, homonymous forms are avoided (defectiveness), where it overrides there are distinct forms (no defectiveness). We can recast these facts about the standard case of deponency and extended deponency, using Archi deponent nouns as an example of extended deponency, as various types and levels of defaults and overrides. From this analysis four deponency properties (DPs) naturally emerge. This is shown in Table 1.

From Table 1 we see that in Latin the mismatch involves voice features, whereas in Archi, our example of extended deponency, nominal number features are involved (DP1). All cells participate in the mismatch in Latin except for the present participle, the future participle, and the future infinitive; for semi-deponents even fewer cells participate in the mismatch; on the other hand, the mismatch in Archi involves all cells (DP2). Whereas Latin deponent forms are identical to the source forms, i.e. the passive form in a deponent is indistinguishable from a passive in a non-deponent, Archi behaves differently by maintaining a formal distinction between number subparadigms even in instances of deponency (DP3). Finally, Latin deponents are defective, whereas Archi deponents are not (DP4).

Corbett's account of extended deponency (this volume) implies a default situation, 'canonical inflection'; and overrides to the default, 'deviations from canonical inflection'. In this paper we take as the starting point the accounts

**Table 1.** Deponency properties (DPs) in terms of defaults and overrides

| Default | Default level | Override | Standard dep. (Latin) | Extended dep. (Archi) | DP |
|---|---|---|---|---|---|
| function ~ form | first order | function ~ form mismatch | *overrides* voice features | *overrides* number features | DP1 |
| function: all morphosyntactic cells involved | second order | subset of cells not involved | *overrides* 1.{pres. part.} {fut. infin.} {fut. part.} 2. more: semi-deponents | *inherits default* | DP2 |
| form: dep. form = source form | second order | non-identity between dep. and source forms | *inherits default* | *overrides* 1. heteroclisis 2. stem shape | DP3 |
| defective paradigm (entailed by DP3) | second order | not defective | *inherits default* | *overrides* formally distinct for number | DP4 |

of extended deponency by Baerman and Corbett, and aim to make explicit the role of defaults and overrides implicit in them. We do this by offering an account of Latin deponent verbs in Network Morphology, a declarative framework for writing default inheritance-based theories of the lexicon, and whose representation is underpinned by a formal semantics. We also offer an account of deponent nouns in Archi, a Nakh-Daghestanian, Lezgian language spoken in the Caucasus, as an example of extended deponency. In this way we show how the idea of extended deponency follows systematically from the starting point of a default-overrides approach to standard deponency. In section 2 we introduce the Network Morphology framework. We use part of our Network Morphology account of Latin regular verbs to illustrate the salient features of its formalism, the lexical knowledge representation language DATR (Evans and Gazdar 1996). Section 3 is then a detailed Network Morphology treatment of Latin deponent and semi-deponent verbs which recasts as a formal system of defaults and overrides the properties of deponency that Baerman draws together. Extended deponency as extension of this system is illustrated by a Network Morphology account of Archi deponent nouns (§ 4). Insights and conclusions stemming from these accounts are summarized in section 5.

# 2. The Formal Framework: Network Morphology

Network Morphology is a declarative framework that situates morphological facts in a network of information sharing nodes, thereby capturing the generalizations that can be made about morphology, while at the same time characterizing exceptionality. This is achieved by setting up hierarchies whose daughter nodes inherit non-monotonically, or by default, from their mothers. The broadest level of generalization stated at the dominating nodes may be overridden by intermediary nodes which themselves can express a narrower level of generalization. In this way Network Morphology provides a framework for uncovering systematicity behind prima facie irregular phenomena such as deponency, and teases apart 'true' exceptionality from semi-regularity. Network Morphology theories are expressed in DATR, a unification-based lexical knowledge representation language designed by Evans and Gazdar to support default and exceptional behaviour (Evans and Gazdar 1996). DATR defines networks by links typed by attribute paths through which information is inherited. Its interpretability comes from an explicit theory of inference, and an explicit declarative semantics. It is therefore computationally implementable, and a variety of interpreters exist for DATR theories (e.g. Cahill and Gazdar 1999: fn. 7). For the Network

Morphology framework, see Corbett and Fraser (1993); Evans, Brown, and
Corbett (2001); and Hippisley (2001) and the references there.

To illustrate, consider the small fragment of our Network Morphology
theory of Latin in (1a, b). It expresses generalizations about stem shapes for
a class of Latin 1st conjugation verbs. Note that the full Network
Morphology theory of Latin verbs and Archi nouns is available online
(Hippisley 2006a, b).

(1a)

```
CONJ_1:
    <stem theme> == ā
    <stem 1> == "<root>" <stem theme>
    <stem 2> == <stem 1> v
    <stem 3> == <stem 1> t.
```

Morphological facts are expressed as attribute paths linked to descriptors.
Facts are collected at nodes to express generalizations. In (1a) we have a node
which is labelled CONJ_1, which contains four facts. The first fact (second
line) is that the theme vowel of this conjugation is a long /a/. This is represented by linking the attribute path <stem theme> to the atomic value ā via
the inference symbol ==. The second fact is about the formation of the first
stem (or 'stem 1') in this conjugation. The descriptor is not an atom, rather a
series of attribute paths; this expresses that the value for <stem 1> will be
the concatenation of the values of the paths <root> and <stem theme>.
Descriptors can also be a combination of attribute paths and atoms, as in the
cases of <stem 2> and <stem 3>. As the first conjugation is the most productive one, we can think of it as the 'default' conjugation. In (1b) we have
the daughter node CONJ_4. Its hierarchical relationship with CONJ_1 is
expressed by an empty path linked to the node CONJ_1, representing the
(default) inheritance of all facts from that node. As DATR defines default
inheritance networks, facts from the mother node may be overridden simply
by specifying them. (1b) shows that CONJ_4 is identical to CONJ_1 in every
regard except for the value of the theme vowel, and the addition of a fact
about the first stem.

(1b)

```
CONJ_4:
    <> == CONJ_1
    <stem theme> == ī
    <stem 1 ext> == <stem 1> ē.
```

We should also note that paths as descriptors may express inheritance of
a value both from the local context, i.e. found at the node where it is situated,
and the global context. Global inheritance is expressed by quoting the path.
In (1a) part of the value of <stem 2> is the value of a path locally declared,

<stem 1>. But the evaluation of <stem 1> depends partly on the quoted path "<root>", and this path is not available at the CONJ_1 node. Its global context is the node representing the query lexical entry. In (2) we give the example of the lexical entry for *amō* 'love', to which we give the perspicuous label Amo. Note that DATR requires that all nodes have an initial uppercase character, and that atoms must always be lower case. As the path <root> is declared at the lexical entry node, its value am can be inherited by the path <stem 1> at the CONJ_1 node.

(2)

    Amo:
        <> == VERB
        <gloss> == love
        <root> == am
        <stem> == CONJ_1.

DATR also supports orthogonal multiple inheritance, i.e. values of paths can be inherited from more than one node. In (2) we see that the primary source of inheritance is from the node VERB, representing the lexical entry's word class membership, and that the conjugation class node is a secondary source of inheritance, orthogonal to the principal source. This allows for more flexibility in the distribution of morphological facts. They can belong to orthogonally related hierarchies, within a single network. (2) shows that in our Network Morphology theory of Latin we have (at least) a hierarchy for word classes, and a separate hierarchy for stem formation facts.

The final point to make concerns DATR's principle of default inference which enables it to define default inheritance networks. It is based on the fact that any path which is an extension of another path receives the same definition as the path it extends, unless otherwise stated. Put another way, by default a path implies any further specification of itself. From (1a, b) we can see that the conjugation class nodes specify an associated theme vowel. For example in CONJ_4 this is ī and for CONJ_1 it is ā. This value is inherited by a lexical entry by setting up a path <stem> that inherits from a conjugation class node. What is inherited is all paths that extend the subpath <stem>, including <stem theme>. In other words <stem> implies <stem 1>, <stem 2>, <stem 3> *and* <stem theme> (for theme vowel). This allows a lexical entry to pick up a natural class of facts collected at a node by identifying them with an attribute that is the leading subpath. The partial theorem of Amo is given in (3) and shows the value of its three stems, and its theme vowel. Note that theorems are the outputs of a DATR theory (description). Whereas theories employ a double equals (==) expressing inference, theorems are the result of making the inference, i.e. the evaluation, and employ single equals (=).

(3)

    Amo:<gloss> = love.
    Amo:<root> = am.
    Amo:<stem theme> = ā.
    Amo:<stem 1> = am ā.
    Amo:<stem 2> = am ā v.
    Amo:<stem 3> = am ā t.
    Amo:<syn active perfect past indicative sg 2> = am ā v istī.
    . . .

# 3. Defaults and Standard Deponency: A Network Morphology Account of Latin Deponent Verbs

We briefly recall the basic facts about Latin deponent verbs that our Network Morphology account must capture. The mismatch is between morphosyntactic voice and its formal expression, specifically *active* morphosyntactic features are realized by *passive* morphology. Second, deponent verbs are defective: there are no forms available for realizing passive categories. Third, certain of the active categories are not involved in the mismatch. For some of these, this is because there is no corresponding form in the passive paradigm: a mismatch is de facto impossible. But this does not result in a gap in a deponent's paradigm since suitable active forms are used in these instances. However for one category, the future infinitive, the active is used even though there is a passive form available. Fourth, a consequence of the mismatch involves the addition of a morphosyntactic category that is generally absent because there is no morphological form to realize it. This is the active perfect past participle, realized by the passive perfect past participle form. Fifth, verbs may be semi-deponents: part of the paradigm involves a mismatch, and part is regular. Which part of the paradigm is deponent varies between verbs.

    We base our account on Baerman's report of Latin deponency (Baerman 2006), who in turn draws on Ernout and Thomas (1953), Flobert (1975), and Kühner (1955). The theorem is validated by checking against the Kennedy Latin primer (Kennedy 1962). We begin by discussing our formal treatment of the verb system to capture generalizations that can be stated over regular verbs. We are then in a position to express deponent verbs as overrides to a high level default on the one hand, and as a class with it own default properties on the other.

### 3.1. The Latin verbal system: a Network Morphology account

We follow Aronoff's (1992) analysis of the four Latin verb conjugations as a function of one of four theme vowels available to build a Latin stem. For the realization of a given morphosyntactic category, the theme vowel is used to imply the correct combination of stem type, stem shape, and the inflectional suffix. Stem types, or indexed stems, are argued for in Aronoff (1994) and are assumed in formal theories of morphology, e.g. Network Morphology (see Hippisley 1998, 2001 and Brown 1998 for Network Morphology accounts of Russian using indexed stems) and Paradigm Function Morphology (Stump 2001).

All verbs inherit ultimately from the node VERB, shown in (4). This node holds the generalization that syntactic features by default correspond to morphological features. The DATR theory expresses how these morphosyntactic features are realized as the combination of a (global) stem path and atomic value, as we will show. The VERB node also contains the generalization that the primary division of the verbal paradigm is in terms of voice. This is expressed by the attribute ordering of paths: the first feature attribute is either active or passive. The path is then extended at active and passive formation nodes, where it is passed on appropriately for further extensions until the full path inherits a value. This allows us to capture the first property of Latin deponents, that the mismatch involves voice (Deponency Property 1, Table 1).

(4)

  VERB:
    &lt;syn&gt; == "&lt;mor&gt;"
    &lt;mor active&gt; == ACT_FORMS:&lt;&gt;
    &lt;mor passive&gt; == PASS_FORMS:&lt;&gt;.

The secondary division of the paradigm is along aspectual lines. Formally this means that attributes expressing aspect features are ordered after those expressing voice features. As we shall see this enables us to capture the fact that semi-deponents are really verbs that are deponent in only one aspect (Deponency Property 2, Table 1). This is formalized in (5a, b).

(5a)

  ACT_FORMS:
    &lt;imperfective&gt; == ACT_IMPF:&lt;&gt;
    &lt;perfect&gt; == ACT_PERF:&lt;&gt;.

(5b)

  PASS_FORMS:
    &lt;imperfective&gt; == PASS_IMPF:&lt;&gt;
    &lt;perfect&gt; == PASS_PERF:&lt;&gt;.

The next division is according to tense; formally an attribute representing a tense feature follows the aspect attribute. This is followed by a mood attribute, then number attribute, and finally person attribute. We illustrate this ordering for the fully specified path <mor active perfective past indicative sg 2> with the nodes in (6). Note that the path <plus> in (6a) expresses the pluperfect tense feature in Latin.

(6a)

    ACT_PERF:
        <past> == ACT_PAST_PERFECT:<>
        <future> == ACT_FUTURE_PERFECT:<>
        <plus> == ACT_PLU_PERFECT:<>.

(6b)

    ACT_PAST_PERFECT:
        <indicative sg 1> == "<stem 2>"ī
        <indicative sg 2> == "<stem 2>"istī
        <indicative sg 3> == "<stem 2>"it
        <subjunctive sg 1> == "<stem 2>"erim
        <subjunctive sg 2> == "<stem 2>"erīs
        <subjunctive sg 3> == "<stem 2>"erit
        <infinitive> == "<stem 2>"isse.

As with all Network Morphology theories, our theory of Latin verbs takes an inferential-realizational approach (Stump 2001). The function is realized as a modification of the stem. Formally this is expressed as the path <mor active perfective past indicative sg 2> inheriting the complex value of (a) the value of the path <stem 2> and (b) the atom istī. We also assume that a lexical entry can have more than one modifiable stem. In this case what is being modified is the value of a path labelled 'stem 2' that is retrievable from the lexical entry being queried; this is what is expressed by the double quotes (see discussion about global inheritance in the previous section). There are (typically) three stems which are used to realize the full set of morphosyntactic features, and the shape of the three stems is generalizable. We capture this using nodes to hold the generalizations and then allowing lexical entries to inherit from them. There is an association between stem shape and conjugation class, and to preserve this association we label the stem formation nodes after the four conjugation classes used in traditional analyses of Latin verbs. These are shown in (7), and were partially discussed in section 2.

(7a)

    CONJ_1:
        <stem theme> == ā
        <stem 1> == "<root>"<stem theme>
        <stem 2> == <stem 1> v
        <stem 3> == <stem 1> t.

(7b)

    CONJ_2:
        <> == CONJ_1
        <stem theme> == ē
        <stem 2> == "<root>" u
        <stem 3> == "<root>" it.

(7c)

    CONJ_3:
        <> == CONJ_1
        <stem theme> == e
        <stem 2> == "<root>" s
        <stem 3> == "<root>" t
        <stem 1 alt> == "<root>" i.

(7d)

    CONJ_4:
        <> == CONJ_1
        <stem theme> == ī
        <stem 1 ext> == <stem 1> ē.

From (7a–d) we can see that each conjugation class node also specifies an associated theme vowel. For example in Conjugation 2 (7b) this is /ē/. The value of the theme vowel for a lexical entry is expressed as the value of a path that extends <stem>, and is used for determining the shape of stem 1 (see section 2). The partial theorem of Amo is given in (8) and shows the value of its three stems, and the realization of the morphosyntactic category 'active perfective past indicative 2nd person singular'.

(8)

    Amo:<gloss> = love.
    Amo:<root> = am.
    Amo:<stem 1> = am ā.
    Amo:<stem 2> = am ā v.
    Amo:<stem 3> = am ā t.
    Amo:<syn active perfect past indicative sg 2> = am ā v istī.
    . . .

We follow Aronoff (1992) in using the theme vowel, the value of the path <stem theme>, not only to build stems but also to determine stem type and inflectional marker combinations when they differ amongst conjugations for a given feature. For example, for the active imperfective future, one set of desinences is attached to Stem 1 for Conjugations 1 and 2, and another set of desinences is attached directly to the root for Conjugation 3 and to Stem 1 for Conjugation 4. This is shown in the partial theorems of four verbs each belonging to one of the four Conjugations. (9a) is a Conjugation 1 verb, (9b) belongs to Conjugation 2, (9c) Conjugation 3, and (9d) Conjugation 4.

(9a)

> Amo:<gloss> = love.
> Amo:<root> = am.
> Amo:<stem 1> = am ā.
> Amo:<syn active imperfective future indicative sg 1> = am ā bō.
> Amo:<syn active imperfective future indicative sg 2> = am ā bis.
> Amo:<syn active imperfective future indicative sg 3> = am ā bit.
> . . .

(9b)

> Moneo:<gloss> = advise.
> Moneo:<root> = mon.
> Moneo:<stem 1> = mon ē.
> Moneo:<syn active imperfective future indicative sg 1> = mon ē bō.
> Moneo:<syn active imperfective future indicative sg 2> = mon ē bis.
> Moneo:<syn active imperfective future indicative sg 3> = mon ē bit.
> . . .

(9c)

> Rego:<gloss> = rule.
> Rego:<root> = reg.
> Rego:<syn active imperfective future indicative sg 1> = reg am.
> Rego:<syn active imperfective future indicative sg 2> = reg ēs.
> Rego:<syn active imperfective future indicative sg 3> = reg et.
> . . .

(9d)

> Audio:<gloss> = hear.
> Audio:<root> = aud.
> Audio:<stem 1> = aud ī.
> Audio:<syn active imperfective future indicative sg 1> = aud ī am.
> Audio:<syn active imperfective future indicative sg 2> = aud ī ēs.
> Audio:<syn active imperfective future indicative sg 3> = aud ī et.
> . . .

The theory for this is given in (10) where (10a) show that evaluation is based on the theme vowel of the lexical entry being queried: <"<stem theme>">. It should be made clear that for the realization of most categories there is no conjugation distinction if a stem indexing approach is taken. In other words, the conjugational distinctions in the formation of the various stem types allow us to make a general statement about stem type and desinence as the spell-out for most categories, which is inherited by default by (regular) verbs of any class. The way we express the realization of 'active perfective past indicative 2nd person singular' in (5) and (6) above is how we are able to handle most of the categories.

(10a)

    ACT_IMPF_FUT:
        \<indicative\> == ACT_IMPF_FUT_INDIC:\<"\<stem theme\>"\>
        \<infinitive\> == "\<mor active imperfective future participle\>" esse
        \<participle\> == "\<stem 3\>" ūrus.

(10b)

    ACT_IMPF_FUT_INDIC:
        \<ā\> == TYPE_1_ACT_FUT_INDIC:\<\>
        \<e\> == TYPE_2_ACT_FUT_INDIC:\<\>
        \<ī\> == TYPE_3_ACT_FUT_INDIC:\<\>
        \<ē\> == \<ā\>.

(10c)

    TYPE_1_ACT_FUT_INDIC:
        \<sg 1\> == "\<stem 1\>" bō
        \<sg 2\> == "\<stem 1\>" bis
        \<sg 3\> == "\<stem 1\>" bit.

(10d)

    TYPE_2_ACT_FUT_INDIC:
        \<sg 1\> == "\<root\>" am
        \<sg 2\> == "\<root\>" ēs
        \<sg 3\> == "\<root\>" et.

(10e)

    TYPE_3_ACT_FUT_INDIC:
        \<sg 1\> == "\<stem 1\>" am
        \<sg 2\> == "\<stem 1\>" ēs
        \<sg 3\> == "\<stem 1\>" et.

To end this preliminary section on our theory of the Latin verbal system, we should briefly note that where possible we capture cases of directional syncretism as path referrals, in the spirit of Network Morphology (see Baerman, Brown, and Corbett 2005: ch. 5). For example, in (10a) the active imperfective future infinitive is partially realized by the active imperfective future participle. In (11a) we show how we capture the fact that for all verbs the active future perfect indicative is syncretic with the active perfect past subjunctive. (11c) shows the identities in form in the theorem for the Conjugation 2 verb *moneō* 'advise'.

(11a)

    ACT_FUTURE_PERFECT:
        \<indicative sg 1\> == "\<stem 2\>" erō

&lt;indicative sg 2&gt; == "&lt;mor active perfect past subjunctive sg 2&gt;"
&lt;indicative sg 3&gt; == "&lt;mor active perfect past subjunctive sg 3&gt;".

(11b)

    ACT_PERF:
        &lt;past&gt; == ACT_PAST_PERFECT:&lt;&gt;
        . . .

    ACT_PAST_PERFECT:
        &lt;subjunctive sg 1&gt; == "&lt;stem 2&gt;" erim
        &lt;subjunctive sg 2&gt; == "&lt;stem 2&gt;" erīs
        &lt;subjunctive sg 3&gt; == "&lt;stem 2&gt;" erit
        . . .

(11c)

    Moneo:&lt;gloss&gt; = advise.
    Moneo:&lt;root&gt; = mon.
    Moneo:&lt;stem 1&gt; = mon ē.
    Moneo:&lt;stem 2&gt; = mon u.
    Moneo:&lt;stem 3&gt; = mon it.
    Moneo:&lt;syn active perfect past subjunctive sg 1&gt; = mon u erim.
    Moneo:&lt;syn active perfect past subjunctive sg 2&gt; = mon u erīs.
    Moneo:&lt;syn active perfect past subjunctive sg 3&gt; = mon u erit.
    Moneo:&lt;syn active perfect future indicative sg 1&gt; = mon u erō.
    Moneo:&lt;syn active perfect future indicative sg 2&gt; = mon u erīs.
    Moneo:&lt;syn active perfect future indicative sg 3&gt; = mon u erit.
    . . .

Having laid out the main points of our Network Morphology account of the verb system, we can now turn to the defining characteristics of deponent verbs and express these formally as the properties of standard deponency as outlined in Table 1 in section 1.

### 3.2. Deponency Property 1: overriding the function ~ form association

The primary characteristic of Latin deponent verbs is that they realize active morphosyntax with passive morphology. In terms of defaults and overrides, they override a first order default that active morphosyntax is realized by active morphology. This default has been formalized in (4) and (5a) above. Deponency Property 1 (DP1) is expressed as an equation at a deponency node from which deponent verbs inherit (12a).

(12a)

    DEPONENT:
        &lt;&gt; == VERB
        &lt;mor active&gt; == PASS_FORMS:&lt;&gt;
        . . .

(12b)

> PASS_FORMS:
>> <imperfective> == PASS_IMPF:<>
>> <perfect> == PASS_PERF:<>.

As deponency only involves a single feature, the voice feature, and not aspect, tense, mood, number, or person, and because in our theory of Latin verbs we have partitioned the paradigm according to voice, we can express deponency parsimoniously by referencing the path <mor active> referring to the node which handles passive morphology. This is because formally <mor active> is the leading subpath that implies all its extensions, e.g. <mor active perfect past indicative sg 2>, and hence gathers together the full set of active morphological features. All these fully specified paths are then evaluated at passive morphology nodes: from (12b) we see that an active imperfective will be evaluated at a passive imperfective node, and an active perfect at a passive perfective node. Note that by positing a special deponency node, we are capturing deponency as a set of second level defaults: the node overrides the broadest level default of function ~ form associations, but contains its own generalizations for the class of deponent verbs. In (13a) we have the lexical entry for the deponent verb *hortor* 'encourage'.

(13a)

> Hortor:
>> <> == DEPONENT
>> <gloss> == encourage
>> <root> == hort
>> <stem> == CONJ_1.

Thus if we compare (13a) with the lexical entry for *amō* 'love' in (2) we see that the only difference between a lexical entry for a deponent verb and a regular verb is the main source of inheritance. Deponent verbs, just as regular verbs, have stem types and theme vowels which are specified by their conjugation class; they also inherit their own set of default facts. The partial theorem of Hortor is given in (13b), and this can be compared to the partial theorem of Amo in (13c). (Note that the lines in bold face will be discussed in § 3.3).

(13b)

> Hortor:<gloss> = encourage.
> Hortor:<root> = hort.
> Hortor:<stem 1> = hort ā.
> Hortor:<stem 2> = hort ā v.
> Hortor:<stem 3> = hort ā t.
> Hortor:<syn active imperfective present indicative sg 2> = hort ā ris.
> Hortor:<syn active imperfective present indicative sg 3> = hort ā tur.

Hortor:<syn active imperfective present infinitive> = hort ā rī.
**Hortor:<syn active imperfective present participle> = hort ā ns.**
**Hortor:<syn active imperfective future infinitive> = hort ā t ūrus esse.**
**Hortor:<syn active imperfective future participle> = hort ā t ūrus.**
Hortor:<syn active perfect past indicative sg 2> = hort ā t us es.
Hortor:<syn active perfect past indicative sg 3> = hort ā t us est.
Hortor:<syn active perfect past participle> = hort ā t us.
. . .

(13c)

Amo:<gloss> = love.
Amo:<root> = am.
Amo:<stem 1> = am ā.
Amo:<stem 2> = am ā v.
Amo:<stem 3> = am ā t.
Amo:<syn active imperfective present indicative sg 2> = am ā s.
Amo:<syn active imperfective present indicative sg 3> = am ā t.
Amo:<syn active imperfective present infinitive> = am ā re.
**Amo:<syn active imperfective present participle> = am ā ns.**
**Amo:<syn active imperfective future infinitive> = am ā t ūrus esse.**
**Amo:<syn active imperfective future participle> = am ā t ūrus.**
Amo:<syn active perfect past indicative sg 2> = am ā v istī.
Amo:<syn active perfect past indicative sg 3> = am ā v it.
. . .

The theorem clearly shows the mismatch between syntactic active function and passive morphology. Recall from the introduction to section 2 that Network Morphology theories aim to uncover systematicity behind irregular phenomena such as deponency. DP1 is expressed as an override of a default, but this override is situated at a node from which lexical entries such as the one for *hortor* inherit. In this way we can express deponency itself as having default properties for a class of items.

### 3.3. Deponency Property 2: cells involved in the mismatch

Once we have established that there is a mismatch (DP1) we could assume that all cells of the paradigm are involved in the mismatch, and view this as a second order default: a default about the behaviour of the exceptional phenomenon. The inheritance or overriding of this default characterizes Deponency Property 2. In standard deponency the default is overridden: three morphosyntactic categories do not participate in the mismatch. These can be clearly seen when we compare the theorem of deponent verb with a regular verb, as in (13b) and (13c). The categories in question are highlighted in boldface. For two of these, the imperfective present participle and the imperfective future participle, the mismatch is impossible because there are no passive equivalents in a verb's paradigm. Deponent verbs then default to active morphology for these categories, thereby avoiding gaps in the paradigm. This is captured by 'defaulting to active formation unless otherwise specified', and is represented in (14a) for the case of present participle (last equation), and in (14b) for the future participle.

(14a)

    PASS_IMPF_PRES:
        <indicative sg 2> == "<stem 1>" ris
        <indicative sg 3> == "<stem 1 alt>" tur
        <subjunctive> == PASS_PRES_SUBJ:<"<stem theme>">
        <imperative sg 2> == VERB:<mor active imperfective present infinitive>
        <imperative pl 2> == "<stem 1 alt>"minī
        <infinitive> == PASS_PRES_INF:<"<stem theme>">
        <> == ACT_IMPF_PRES.

(14b)

    PASS_IMPF_FUT:
        <indicative> == PASS_FUT_INDIC:<"<stem theme>">
        <infinitive> == "<stem 3>" um īrī
        <> == ACT_IMPF_FUT.

The empty path in the last lines of (14a) and (14b) expresses any extension of the subpath not defined at the node; this is referred to an equivalent active formation node for its value. In (14b) this will be the (future) participle as the indicative and infinitive are defined, and there are no active future imperative or subjunctive categories. And in (14a) this will be the (present) participle as it is the only feature not defined at the node. However, (14b) shows quite clearly that there is in Latin a passive future infinitive form, and we see it in the theorem of Amo in (13c). Despite its availability, for deponent verb Hortor the active form is used, *hortātūrus esse* (compare Amo's theorem). In this case we have a category not involved in the mismatch when the equivalent passive form is available. This is a stipulation we must therefore make for deponent verbs, and *is* expressed at the Deponent node, a more complete version of which is now given in (15).

(15)

    DEPONENT:
        <> == VERB
        <mor active> == PASS_FORMS:<>
        <mor active imperfective future infinitive> == VERB
        <syn active perfect past participle> ==
            VERB:<mor passive perfect past participle>
        . . .

We could think of this as a 'true' overriding of the second order default, whereas the other two categories override by virtue of the inheritance of another default, i.e. use active morphology in the absence of passive morphology. We noted in section 1 that DP2 is different for Greek in that it inherits the default that the mismatch will involve all cells. This can now be explained in terms of the availability of mediopassive morphology: the same set of active features is present for the mediopassive. Alongside this fact about Greek regular morphology is the fact that the deponent verbs do not stipulate non-participation in the mismatch of a particular category. This means that the statement <mor active> == MEDIO_PASSIVE_FORMS:<> would suffice to account for the mismatch in Greek.

While there are two categories in the active paradigm which are missing in the passive paradigm, there is one category in the passive missing from the active. This is the perfect past participle. This means that as a consequence of a mismatch with passive morphology, deponent verbs are able to realize a category that cannot be realized for regular verbs, namely the active past participle. Latin has a form for passive past participle, which is used. This is expressed as a syntactic function in (15), where the leading subpath is <syn>, inheriting from a passive form, where the leading subpath is <mor>. Since this is the only place where the extension of this <syn> path is specified, the absence of morphology for this function for non-deponent verbs results in it not appearing in their theorems.

### 3.3.1. Deponency Property 2 and semi-deponent verbs

For semi-deponent verbs it is not just a few cells that are not involved in the mismatch, but half the paradigm. Semi-deponents can therefore be seen as one extreme of Deponency Property 2. The division of the paradigm could be seen as being one of aspect. Another view is to see the division based on Stem 2 forms, but as they only involve realization of perfect categories (in the active), it makes no additional claim: in either case the perfect is involved. This is different to Archi, for example, where the deponency is a function of the stem types as we shall see in section 4. To illustrate we show the theory for the verb *audeō* 'dare', which is deponent for perfective morphosyntax, and regular for imperfective features, and the verb *revertor* 'return' which is the converse: it is deponent for imperfective morphosyntactic features, and regular for perfective. (16a) and (16b) give the nodes that express generalizations about these two types of semi-deponent verb. It should be noted that semi-deponents traditionally refer to what I call Perfect Deponent, and what I call Imperfect Deponent is discussed as allied phenomena.

(16a)

    PERFECT_DEPONENT:
        <> == DEPONENT
        <mor active imperfective> == VERB.

(16b)

> IMPF_DEPONENT:
>     <> == DEPONENT
>     <mor active perfect> == VERB.

The node in (16a) expresses that deponency properties are inherited by default, except that the active imperfective forms override the generalization that their values are those of passive forms; instead they behave like any other verb. (16b) is the converse: this time active perfect forms override the mismatching generalization stated at the Deponent node. This analysis makes the claim that semi-deponency is a type of deponent verb, with some overrides. The lexical entry for perfect deponent *audeō* 'dare' and its partial theorem is given in (17a, b).

(17a)

> Audeo:
>     <> == PERFECT_DEPONENT
>     <gloss> == dare
>     <root> == aud
>     <stem 3> == aus
>     <stem> == CONJ_2.

(17b)

> Audeo:<gloss> = dare.
> Audeo:<root> = aud.
> Audeo:<stem 1> = aud ē.
> Audeo:<stem 2> = aud u.
> Audeo:<stem 3> = aus.
> Audeo:<syn active imperfective present indicative sg 2> = aud ē s.
> Audeo:<syn active imperfective present indicative sg 3> = aud ē t.
> Audeo:<syn active imperfective present infinitive> = aud ē re.
> Audeo:<syn active imperfective present participle> = aud ē ns.
> Audeo:<syn active imperfective future infinitive> = aus ūrus esse.
> Audeo:<syn active imperfective future participle> = aus ūrus.
> Audeo:<syn active perfect past indicative sg 2> = aus us es.
> Audeo:<syn active perfect past indicative sg 3> = aus us est.
> Audeo:<syn active perfect past participle> = aus us.
>     . . .

For the imperfect deponent verb *revertor*, only the imperfective cells are involved in the mismatch. At the same time, we have seen that a higher level default for deponent verbs states that three imperfective categories are not involved (Deponency Property 3). As *revertor* is expressed as a type of deponent verb, it inherits this default with the result that it has even fewer deponent forms than a semi-deponent verb like *audeō*. In other words, it displays an extreme version of the Deponency Property 3 default, that all cells are involved in the mismatch, by overriding it for the majority of cells. In addition, Revertor inherits a syntactic active perfect past participle, spelled out as a passive form: *reversus*. This is possible despite Revertor's perfect subparadigm not being involved in the mismatch because realization of a syntactic active perfect past participle is a fact stated at the node Deponency.

(18a)

    Revertor:
           <> == IMPF_DEPONENT
           <gloss> == return
           <root> == revert
           <stem 2> == <root>
           <stem 3> == <root> s
           <stem> == CONJ_3.

(18b)

           Revertor:<gloss> = return.
           Revertor:<root> = revert.
           Revertor:<stem 1> = revert e.
           Revertor:<stem 2> = revert.
           Revertor:<stem 3> = revert s.[†]
           Revertor:<syn active imperfective present indicative sg 2> = revert e ris.
           Revertor:<syn active imperfective present indicative sg 3> = revert i tur.
           Revertor:<syn active imperfective present infinitive> = revert ī.
           **Revertor:<syn active imperfective present participle> = revert e ns.**
           **Revertor:<syn active imperfective future infinitive> = revert s ūrus esse.**
           **Revertor:<syn active imperfective future participle> = revert s ūrus.**
           Revertor:<syn active perfect past indicative sg 1> = revert ī.
           Revertor:<syn active perfect past indicative sg 2> = revert istī.
           Revertor:<syn active perfect past indicative sg 3> = revert it.
           Revertor:<syn active perfect past participle> = revert s us.[†]

      ...

[†] Surface form *reversus*.

### 3.4 Deponency Properties 3 and 4: defectiveness

In our theory defectiveness is captured by adding a fact at the deponency node, as shown in (19). Here the path <mor passive> implies all its extensions, the full set of passive features, and is assigned the value undefined.

(19)

    DEPONENT:
           <> == VERB
           <mor active> == PASS_FORMS:<>
           <mor active imperfective future infinitive> == VERB

<syn active perfect past participle> == VERB:<mor passive perfect past participle>
<mor passive> == undefined.

As indicated in Table 1, however, defectiveness should really be seen as a natural consequence of inheriting another default. Once we have established that there is a mismatch in function and form, we can make generalizations about the function, outlined as Deponency Property 2 in Table 1, and generalizations about the form, outlined as Deponency Property 3 (Table 1). The form type of generalization is that the deponent form is non-distinct from the source form. This can be stated as a second order default, and in standard deponency (Latin) it is not overridden. This default is bound in with the way the first order default, namely that active inherits passive morphology, is expressed (12a, b). We can see this by comparing the deponent active forms for *hortor* in (13b) with the passive forms of the regular verb *amō* in (20)

(20)

Amo:<gloss> = love.
Amo:<root> = am.
Amo:<stem 1> = am ā
Amo:<stem 2> = am ā v.
Amo:<stem 3> = am ā t.
Amo:<syn passive imperfective present indicative sg 2> = am ā ris.
Amo:<syn passive imperfective present indicative sg 3> = am ā tur.
Amo:<syn passive imperfective present infinitive> = am ā rī.
Amo:<syn passive imperfective future infinitive> = am ā t um īrī.
Amo:<syn passive perfect past indicative sg 2> = am ā t us es.
Amo:<syn passive perfect past indicative sg 3> = am ā t us est.
Amo:<syn passive perfect past participle> = am ā t us.
. . .

# 4. Defaults and Extended Deponency: A Network Morphology Account of Archi Deponent Nouns

Archi deponent nouns involve the mismatch between morphosyntactic number and its formal expression. This is an example of extended deponency because it displays Deponency Property 1, i.e. that the default function ~ form association is being overridden, but this override extends beyond voice features. It also displays Deponency Property 2, but again in the 'extended' sense: it inherits the second level default that all morphosyntactic cells are involved in the mismatch, unlike Latin. For Deponency Property 4, rather than inheriting the default of defective paradigms it overrides with non-defectiveness. This is entailed by displaying Deponency Property 3 in the extended sense: unlike Latin there is a distinction between the deponent forms, used to express one number, and the source forms, used to express the other number. The distinction is by virtue of heteroclisis. But it is also due to the fact that Archi nouns may have a version of the root associated with a particular number, seen in cases of weak and strong suppletion. In this event, there is no mismatch between morphosyntactic number and its formal expression at the level of the root, even in a deponent noun.

In this section we present our Network Morphology account of the Archi noun system as an example of a formal defaults-overrides account of extended deponency. The analysis of the Archi data is taken from Baerman (2006b) which in turn draws on Kibrik (1977a; 1977b).

### 4.1 The Archi nominal system: a Network Morphology account

Archi nouns have distinct singular and plural stems on which are built the case inflectional markers. Number distinctions are therefore expressed by the stem. Oblique case markers are based on the ergative word-form. There are no inflectional classes as such: all nouns that can inflect for a morphosyntactic feature inflect in the same way. However there are three main stem formation classes that provide suitable number distinguishing stems for inflection. Regardless of class, by default the absolute singular form is based directly on the root. Where a noun has a distinct root for all plural forms, i.e. in weak and strong suppleting nouns, the absolute singular is formed on the singular root. For some nouns there is a distinct root used for the absolute singular. These facts about Archi are formalized in (21) to (24) below. In (21) we express the default dependence of a morphological word-form on the lexeme's stem, and in this way formalize number marking through the stem. This is because the path <mor> implies any extension of itself, as does the path <stem>. This expresses the fact that, for example, the path <mor sg> takes as its value the value of the path <stem sg>. The implication is that all singular word forms, regardless of case, will begin with a singular stem. The quotes indicate global inheritance expressing that <stem> and its extensions, <stem sg> and <stem pl> and as we shall see later <stem sg erg>, are retrieved from the lexical entry being queried. Finally, the 'exception' is the absolute singular which is formed directly on a root form: in the case of some items, on the bare root, for others a special form of the root used in the singular only, and for others a special root used for the absolute singular only. These three possibilities correspond to the subpath <root>, its extension <root sg> and its further extension <root sg abs>. Again, the quotes indicate that the path is lexically specified.

(21)

> NOUN:
> > \<mor> == "\<stem>"
> > \<mor sg abs> == "\<root sg abs>".

With respect to the formation of the absolutive and ergative, Archi can be said to have three major noun classes. These generalize the formation of the stem when it combines with inflections to express the full set of morphosyntactic features. One class is for lexemes with consonant final roots, which we call Class 1. Another is for lexemes with vowel final roots (Class 2). There is also a special class for substantivized adjectives, and these lexemes have frozen gender markers (Class 3). The three stem formation classes are given in (22) and (23) below. In (22a) the first class, Class 1, inherits facts about nouns, including those discussed above, and specifies singular and plural stem building generalizations. The singular stem is based on the lexically specified ergative root, in those instances where this is distinct, and the plural on a plural root, again in instances where there is a distinction in the roots, to which is added the formative *-mul-*.

(22a)

> CLASS_1:
> > \<> == NOUN
> > \<stem sg> == "\<root sg erg>" CLASS_1_SG:\<>
> > \<stem pl> == "\<root pl>" mul CLASS_1_PL:\<>.

For singular stem formation, referral is made to a special node (22b) where by default the formative *-li-* is added to the root, and then case endings are picked up at a separate node (discussed below). However, for the absolutive nothing is added to the root, and no reference is made to inflectional material to mark case ending.

(22b)

> CLASS_1_SG:
> > \<> == li NOUN_FORMS:\<>
> > \<abs> == .

Plural stem formation is expressed similarly with the important difference that the formative *-čaj-* is added to all stems; the exception is the absolutive marker which is zero (22c).

(22c)

> CLASS_1_PL:
> > \<> == čaj NOUN_FORMS:\<>
> > \<abs> == .

Singular and plural stem formation operates differently in the other two classes, and this is shown in (23). Note that Class 2 operates in the same way as Class 1 for singular stem formation, and this is expressed by using the empty path.

(23)

```
CLASS_2:
    <> == CLASS_1
    <stem pl> == "<root pl>"CLASS_2_PL:<>.
CLASS_2_PL:
    <> == t:aj NOUN_FORMS:<>
    <abs> == t:u.
CLASS_3:
    <> == NOUN
    <stem sg> == "<root sg erg>"CLASS_3_SG:<>
    <stem pl> == "<root pl>"CLASS_3_PL:<>.
CLASS_3_SG:
    <> == mu NOUN_FORMS:<>.
CLASS_3_PL:
    <> == maj NOUN_FORMS:<>
    <abs> == .
```

Each stem is ultimately referred to a list of case features and corresponding inflections, shown in (24). As word-forms are based on the ergative word-form, the ergative receives no additional marker.

(24)

```
NOUN_FORMS:
    <erg> ==
    <gen> == n
    <dat> == s
    <comit> == ɬ:u
    <comp> == xur
    <perm> == kɬ'əna
    <part> == qˤiš
    <superlat> == t:ik
    <sublat> == kɬ'ak.
```

Having provided a formal account of the noun system, we can now show how lexical entries inherit these facts. Lexical entries are represented as nodes which are labelled to indicate the lexeme being represented. Each lexical entry is furnished with a root. For some, a special version of the root is used for building the oblique singular stems and another for building plural stems. This is true for *kɬ'ánnu* 'lover'. Lexical entries inherit from one of the three stem formation classes. This is shown in (25a–c).[1]

---

[1] Note that accented characters as title-case in nodes names cannot be expressed in DATR and are used here purely for exposition

(25a)

    Árum:

        <> == CLASS_1
        <gloss> == sickle
        <root> == áˤrum .

(25b)

    Aˤri:

        <> == CLASS_2
        <gloss> == military division
        <root> == áˤri.

(25c)

    Kɬ'ánnu:

        <> == CLASS_3
        <gloss> == lover
        <root> == kɬ'ánnu
        <root sg erg> == <root> m
        <root pl> == kɬ'ánnib.

## 4.2 Extended deponency in Archi

The mismatch between morphosyntactic feature and formal expression involves number. The formal part of the mismatch lies at the level of the stem. In other words the mismatch is between stem shape and the number feature normally identified with it. The word *xali* 'family' is a deponent noun whose singular morphosyntax is realized by what appear to be plural forms. So the dative singular is *xal-majs* which is formally similar to Class 3 plural nouns, such as *kɬ'ánnib-majs* (DAT. PL.) 'lovers'. This is clear evidence that the first level default is being overridden, the function ~ form association. As it does not involve voice features, it is an extended version of DP1. At the same time, every cell in the paradigm is involved in the mismatch. In other words, it inherits the default associated with DP2, and so displays an extended version of DP2. An interesting feature of Archi deponency is that there are no defective paradigms, as with Latin. While a noun may have a deponent plural form with singular meaning, it also has a full subparadigm of plural forms with plural meaning. This is shown in the theorem of the lexical entry for *xali* generated by our Network Morphology theory of Archi.[2]

(26)

    Xali:<gloss> = family.
    Xali:<mor sg abs> = xali.

---

[2] The theory does not take into account the regular /aj/ ~ /e/ alternation before a consonant.

Xali:<mor sg erg> = xal maj.
Xali:<mor sg gen> = xal maj n.
Xali:<mor sg dat> = xal maj s.
Xali:<mor sg comit> = xal maj ɬ:u.
Xali:<mor sg comp> = xal maj xur.
Xali:<mor sg perm> = xal maj kɬ'əna.
Xali:<mor sg part> = xal maj qˤiš.
Xali:<mor sg superlat> = xal maj t:ik.
Xali:<mor sg sublat> = xal maj kɬ'ak.
Xali:<mor pl abs> = xali t:u.
Xali:<mor pl erg> = xali t:aj.
Xali:<mor pl gen> = xali t:aj n.
Xali:<mor pl dat> = xali t:aj s.
Xali:<mor pl comit> = xali t:aj ɬ:u.
Xali:<mor pl comp> = xali t:aj xur.
Xali:<mor pl perm> = xali t:aj kɬ'əna.
Xali:<mor pl part> = xali t:aj qˤiš.
Xali:<mor pl superlat> = xali t:aj t:ik.
Xali:<mor pl sublat> = xali t:aj kɬ'ak.

This is possible because the two subparadigms belong to different stem formation classes. In other words, in the case of Deponency Property 3, Archi
overrides the default that the deponent forms in a lexeme's paradigm are non-
distinct from the source forms in the same paradigm *by virtue* of heteroclisis.
The Network Morphology account of the deponent lexeme is given in (27).
The lexeme is a Class 3 noun the singular, and is treated as a Class 2 noun for
the plural (last two lines). We should also note that this lexical item has a distinct ergative singular root on which all singular forms apart from absolutive
singular are built. Examples where a distinct root is used for the entire
singular subparadigm are discussed in the next section.

(27)

Xali:
    <> == NOUN
    <gloss> == family
    <root> == xali
    <root sg erg> == xal
    <stem sg> == <root sg erg> CLASS_3_PL:<>
    <stem pl> == <root pl> CLASS_2_PL:<>.

### 4.3. Number marking maintained in the mismatch

We have seen how heteroclisis in deponent nouns is responsible for overriding the default that source and deponent forms are non-distinct. The subparadigms of deponent nouns are distinguished for another reason. In Archi
some nouns have more than one root form, i.e. forms which are not general-

izable by the stem formation classes. In other words these items are examples of suppleting lexemes. In such cases one version of the root is used for singular realizations, and the other for plural realizations. This is important for our next example of deponency in Archi, and to help illustrate it we can use the non-deponent suppletive noun for 'corner of a sack': *bič'ni* (ABS SG.) and *boždo* (ABS PL) (see Hippisley et al. 2004 for a fuller discussion of suppletion and paradigmatic organisation, including this Archi example). We express the distinction at the level of the lexeme, as shown in (28a) which is the lexical entry for *bič'ni* 'corner of a sack'. There is one form for the singular, the 'singular root', and one for the plural, 'plural root'. The theorem is shown in (28b).[3]

(28a)

    Bič'ni:
        <> == CLASS_1
        <gloss> == corner of sack
        <root sg> == bič'ni
        <root pl> == boždo
        <stem pl> == <root pl> CLASS_1_PL:<>.

(28b)

    Bič'ni:<gloss> = corner of sack.
    Bič'ni:<mor sg abs> = bič'ni.
    Bič'ni:<mor sg erg> = bič'ni li.
    Bič'ni:<mor sg gen> = bič'ni li n.
    Bič'ni:<mor sg dat> = bič'ni li s.
    Bič'ni:<mor sg comit> = bič'ni li ɬ:u.
    Bič'ni:<mor sg comp> = bič'ni li xur.
    Bič'ni:<mor sg perm> = bič'ni li kɬ'əna.
    Bič'ni:<mor sg part> = bič'ni li qˤiš.
    Bič'ni:<mor sg superlat> = bič'ni li t:ik.
    Bič'ni:<mor sg sublat> = bič'ni li kɬ'ak.
    Bič'ni:<mor pl abs> = boždo.
    Bič'ni:<mor pl erg> = boždo čaj.
    Bič'ni:<mor pl gen> = boždo čaj n.
    Bič'ni:<mor pl dat> = boždo čaj s.
    Bič'ni:<mor pl comit> = boždo čaj ɬ:u.
    Bič'ni:<mor pl comp> = boždo čaj xur.
    Bič'ni:<mor pl perm> = boždo čaj kɬ'əna.
    Bič'ni:<mor pl part> = boždo čaj qˤiš.

---

[3] In the plural there should be an epenthetic /r/ between the root final vowel and the initial consonant of the *-čaj-* formative, e.g. *boždorčaj* (PL, ERG) but this allomorphy is not lexical and is therefore not accounted for by the theory.

Bič'ni:<mor pl superlat> = boždo čaj t:ik.
Bič'ni:<mor pl sublat> = boždo čaj k+'ak.

There is one deponent noun which also has suppletive roots. The noun *xˤon*
'cow' has the suppletive root *buc:'i* used in realizations of plural morphosyntax. The lexical entry for this noun is given in (29a) with its theorem in (29b).

(29a)

Xˤon:
        <> == NOUN
        <gloss> == cow
        <root sg abs> == xˤon
        <root sg erg> == xˤini
        <root pl> == buc:'i
        <stem sg> == <root sg erg> NOUN_FORMS:<>
        <stem pl> == <root pl> CLASS_1_SG:<>.

(29b)

Xˤon:<gloss> = cow.
Xˤon:<mor sg abs> = xˤon.
Xˤon:<mor sg erg> = xˤini.
Xˤon:<mor sg gen> = xˤini n.
Xˤon:<mor sg dat> = xˤini s.
Xˤon:<mor sg comit> = xˤini +:u.
Xˤon:<mor sg comp> = xˤini xur.
Xˤon:<mor sg perm> = xˤini k+'əna.
Xˤon:<mor sg part> = xˤini qˤiš.
Xˤon:<mor sg superlat> = xˤini t:ik.
Xˤon:<mor sg sublat> = xˤini k+'ak.
Xˤon:<mor pl abs> = buc:'i.
Xˤon:<mor pl erg> = buc:'i li.
Xˤon:<mor pl gen> = buc:'i li n.
Xˤon:<mor pl dat> = buc:'i li s.
Xˤon:<mor pl comit> = buc:'i li +:u.
Xˤon:<mor pl comp> = buc:'i li xur.
Xˤon:<mor pl perm> = buc:'i li k+'əna.
Xˤon:<mor pl part> = buc:'i li qˤiš.
Xˤon:<mor pl superlat> = buc:'i li t:ik.
Xˤon:<mor pl sublat> = buc:'i li k+'ak.

The default associated with Deponency Property 3 rules out such examples:
source and deponent forms are non-distinct, therefore suppletion based on
the function involved in the mismatch is not possible. In Latin a verb cannot
be both deponent and suppletive. As this default is overridden in Archi any-
way due to heteroclisis, with the result that there are formally distinct subparadigms, suppletion is maintained even in deponent nouns. We should note
that for *xˤon* 'cow' the heteroclisis involves the singular subparadigm not

belonging to any of the three stem formation classes, and inheriting directly from a node generalizing over all nouns, but the plural belonging to Class 1. In sum, the extended version of Deponency Property 3 allows for deponent items to be suppletive. Another example of a deponent noun which is suppletive is *c'aj* 'goat' which has the suppletive root *c'ohor* for the plural. The lexical entry is given in (30), and expresses its suppletion, heteroclisis, and deponency behaviours.

(30)

    C'aj:
        <> == NOUN
        <gloss> == goat
        <root> == c'aj
        <root pl> == c'ohor
        <stem sg> == <root sg erg> CLASS_2_PL:<>
        <stem pl> == <root pl> CLASS_1_PL:<>.

# 5. Concluding Remarks

We have attempted to make explicit the role that defaults and overrides play in the notion 'extended deponency'. We have done this by recasting the characteristics of standard and extended deponency as sets of defaults and overrides operating at different levels of generalization, which we have then formalized within the declarative defaults-based framework of Network Morphology. We have presented Network Morphology accounts of standard deponency (Latin) and extended deponency (Archi). At the broadest level, deponency is a mismatch of function and form. We have expressed deponency as the overriding of a default operating at the highest level of generalization. We can then state two generalizations about deponent items: first, they involve all cells in the paradigm, and second within a deponent lexeme's paradigm the deponent forms are indistinguishable from the source forms. These two properties are expressed as second level defaults, defaults about deponent items themselves. Standard deponency and extended deponency can be characterized in the ways in which these secondary level defaults are inherited or overridden, and if overridden, the extent to which they are overridden. Semi-deponency is directly connected with the first of these second level defaults, that all cells participate in the mismatch, and is where an item overrides the default to the extent that half its paradigm is not involved in the mismatch. And defectiveness is directly connected to the second default: inheriting it leads to potential mass inflectional homonymy between two subparadigms, so one of the subparadigms is 'laid aside'. In our example of extended deponency, this default is overridden due to heteroclisis and the function (number) being expressed by the root. The result is the use of the deponent form for its source function. In this way we have shown how the definition of extended deponency is stateable in terms of defaults and overrides, allowing for the possibility of formal, computationally tractable accounts of deponency phenomena.

# References

Aronoff, Mark. 1992. Stems in Latin verbal morphology. *Morphology now*, ed. by Mark Aronoff, 5–32. New York: SUNY.

—— 1994. *Morphology by itself: stems and inflectional classes*. Cambridge, Mass.: MIT Press.

Baerman, Matthew. 2006a. Latin deponency language report. [Available at www.smg.surrey.ac.uk/deponency/Examples/Latin.htm].

—— 2006b. Archi deponency language report [Available at www.smg.surrey.ac.uk/deponency/Examples/Archi.htm]

—— This volume. Morphological typology of deponency.

Baerman, Matthew, Dunstan Brown, and Greville G. Corbett. 2005. *The syntax-morphology interface: a study of syncretism*. Cambridge: CUP.

Brown, Dunstan. 1998. Stem indexing and morphonological selection in the Russian verb. *Models of inflection*, ed. by Ray Fabri, Albert Ortmann, and Teresa Parodi, 196–221. Niemeyer: Tübingen.

Cahill, Lynn, and Gerald Gazdar. 1999. German noun inflection. *Journal of Linguistics* 35.1–42.

Corbett, Greville G. This volume. Deponency, syncretism, and what lies between.

Corbett, Greville G., and Norman Fraser. 1993. Network Morphology: a DATR account of Russian nominal inflection. *Journal of Linguistics* 29.113–42.

Ernout Alfred, and François Thomas. 1953. *Syntaxe latine* (2nd edn). Paris: Klincksieck.

Evans, Nicholas, Dunstan Brown, and Greville G. Corbett. 2001. Dalabon pronominal prefixes and the typology of syncretism. *Yearbook of Morphology 2000*, ed. by Jaap van Marle and Geert Booij, 187–231. Dordrecht: Kluwer:.

Evans, Roger, and Gerald Gazdar. 1996. DATR: a language for lexical knowledge representation. *Computational Linguistics* 22.167–216.

Flobert Pierre. 1975. *Les verbes déponents latins des origines à Charlemagne*. Paris: Société d'Édition 'Les Belles Lettres'.

Hippisley Andrew. 1998. Indexed stems and Russian word formation: a Network Morphology account of Russian personal nouns. *Linguistics* 36.1039–1124.

—— 2001. Word Formation Rules in a default inheritance framework: a Network Account of Russian personal nouns. *Yearbook of Morphology 1999*, ed. by Jaap van Marle and Geert Booij, 221–61. Dordrecht: Kluwer.

—— 2006a. A formal account of Latin deponent verbs. [Available at www.smg.surrey.ac.uk/deponency/DATR_analyses/Archi/Latin_report.pdf]

—— 2006b. A formal account of Archi deponent nouns. [Available at www.smg. surrey.ac.uk/deponency/DATR_analyses/Archi/Archi_report.pdf]

Hippisley, Andrew, Marina Chumakina, Greville G. Corbett, and Dunstan Brown. 2004. Suppletion: frequency, categories and distribution of stems. *Studies in Language* 28.389–421.

Kennedy, Benjamin. 1962. *Revised Latin primer* (edited and further revised by J. Mountford). Harlow: Longman.

Kibrik, Aleksandr E. 1977a. *Opyt strukturnogo opisanija arčinskogo jazyka:* II: *taksonomičeskaja grammatika.* (Publikacii otdelenija strukturnoj i prikladnoj lingvistiki 12). Moscow: Izdatel'stvo Moskovskogo Universiteta.

—— 1977b. *Arčinskij jazyk: teksty i slovar'.* Moscow: Izdatel'stvo Moskovskogo Universiteta.

Kühner, Raphael. 1955. *Ausführliche Grammatik der lateinischen Sprache* (part 2, 1, revised by Andreas Thierfelder). Hamburg: Hahn.

Stump, Gregory. 2001. *Inflectional morphology: a theory of paradigm structure.* Cambridge: CUP.

# 8

# The Limits of Deponency:
# A Chukotko-centric Perspective*

JONATHAN DAVID BOBALJIK

## 1. Introduction

DEPONENCY, WITH REFERENCE TO LATIN VERBS, is characterized by Baerman (this volume) as in (1).

(1)    Deponency is a mismatch between form and function. Given that there is a mor-
       phological opposition between active and passive that is the normal realization of
       the corresponding functional opposition, deponents are a lexically-specified set of
       verbs whose passive forms function as active. The normal function is no longer
       available.

The Latin example in (2) illustrates the phenomenon. The verb bears morphology from the passive paradigm, yet the syntax of the clause is active, as
evidenced, for example, by the accusative case-marking on the pronoun.

(2)    me=que       hort-antur   ut      magn-o       anim-o        sim
       me.ACC=and   exhort-3PL   that    great-ABL.SG  spirit-ABL.SG  be.1SG.SBJV
       'and they exhort me to be of good courage'
       (Cicero, *Epistulae ad Atticum,* book 11, letter 6; via Baerman this volume)

This paper aims to shed a small amount of light on two questions regarding
the phenomenon of deponency, as given in (3).

* For useful comments and suggestions, I thank the audience at the deponency workshop and
particularly to Andrew Spencer, Susi Wurmbrand, and Phil Branigan, my collaborator in developing the analysis of Chukchi reported here. Comments from the editors of this volume have
been particularly useful in attempting to identify and frame the issues. I also thank Itziar Laka
for suggesting the similarity to Basque. Funding for portions of this research were provided by
the Social Sciences and Humanities Research Council, grant number 410-2002-0581. All errors
are my own responsibility.

(3)  a.  Do deponent paradigms constitute evidence for special devices in an autonomous morphological component, or can they be handled in some other way?

b.  Do deponent paradigms constitute a natural class, with a common morpho-syntactic analysis or is deponency a descriptive cover for distinct phenomena with different analyses in different languages?

The first of these questions constitutes one of the motivations for the present volume. The second question is related to the first, but differs in emphasis, focusing instead on separating the universal from the language-particular. This second question looms large in research traditions that stress the universal, such as versions of generative grammar that seek universal principles as a partial answer to the logical problem of language acquisition, and will be the main focus here. Of course, approaching question (3b) in particular requires a definition of *deponent* that extends beyond Latin, yet is limited enough in scope so as to make (3b) a reasonable question to pursue. Thus, the definition of 'extended deponence' offered by Baerman (this volume) and Corbett (this volume), is so broad that a negative answer to (3b) on that definition seems a safe bet. The research strategy pursued here is to approach (3b) with reference to a more restricted subset of what Baerman and Corbett would term 'extended deponency', namely those that involve verbs whose non-active form assumes an active function. At the risk of compounding terminological confusion, I thus define the term *v-deponent* to refer to this particular range of (extended) deponency.[1]

(4)  v-deponent$_{def}$

Given a morphological opposition between active and non-active that is the normal realization of the corresponding functional opposition, *v-deponents* are those verbs whose non-active forms function as active.

With the sense of 'deponent' limited to 'v-deponent', it seems to me that (3b) is a reasonable question to ask. My specific target of investigation is an apparently (v-)deponent configuration in the Chukotko-Kamchatkan languages, the 'spurious antipassive' (henceforth, SAP). With regard to (3a), I will conclude that no special deponency devices are necessary for the analysis of this construction, and that its properties arise from the independently observed properties of Chukchi grammar interacting in a predictable fashion

---

[1] The definition is modelled on Baerman's, above (1). The choice to consider the active use of non-active voice as the defining criterion is not specific to the current paper, but rather seems to me to be the most commonly used sense of the term in the grammatical literature. Compare the definition of 'deponent' in the *Oxford English Dictionary*:

*deponent*, adj. Gram. Of verbs: Passive or middle in form but active in meaning: originally a term of Latin Grammar. (Online edition, consulted July 2006).

with independent principles of morphology and syntax. I will also reach a negative conclusion regarding (3b), arguing that deponent constructions (even in the limited sense of v-deponent), despite sharing characteristics at a descriptive level, do not constitute a natural class, subject to a uniform analysis, but instead, deponent configurations may arise in different languages for a variety of unrelated reasons.

The paper is organized as follows. In section 2, I lay out the basic case for treating the SAP as an instance of deponency as I am using the term, providing just as much discussion of the complicated morphosyntax of Chukchi as is necessary to appreciate the pattern. Some further information on verbal agreement, with sample paradigms, is presented in the appendix. I then touch briefly on differences between Chukchi and Latin. In section 4, I turn to the first of the questions in (3), namely, the detailed theoretical analysis of the Chukchi SAP. The analysis is presented in detail in Bobaljik and Branigan (2006), and I will simply report the highlights here, with a particular emphasis on how the deponent pattern is handled with no new theoretical devices. That section brings us to the conclusion that the considerations that yield the v-deponent pattern in Chukchi are independent of whatever underlies (v-)deponency in Latin and Greek. Confirming evidence that surface deponency in Chukchi is derived by considerations independent of deponency as such comes, perhaps, from a consideration of the phenomenon of ergative displacement in Basque, discussed in section 5. This peculiar phenomenon has all of the important characteristics of the Chukchi SAP, save the spurious morphological marking of a voice alternation.

## 2. A Deponency Mismatch in Chukotkan

The phenomenon of interest for the present study is a construction in the Chukotkan languages dubbed the *spurious antipassive* by Ken Hale (Halle and Hale 1997), and referred to by many others as an 'inverse' alignment (following Comrie 1980). Examples from Chukchi are given in (5).[2] In this pattern, the verb form is drawn from the non-active paradigm (note the antipassive prefix *ine-* boldfaced in the examples), yet the verb-external morphosyntax remains active and transitive, illustrated (as in Latin) by case-marking.[3]

---

[2] The SAP also occurs in Koryak, though with more limited distribution. Most of the points made here carry over to the Koryak SAP. See Comrie (1979), Spencer (2000) for the Koryak facts, and Zhukova (1972, 1980) for the standard description of Koryak.

[3] Chukchi examples are offered in broad transcription. Glosses are simplified somewhat for expository reasons. Certain phonological processes have not been factored out, hence the same underlying morpheme may be represented with various surface forms in the examples. Thus, *ine-* and *ena-* are vowel harmony alternants, as are *-ɣʔi* in (5a) and *-ɣʔe* in (7b), the final vowel

(5)  a.   ə-nan          γəm          Ø-ine-ɬʔu-γʔi
          he-ERG         I (ABS)      3SG.SUB(I)-AP-see-3SG.SUB(I)
          'He saw me.'                                    (Skorik 1977: 44)

     b.   torγə-nan      γəm          q-in-imti-tək
          you.PL-ERG     I (ABS)      2.SUB-AP-carry-2PL.SUB(I)
          '(You PL) Carry me!'                            (Skorik 1977: 83)

     c.   ə-nan          γəm          Ø-r-ine-ɬʔu-rkən
          he-ERG         I (ABS)      3SG.SUB(I)-FUT-AP-see-PROG
          'He will be seeing me.'                         (Skorik 1977: 57)

In the next subsections, I present a brief overview of the points of Chukchi morphosyntax that are relevant for establishing that the forms in (5) qualify as deponent, as defined in (4), turning then to a comparison with deponency in Latin.

## 2.1. Case

In terms of case-marking, Chukchi follows an ergative alignment.[4] The subject of a transitive clause bears a special case-marking (ergative), while objects and intransitive subjects both stand in the unmarked (absolutive / nominative) case, as illustrated in transitive (6) versus intransitive (7).[5]

---

of *ine-* is elided before another vowel, as in (5b), and schwa is generally epenthetic, but assigned in the examples to one morpheme or another arbitrarily. Note that although Chukchi has no conjugation classes (all verbs take the same inflectional morphology), inflectional morphology shows significant internal allomorphy, with agreement markers showing allomorphy for tense, aspect, and mood. Only those aspects of this allomorphy directly relevant to the discussion are indicated here, thus the reader may note the same features in the gloss having different phonological forms. (The suffix for 3SG.SUB(I) is *-γʔi* in the aorist, but *-Ø*, or *-n*, in other paradigms.) Some morphemic glosses are subject to further segmentation, not affecting the argument made here. Zero inflectional affixes have been added for expository reasons, where well motivated, and are not crucial to the analysis. Note that word order in Chukchi is reported to be free. Thus examples are presented here as given in the sources and I take surface order in Chukchi to be unenlightening for the issues under investigation.

[4] For far more detailed descriptions of Chukchi, see particularly Skorik (1977) and Dunn (1999). Prior descriptions and accounts of the SAP (not all under this name) are offered in Comrie (1979, 1980), Halle and Hale (1997), Spencer (2000), Hale (2002), and Bobaljik and Branigan (2006).

[5] Only pronouns have a morphologically distinct ergative case; other nouns use either the instrumental or locative suffixes in this function. Nevertheless the transitive subject is always distinguished from NPs in the absolutive function. It is worth noting that Chukchi case-marking is canonically ergative in the sense that case tracks surface transitivity and is, if at all, only indirectly tied to argument structure or thematic role (see Nedjalkov 1976). In contrast to languages such as Georgian, Hindi, and Basque, in Chukchi, intransitive subjects are never ergative (even if agentive), and transitive subjects are ergative regardless of thematic role.

(6) a. γəm-nan      γət      tə-ɬʔu-γət
     I-ERG      you.SG(ABS)      1SG.SUB-see-2SG.OBJ
     'I saw you.'                                             (Skorik 1977: 44)

     b. ərγə-nan      γəm      ne-ɬʔu-γəm
     they-ERG      me(ABS)      3.SUB(T)-see-1SG.OBJ
     'They saw me.'                                         (Skorik 1977: 45)

(7) a. γəm                   tə-kətγəntat-γʔak
     I (ABS)               1SG.SUB-run-1SG.SUB(I)
     'I ran.'                                                  (Skorik 1977: 20)

     b. ətɬjon             Ø-kətγəntat-γʔe
     he.ABS            3.SUB(I)-run-3SG.SUB(I)
     'He ran.'                                               (Skorik 1977: 20)

The examples in (6)–(7) also illustrate aspects of Chukchi verbal agreement. Finite predicates show agreement with both subject and object (if there is one). As a rough approximation, agreement is typically marked twice on the finite predicate: a prefix (sometimes zero) marks subject agreement for transitive and intransitive verbs alike, while an agreement suffix marks agreement with the object if there is one, else with the subject. This yields a characteristic quirk of the Chukotko-Kamchatkan languages, whereby intransitive subjects are cross-referenced twice on the verb, once by a prefix and again by a suffix (see Bobaljik 1998, Bobaljik and Wurmbrand 2002). Representative paradigms for agreement are given in the appendix.

## 2.2. Voice

As is typical for ergative languages, the major voice alternation in Chukchi is between active and antipassive (rather than passive). This is illustrated in (8). The (a) example is an active clause, with an ergative-absolutive case array and transitive agreement on the verb. Example (8b) is the corresponding antipassive; the logical object is demoted (expressed in an oblique case) and the clause is correspondingly intransitive in both case-marking and agreement properties.

(8) a. ʔaaček-a      kimitʔ-ən      ne-nɬʔetet-ən
     youth-ERG      load-ABS      3.SUB(T)-carry-3SG.OBJ
     '(The) young men carried away the load.'

     b. ʔaaček-ət      Ø-ine-nɬʔetet-γʔet      kimitʔ-e
     youth-PL (ABS)      3.SUB(I)-AP-carry-3PL.SUB(I)      load-INSTR
     '(The) young men carried away a load.'      (Kozinsky et al. 1988: 652)

There is a second antipassive, marked by the suffix *-tku,* typically described as having an iterative function (Dunn 1999: 216). The active / antipassive alternation with this suffix is illustrated in (9).

(9)  a.  morɣə-nan      mət-viriŋ-ərkən-et                    tumɣ-ət
         we-ERG         1PL.SUB-defend-PROG-3PL.OBJ          comrade-PL.ABS
         'We are defending our comrades.'

     b.  muri           mət-viriŋə-tku-rkən                   (tomɣ-etə)
         we.ABS         1PL.SUB-defend-AP-PROG               comrade-PL.DAT
         'We are defending our comrades.'              (Skorik 1977: 124–5)

Note that both antipassives are morphologically marked (they bear an overt morpheme) relative to the unmarked active. In all other respects, the true antipassive is identical in form to intransitives, showing regular intransitive inflectional morphology in all (or nearly all) cells of the paradigms.[6] Note in addition that the antipassive morphemes occupy a different position in the verbal template than agreement morphemes. Agreement morphemes (both prefixes and suffixes) occur peripherally in the word, for example outside of tense and aspect markers, while the antipassive morphemes occur between tense/aspect and the verb root. This is not evident in (8b), but can be seen in the suffix orders in (9), and is readily demonstrable from the paradigms in Skorik (1977) and Dunn (1999), see also Spencer (2000). Thus the template for Chukchi verbs is as in (10).

(10)  Agreement—Mood—Tense—$AP_{ine}$—verb.root—$AP_{tku}$—Aspect—
      Agreement

As a final remark on the true antipassive, it should be noted that the antipassive morphology is not incompatible with transitive agreement. The antipassive construction involves the demotion of the underlying direct object to an oblique function. All else being equal, this yields a construction that is morphologically and syntactically intransitive, as seen above, and again in (11a–b). However, as Kozinsky et al. (1988) and Dunn (1999) note, it is also possible for the antipassive to co-occur with applicativization (not marked morphologically) whereby an underlying oblique is promoted to surface direct object status when the underlying direct object has been demoted. This yields so-called 'conversive' antipassives, which are formally transitive on the surface and thus have transitive agreement morphology, where object agreement picks out the promoted object *utkuč?-ən* 'trap' in (11c).

(11)  a.  ətɬəɣ-e        təkeč?-ən      utkuč?-ək      peɬa-nen
          father-ERG     bait-ABS       trap-LOC       leave-3SG>3SG
          'Father left the bait at/in the trap.'

---

[6] Although this is the standard presentation (see especially Skorik 1977: 113ff.), 3 of the 120 forms of Skorik's antipassive paradigms are given (without comment) in forms that differ slightly from the corresponding intransitives, pp. 20–38 and 76–94.

b.  ətłjon           təkečʔ-a        Ø-ena-peła-γʔe
    he.ABS          bait-INSTR      3.SUB(I)-AP-leave-3SG.SUB(I)
    'He left the bait.'

c.  ətłəγ-e          təkečʔ-a        utkučʔ-ən       ena-peła-nen
    father-ERG      bait-INSTR      trap-ABS        AP-leave-3SG>3SG
    'Father left the bait at/in the trap.'

                                                    (Kozinsky et al. 1988: 663–5)

## 2.3. The SAP

With this much background in Chukchi morphosyntax, we may now return
to the SAP in (5), repeated here, with an additional example, illustrating an
SAP with the -*tku* suffix.[7]

(12)  a.  ə-nan           γəm             Ø-**ine**-łʔu-γʔi
          he-ERG          I (ABS)         3SG.SUB(I)-AP-see-3SG.SUB(I)
          'He saw me.'                                    (Skorik 1977: 44)

      b.  torγə-nan       γəm             q-**in**-imti-tək
          you.PL-ERG      I (ABS)         2.SUB-AP-carry-2PL.SUB(I)
          '(You PL) Carry me!'                            (Skorik 1977: 83)

      c.  ə-nan           γəm             Ø-r-**ine**-łʔu-rkən
          he-ERG          I (ABS)         3SG.SUB(I)-FUT-AP-see-PROG
          'He will be seeing me.'                         (Skorik 1977: 57)

      d.  γə-nan          muri            Ø-łʔu-**tku**-rkən
          you.SG-ERG      us.ABS          2.SUB-see-AP-PROG
          'You see us.'                                   (Skorik 1977: 50)

Inspection of these examples shows that each clause bears a regular, transitive, active case array (ergative subject, absolutive object) while the verb bears
antipassive morphology (prefix *ine-* or suffix *-tku*) and the corresponding
intransitive agreement. None of the examples in (12) has an object agreement
suffix, such as *-γəm* (1SG.OBJ, compare (6b)) or *-mək* (1PL), and instead the
agreement morphology is drawn from the intransitive paradigm, with prefixes
and suffixes cross-referencing the subject (compare (7)). Thus, there is in
effect a double mismatch here. One mismatch is that the verbal agreement is
intransitive, though the clause is transitive. The second mismatch is that the
intransitive agreement morphology, which normally cross-references absolutive nominals, references instead the ergative subject in the SAP.[8] As noted by
Comrie (1979: 231) and Nedjalkov (1979: 254), examples like (12c,d) show

---

[7] This use is not attested in the Khatyrka dialect of Chukchi (Skorik 1977: passim) nor in Koryak
(Comrie 1979: 238).
[8] There is exactly one partial exception. The combination 3SG>3PL in the habitual triggers the
SAP, but the plural morpheme there is controlled by the absolutive nominal, i.e. the object
(Comrie 1979). I return to this briefly in section 5.

that the spurious antipassive morphemes occupy the position of the true antipassives (inside the tense prefix or aspectual suffix) and are not in the more peripheral positions occupied by agreement prefixes (this is demonstrably systematic).

I will return to the distribution of the SAP below (see also the agreement paradigms in the appendix). At this point, I believe it is fair to conclude that the SAP in Chukchi straightforwardly meets the descriptive definition of v-deponency offered in (4), constituting a mismatch of non-active verbal morphology alongside active syntax.


# 3. Chukchi and Latin: Points of Difference

Before turning to the analysis of the Chukchi SAP, I present a few brief remarks on the difference between the manifestations of deponency in Chukchi and Latin. The research question does not hinge on questions of terminology, of course, and could be rephrased even if the term 'deponent' is to be limited to Latin and Greek: given that the Chukchi SAP shares with Latin deponent verbs the peculiarity of a mismatch of non-active form with active morphosyntax ('meaning'), do they share a common analysis at some useful level of abstraction? Nevertheless a comparison of the definition of v-deponency offered in (4) to Baerman's characterization of Latin deponency in (1) serves as a useful means to frame the discussion.

There are three points of difference between (1) and (4): (i) passive versus non-active; (ii) lexical specification, and (iii) loss of original function. The first of these differences is relevant for an extension of the investigation to languages with voice systems other than active-passive, for example ergative languages with an antipassive as the non-active voice, and I take this extension to require no further comment. Brief remarks on the other two differences follow.

### 3.1. Triggers

The triggering factor for deponent verb forms differs significantly between Latin and Chukchi. In Latin (and Greek), as noted above, the deponent verbs constitute a lexically listed class.[9] In Chukchi, by contrast, the SAP is an

---

[9] It bears mention that the class, though lexically listed, is by no means small. The 'comprehensive list of deponent verbs' at the Saint Louis University Latin Teaching Materials Site <http://www.slu.edu/colleges/AS/languages/classical/latin/tchmat/grammar/dep.html>, [last accessed May 2006], lists 421 deponent verbs for Latin. Some verbs are deponent in part of their paradigm only (see Matthews, this volume). Xu et al. (2006) argue for a partial basis for deponency in lexical semantics.

integral part of the agreement system of the language—the SAP is the obligatory means of expressing certain combinations of subject and object in
certain tenses (see the transitive paradigms in (31) in the appendix). In the
active (i.e. non-stative) inflections such as the aorist, the pairings that require
the SAP are as listed in (13); they are formulated specifically as filters for
reasons that will become clear below.

(13)   subject-object agreement combinations requiring SAP (non-participial tenses)[10]

    a.   * 3 SG > 1 SG          requires SAP with *ine-*
    b.   * 2 > 1 SG             requires SAP with *ine-*
    c.   * 2 > 1 PL             requires SAP with *-tku*

These combinations form a subset of the 'inverse' environments, i.e. where
the object outranks the subject on the person hierarchy (1>2>3). On these
grounds, Comrie (1979) (and subsequent authors) have thus referred to the
SAP as a species of inverse construction. I will follow this tradition, with
some trepidation, in positing a set of 'inverse filters' that disallow the morphological expressions of particular combinations of subject and object. The
main aim of the analysis in section 4 is to show that the SAP arises as the
automatic consequence of such filters; given particular, independently motivated assumptions about universal grammar and Chukchi; the hope is that
positing such filters is all that needs to be said in order for the SAP to arise,
thus answering (3a) in the negative, for Chukchi.

The hesitation in labelling these filters 'inverse' concerns the expanded
range of SAP environments when the habitual tense/aspect is brought under
consideration. In this conjugation (see (31)), the SAP is required in many non-
inverse contexts in addition to those in (13), including for example, 1SG > 3SG,
the reverse of (13a) and the construction that is least inverse in terms of the
person hierarchy. This point notwithstanding, the trigger for deponency in
Chukchi is a question of feature combinations of subject and object, and
unlike Latin is not a matter of lexical specification.[11]

### 3.2. Retention

Another point of difference in the definitions (and the languages) concerns
the question of retention of original function of the non-active morphology.

---

[10] In the Khatyrka dialect of Chukchi, 2SG/PL>1PL forms are syncretic with 3>1PL, and are thus
not SAP environments.
[11] Indeed, it may be the case that certain transitive verbs in Chukchi are lexically specified not to
undergo true antipassivization, namely the 'labile' verbs, which may freely occur in ERG-ABS case
frames (with transitive morphology) or in ABS-OBL case frames, with intransitive morphology
(Nedjalkov 1979: 244). However, all descriptions of Chukchi verb inflection imply that in their
transitive array, even these verbs will indeed participate in the SAP. I have not located relevant
examples yet.

In other words, is a deponent verb one that is non-active in form and exclusively active in syntax, or should the definition encompass verbs that are non-active in form but syncretic in distribution, occurring in both active and non-active syntax with no morphological distinction? Although Baerman's definition of a canonical deponent verb excludes the latter (following the apparent original sense of *deponent* as 'put aside', see Matthews (this volume)), some modern descriptions of Latin include the 'common' verbs under the label deponent, and thus one finds: '[s]ome deponents are occasionally used in a passive sense: as, *críminor*, "I accuse", or "I am accused"' (Greenough et al. 1903: §190). As far as the question is applicable to Chukchi, it seems that the Chukchi forms in question do retain their original function as antipassives. This is trivially true at the level of word-form: the individual forms used to construct the spurious antipassive are drawn from the regular antipassive paradigm, and thus the individual verb forms are all ambiguous between true and spurious antipassives. A somewhat subtler take on the question (suggested by Andrew Spencer) might be whether a given form may serve both an active and a (true) antipassive function with the same syntactic arguments. This is probably not testable in the core (non-stative) conjugations, since it is only first person objects that require the SAP, and these make poor choices as logical objects in the antipassive construction on independent grounds (topicality, perhaps). Yet this is testable for the habitual conjugations, where the SAP pervades the transitive paradigm. And indeed what we do find is that the same form serves both the true and spurious antipassive functions. Thus, with a first person subject and third person (logical) object, the morphology in (14) (where $\sqrt{}$ is a place holder for the root) occurs in the true antipassive paradigm (Skorik 1977: 115) and in the SAP function within the active paradigm (Skorik 1977: 67; Dunn 1999: 192).

(14)   n-ine-$\sqrt{}$-muri
        PRESII-AP-VERB-1PL.SUBJ

Within the terminology established by Baerman and Corbett, the Chukchi SAP forms are thus both deponent and syncretic, to the extent that this is testable (see especially Baerman, this volume, § 7.3).

  In sum, to this point I have argued that the Chukchi SAP shares with Latin deponent verbs the key property of non-active morphology with active syntax. A comparison with Baerman's Latin-based characterization of deponency highlights points of difference between the two phenomena. We now have before us sufficient understanding to proceed to finer questions of analysis. In the next section, I will briefly outline the analysis of the Chukchi SAP as presented in Bobaljik and Branigan (2006), showing how the various properties of the construction arise from independently justifiable assumptions. As it happens, these considerations will lead us away from Latin, thus suggesting the negative answer to the question of unification.

## 4. The Chukchi SAP: Analysis

In this section, I highlight the key properties of the analysis of the Chukchi SAP put forward in Bobaljik and Branigan (2006, henceforth B&B). The presentation here will be rather cursory, and the reader is referred to the work cited for justification, additional detail, and consideration of alternatives.

Distilled to its core, the intuition behind the B&B analysis is that the detransitivization of the verb (in its morphology, but not its syntax) is a predictable response of the morphological component to the 'inverse filters' such as those in (13) (cf., Comrie 1979). We take it that the syntactic structure is logically prior to morphology, and thus adopt a realizational theory of morphology (specifically, Distributed Morphology, though on this point, any theory in which the morphology realizes, sometimes imperfectly, the feature structure generated by the syntax will suffice). The syntax applies unremarkably in all transitive clauses, but certain combinations are barred from controlling transitive agreement morphology on the verb. For SAP configurations, deletion of the offending features, in the morphological component, 'repairs' the morphological structure, so that it no longer violates the inverse filters, but this results in a morphological agreement pattern that is effectively intransitive, thus yielding the observed mismatch. The tricky part of the analysis, as Spencer (2000) points out, lies not in the detransitivization as such (which can be achieved in many theories), but in having the deletion of agreement features force the appearance of the syntactically unmotivated antipassive morphology. B&B argue that recent advances in the study of movement dependencies and their interaction with phonological considerations point to a solution to this part of the puzzle, and more specifically, a solution which all but necessitates that it is the antipassive (as opposed to any other morpheme) that must occur spuriously as the signal of the morphological detransitivization.

The B&B analysis is set within the general Government and Binding (GB)/Minimalist syntactic framework, supplemented by a realizational approach to morphology, as noted above. This framework includes a commitment to a model of grammar whereby syntactic structures are generated by the syntactic component, and the output of this component is then subject to interpretation by a semantic (LF) and a morpho-phonological (PF) component, as in the familiar 'Y' model in (15) and related models.

(15)  'Y' Model of Grammar

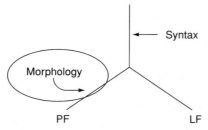

These commitments take matching of form and meaning to be the null case, with mismatches to be explained with a theoretical apparatus that is permissive enough to account for observed variation, yet restrictive enough to generate (correct) predictions about new phenomena. As a realizational theory, the syntactic structures are taken to be abstract (thus syntax manipulates features and nodes, not 'words'), and the interpretive components assign to these structures appropriate sound and meaning representations. Within this architecture, one source of potential form-meaning mismatches lies in the 'morphology', that is, the mapping procedure that assigns morpho-phonological representations to syntactic structures. We exploit this potential for mismatch in the account of the SAP.

In line with recent theorizing in this general framework, we assume that core (i.e. non-oblique) nominal arguments in active clauses enter into two local relationships, which we express in terms of phrase structure and movement (or chain formation). After movement, the nominal features are inactive in their lower position, which we indicate in the trees below with strikethrough; for present purposes, this is equivalent to traces in GB. It should be noted that these structures define relations among features, and do not necessarily indicate word-order; they are thus partially analogous to f-structures in Lexical Functional Grammar (LFG) and similar constructs, although the framework differs from LFG in taking these structures to be fundamentally hierarchical in the phrase-structural sense. The diagram at (16) illustrates the basic derivation we would assign to a basic intransitive clause.[12]

(16)  Intransitive Clause

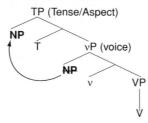

---

[12] An unaccusative clause would be minimally different in that the lower position of the sole NP argument would be in the complement of VP, rather than the specifier of *v*P.

'Subject agreement' in general, and more narrowly, the suffixal agreement in Chukchi, is a property of the T node, and is controlled exclusively by the features of the nominal that enters into a local dependency with this node, as sketched in this diagram. For Chukchi, we assume an additional CP layer dominating the TP in (16). I assume that the subject agreement prefixes are part of this higher projection. Evidence for this includes the observation that the (subject) agreement prefixes show a significant degree of fusion with markers of mood, but no significant interactions with lower features (tense, aspect), in contrast to the agreement morphology realized at T. For additional discussion of the internal hierarchical structure of the Chukotko-Kamchatkan verb, see Bobaljik (2000) and Bobaljik and Wurmbrand (2001). I omit further discussion of the CP layer.[13]

The next tree indicates the structure we assign to an active, transitive derivation in Chukchi (with CP omitted). The labels 'subject' and 'object' are for expository convenience, and serve no role in the formal analysis, beyond identifying the features associated with particular nominals.

(17)  Transitive Clause (Active, Ergative)

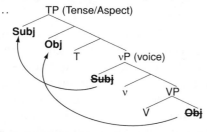

This derivation incorporates the premise that the relationship of syntactic configurations to argument structure is universal, and that ergative languages do not vary from nominative ones in this regard. In current terms, this means that the internal argument is merged in VP and the external argument is introduced in the specifier of a functional projection, *v*P. The difference between (the abstract structures underlying) ergative and accusative case arrays lies in the formal licensing relations in the higher part of the tree. For familiar nominative-accusative systems, a standard assumption within this framework is that the functional head *v* is responsible for formal licensing of the object ('structural accusative case', see Wurmbrand 2006 for evidence and

---

[13] By treating the subject agreement prefixes as occurring in CP, we treat the double agreement in intransitive clauses in particular as analogous to, e.g. the complementizer agreement phenomena found, for example, in various Germanic languages, as illustrated in (i), from Bavarian.

(i)    ...    ob-**st**         noch    Minga    kumm-**st**
              whether-2sg      to      M.       come-2sg
              'whether you're coming to M.'                        (Bayer 1984)

discussion). B&B propose, following Bok-Bennema (1991) and Nash (1995), that the basic property that differentiates the ergative system in Chukchi is that in Chukchi, the *v* head cannot check/license object case. Given this assumption, both subject and object raise to the domain of T° for checking. The specific ordering of subject above object within TP is determined by the principle of 'Tucking In' (Richards 2001).We argue that independent evidence for this multiple-checking by T, comes from the existence of portmanteau morphology (for subject–object combinations) on the agreeing head T°.

A special case of an intransitive derivation is the (true) Antipassive, such as (8b), for which the derivation is given in (18).

(18)   True Antipassive Clause

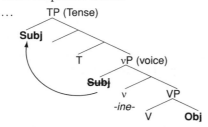

Salient properties of the antipassive derivation include the following. The syntactic representation of the argument structure is the same as that of a transitive clause, with a subject and object, base-generated ('merged') in the appropriate positions. Unlike an active clause, though, in the antipassive, the object does not raise out of the VP/*v*P into the functional domain. As the object remains in VP, it is not formally licensed by T, and requires a special licensing, namely, an oblique case.[14] Since the object remains in the VP, the TP domain (where, by hypothesis, agreement relations are calculated) is formally intransitive, despite the transitive argument structure lower in the tree. Recall that we assume a realizational theory of morphology, and under this view, the overt antipassive morpheme *-ine-* does not cause the syntactic configuration in (18), rather the morpheme is introduced as a reflection of the antipassive syntax. One may think of *-ine-* as the *exponent* or *spell out* of the *v* head when there is an object in its local domain, the head being spelled out as Ø otherwise (e.g. when there is no object or when the object has raised out).

---

[14] Within the framework we are assuming, see (15), syntactic structure underlies both morphological realization and semantic interpretation. Since all structures are hierarchical, this perspective on the antipassive not only characterizes the morphological form of the verb, but also finds confirmation in properties that demonstrate that the logical object of an antipassive is in a position lower than the corresponding object in an active clause. This has been demonstrated for languages other than Chukchi (see Bittner 1994; Bittner and Hale 1996; Wharram 2003), and the available Chukchi evidence is consistent with this view.

At this point, most of the pieces are in place for our analysis of the SAP, which we sketch in (19).

(19)  Spurious Antipassive

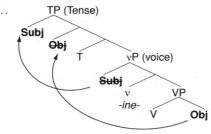

In our view, the SAP is a normal transitive clause syntactically. Thus, it has a normal transitive derivation, as the arrows indicate: both subject and object raise to T for case-checking, as in (31). What 'goes wrong' is the morphological interpretation of such a clause. As pointed out above, the SAP is obligatory with certain combinations of subject and object. We propose that such inverse filters are computed locally, i.e. when the two arguments are in a checking relationship with the same functional head. The offending configuration is resolved, in the mapping to the morphological component, by deleting the features of one of the arguments (the lower one) at the checking head. This is indicated by strikethrough of the top copy of the object in (19). If we focus on the T domain, the deletion of the object features makes T (the locus of agreement) appear intransitive.

Now, the key to understanding what happens in the lower part of the tree comes from recent work in the syntax of chains which has shown that the automatic consequence of the deletion of a higher copy in a chain is the exceptional activation of a lower copy. A straightforward example can be drawn from multiple *wh*-questions in certain Slavic languages, including Serbo-Croatian (examples and analysis from Bošković 2002).[15]

In Serbo-Croatian, as in some other Slavic languages, there is a syntactic requirement that all *wh*-words in a multiple question must front, as in (20). Failure to do so yields unacceptability, except perhaps under certain special interpretations such as echo questions.

(20)  a.  Ko  šta$_i$  kupuje  $t_i$?        b.  ?*Ko kupuje  šta?
          who what  buys                     who buys     what
          'Who buys what?'                   'Who buys what?'     (p. 355)

---

[15] Other phenomena illustrating this effect include restrictions on Object Shift in Germanic (Bobaljik 1995, 2002), on *wh-in situ* in English multiple questions (Pesetsky 1998), and on unexpectedly 'low' clitics in Slavic (Franks 1998).

The requirement that all *wh*-words front appears to be relaxed just in case the fronting would yield a sequence of homophonous *wh*-words, as in (21).[16] In exactly this environment, the object *wh*-word is pronounced in its lower, rather than its higher position.

(21)  a.  *šta  šta    uslovljava   $t_i$?          b.  šta    uslovljava   šta?
         what what   conditions                       what  conditions   what
         'What conditions what?'                       'What conditions what?'        (p. 364)

Bošković's account (with subject traces/copies suppressed) is given in (22). In a normal clause, all *wh*-words front, creating chains that consist of sequences of copies of the moved item. In the normal case, all but the highest of these copies are deleted as in (22a), yielding the surface order in (20). The interpretation of (21b) as a regular multiple-question indicates that the representation which feeds semantic interpretation is that arising from movement. Post-syntactically, then, where highest-copy pronunciation is expected, a morphological anti-homophony filter applies, blocking pronunciation of the highest copy, and automatically triggering the pronunciation of the next lower copy, as in (22b).

(22)  a.  Ko    šta$_i$    kupuje      ~~šta~~$_i$
         who   what      buys        what
         'Who buys what?'

      b.  šta   ~~šta~~$_i$   uslovljava   šta$_i$?
         what  what       conditions   what
         'What conditions what?'

In sum, the automatic consequence of deletion of an element in a high position, to satisfy a PF filter, is the exceptional reactivation or reappearance of that element in its low (trace) position. That this occurs on the 'left branch' of the derivation in (15) is evidenced by the observation that to the extent that wh-words can remain in situ with special effects (echo questions), such special effects are conspicuously absent *just when* the anti-homophony constraint forces high deletion and thus the lower pronunciation.

It is this effect which fills in the missing pieces of the SAP derivation in (19). In a normal transitive derivation, as in (17), the features of the object are active in the TP domain, yielding object agreement, and are thus deleted from the VP domain, which contains only traces of arguments. In the SAP, although the object has syntactically undergone movement to the TP domain (unlike a true antipassive), deletion of the object's features in the TP domain, to satisfy the inverse filters, has the automatic consequence that the lower

---

[16] See Menn and MacWhinney (1984) for an extensive survey of constraints on repeated morphemes, and various responses / repair strategies that are used.

instantiation of those features is reactivated, but only in the morphology. In this regard, the *v*P domain for an SAP 'looks like' an antipassive clause (18), rather than a true transitive clause: the *v*P contains an active (non-strike-through) object, but only a trace of the subject. Recall now that we assumed for (18) that the appearance of antipassive morphology is a reflection of the feature structure of the clause, rather than the cause of that structure. Since the outcome of deletion in (19) looks like an antipassive, the same consideration will trigger the insertion of the antipassive morpheme in the morphology. Like the Serbo-Croatian multiple question paradigm, the effects here happen in the post-syntactic, morphological realization of syntactic structure, and thus the syntactic and semantic effects of true antipassivization are conspicuously absent.[17]

In sum, the core theoretical devices used in the Bobaljik and Branigan (2006) analysis of the Chukchi SAP are general devices none of which is specifically tailored to derive deponency. Under our conception of things, the deponent pattern (spurious detransitivization) arises in Chukchi because of a confluence of independent properties. Key among these is the filters that regulate the morphological expression of combinations of arguments that undergo checking/licensing at a single functional head. This consideration provides some predictive power regarding the distribution of this type of deponent pattern.

Recall from the discussion of (17) that we assume that the licensing of subject and object by T is a property of ergative systems, where the syntax underlying nominative-accusative alignments involves checking at distinct heads. If this is correct, we are led to expect that the kind of feature-driven detransitivization exemplified by the Chukchi SAP will be limited to ergative arrays. A possible consideration in favour of this view comes from Itelmen, Chukchi's southern cousin.[18] The Itelmen agreement morphology is clearly

---

[17] One remaining question is in the distribution of *ine-* vs -*tku* allomorphs of *v* in the SAP. In all conjugations except the habitual, the SAP is used only with first person objects, and the allomorphy reflects number. It is thus tempting (cf. Comrie 1979) to relate this to the iterative function of the -*tku* antipassive. A proposal implementing this within *phase* theory is hinted at in Bobaljik and Branigan (2006: 77 fn. 23). Formalizing this presents various hurdles. Most glaringly, treating the *ine-* vs -*tku* as number agreement on *v* works for all the non-stative moods but fails for the habitual, where 2PL and 3PL objects trigger the *ine-* SAP (though 3PL objects are special in other regards, see n. 8 above). Note also that while -*tku* may carry iteratve meaning (related to plurality or pluractionality), it is not reported that number of the logical object plays a role in choice of antipassive among true antipassives. This issue is thus left as an unresolved problem for the analysis.

[18] This should be set against the possible counter-evidence from Yurok, as described by Baerman (this volume). Yurok is not ergative, and may have a deponent aspect to its agreement paradigm, conditioned by subject-object interactions. As Baerman notes, though, there are a variety of qualifications to be made in considering the forms in question to be morphologically passive.

cognate to Chukchi and shares most of the quirks that are characteristic of this family (see Comrie 1983, Bobaljik 1998). However, Itelmen is alone among the Chukotko-Kamchatkan languages in lacking ergative morpho-syntax, and in addition, lacks any analogue to the SAP, with regular transitive morphology throughout the transitive paradigm. This state of affairs is of course what is predicted by the view sketched here.[19]

A related prediction concerns the status of ergativity as a natural class. The emerging consensus appears to be that there is no single unified account of ergativity that holds for all languages with an ergative case array (see the papers collected in Johns et al. 2006). While ergative case in Chukchi is clearly structural, it appears there are other languages in which ergative may be a thematic case, restricted by theta-role rather than surface transitivity, and with a passive-like derivation rather than the active derivation in (17) (Hindi-Urdu has been suggested as such a language). If such languages exist, then they would not involve multiple licensing by a single functional head, and hence would not be subject to the kinds of filters posited in (13), and hence could not have a construction like the SAP (even if they have an antipassive). Considerations such as those mentioned in this and the previous paragraph thus go some way to answering the question of why deponency seems so rarely attested. It arises only when a particular constellation of other conditions are met.

Thus, the Chukchi SAP has the properties it has, and in particular, the property of active syntax with derived, non-active morphology, as a result of the application of a set of language particular filters, interacting with the cross-linguistic principle that suppression of the higher copy of a moved element triggers activation of the lower copy (trace) of that element. There is no reason to suspect that these mechanisms are at play in Latin (and Greek) deponent verbs.[20] Thus, we reach the conclusion that despite sharing the descriptive property of v-deponency, at the level of formal analysis, Latin deponent verbs and the Chukchi SAP have nothing in particular in common. A further consideration in favour of this (negative) conclusion is presented in the next section.

---

[19] Note that various authors have proposed that in nominative-accusative languages, the direct and indirect object may be licensed by the same functional head (see, e.g. Anagnostopoulou 2002). Thus, where filters restricting combinations of subject and object are expected in ergative languages, the analogue for nominative-accusative languages would be conditions on the morphological expression of various combinations of direct and indirect objects. The Person Case Constraint family of phenomena (such as the French *me-lui* restriction on clitics, see Bonet 1994) seem at first blush to fit the bill.

[20] For an account of Latin deponency set within the general framework adopted here, see Embick (2000).

## 5.  Basque: SAP Without Antipassive

Armed with the analysis of the Chukchi SAP presented above, we may now turn to another phenomenon in an ergative language involving apparent detransitivization in response to agreement filters. The relevant construction is the 'ergative displacement' in Basque (for detailed description, and prior accounts, see Laka 1993, Rezac 2003, and Hualde and Ortiz de Urbina 2003). A synopsis of the defining characteristics of this phenomenon is given in (23); according to the available descriptions, Ergative Displacement is obligatory when the conditions in the first line are met.

(23)    Ergative Displacement (Basque)
        If clause is non-present, and subject>object = {1,2} > 3
        then
        The ergative subject governs absolutive agreement
        The absolutive object fails to govern (absolutive) agreement

The similarity to the Chukchi SAP is striking. Agreement morphology is intransitive, while verb-external syntax is transitive, as witnessed by case-marking. Moreover, in precisely this configuration, the intransitive agreement morphology is controlled by the ergative, rather than the absolutive, argument. There is, however, one remarkable difference between the two constructions, namely that the Chukchi SAP involves a morphological mark of detransitiviation (the antipassive morpheme), and it is in virtue of this property that the SAP qualifies as deponent (see Matthews, this volume for remarks on the implicit role of morphological marking in the attention paid to deponency). Basque ergative displacement involves no mark of a voice alternation, and thus does not meet the criteria for deponency, even under the definition in (4). I argue here that this difference is superficial, Basque lacks any morphologically marked voice opposition, and hence, the alternation in Basque may receive the same analysis as the Chukchi SAP, up to the morphological realization of the functional head $v$, which in Basque remains null whether or not an object is in its local domain. Not only does the Chukchi SAP lack a formal affinity to Latin deponency (despite the superficial resemblance in terms of v-deponency (4)), the family of constructions with which it does form a natural class are not necessarily deponent even in the broad sense. The following paragraphs sketch just enough information about the Basque to admit this conclusion, and then note one final curious point of similarity between Chukchi and Basque that falls outside of the analysis offered here, for both languages.

Basque ergative displacement is exemplified in (25). Example (25a–b) are controls, illustrating the normal agreement pattern in the present tense. This conforms to the template in (24), from Laka (1993: 35). Ergative and absolutive agreement morphology are distinguished both by their form and their position in the word, with the absolutive agreement (object) occurring as a prefix. The example in (25c) illustrates ergative displacement. Although the syntax and semantics of the clause are transitive, the verbal morphology is from the intransitive paradigm, with an absolutive prefix cross-referencing the subject, even though the latter is ergative.

(24)  ABSOLUTIVE——VERB——DATIVE——MODAL——ERGATIVE——TENSE
      AGREEMENT    ROOT    AGREEMENT              AGREEMENT

(25)  a  (nik)      **d**-akar-**t**
         I.ERG      3SG.ABS-bring-1SG.ERG
         'I bring it.'

      b. **n**-akar
         1S.ABS-bring
         'He brings me.'

      c. (nik)      **n**-ekarren
                    1SG.ABS-bring.past
         'I brought it'              (Hualde and Ortiz de Urbina 2003: 208–10)

In addition to the transitive case array, Laka shows that the distribution of reflexives continues to treat the ergative displacement examples (such as (26b)) as transitive.

(26)  a. Nik       neure     burua      ikusten    d-u-t
         1SG.ERG   my.own    head.ABS   see.IMPF   3.ABS-have-1.ERG
         'I see myself.'

      b. Nik       neure     burua      ikusten    n-u-en
         1SG.ERG   my.own    head.ABS   see.IMPF   1.ABS-have-PAST
         'I saw myself.'                          (Laka 1993: 54)

The tree in (27) applies the analysis of the Chukchi SAP to Basque ergative displacement. The syntactic and morphological derivations are identical, with the exception that the filters that apply in Basque pick out a different set of person-number combinations of subject and object. The only difference between the derivation in (27) and that in (19) is in the phonological realization of the head *v*; Chukchi has an antipassive morpheme, which is thus used in this environment, where Basque has no such morpheme. The construction in Basque should, and does, look simply like an intransitive verb in terms of its agreement morphology.

(27) Ergative Displacement

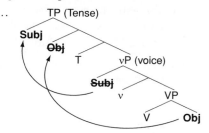

Further Basque facts indicate the fine line between syntax and morphology, which is central to the view espoused here. In Basque, the agreement morphology normally surfaces on an auxiliary, rather than on the main verb (as it does in Chukchi). As in other languages, Basque displays a phenomenon of auxiliary selection, governed by argument structure. As Laka stresses (p. 54), although the agreement morphology in ergative displacement constructions is drawn from the intransitive array, the auxiliary used is nevertheless the transitive auxiliary *ukan* 'have', rather than the auxiliary *izan* 'be' which is expected when there is only an absolutive agreement marker (the form of this auxiliary in (26b) would be *n-intz-en*). The analysis presented here makes the right cut between these two morphological signals of transitivity.[21] The choice of auxiliary is determined by argument structure, a property that is unaffected by the filters and their resulting deletion operations, hence auxiliary selection remains transitive. It is only agreement morphology (and voice, relevant only to Chukchi) that is intransitive.[22]

Before closing this section, I note one loose end for which I have no account. In Basque, there is a special plural morpheme, not indicated in the template in (24), which occurs between the absolutive agreement marker and the verb root. Ergative displacement does not affect this morpheme: even though the absolutive agreement marker is controlled by the ergative nominal

---

[21] The proposal here thus shares some measure of affinity to the suggestion in Heath (1976) that ergative displacement is a species of antipassive. Objections to that analysis have been on the grounds that the construction displays none of the canonical syntactic, semantic, or verb-external morphosyntatic properties of an antipassive. Of course, this is exactly the characteristic behaviour of a spurious antipassive.

[22] Compare the Basque case with the Sanskrit periphrastic perfectives discussed by Stump (this volume). In Basque Ergative Displacement, there is a mismatch internal to the form of the auxiliary: the form of the root is justified by the syntactico-semantic context (transitive), while the agreement is unjustifiably intransitive. I take this as evidence that the apparent detransitivization in the agreement is morphological, not syntactic in nature. In the Sanskrit perfectives discussed by Stump (as I understand it), the mismatch is at a different level, with both auxiliary and main verb showing the surface form that arguably fails to match the semantics (argument structure or voice). The differing nature of the facts in the two languages leads to different theoretical treatments.

in the construction, the appearance of the plural morpheme is still controlled by the absolutive NP. This is shown in (28b), with the morpheme in question boldfaced. Example (28a) is a present tense control, where both the absolutive agreement and absolutive number are controlled by the absolutive NP.

(28)  a.  Nik       liburuak      irakurri      d-**it**-u-t
          I.ERG     books.ABS     read          3.ABS-**PL**-have-1.ERG
          'I read the books.'

      b.  Nik       liburuak      irakurri      n-**it**-u-en
          I.ERG     books.ABS     read          1.ABS-**PL**-have-PAST
          'I have read the books.'                          (Ortiz de Urbina 1989)

Two avenues of exploration present themselves. On the one hand, we may seek evidence for further articulation of the functional structure of the clause, with a number agreement projection distinct from the locus of the other agreement morphology. The filters may not apply to this node. Care must be taken in fleshing this out so as not to undermine the necessary feature movement chains and their consequences for the post-deletion morphological representation. On the other hand, we might suspect verbal number (pluractionality) here. As noted by Corbett (2000: 253) (see also Durie 1985), it is not uncommon for verbal number to pick out absolutives regardless of what agreement morphology may be doing.

    Note incidentally that the same issue arises in Chukchi (as mentioned in fn. 8, above). In the combination of 3SG subject acting on 3 object in the habitual mood, the SAP is required, and the agreement morphology conforms to the intransitive agreement paradigm, except that the absolutive plural marker is still governed by the absolutive NP (see (29b)).

(29)  a.  ənan          ətłjon        n-ine-ɬʔu-qin
          3SG.ERG       3SG.ABS       MOOD-AP-see-3SUBJ
          'He sees him.'

      b.  ənan          ətri          n-ine-ɬʔu-qin-**et**
          3SG.ERG       3PL.ABS       MOOD-AP-see-3SUBJ-**PL**
          'He sees them.'                                   (Skorik 1977: 66)

I will leave further investigation of this issue as a topic for future research.


# 6. Summary and Conclusions

This paper has examined in some detail a construction which meets the main criterion for deponency, namely, a set of verb forms with non-active, intransitive morphology occurring in syntactic environments that are active and transitive. I have offered two conclusions here. First, I have shown that the pattern can be derived with no special morphological devices, and is in fact even expected from certain theoretical perspectives, given a certain constellation of properties. Second, I have argued that at the level of theoretical analysis, the key properties of the Chukchi SAP have no obvious point of connection to deponency in Latin and Greek, and if anything, are related to other person-governed transitivity mismatches, such as Basque ergative displacement, which fail to meet the criteria of deponency even in the sense defined in (4). Thus, I conclude that 'v-deponency' as defined in (4) may serve as a useful descriptive label for identifying intriguing patterns, presenting challenging problems for morphological and syntactic accounts, but does not pick out a natural class of phenomena with a common underlying analysis. Both questions with which the paper started are thus answered in the negative for the case at hand, pending resolution of the various loose ends mentioned above.

## 7. Appendix: Chukchi Verb Agreement Paradigms (Partial)

Verbs in Chukchi inflect for ten combinations of tense, mood, and aspect, in addition to agreement. There are no conjugation classes, and thus the inflectional morphology is the same for all verbs, aside from phonological interactions. Illustrative paradigms for intransitive verbs are given in (30), and the corresponding paradigms for transitive verbs are given in (31). The Aorist (Skorik's 'Past I') is the morphologically unmarked conjugation (in the sense that there are no tense, aspect, or mood markers) but involves a variety of thematic suffixes that have an odd distribution. The Future Progressive (Skorik's 'Future 2') shows both a tense prefix (*re-*) and an aspectual suffix (*-rkən*) in addition to the agreement morphology. Note that agreement markers (prefixes and suffixes alike) are always peripheral to tense, aspect and mood (not shown), while the antipassive markers *ine-* and *-tku*, even in their guise as SAP morphemes, occur inside tense and aspect. The aorist and future progressive are what Dunn (1999) refers to as active inflections (as contrasted with 'stative' inflections, not to be confused with the active-antipassive voice alternation). The morphology in the active inflections is specific to verbal inflection. The third column ('habitual', Skorik's 'Present 2') exemplifies one of the two stative conjugations. These conjugations lack agreement prefixes, and the agreement suffixes are largely the same as those used for predicative nouns and adjectives. The primary source for these paradigms is Skorik (1977).

(30)  Chukchi intransitive verb agreement

| SUBJ | Aorist | | Future Progressive | | Habitual | |
|------|--------|--------|--------------------|--------|----------|--------|
| 1sg | t- | √ -γʔek | t-re- | √ -rkən | n- | √ -iɣəm |
| 2sg |   | √ -γʔi | re- | √ -rkən | n- | √ -iɣət |

| SUBJ | Aorist | | Future Progressive | | Habitual | |
|---|---|---|---|---|---|---|
| 3SG | | √ -γʔi | re- | √ -rkən | n- | √ -qin |
| 1PL | mət- | √ -mək | mət-re- | √ -rkən | n- | √ -muri |
| 2PL | | √ -tək | re- | √ -rkəni-tək | n- | √ -turi |
| 3PL | | √ -γʔe-t | re- | √ -rkəni-ŋə-t | n- | √ -qin-et |

The corresponding paradigms for transitive verbs are given here.

(31)   Chukchi transitive verb agreement

| SUBJ | OBJ | Aorist | | Future Progressive | | Habitual | |
|---|---|---|---|---|---|---|---|
| 1SG | 2SG | t- | √ -γət | t-re- | √ -rkəni-γət | n-ine- | √ -iγəm |
| | 2PL | t- | √ -tək | t-re- | √ -rkəni-tək | n-ine- | √ -iγəm |
| | 3SG | t- | √ -γʔen | t-re- | √ -rkən | n-ine- | √ -iγəm |
| | 3PL | t- | √ -net | t-re- | √ -rkən-et | n-ine- | √ -iγəm |
| 1PL | 2SG | mət- | √ -γət | mət-re- | √ -rkəni-γət | n-ine- | √ -muri |
| | 2PL | mət- | √ -tək | mət-re- | √ -rkəni-tək | n-ine- | √ -muri |
| | 3SG | mət- | √ -γʔen | mət-re- | √ -rkən | n-ine- | √ -muri |
| | 3PL | mət- | √ -net | mət-re- | √ -rkən-et | n-ine- | √ -muri |
| 2SG | 1SG | ine- | √ -γʔi | r-ine- | √ -rkən | n-ine- | √ -iγət |
| | 1PL | | √ -tku-γʔi | re- | √ -tku-rkən | n- | √ -tku-iγət |
| | 3SG | | √ -γʔen | re- | √ -rkən | n-ine- | √ -iγət |
| | 3PL | | √ -net | re- | √ -rkən-et | n-ine- | √ -iγət |
| 2PL | 1SG | ine- | √ -tək | r-ine- | √ -rkəni-tək | n-ine- | √ -turi |
| | 1PL | | √ -tku-tək | re- | √ -tku-rkəni-tək | n- | √ -tku-turi |
| | 3SG | | √ -tkə | re- | √ -rkəni-tkə | n-ine- | √ -turi |
| | 3PL | | √ -tkə | re- | √ -rkəni-tkə | n-ine- | √ -turi |
| 3SG | 1SG | ine- | √ -γʔi | r-ine- | √ -rkən | n-ine- | √ -qin |
| | 1PL | ne- | √ -mək | ne-re- | √ -rkəni-mək | n- | √ -muri |
| | 2SG | ne- | √ -γət | ne-re- | √ -rkəni-γət | n- | √ -iγət |
| | 2PL | ne- | √ -tək | ne-re- | √ -rkəni-tək | n- | √ -turi |
| | 3SG | | √ -nin | re- | √ -rkən-in | n-ine- | √ -qin |
| | 3PL | | √ -nin-et | re- | √ -rkən-in-et | n-ine- | √ -qin-et |
| 3PL | 1SG | ne- | √ -γəm | ne-re- | √ -rkəni-γəm | n- | √ -iγəm |
| | 1PL | ne- | √ -mək | ne-re- | √ -rkəni-mək | n- | √ -muri |
| | 2SG | ne- | √ -γət | ne-re- | √ -rkəni-γət | n- | √ -iγət |
| | 2PL | ne- | √ -tək | ne-re- | √ -rkəni-tək | n- | √ -turi |
| | 3SG | ne- | √ -γʔen | ne-re- | √ -rkən | n- | √ -qin |
| | 3PL | ne- | √ -net | ne-re- | √ -rkən-et | n- | √ -qin-et |

# References

Anagnostopoulou, Elena. 2002. *The syntax of ditransitives: evidence from clitics.* Berlin: Mouton de Gruyter.

Baerman, Matthew. This volume. Morphological typology of deponency.

Bayer, Josef. 1984. COMP in Bavarian syntax. *The Linguistic Review* 3.209–74.

Bittner, Maria. 1994. *Case, scope and binding.* Dordrecht: Kluwer.

Bittner, Maria, and Ken Hale. 1996. The structural determination of case and agreement. *Linguistic Inquiry* 27.1–68.

Bobaljik, Jonathan David. 1995. *Morphosyntax: the syntax of verbal inflection.* Cambridge, Mass.; MIT Dissertation.

—— 1998. Pseudo-ergativity in Chukotko-Kamchatkan agreement systems. *Ergativity: Recherches Linguistiques de Vincennes* 27, ed. by Lea Nash, 21–44.

—— 2000. The ins and outs of contextual allomorphy. *University of Maryland Working Papers in Linguistics: 10*, ed. by Kleanthes K. Grohmann and Caro Struijke, 35–71.

—— 2002. A-chains at the PF-interface: Copies and 'covert' movement. *Natural Language and Linguistic Theory* 20.197–267.

Bobaljik, Jonathan David, and Phil Branigan. 2006. Eccentric agreement and multiple case checking. *Ergativity: emerging issues*, ed. by Alana Johns, Diane Massam, and Juvenal Ndayiragije, 47–77. Dordrecht: Springer.

Bobaljik, Jonathan David, and Susi Wurmbrand. 2001. Seven prefix-suffix asymmetries in Itel'men. *CLS 37: The Panels. Papers from the 37th Regional Meeting of the Chicago Linguistics Society*, ed. by Mary Andronis, Christoper Ball, Heidi Elston, and Sylvain Neuvel, 205–19.

—— and —— 2002. Notes on agreement in Itelmen. *Linguistic Discovery* 1. Online journal: <http://linguistic-discovery.dartmouth.edu/WebObjects/Linguistics>.

Bok-Bennema, Reineke. 1991. *Case and agreement in Inuit.* Berlin: Foris.

Bonet, Eulàlia. 1994. The person-case constraint: a morphological approach. *The morphology-syntax connection*, ed. by Heidi Harley and Colin Phillips, MIT Working Papers in Linguistics, 33–52.

Bošković, Željko. 2002. On multiple *wh*-fronting. *Linguistic Inquiry* 33.351–83.

Comrie, Bernard. 1979. Degrees of ergativity: Some Chukchee evidence. *Ergativity: towards a theory of grammatical relations*, ed. by Frans Plank, 219–40. London/New York: Academic Press.

—— 1980. Inverse verb forms in Siberia: Evidence from Chukchee, Koryak, and Kamchadal. *Folia Linguistica Historica* 1.61–74.

—— 1983. The genetic affiliation of Kamchadal: some morphological evidence. *Papers in Linguistics* 16.109–20.

Corbett, Greville G. 2000. *Number.* Cambridge: Cambridge University Press.

—— This volume. Deponency, syncretism, and what lies in between.

Dunn, Michael. 1999. *A grammar of Chukchi.* Canberra: Australian National University Dissertation.

Durie, Mark. 1985. The grammaticalization of number as a verbal category. *Proceedings of the Twelfth Annual Meeting of the Berkeley Linguistics Society*, ed. by Vassiliki Nikiforidou, Mary VanClay, Mary Niepokuj, and Deborah Feder, 355–70. Berkeley: Berkeley Linguistics Society.

Embick, David. 2000. Features, syntax, and categories in the Latin perfect. *Linguistic Inquiry* 31.185–230.

Franks, Steven. 1998. Clitics in Slavic. Paper presented at Comparative Slavic Morphosyntax: the State of the Art, Spencer, IN.

Greenough, J. B., G. L. Kittredge, A. A. Howard, and Benj. L. D'Ooge. (eds.) 1903. *Allen and Greenough's new Latin grammar*. Ginn and Company. Online version: <http://www.perseus.tufts.edu/cgi-bin/ptext?doc=Perseus%3Atext%3A1999.04.0001> accessed 4 Jan. 2007.

Hale, Ken. 2002. *Eccentric agreement. Kasu eta komunztaduraren gainean* [On Case and Agreement], ed. by Beatriz Fernández and Pablo Albizu, 15–48. Vitoria-Gasteiz: Euskal Herriko Unibetsitatea.

Halle, Morris, and Ken Hale. 1997. Chukchi transitive and antipassive constructions. Cambridge, Mass.: MIT, ms.

Heath, Jeffrey. 1976. Antipassivization: a functional typology. *Proceedings of the Second Annual Meeting of the Berkeley Linguistics Society*, ed. by Henry Thompson, Kenneth Whistler, Vicki Edge, Jeri Jaeger, Ronya Jaykin, Miriam Petruck, Christopher Smeall, and Robert D. Jr. Van Valin, 202–11. Berkeley: Berkeley Linguistics Society.

Hualde, José Ignacio, and Jon Ortiz de Urbina. (eds.) 2003. *A grammar of Basque*. Berlin: Mouton.

Kozinsky, Issac S., Vladimir Nedjalkov, and Maria S. Polinskaja. 1988. Antipassive in Chuckchee: oblique object, object incorporation, zero object. *Passive and voice*, ed. by Masayoshi Shibatani. Amsterdam: John Benjamins.

Laka, Itziar. 1993. The structure of inflection: a case study in X° syntax. *Generative studies in Basque linguistics*, ed. by José Ignacio Hualde and Jon Ortiz de Urbina, 21–70. Amsterdam/Philadelphia: John Benjamins.

Matthews, P. H. This volume. How safe are our analyses?

Menn, Lise, and Brian MacWhinney. 1984. The repeated morph constraint: toward an explanation. *Language* 60.519–41.

Nash, Lea. 1995. *Portée argumentale et marquage casuel dans les langues SOV et dans les langues ergatives: l'exemple du géorgien*. Paris: Université Paris 8 Dissertation.

Nedjalkov, Vladimir P. 1976. Diathesen und Satzstruktur im Tschuktschischen. *Studia Grammatica* 13.181–213.

—— 1979. Degrees of ergativity in Chukchee. *Ergativity: towards a theory of grammatical relations*, ed. by Frans Plank, 241–62. London/New York: Academic Press.

Ortiz de Urbina, Jon. 1989. *Parameters in the grammar of Basque*. Dordrecht: Foris.

Pesetsky, David. 1998. Some optimality principles of sentence pronunciation. *Is the best good enough*? ed. by Pilar Barbosa, Danny Fox, Paul Hagstrom, Martha McGinnis, and David Pesetsky, 337–83. Cambridge Mass.: MIT Press and MITWPL.

Rezac, Milan. 2003. The fine structure of cyclic Agree. *Syntax* 6.156–82.

Richards, Norvin. 2001. *Movement in language: interactions and architectures*. Oxford: Oxford University Press.

Skorik, Piotr Ja. 1977. *Grammatika čukotskogo jazyka, čast' II: glagol, narečie, služebnye slova* [Grammar of Chukchi, part II: verb, adverb and auxiliary words]. Leningrad: Nauka.

Spencer, Andrew. 2000. Agreement morphology in Chukotkan. *Morphological analysis in comparison*, ed. by Wolfgang U. Dressler, Oskar E. Pfeiffer, and Markus A. Pochtrager, 191–222. Amsterdam: John Benjamins.

Stump, Gregory T. This volume. A non-canonical pattern of deponency and its implications.

Wharram, Douglas. 2003. *On the interpretation of (un)certain indefinites in Inuktitut and related languages*. Storrs, CT: UConn Dissertation.

Wurmbrand, Susi. 2006. Licensing case. *Journal of Germanic Linguistics* 18. 174–234.

Xu, Zheng, Mark Aronoff, and Frank Anshen. 2006. Deponency in Latin. Paper presented at Deponency and Morphological Mismatches, London.

Zhukova, Alevtina N. 1972. *Grammatika korjakskogo jazyka: fonetika, morfologija* [Grammar of Koryak: Phonetics and Morphology]. Leningrad; Nauka.

—— 1980. *Jazyk palanskix korjakov* [The Language of the Palana Koryaks]. Leningrad: Nauka.

# 9

# Slouching Towards Deponency:
# A Family of Mismatches in the Bantu
# Verb Stem*

JEFF GOOD

## 1. Introduction

MOST BANTU LANGUAGES HAVE A SET OF highly productive verbal derivational suffixes which alter the argument structure and semantics of basic verb
roots. One example of such a suffix is the Causative, which gives a verb stem
causative semantics and allows it to take an extra causer argument. A prototypical instance of the use of the Causative, drawn from Chichewa (Baker
1988:10), is given in (1).[1]

(1)  a.  *Mtsuko*      *u-na-gw-a.*
           3.waterpot   3-PST-fall-FV
           'The waterpot  fell.'

      b.  *Mtsikana*   *a-na-gw-**ets**-a*        *mtsuko.*
           1.girl       3SG-PST-fall-CAUS-FV   3.waterpot
           'The girl      made the waterpot   fall.'

---

* This paper owes an enormous debt to Larry Hyman, whose work on the morphophonology of
the Bantu verb stem was a prerequisite to identifying the cases of deponency discussed here.
Johanna Nichols should also be acknowledged for pointing out to me several years ago that
'pseudo-' verb stems in Bantu could be given the label 'deponent'. Discussions with Matthew
Baerman and comments from attendees of the Conference on Deponency and Morphological
Mismatches also contributed to this paper.
[1] As seen in (1), surface forms of verbs in Bantu languages typically end in an inflectional Final
Vowel, glossed FV, which is not classified here as part of the verb stem. Most surface forms also
appear with a number of verbal prefixes. These will not factor into the discussion here in any
crucial way.

*Proceedings of the British Academy* **145**, 203–230. © The British Academy 2007.

The verb root in sentence (1a), -*gw*- 'fall', is not followed by any derivational suffixes and, thus, retains it basic valency and semantics. In (1b) the Causative suffix -*ets*- appears after -*gw*-, giving causative semantics to the verb and shifting its valency from intransitive to transitive.

This paper will discuss some morphological idiosyncrasies involving the four Bantu verbal suffixes listed in Table 1. The forms of the suffixes given in the table follow the Proto-Bantu reconstructions of Meeussen (1967: 92). The symbol *i̧* seen in the reconstruction of the Transitive suffix represents the highest front vowel in a symmetric seven-vowel system.

Following a convention seen in Table 1, throughout the paper, I will use lower-case terms like *passivization* and *applicativization* to refer to abstract morphological processes which can apply to basic verb roots to create derived verb stems showing the syntax and semantics associated with those terms. The capitalized terms Causative, Applicative, Transitive, and Passive, by contrast, will be used to refer to the specific Proto-Bantu morphemes given in Table 1 or to the reflexes of those morphemes in the Bantu daughter languages.[2] Since the functions of the Causative and the Transitive largely overlap and the two morphemes can interact in intricate ways to mark a single stem as causativized, as will be briefly discussed in section 2.2, a single abstract term, *causativization*, will be used for the syntax and semantics that they encode. Thus, for example, the *Transitive* will often be described as *causativizing* a given verb.[3]

A prototypical use of the Causative suffix was given in (1). As just mentioned, the Transitive suffix typically has a function similar to the Causative, and an example of its use will be seen below in (3). The prototypical function of the Passive is as a straightforward passivizing morpheme: the logical object of a verb marked with the Passive is promoted to subject and the

**Table 1.** Reconstructed Bantu verbal suffixes

| PROTO-BANTU | FUNCTION | LABEL |
|---|---|---|
| *-ic- | causativization | Causative |
| *-id- | applicativization | Applicative |
| *-i̧- | causativization | Transitive |
| *-u- | passivization | Passive |

[2] The attested forms of these suffixes vary from language to language, of course, and they will sometimes bear rather opaque relationships to the Proto-Bantu forms, as will become clear over the course of the paper.

[3] The use of the term Transitive for the reconstructed Proto-Bantu morpheme *-i̧- was introduced in Good (2005) to avoid terminological confusion where both *-i̧- and *-ic- were referred to as 'causatives'. In other work, these suffixes are sometimes distinguished through the use of modifiers like 'short' and 'long' or through similar devices.

logical subject is either unexpressed or expressed as an oblique argument (typically as an instrumental prepositional phrase). Following Peterson (1999: 120), the Applicative can generally be characterized as making 'intransitive verbs transitive and transitive verbs "supertransitive" in that they [will have] two direct objects'. (Importantly, the Applicative makes intransitive verbs transitive by letting them take an object—not by adding a subject argument, as seen for causativization in (1b).) A prototypical example of the use of the Applicative, again from Chichewa, taken from Alsina and Mchombo (1993: 18), is given in (2).

(2)   a.   *Chitsîru    chi-na-gúl-á    mphátso.*
          7.fool       7-PST-buy-FV    9.gift
          'The fool bought a gift.'

      b.   *Chitsîru    chi-na-gúl-ir-á    atsíkana    mphátso.*
          7.fool       7-PST-buy-APPL-FV   2.girl     9.gift
          'The fool bought the girls a gift.'

In (2b) the presence of the Applicative allows the verb *-gúl-* 'buy' to take an unmarked benefactive object (*atsíkána* '2.girl'), in addition to an unmarked theme (*mphátso* '9.gift'). When the Applicative is not present on that verb, as in (2a), only one unmarked object (a theme) is permitted. (A marked benefactive object, introduced by the preposition *kwa* 'for', would be permitted in a sentence like the one in (2a).)

In descriptions of Bantu languages one can find the use of labels like *pseudo-passive* or *pseudo-causative* to describe verb stems which look as if they are marked with one of the verbal suffixes given in Table 1 but which are not clearly associated with corresponding 'bare' roots. The data in (3) from Kinande (Hyman 1993: 12–13) give an example of such a stem, *-song-į-* 'gather', which is classified as a pseudo-causative since it is marked with an instance of the Transitive. This stem is contrasted with the regular verb root *-tsap-* 'wet'.

(3)

| STEM | GLOSS | TRANSLATION |
|---|---|---|
| *-tsap-* | 'wet' | 'get wet' |
| *-tsap-į-* | 'wet-TRANS' | 'make wet' |
| *-tsap-an-į-* | 'wet-RECP-TRANS' | 'wet each other' |
| *-song- | — | NO MEANING |
| *-song-į-* | 'SONG-TRANS' | 'gather (trans.)' |
| *-song-an-į-* | 'SONG-RECP-TRANS' | 'gather each other' |

The data in (3) show the regular verb root *-tsap-* 'wet' being causativized by the addition of the Transitive suffix and also reciprocalized with the Reciprocal suffix. The morphologically complex stem *-song-į-*-'SONG-TRANS', if regular, would be similarly associated with a bare root *-song-*. However this

root is never attested without the Transitive suffix and has no meaning on its
own. Furthermore, as seen, the Reciprocal suffix can intervene between *song*
and *i* in this stem, clearly indicating that it is synchronically analysable as
consisting of two morphemes, a root followed by the Transitive. The stem
-*song-i*-, therefore, looks like it has been causativized with the Transitive even
though it is evidently not derived from some more basic verb root, making it
reasonable to assign it the label pseudo-causative.

Taken at face value, verb stems like -*song-i*- would seem to be good candidates for the label *deponent*, since they apparently exhibit a form-function
mismatch where their morphology signals they belong to a morphosyntactic
class they are not 'truly' members of. However, there are a number of analytical issues raised by 'pseudo-' verb stems in Bantu which make finding
unequivocal instances of deponency far from straightforward. For example,
with respect to the data in (3), the fact that -*song-i*- is transitive makes it
amenable to a treatment where it is, in fact, understood to be causativized—
as its morphology would suggest—and the lack of a bare root with form
-*song*- evinces a simple morphological gap. Under such an analysis, there
would be no actual mismatch between the morphology and the syntax.
Rather, the transitive syntax of -*song-i*- would be in line with the presence of
morphology which elsewhere is known to derive transitives from intransitives
(along the lines of what was seen in (1b)).

Despite such issues, however, it will be shown here that there do appear to
be unequivocal cases of deponency in Bantu. It will be further shown that
deponency is not an isolated phenomenon in the family but, rather, is just one
exponent of a wider pattern of morphological irregularities. In section 2 of
this paper further background information on the Bantu verb stem will be
given in order to make the rest of the discussion clearer. In section 3 one of
the simpler sorts of morphological irregularities found in the verb stem will
be described: lexicalization of root+suffix combinations. In section 4 a number of apparent morphological mismatches in the verb stem will be discussed,
which, while not being cases of deponency, will help set the stage for understanding the data in section 5, where various classes of deponent verb stems
will be covered. Finally, section 6 will offer a brief conclusion.

# 2. The Bantu Verb Stem

## 2.1. Morphosyntactic stems and morphophonological stems

The Bantu verb stem can be described with respect to both its morphosyntactic and its morphophonological properties. In general, these two sets of
properties will coincide in a given morphological form. However, as we shall

see in following sections, under certain conditions they can diverge, leading to, in some cases, deponency.

Within the realm of Bantu morphosyntax, the stem is important as the domain in which verbal argument structure is determined. Specifically, as seen in examples like (1) and (2), verb roots in Bantu can be associated with a basic valency, and the addition of suffixes on the root creates stems whose argument structure is predictable from an examination of the root+suffix combination. This morphosyntactic interaction between the verb root and its suffixes has received a fair amount of attention in work on theoretical syntax (see, e.g. Baker (1988) or Alsina (1999)), underscoring the verb stem's importance as a morphosyntactic unit.

At the same time, the Bantu verb stem has long been considered to also be important with respect to morphophonology—specifically, it is the domain over which a number of important phonological phenomena are operative. A selection of these phenomena, drawn from Hyman (1993: 25), is given in (4). (See also Downing (1999).)

(4)  a.  Vowel height harmony is observed in some Bantu languages within (but not outside of) the verb stem.
    b.  Vowel coalescence often applies differently within the verb stem than it does elsewhere.
    c.  All vowels between the initial vowel of the verb stem and the obligatory Final Vowel are underlyingly toneless.

In the following sections, we shall see further, language-specific morphophonological properties of verb stems relevant to detecting instances of deponency in the family.

## 2.2. Some features of Proto-Bantu verbal phonology and morphology

In addition to acknowledging that the Bantu verb stem can be conceptualized both as a morphosyntactic and as a morphophonological entity, it will also be important here to be aware of several aspects of Proto-Bantu verbal phonology and morphology. Table 2 gives the reconstructed consonant inventory for Proto-Bantu, following Schadeberg (2003: 146). The columns in the table break down the consonants by four reconstructed places of articulation: labial, alveolar, palatal, and velar.[4]

---

[4] How to reconstruct the phonetic realization of the consonants *c and *j is not clear, especially with regards to whether they should be interpreted as palatal stops or palatal affricates—and it is even possible that they were not palatal at all (Hyman 2003a: 42). In orthographic representations of the Bantu daughter languages, *c* and *j* are generally used to represent (alveo-)palatal affricates.

**Table 2.** Proto-Bantu consonant inventory

| p  | t   | c   | k  |
|----|-----|-----|----|
| b  | l/d | y/j | g  |
| m  | n   | ny  |    |
| mp | nt  | nc  | nk |
| mb | nd  | nj  | ng |

As indicated in table 2, fricatives are not generally reconstructed for Proto-Bantu (but see Schadeberg (2003: 147) about the reconstructions of the palatal stops). Fricatives, however, are widely attested in the daughter languages, often as a result of historical palatalization effects, with a reconstructed 'super-high' vowel *į particularly prone to triggering palatalization. We shall see below that this latter fact is important to understanding instances of deponency involving the Transitive, whose reconstructed form *-į- consists solely of this vowel.

In fact, not infrequently, the *only* reflex of the Transitive in a given language is as palatalization on a consonant that it would have followed historically—that is, it has no segmental reflex at all.[5] This can be seen in, for example, the data in (5), taken from the Korekore dialect of Shona (Dembetembe 1987: 58). The causativized forms of certain verbs in this language are derived via a palatalizing mutation of the root-final consonant, corresponding, historically, to palatalization triggered by a Transitive suffix immediately following the verb root.

(5)  | ROOT    | TRANSLATION     | CAUS. STEM | TRANSLATION                        |
     |---------|-----------------|------------|------------------------------------|
     | -svik-  | 'arrive'        | -svits-    | 'make arrive, help to arrive'      |
     | -rir-   | 'sound, ring'   | -ridz-     | 'cause to sound, ring'             |
     | -wand-  | 'be plentiful'  | -wanz-     | 'increase'                         |
     | -net-   | 'get tired'     | -nets-     | 'cause trouble, be troublesome'    |
     | -yimb-  | 'rely on'       | -yinzv-    | 'cause to rely on'                 |
     | -rep-   | 'be long'       | -redzv-    | 'make long, lengthen'              |

An additional complication regarding the Transitive is that, in many languages—perhaps reflecting an inheritance from Proto-Bantu (see Good (2005: 14–15))—it obligatorily appears on any verb stem marked with the Causative suffix, in a complex morphemic combination with shape *-ic-į-. Other verbal suffixes, like the Applicative, can appear between these two

---

[5] Throughout the paper, I will use the term palatalization to refer to the effects of the vowel *į* on preceding consonants. In a few cases, this will include non-prototypical uses of the term to refer to cases where a labial stop alternates with a labial fricative.

suffixes, clearly indicating that the combination is bimorphemic.[6] In languages where the Transitive triggers palatalization, this can lead to complex patterns in surface verb forms where a consonant may be palatalized in one stem formed on a given verb root, but not on a morphologically related stem, depending on whether or not it is (or was historically) immediately followed by the Transitive. The data in (6) from Ciyao (Ngunga 2000: 236) illustrate this. (The reconstructions in (6) are my own.)

(6)

| STEM | | PROTO-BANTU | GLOSS |
|---|---|---|---|
| -won- | < | *-bon- | 'see' |
| -won-el- | < | *-bon-id- | 'see-APPL' |
| -won-es-y- | < | *-bon-ic-i̦- | 'see-CAUS-TRANS' |
| -won-ec-es-y- | < | *-bon-ic-id-i̦- | 'see-CAUS-APPL-TRANS' |

The data in (6) show that the general form of the Applicative in Ciyao ends in an *l*. However, in verbs like *-won-ec-es-y-* 'see-CAUS-APPL-TRANS', which is marked as causativized and applicativized, the Applicative ends in an *s*, consistent with a historical palatalization process, triggered by the Transitive, affecting the single consonant of the reconstructed Applicative form *-id-. Note also that, in this context, the final consonant of the Causative shifts from *s* to etymologically predicted *c*—a kind of depalatalization consistent with the fact that the Causative is not directly followed by the Transitive in this form, unlike in the basic causativized form *-won-es-y-* 'see-CAUS-TRANS'.

The palatalization processes triggered by the Transitive, as we shall see, are not always reflected in regular ways in the Bantu daughter languages. They are often reanalysed as being morphologically conditioned, and, in more extreme cases, they can be analogically extended to forms where there would have been no palatalization historically. (See Hyman (2003b) for detailed discussion.) This sort of analogical extension appears to have played an important role in some of the cases of deponency to be discussed in section 5.

# 3. Lexicalization of Suffixes on the Verb Stem

Given their morphophonological integration with the verb root, it is not surprising to find that the verbal suffixes focused on here often become lexicalized in particular stems. The data in (7) from Luvale, adapted from Horton (1949: 87), provide a relevant example.

---

[6] See §4.1 for a discussion of principles determining how the verbal suffixes are ordered with respect to one another.

(7)   STEM              GLOSS                     TRANSLATION
      *-lw-a-*           'fight'                   'fight'
      *-lw-il-*          'fight-APPL'              'save'
      *-lw-il-is-*       'fight-APPL-CAUS'         'cause to save'
      *-lw-ish-il-*      'fight-CAUS-APPL'         'cause to fight for'

In Luvale, the productive order for the Causative (C) with respect to the Applicative (A) is CA. However, AC order becomes possible 'when a derived form has largely lost its derivative significance (Horton 1949: 87)'. This can be seen in the verb stem *-lw-il-* 'fight-APPL', given in (7), where the Applicative has lexicalized with the verb root meaning 'fight' to take on the meaning 'save'. This lexicalization is associated both with the rise of a non-compositional meaning of the root+suffix combination and with a fusion of the combination which allows the morphotactic restriction against Applicative-Causative order to be violated in the form *-lw-il-is-* 'fight-APPL-CAUS', which has the meaning 'cause to save'. By contrast, the verb stem *-lw-ish-il-* 'fight-CAUS-APPL', which is based on the same root and instantiates the productive Causative-Applicative order, has a fully compositional meaning.

Importantly, lack of semantic compositionality of a root+suffix combination does not necessarily lead to morphological fusion of the sort seen in Luvale. This is illustrated by the Chichewa data in (8) (Hyman and Mchombo 1992: 359).

(8)   STEM              GLOSS                     TRANSLATION
      *-uk-*             'wake_up'                 'wake up'
      *-uk-ir-*          'wake_up-APPL'            'rebel against'
   *-*uk-ir-its-*        'wake_up-APPL-CAUS'
      *-uk-its-ir-*      'wake_up-CAUS-APPL'       'cause to rebel against'

The root+suffix combination *-uk-ir-* 'wake_up-APPL' has become lexicalized with the meaning 'rebel against' in Chichewa. Despite this, when the stem is causativized, the Causative suffix appears between the root and the Applicative suffix, following a morphotactic constraint found throughout Bantu—which is especially strong in Chichewa and was seen in a weaker form in Luvale just above—where the Causative typically must precede the Applicative, even in many cases where this would be unexpected on semantic grounds (see Hyman (2003c), Good (2005)). This issue will be taken up again in section 4.1.

The sort of pattern just illustrated by the data in (8) is interesting in the present context since it points out one possible pathway to deponency-like phenomena in Bantu. If the plain root *-uk-* 'wake_up' were to drop out of

Chichewa but -*uk*-*ir*- meaning 'rebel against' were to remain in the lexicon as a bimorphemic entity, this form would superficially appear to be deponent in the sense that it would look like an applicativized verb but would not be associated with a corresponding non-Applicative root (much like the way in which the Kinande pseudo-causative in (3) lacks a corresponding non-Transitive root). It would, however, fall short of unequivocal deponency since a verb stem meaning 'rebel against' would be transitive, allowing one to argue the Applicative suffix was still synchronically playing a role in determining the stem's overall valency.

Below, we shall see some cases of apparent deponency which may have followed a path like the one just outlined—with the crucial difference being that the semantics of the lexicalized root+suffix combination is not straightforwardly amenable to an analysis where the suffix is making any contribution, even an abstract one, to the stem's syntax and semantics.

## 4. Mismatches in the Bantu Verb Stem

In this section, I will discuss various kinds of 'mismatches' found in Bantu which form part of a larger pattern wherein verb stems fall into different morphophonological classes closely associated with morphological types like Causative, Passive, etc. Three kinds of mismatches will be discussed in turn: templatic suffix ordering, long-distance effects of the Transitive suffix, and the appearance of meaningless formatives under special morphophonological conditions. Unlike the examples of deponency to be discussed in section 5, most of the mismatches here involve what might be termed phonology-morphology mismatches, where the phonological exponence of a morpheme is more complicated than its segmental form simply being concatenated on to the verb root.

Even though these mismatches do not involve the syntactic properties of verb stems, we shall see in section 5 that the existence of mismatches like these will prove useful in establishing unequivocal cases of deponency. Specifically, such mismatches will allow us to make use of criteria for categorizing potentially deponent forms as 'Causative' or 'Passive', etc., which go beyond simply showing that their segmental phonology resembles that of true Causatives, Passives, etc. In some cases, the candidate deponent forms will also participate in morphophonological alternations, of the sort described in this section, which are otherwise only associated with their non-deponent counterparts—giving us strong evidence that both sets of forms truly belong to the same morphological class.

## 4.1. Templatic morpheme ordering

One of the more well-studied areas of mismatch in the Bantu verb stem is apparent templatic ordering of the verbal suffixes of interest to us here (Hyman 2003c; Good 2005). Specifically, a primary determining factor of allowable suffix combinations is a relative order template which can be schematized as a series of linear precedence statements indicating how any set of suffixes should be ordered with respect to each other when multiple suffixes appear in the same verb stem. Such a schema is given in (9).

(9)   CAUS (\*-ic-) > APPL (\*-id-) > RECP (\*-an-) > TRANS (\*-j-) > PASS (\*-u-)

While the template in (9) can be violated in some cases in some languages, overall, it characterizes the possible orderings of the suffixes more accurately than another principle suggested as relevant to their order—semantic scope (Baker 1988; Alsina 1999). One important effect accounted for by the template, worth highlighting here, is that suffix orders consistent with it may be ambiguous for the scope of the semantics associated with the suffixes. This is exemplified by the Chichewa data in (10) (for further discussion see Hyman (2003c)).

(10)  | STEM | GLOSS | TRANSLATION |
|---|---|---|
| *-mang-its-* | 'tie-CAUS' | [X cause Y to tie] |
| *-mang-ir-* | 'tie-APPL' | [Y tie for Z] |
| *-mang-its-ir-* | 'tie-CAUSE-APPL' | [X cause [Y to tie with Z]] *or* |
| | | [X [cause Y tie] with Z] |
| *\*-mang-ir-its-* | 'tie-APPL-CAUS' | — |

As seen in (10), consistent with the template in (9), Causative-Applicative order is permitted in Chichewa but Applicative-Causative order is not. However, this restriction does not appear to be connected to the syntax or semantics of causativization and applicativization since, as indicated, the form *-mang-its-ir-* is ambiguous for scope of applicativization with respect to causativization.

Depending on one's theoretical persuasion, a relative order template like the one given in (9) might be considered to trigger the presence of deponency in a given language. For instance, if one were to assume that morphological ordering should, in general, reflect semantic scope, along the lines of Baker's (1988) Mirror Principle, a reading like '[X cause [Y to tie with Z]]' for the verb *-mang-its-ir-*, as seen in (10), would represent a morphology-syntax mismatch since a morpheme closer to the verb root (the Causative) apparently has scope over a morpheme further from the verb root (the Applicative). Such templatic ordering effects are, however, clearly not ideal sources for examples of deponency since the classification of the relevant forms as deponent relies on a theoretical approach to morphosyntax which is not universally accepted.

Putting aside the issue as to whether or not order/scope mismatches conditioned by the template in (9) should qualify as instances of deponency, we shall see in section 5 that some parts of the template will still have an important role to play in some less theory-dependent cases of deponency. Specifically, the typical positioning of the Transitive and Passive near the end of the verb stem will help us to strengthen the arguments for a morphology/syntax mismatch in certain forms by giving us stronger criteria for treating them as marked with the Transitive or Passive than their simply having the 'right' segmental phonology.

### 4.2. Long-distance effects of the Transitive suffix

A fairly striking set of morphophonological patterns found in some Bantu languages involves apparent 'long-distance' effects of the Transitive suffix. To understand the nature of these effects, it is helpful to begin with data from an etymologically 'well-behaved' language. Such data can be seen in (11) where examples from Mongo of verb stems marked with only the Transitive and of verb stems marked with both the Applicative and the Transitive are given. The examples are drawn from Hulstaert (1965), as collected by Hyman (2003b: 60). As seen in (11), the productive order of the Applicative (A) and Transitive (T) in Mongo is AT, consistent with the template schematized in (9), just discussed above in section 4.1.

| (11) | ROOT | TRANS | APPL-TRANS | ROOT GLOSS |
|---|---|---|---|---|
| | -kɔt- | -kɔts-į- | -kɔt-ɛj-į- | 'cut' |
| | -kút- | -kúts-į- | -kút-ej-į- | 'cool' |
| | -kál- | -káj-į- | -kál-ej-į- | 'dry' |
| | -kɛl- | -kɛj-į- | -kɛl-ej-į- | 'flow' |
| | -kɛnd- | -kɛnj-į- | -kɛnd-ej-į- | 'go' |
| | -kínd- | -kínj-į- | -kínd-ej-į- | 'eat one's fill' |

The Mongo data in (11) show a similar pattern to the Ciyao data given in (6) where the Transitive triggers palatalization on the consonant immediately preceding it, whether this is a root-final consonant or the consonant of an Applicative suffix. Mongo is referred to as etymologically 'well-behaved' here because the palatalized root-final consonants in the forms marked only with the Transitive revert to ending with their 'underlying' consonants when the Applicative intervenes between the root and the Transitive—as expected if palatalization is conceived of as a purely local phenomenon.

A language like Mongo can be contrasted with a language like Bemba, which is etymologically poorly behaved (examples from Hyman (2003b: 61), see also Hyman (1994)). As seen in (12), when a Transitive does not immediately follow the root in Bemba due to the presence of an intervening Applicative, the root-final consonant remains palatalized. (In non-causativized contexts, the Applicative in Bemba has form *-il-/-el-* (Hyman 2003b: 62).) The data in (12) are divided between labial-final stems, which 'palatalize' to a final *f*, and alveolar and velar stems, which palatalize to a final *š*. (The use of *š*, as opposed to *sh*, in examples like that in (12) follows the original source.)

| (12) | ROOT | TRANS | APPL-TRANS | ROOT GLOSS |
|---|---|---|---|---|
| | *-leep-* | *-leef-y-* | *-leef-eš-y-* | 'be long' |
| | *-lub-* | *-luf-y-* | *-luf-iš-y-* | 'be lost' |
| | *-fiit-* | *-fiiš-y-* | *-fiiš-iš-y-* | 'be dark' |
| | *-cind-* | *-cinš-y-* | *-cinš-iš-y-* | 'dance' |
| | *-lil-* | *-liš-y-* | *-liš-iš-y-* | 'cry' |
| | *-buuk-* | *-buuš-y-* | *-buuš-iš-y-* | 'get up (intr.)' |
| | *-lúng-* | *-lúnš-y-* | *-lúnš-iš-y-* | 'hunt' |

Data like that in (12) show that, in some cases, the exponence of the Transitive can include idiosyncratic, morphologically- conditioned phonological effects. We shall see comparable effects in the discussion of deponent forms section 5.1, where they will prove useful in establishing that candidate deponent forms really do belong to the same morphological class as their non-deponent counterparts.

### 4.3. Meaningless formatives

A final interesting kind of morphological complication found in the exponence of verbal suffixes in Bantu worth mentioning here is the appearance of meaningless morphological formatives whose existence is apparently phonologically conditioned.

This phenomenon is reported for Nyakyusa. In order to understand the relevant data, it is first helpful to look at verb stems like those in (13), which are discussed by Hyman (2003b: 74) and were originally reported by Schumann (1899) and Meinhof (1932). Forms are adapted from Meinhof (1932: 147–9); daggers indicate forms I have constructed on the basis of the description. The Nyakyusa forms in (13) are comparable to the Bemba forms just discussed in (12) where interesting morphophonological effects are found when some suffix (here the Applicative) intervenes between the stem and the Transitive suffix.

| (13) | ROOT | TRANS | APPL | APPL-TRANS | ROOT GLOSS |
|---|---|---|---|---|---|
| | *-sok-* | *-sos-y-* | *-sok-el-* | *-sok-es-y-* | 'go out' |
| | *-lek-* | †*-les-y-* | *-lek-el-* | *-lek-es-y-* | 'let go' |
| | *-syut-* | *-syus-y-* | †*-syut-el-* | †*-syuk-es-y-* | 'swing' |
| | *-kind-* | *-kis-y-* | †*-kind-il-* | *-kik-is-y-* | 'pass' |
| | *-jong-* | *-jos-y-* | †*-jong-el-* | *-jok-es-y-* | 'run away' |
| | *-ag-* | *-as-y-* | †*-ag-il-* | *-ak-is-y-* | 'come to an end' |

| ROOT | TRANS | APPL | APPL-TRANS | ROOT GLOSS |
|------|-------|------|------------|------------|
| *-tup-* | *-tuf-y-* | †*-tup-il-* | *-tuk-**if**-y-* | 'become stout' |
| *-pub-* | *-puf-y-* | †*-pub-il-* | *-puk-**if**-y-* | 'get used to' |

As can be seen in (13), Nyakyusa, like Mongo (see (11)), depalatalizes a root-final consonant in a causativized verb when the root is not immediately followed by the Transitive due to the presence of an intervening Applicative. However, unlike Mongo, it always depalatalizes to the same consonant, *k*.[7] In addition, Nyakyusa shows an interesting pattern where the 'palatalization' of the Applicative triggered by the Transitive is sensitive to the underlying form of the root-final consonant. Roots underlyingly ending in alveolar or velar stops marked with the Transitive show an Applicative with form *-is-* (a form consistent with the broader pattern where alveolars palatalize to *s*). Roots underlyingly ending in a labial, however, appear with Applicative form *-if-*, showing the same consonant the root would have surfaced with if it were followed immediately by the Transitive. Superficially, at least, it is as if the final consonant of the root is being transferred to the end of the stem. (See Hyman (2003b: 75) for a historical analysis of these facts.)

An additional complication, of particular interest in the present context, is found in verbs ending in nasal consonants, which do not palatalize when followed by the Transitive suffix. The Nyakyusa forms in (14), adapted from Hyman (2003b: 76), give relevant examples. (As in (13), daggers indicate forms I have constructed on the basis of the description.)

(14)

| ROOT | TRANS | APPL | APPL-TRANS | ROOT GLOSS |
|------|-------|------|------------|------------|
| *-lim-* | *-lim-y-* | †*-lim-il-* | *-lim-**ik**-is-y-* | 'cultivate' |
| *-lum-* | *-lum-y-* | †*-lum-il-* | *-lum-**ik**-is-y-* | 'bite' |

The data in (14) indicate that there is a general morphophonological constraint in Nyakyusa specifying that all forms marked with the Applicative and Transitive should contain a sequence like *-kis-* or *-kif-*. When this constraint cannot be fulfilled 'naturally' because the root-final consonant never palatalizes and, therefore, can never depalatalize to a *k*, a meaningless *-ik-* formative is inserted. Meaningless formatives like Nyakyusa *-ik-* represent an interesting kind of phonology-morphology mismatch wherein an element which looks like a morpheme, but does not appear to have any morphological function, must appear solely in order to satisfy a phonological shape requirement.

While the instances of deponency to be discussed in section 5 will not be associated with morphophonological alternations as complex as this, the

---

[7] This sort of phenomena is attested elsewhere, for example in Ciyao where the replacive consonant is *c* (Ngunga 2000: 240–2) (see also Hyman (2003b: 73)).

Nyakyusa facts underscore the general point that the morphophonology of the Bantu verb stem sometimes seems to have 'a mind of its own', taking on properties not predictable from more general principles of a language's morphology or morphosyntax. Given this, it should not be surprising that, under the right conditions, the morphophonological behaviour of a verb stem can fall out of line with its morphosyntactic interpretation, resulting in, as we shall see, a kind of deponency.

### 4.4. Summary

We have seen in this section that being, for example, a 'causative', 'applicative', or 'passive' verb form in Bantu is not always as simple as being a verb form with a Causative, Applicative, Transitive, or Passive suffix. Such verb forms can also be associated with special morphological and morphophonological restrictions including (i) templatic stipulations on the relative order of the suffixes and (ii) participation in idiosyncratic morphologically conditioned phonological processes. While the data seen in this section did not include instances of deponency, they point to an important pattern wherein a verb form like a Transitive or Applicative can sometimes be identified both by its segmental content and by its morphophonological behaviour. The goal of the next section will be to analyse cases wherein verb forms which both segmentally and morphophonologically appear to belong to a particular class (e.g. Transitives) do not appear to belong to that class syntactically—that is, where we seem to have instances of deponency in the Bantu verb stem.

## 5. Possible Cases of Deponency in Bantu

In this section, I will discuss instances of deponency which have been uncovered in Bantu verb stems involving pseudo-causatives and pseudo-passives. I will also discuss the possibility that certain pseudo-applicatives may be examples of deponency. Each of these classes of 'pseudo-' verbs are discussed in turn.

### 5.1. Pseudo-causatives

All of the cases of pseudo-causatives I have encountered in Bantu languages to this point involve, either synchronically or diachronically, the Transitive, not the Causative, suffix. The Kinande data in (15), repeated from (3), provide a good example of a pseudo-causative where the Transitive still has a clear segmental reflex. A similar pattern is found in Ciyao (Ngunga 2000:

234) (and certainly elsewhere—but a systematic survey of pseudo-causatives in Bantu has not been undertaken here).[8]

(15)

| STEM | GLOSS | TRANSLATION |
| --- | --- | --- |
| *-tsap-* | 'wet' | 'get wet' |
| *-tsap-į-* | 'wet-CAUS' | 'make wet' |
| *-tsap-an-į-* | 'wet-RECP-CAUS' | 'wet each other' |
| *-song-* | — | no meaning |
| *-song-į-* | 'SONG-CAUS' | 'gather (trans.)' |
| *-song-an-į-* | 'SONG-RECP-CAUS' | 'gather each other' |

As discussed in section 1, verb forms like *-song-į-* are not unequivocal instances of deponency—one could instead suggest that there is simply a morphological gap for the bare stem *-song-* in Kinande, something which would not be particularly striking given the general tendency of the Bantu verbal suffixes to lexicalize, as discussed in section 3. The challenge is to find cases comparable to Kinande *-song-į-* involving verb stems which would be quite difficult to reasonably classify as being syntactically or semantically 'causativized'—i.e. cases where the Transitive cannot be easily said to be making any contribution to the verb stem's syntax or semantics. I am, in fact, aware of several such cases. For example, Kinyamwezi causativized verbs are described as follows:

> Semantically and syntactically most [c]ausative verbs are regular. The [Transitive or Causative] extension adds an agent to the argument structure, the subject of the underived verb becomes the object of the [c]ausative verb. However, there are quite a number of formally [c]ausative verbs for which no corresponding underived verb is in use, and in some cases the typical causative argument structure has been obscured.   (Maganga and Schadeberg 1992: 155)

The examples in (16) (adapted from Maganga and Schadeberg (1992: 155)) give instances of such pseudo-causatives in Kinyamwezi. They are treated as formal causatives by Maganga and Schadeberg because they all have a final palatal articulation that is consistent with their being suffixed with a Transitive. As can be seen, while some of these verbs (e.g. *-goóŋóóɲ-* 'knock') would be amenable to a morphological gap analysis, others (e.g. *-kúmy-* 'be surprised') are apparently intransitive and, therefore, not amenable to one. Such verbs seem to represent instances of deponency. Kinyamwezi, however, does not offer the strongest possible evidence for deponent pseudo-causatives since, unlike the cases discussed immediately

---

[8] Ciyao is further described as showing a pattern of depalatalization of a stem-final consonant, like what was seen for Nyakyusa in section 4.3, involving a single replacive consonant, *c*. This process affects the final consonant of pseudo-causatives in addition to real Causatives (Ngunga 2000: 242), indicating that both are in the same morphological class.

below, the basis for the classification of a given verb stem as being marked
with the Transitive involves only segmental phonology and does not also
include special morphophonological alternations of the sort discussed in
section 4. Given that the relevant segmental form is simply a final palatal
articulation, one could reasonably argue that, at least in some cases, the
formal resemblance between apparent pseudo-causatives and verbs marked
with the Transitive is simply accidental.

(16)  STEM                  GLOSS
      *-amby-*              'help'
      *-andy-*              'begin'
      *-ßoonj-*             'taste'
      *-daahy-*             'bid farewell'
      *-dúj-*               'be able'
      *-goóŋóóɲ-*           'knock'
      *-kúmy-*              'be surprised'
      *-kuúmy-*             'touch'
      *-weej-*              'can'

Kinyamwezi also makes use of a reflex of the Causative, with form
*-iish-*, to mark causativization. However, this suffix does not appear to be
implicated in any deponency-like phenomena in the language. As mentioned
above, I am not, in fact, aware of any cases of deponent pseudo-causatives in
Bantu involving a reflex of the Causative suffix.

A similar pattern to what is seen in Kinyamwezi can be found in
Chimwiini (Abasheikh 1978). In the case of this language, the relevant verb
stems again show final consonants that make them appear to be formally
marked with the Transitive. In addition, as we shall see, they show a special
morphological selection pattern otherwise only associated with truly
causativized stems, giving us strong evidence that they belong to the
same morphological class as such stems. Examples of Chimwiini
pseudo-causatives are given in the first half of the table in (17) (Abasheikh
1978: 66).

(17)  STEM                  GLOSS
      *-pas-*               'borrow'
      *-anz-*               'begin'
      *-ṭosh-*              'suffice'
      *-fa:ñ-*              'do'

      *-pis-*               'cause to pass'
      *-las-*               'cause to divorce'
      *-la:ñ-*              'cause to quarrel'

The verbs in the first half of the table in (17) are all explicitly described as
being 'non-causative' (Abasheikh 1978: 66). However, as just mentioned, they
end in consonants typically associated with causativized forms marked with

the Transitive. (Recall that, as seen in Table 2, Proto-Bantu is not generally reconstructed with fricatives. Root-final fricatives in verbs are, therefore, often associated, historically at least, with causativization marked with the Transitive.) They also select for a special allomorph of the Applicative normally only associated with causativized verbs (including verbs causativized with a reflex of the Causative, which has the form *-ish-/-esh-* in Chimwiini (Abasheikh 1978: 55–7)).[9] Abasheikh (1978: 66) describes the use of this special Applicative form as follows:

> [T]he [Applicative] suffix basically has the shape *-ił-* (*~-eł-*). However a special allomorph *-iłiz-* (*~-ełez-*) appears after the verb stem ending in *s*, *z*, *sh*, and *ñ* . . . This allomorph is consequently the one that is used in causative [applicative] verbs, since the causative verb stem always ends in a consonant that belongs to the above mentioned group of consonants.

The verbs described by Abasheikh as non-causativized in the first half of the table in (17) are good candidates for deponent stems, resembling clearly causativized forms both in terms of their segmental phonology and their morphological selection. As with the earlier cases, however, they can not all be considered unequivocal instances of deponency since the apparent transitivity of some of the verbs makes them amenable to being treated as syntactically or semantically causativized, with a morphological gap accounting for the lack of a non-causativized root. The verb *-ṭosh-* 'suffice' is the best potential case of a deponent stem in (17), since its translation implies it is intransitive, making it a poor candidate for being analysed as causativized in any way.

I have encountered one other language, Ganda, with apparent pseudo-causative deponent stems, and, in this case, the evidence for this is especially strong. This language has verb stems which resemble truly causativized stems both in terms of their form and their morphophonological patterning but which (i) have been explicitly described as intransitive—in the other cases here intransitivity has been inferred from glosses—and (ii) have, in some cases, clearly been transferred into the same morphological class as causativized verb stems as the result of a historical innovation. As with the other cases discussed, the relevant verbal suffix is the Transitive, not the Causative. The data are somewhat complex and can only be easily understood given some background on more general issues of Ganda morphophonology. The data and basic analysis of the Ganda facts given here are drawn from Hyman (2003b: 81–5).

---

[9] Historically, the form *-ish-/-esh-* almost certainly reflects a palatalization of *-ic- triggered by the frequent presence of a following Transitive, along the lines of what was described in §2.2. Therefore, a verb marked with the Causative could be understood to also be marked with the Transitive, at least from an etymological perspective.

The first set of facts which is important for understanding deponency in Ganda involves the phonological effects of (i) palatalization triggered by the Transitive and (ii) the suffix's subsequent 'absorption' into roots ending in certain consonants, giving it no overt segmental reflex. This process is schematized in (18), following Hyman (2003b: 82). The sequences in the top half of (18) represent the final consonant of a verb root, followed by the Transitive suffix, followed in turn by the inflectional Final Vowel -*a*. The bottom half of the table schematizes how roots ending in Proto-Bantu *c and *j which were not marked with the Transitive are realized in Ganda.

(18)  | PROTO-BANTU | | STAGE I | | STAGE II | | STAGE III |
|---|---|---|---|---|---|---|
| *t-i̧-a | > | *s-i̧-a | > | *s-y-aa | > | s-aa |
| *k-i̧-a | > | *s-i̧-a | > | *s-y-aa | > | s-aa |
| *d-i̧-a | > | *z-i̧-a | > | *z-y-aa | > | z-aa |
| *g-i̧-a | > | *z-i̧-a | > | *z-y-aa | > | z-aa |
| *c-a | > | | | *š-a | > | s-a |
| *j-a | > | | | *ž-a | > | y-a (j-a after nasal) |

As indicated in (18), the regular reflex of Proto-Bantu *c in Ganda is *s*, but Ganda *s* may also derive from the regular reflex of *ki̧ or *ti̧ (Guthrie 1971: 44). Given that the reconstructed form of the Transitive is *-i̧-, there should be at least two sources of root-final *s* in Ganda verbs, one of which is associated with causativization and the other which is not. Furthermore, in principle, it should be possible to synchronically distinguish between root-final *s* in Ganda which is a reflex of Proto-Bantu *c and root-final *s* which is a reflex of Proto-Bantu *k-i̧- or *t-i̧-. This is because there are three phonological processes found in the language which are sensitive to the (historical) presence of the Transitive.

One such process involves compensatory lengthening of a Final Vowel following the Transitive -*i̧*-, both when the suffix surfaces as a glide and when it is absorbed. Utterance-final long vowels will be realized as short before a pause in Ganda (Hyman 2003b: 83). Therefore, determining whether or not a verb ends in an underlyingly long Final Vowel requires that it be 'protected' from appearing utterance finally. This can be done by placing a clitic after the verb. Representative data are given in (19) (Hyman 2003b: 83).[10]

(19)  | VERB | TRANSLATION |
|---|---|
| *ku-láb-à=kí* | 'to see what?' |
| *kw-áák-à=kô* | 'to blaze a bit' |
| *ku-láb-y-àà=kí* | 'to make see what?' |
| *ku-láb-y-àà=kô* | 'to make see a bit' |

---

[10] The long vowels seen in the verb root -*ák*- 'blaze' and the related causativized stem -*ás*- 'blaze.TRANS' in (19) are the result of compensatory lengthening triggered by the gliding of the *u* in the infinitival prefix *ku*-.

| *kw-áás-àà=kí* | 'to make blaze what?' |
| *kw-áá-àà=kô* | 'to make blaze a bit' |

The first pair of verbs in (19) is not marked—overtly or abstractly—with the Transitive. Each can be seen to end in an underlying short vowel since the Final Vowel of the verb surfaces as *à* even when it is protected by a postverbal clitic. The second pair of verbs shows the effects of the Transitive, when surfacing as the glide -*y*-, on the Final Vowel of the verb, which is lengthened in this context. Lengthening can also be observed in the last pair of verbs. While these verbs do not contain an overt segmental reflex of the Transitive, their form indicates that, at least historically, they were subject to palatalization triggered by the Transitive being suffixed to the non-causativized root -*ák*- 'blaze', seen in the first pair of verbs in (19). Thus, these verbs can be understood to contain an absorbed Transitive, which is what causes their Final Vowel to be subject to the observed lengthening.

A second phonological process sensitive to the presence of the Transitive in Ganda involves applicativization. Specifically, the language behaves like some of the languages discussed earlier, for example Ciyao (see the data in (6)), where the form of the Applicative is different in causativized as opposed to non-causativized environments. Relevant data are given in (20) where the italicized stems represent underlying and/or historical verb forms and the bracketed stems represent surface forms not appearing utterance finally (Hyman 2003b: 82–3). Of interest here is the alternation between the -*ir*- and -*iz*- forms of the Applicative.

| (20) | VERB STEM | | APPLICATIVE | | STEM GLOSS |
|---|---|---|---|---|---|
| | *-láb-* | [láb-a] | *-láb-ir-* | [láb-**ir**-a] | 'see' |
| | *-láb-i̧-* | [láb-y-aa] | *-láb-ir-i̧-* | [láb-**iz**-aa] | 'make see' |
| | *-ák-* | [ák-a] | *-ák-ir-* | [ák-**ir**-a] | 'blaze' |
| | *-ás-i̧-* | [ás-aa] | *-ás-ir-i̧-* | [ás-**iz**-aa] | 'make blaze' |

As can be seen in (20), an Applicative suffix appearing on a verb stem which contains a Transitive surfaces as -*iz*- instead of -*ir*-, due to the same basic process of palatalization of the Proto-Bantu form *-id- seen above in (6). Also relevant here are the facts discussed in section 4.1 involving templatic suffix ordering, which help make clear the reason why the Transitive follows the Applicative in the forms in the second column of (20).

In addition to these two processes, Hyman (2003b: 82–4) discusses a third phenomenon sensitive to the presence of the Transitive, involving the Perfective marker *-i̧d-e, which shows a similar alternation to the Applicative in causativized versus non-causativized contexts.

As discussed above, etymologically, there are at least two classes of *s*-final verb roots in Ganda, those which developed from *c-final roots and those which developed from *kį or *tį sequences where the *į* was the exponent of the Transitive. Those developing from *c-final roots, of course, should behave as though they have not 'absorbed' a reflex of the Transitive. That is, they should not show long Final Vowels or take the special -*iz*- form of the Applicative, unlike, for example, the causativized verb -*ás*- 'make blaze' seen in (19) and (20). However, it turns out that, synchronically, there is only one class of *s*-final roots in Ganda. All roots with this shape behave as though they have absorbed a Transitive suffix.[11] Relevant examples of reconstructed *c-final roots and their Ganda reflexes, adapted from Hyman (2003b: 84), are given in (21). As can be seen, the morphophonological behaviour of these roots indicates that they have been analogically shifted into the class of roots with an absorbed Transitive, even though historically they would not have been marked with this suffix.

(21)  PRONTO-BANTAU              GANDA      *what* ENCLITIC      APPLICATIVE
      *-dác- 'shoot (arrow)'  >   -lás-     ku-lás-àà=kí        lás-iz-aa
      *-píc-, *-bíc- 'hide'   >   -bis-     ku-bis-aa=kí        bis-iz-aa

Hyman (2003b: 84) describes the Ganda situation quite explicitly as follows:

> As seen, all three criteria establish that PB *-CVc- roots, pronounced -CVs- in Ganda, have been reanalyzed as -CVs-į-, that is, as pseudo-causatives. This is true even of the few [-]CVs- verbs which are intransitive, and hence not likely to be morphological causatives at all, e.g., *kuus-a* 'be hypocritical', *myáas*[-]*a* 'flash' (of lightning).

Ganda, thus, gives us three reasons for claiming its lexicon includes pseudo-causative deponent forms: (i) the criteria for membership in the class of Transitive verbs goes beyond segmental features and includes participation in morphophonological alternations otherwise only associated with verbs that are truly causativized, (ii) there are explicitly indicated examples of intransitive pseudo-causatives which cannot be straightforwardly analysed as cases where there is simply a morphological gap for the more 'basic' root to which causativization would apply, and (iii) there is clear evidence that verbs which were historically not causativized have been moved into the same morphophonological class as verbs marked with the Transitive.[12] The conjunction of the latter two points allows us to say that Ganda exhibits deponency on

---

[11] For discussion of why Ganda underwent this apparent analogical process, but languages showing similar patterns did not, see Hyman (2003b: 84–7).

[12] Hyman (2003b) gives no example of a historically intransitive verb analogically moved into the Transitive-marked class. I have no reason to believe this is or is not an accidental omission. The translation of the form *ku-bis-aa=kí* given by Hyman (2003b: 84) is 'to hide what?', implying it is transitive.

two distinct levels: in terms of its synchronic grammar and in terms of diachronic change.

Overall, then, it would appear to be the case that at least some Bantu pseudo-causatives are examples of deponent stems, with Ganda showing the clearest evidence for this. Finding unequivocal cases of deponency was far from trivial however since (i) it was not straightforward to establish strong criteria for classifying a given stem as formally causativized given that the most salient exponent of causativization is often simply a final palatal articulation and (ii) even when there were such criteria, it was not always easy to establish a morphology-syntax mismatch since the syntax and semantics of causativization are such that one could argue that any transitive verb is a 'causative'.

## 5.2. Pseudo-passives

Pseudo-passive verbs in some Bantu languages also offer some reasonable candidates for deponent stems. On a purely segmental level, possible pseudo-passives are quite easy to find by looking through dictionaries for stems with 'extraneous' final *w*'s, analysable as deriving from the Proto-Bantu Passive \*-u-, which are not accompanied by related stems without final *w*. Of course, such stems, on their own, are weak candidates for deponency since such final *w*'s could represent accidentally homophonies with the Passive and, even when they do not, the existence of *w*-final stems without bare counterparts could evince a morphological gap instead of deponency.

Analogous to pseudo-causatives, if pseudo-passive stems in a given language meet the following three criteria, it will be possible to make a fairly strong case for deponency: (i) membership in the Passive morphological class should go beyond mere presence of a segment which is apparently a reflex of \*-u-, (ii) there should be verb stems which are not amenable to being analysed synchronically as passivized and lacking an associated plain stem due to the presence of a morphological gap, and (iii) there should be evidence that non-passivized Proto-Bantu forms ending in sequences accidentally homophonous with the Passive morpheme were analogically moved into the Passive class.[13]

I am aware of one language with pseudo-passives which seem to meet all three criteria, Kinyamwezi. As a systematic survey of pseudo-passives in Bantu has not been undertaken here, there are almost certainly others.[14]

---

[13] I do not mean to suggest that these are the only kind of criteria we could use to argue for deponency in Bantu. Rather, these are the best criteria I am aware of at present.

[14] Larry Hyman (personal communication), for example, has found a comparable phenomenon in Bemba to what is described here for Kinyamwezi.

Maganga and Schadeberg (1992: 149) describe the basic situation in Kinyamwezi as follows:

> There are a few verbal bases ending in *w* without being passives, at least in a synchronic perspective. In as far as passives can be derived from such verbs this is done by substituting *-iw-* for *-w-*.

The forms in (22), adapted from Maganga and Schadeberg (1992: 149–51), are examples of such pseudo-passives in Kinyamwezi. A '—' in the table indicates that the possibilities for passivization of the verb were not given. The association of Proto-Bantu roots with Kinyamwezi stems is my own, with the reconstructions drawn from Guthrie (1970: 146,176). As indicated in the gloss column, Maganga and Schadeberg associate some of these verbs with corresponding bare stems but treat them as pseudo-passives because the Passive stems have undergone semantic shifts.

(22)

| STEM | PASSIVE | GLOSS | PROTO-BANTU |
|---|---|---|---|
| *-gay-iw-* | none | 'lack' (cf. *-gay-* 'die') | |
| *-chil-w-* | none | 'hate' | |
| *-íg-w-* | *-igíw-* (?) | 'hear' | *-jígʉ- |
| *-tóg-w-* | *-togíw-* | 'like' | |
| *-i-kúúmb-w-* | — | 'REFL-wish' | |
| *-lemeel-w-* | — | 'fail' (cf. *-lemeel-* 'be too difficult') | *-dèm- (plus APPL?) |
| *-zilí-w-* | — | 'be in need' | |

The lack of a corresponding passivized form for the first two verbs in (22) makes them good candidates for an analysis where they are, in fact, passivized but there is a morphological gap for the bare stem. However, the fact that the second two verbs can be passivized makes such an analysis more difficult for them. This would imply they could be doubly passivized, which is problematic on syntactic grounds. (Of course, such an analysis would be easier for the verb *-íg-w-* 'hear' than for the verb *-tóg-w-* 'like' since its Passive form is indicated as being marginal.) For the two verbs explicitly indicated as having undergone semantic drift, it is not clear how the existence of the bare stems with considerably different meanings impacts their classification as deponent. Making such a determination would, of course, require a theory as to when the meaning of two historically related elements diverges significantly enough to consider them morphologically distinct. I leave this matter unresolved here, though it is obviously of potential interest for general models of deponency.

One of the roots in (22), *-íg-w-* 'hear', is reconstructed in Proto-Bantu as having a final 'superhigh' back vowel *ʉ not associated with the Proto-Bantu Passive *-u-. This root, therefore, appears to be a good candidate for deponency on a diachronic level since it was not originally a Passive form but

entered the Passive class as a result of morphophonological analogy triggered by its surfacing with a final *w*—a stem-final consonant otherwise
closely associated with true Passives in Kinyamwezi.

As indicated above, the evidence that forms like those in (22) should be
classified as Passives goes beyond their simply having a segmental form that
appears to contain a Passive suffix. Such verbs also participate in special
morphophonological alternations involving the Pre-Final element *-ag-* and
the Perfective marker *-il-e* (both of which play a role in TMA-marking)
(Maganga and Schadeberg 1992: 150–1). Maganga and Schadeberg (1992:
150) describe the situation for *-ag-* as follows:

> If a conjugated verb contains the [P]re-Final element *-ag-*, the Passive I exten-
> sion *-w-* occupies the position after *-ag-* and before the Final [Vowel]. This is
> also true for petrified or pseudo-passives as in [*kʊ-togw-á*] 'to like'.

The forms in (23), adapted from Maganga and Schadeberg (1992: 150),
illustrate this pattern. The first verb exemplifies a true Passive and the second
two verbs are pseudo-passives. The relevant feature of these forms is that the
segmental exponent of the Passive, *w*, appears after the Pre-Final element
*-ag-* instead of immediately after the root. This shift of the Passive *-w-* to a
position near the end of the stem is related to the fact that the suffix has the
final position in the relative-order template discussed in section 4.1.

| (23) | VERB | MEANING | STEM |
|------|------|---------|------|
| | *yaatʊmágwa* | 'it was sent' | *-tʊm-w-* (cf. *-tʊm-* 'send') |
| | *waanitogágwa* | 'she has liked me' | *-tóg-w-* |
| | *waániigágwa* | 'she has heard me' | *-íg-w-* |

As indicated in the above quotations, Maganga and Schadeberg distinguish between two Passive suffixes in Kinyamwezi, one with form *-w-* and the
other with form *-iw-*.[15] One of the pseudo-passive forms they give *-gayiw-*
'lack' makes use of this longer suffix. Though they do not explicitly give an
example of it containing the Pre-Final element *-ag-*, their description implies
it should behave like the Passive of the verb *-hay-* 'say', which has the form
*-hay-iw-*. The stem form of this verb with the Pre-Final is *-hay-iw-ag-w-*,
containing two exponents of passivization, the long Passive morpheme *-iw-*
before *-ag-* and the short Passive after *-ag-* (Maganga and Schadeberg 1992:
150).

The Perfective marker *-il-e* shows a comparable pattern with respect to
Passive marking as that found for the Pre-Final element *-ag-*.[16] The verb

---

[15] While the *w* in the long form of the Kinyamwezi Passive is almost certainly derived from the
Proto-Bantu Passive *-u-, the source of the *i* is not clear.

[16] As with the Pre-Final *-ag-*, the shift in the position of the Passive in Perfective stems is
connected to the existence of the verbal suffix template discussed in §4.1.

*waatógílwé*, for example, 'she has liked' is based on the pseudo-passive stem *-tóg-w-* 'like'—as with verbs marked with *-ag-*, the *w* marking passivization in verbs marked with *-il-e* 'jumps' towards the end of the stem. The general pattern for the Perfective, however, is distinct from the pattern for the Pre-Final in that both the short and long forms of the Passive—i.e. both the *-w-* form and the *-iw-* form—'disappear' root finally, resulting in only one exponent of passivization for all regular Passive Perfective stems, a *-w-* immediately following the *-il-* of the Perfective (Maganga and Schadeberg 1992: 150).

However, the one pseudo-passive verb given as taking the *-iw-* Passive, *-gay-iw-* 'lack' is exceptional in this regard. The suffix *-iw-* 'remains in its place and in addition we find the Passive-Perfective Final [*-il-w-e*]' (Maganga and Schadeberg 1992: 150). This is illustrated in (24). (The Augment prefix marking the noun in 24 plays a role in its interpretation as definite.)

(24)   *naágáyiwílwé*            *ɪ-héla*
       1SG.PST.lack.PFV         AUG-money
       'I lacked the money.' (Maganga and Schadeberg1992: 150; glossing my own)

Clearly, the overall picture is quite complex, but, nevertheless, there is good evidence that being a Passive verb in Kinyamwezi involves more than just containing a stem-final *w*. It also means taking part in a special set of morphophonological alternations. Since pseudo-passives generally participate in the same set of idiosyncratic morphophonological alternations as truly passivized verbs, they meet the first criterion for deponency given above.

While it is not clear that all the pseudo-passives listed in (22) are deponent forms, since some do not clearly meet either the second or the third criteria, at least two are very good candidates for being categorized as deponent stems: *-íg-w-* 'hear' and *-tóg-w-* 'like'. Both can be associated with separate Passive forms, strongly indicating they themselves are not understood to be syntactic passives, and one of them *-íg-w-* 'hear', meets the additional criterion that its membership in the Passive class is apparently a historical innovation. Thus, it seems reasonable to say that Kinyamwezi is a language with pseudo-passive deponent verb stems.

An interesting issue raised by the Kinyamwezi facts, for which, unfortunately, I have no data, is whether or not there are some *w*-final verb forms which do not participate in the morphophonological alternations described above. If they did exist, it would make the case that forms like *-íg-w-* 'hear' and *-tóg-w-* 'like' are deponent stronger since it would imply that their designation as morphological Passives is not simply determined by their having a specific phonological shape but, rather, results from their being assigned to an abstract, unpredictable morphological class otherwise only associated with true Passives—a class which would correlate with, but not be precisely the same as, the class of stems having a final $w$.[17]

## 5.3. Pseudo-applicatives?

While one can quite easily find cases where suffixes other than the Transitive or Passive are found on verb stems which are not accompanied, synchronically at least, by corresponding bare roots, it is rather more difficult to devise convincing arguments that such stems are exhibiting deponency. The Applicative provides a good example of the sorts of complications that arise when trying to do this. Lexicalized Applicatives are quite frequent in Bantu and can be found through even cursory inspections of dictionaries. It is not surprising, therefore, that one also often encounters cases where stems containing lexicalized Applicatives are not associated with a bare root.

Drawing again on Kinyamwezi, consider, for example, the forms in (25), adapted from Maganga and Schadeberg (1992: 158) (presence/absence of bare stem determined based on examination of word list included in Maganga and Schadeberg (1992)). These forms are instances of apparent intransitive pseudo-applicative verb stems.

(25)
| APPL. STEM | GLOSS | BARE STEM |
|---|---|---|
| -angíl- | 'be not enough' | — |
| -βuúkʊl- | 'rise slowly' | -βuúk- 'rise' |
| -leembel- | 'be quiet' | — |
| -laálɪl- | 'go to sleep hungry' | -laál- 'sleep' |

If one assumes that the Bantu Applicative suffix should *always* allow a verb to take an 'extra' object then, perhaps, the fact that the stems in (25) are intransitive makes them examples of deponency. However, it is not clear that the use of the Applicative is quite that syntactically straightforward—see Marten (2003) for relevant discussion. Without a very clear sense of what the syntax and semantics 'should' be for the Applicative, it is impossible to be sure when there is a mismatch between the morphological form and the syntactic function of an applicativized stem. In the case of pseudo-causatives, it was assumed that an intransitive verb is a poor candidate for being syntactically causative. In the case of pseudo-passives, it was assumed that a verb that could independently passivize, using a different marking strategy from its

---

[17] The existence of Ganda $s$-final verbs not subject to the morphophonological processes described in §5.1 would be similarly useful. However, as indicated in the discussion in that section, Hyman (2003b) reports that all $s$-final verbs in Ganda, in fact, behave as if they were marked with the Transitive.

'lexical' marking, was a poor candidate for being syntactically passive. There is no such straightforward criterion for being a 'true' syntactic applicative.[18]

An additional complication in looking for examples of deponent pseudo-applicatives is that, for whatever reason, it is harder to find cases where suffixes with the shape -VC-, like the Causative and Applicative, participate in special morphophonological processes like what was seen for the Ganda Transitive in section 5.1 or the Kinyamwezi Passive in section 5.2. It is harder, therefore, to establish for these suffixes that apparent cases of 'pseudo-' stems are not, instead, simply forms which accidentally resemble roots followed by the relevant verbal suffix.

None of this is to say that there are no instances of suffixes other than the Transitive or the Passive playing a central role in deponency phenomena in some Bantu languages. Rather, it is simply harder to find solid cases of these on methodological grounds.

# 6. Conclusion

We have seen here that there appear to be good candidates for deponency in Bantu involving pseudo-causatives and pseudo-passives. The Proto-Bantu Transitive *-i- and Passive *-u- were the morphemes involved in the clearest cases. Deponency does not seem to be an isolated morphological phenomenon in Bantu languages but, rather, is one part of a general 'syndrome' where stem+suffix combinations can be associated with phonological processes that effectively partition them into different morphophonological classes. In most cases, such classes will show a complete correspondence with associated morphosyntactic classes. However, under certain conditions, the morphophonological and morphosyntactic classes can become disjoint, resulting in deponent forms.

Since the phenomena discussed here were drawn from derivational, not inflectional, morphology, the analysis of deponency did not invoke paradigmatic mismatches, of the sort found in classic cases of deponency, like those seen in Latin. It did, however, make extensive use of the notion of morphophonological class and would, thus, appear to be broadly in line with Kiparsky's (2005) suggestion that the devices of lexical phonology and morphology are adequate for the analysis of deponency. Given that some analyses of deponent forms in inflectional morphology have made crucial reference to paradigmatic relations (see, for example, Sadler and Spencer (2001), Stump

---

[18] This basic problem is again encountered when trying to find possible cases of deponency involving another verbal suffix, not discussed here, the *-ik- Stative, which is also frequently found lexicalized on verb stems not accompanied by corresponding bare stems.

(2001: 171–6, this volume), Corbett (this volume) and Spencer (this volume)), this raises the question as to whether or not deponency in derivational morphology may have distinct properties from inflectional deponency.[19] Finding an answer to this question will require collecting more cases of deponency involving morphological phenomena not easily characterized with respect to paradigms—assuming they can be found.

A final point worth making about the Bantu data seen here is how it illustrates a possible historical pathway to deponency, distinct from the classic cases: morphophonological analogy. Specifically, accidental phonological resemblances between a given form and forms belonging to a well-defined morphosyntactic class may result in that form taking on special morphophonological properties normally only associated with that class. (See Bermúdez-Otero (this volume) for a similar pattern in Spanish.)

# References

Abasheikh, Mohammed. 1978. The grammar of Chimwi:ni causatives. Urbana-Champaign, Ill.: University of Illinois Ph.D. Dissertation.

Alsina, Alex. 1999. Where's the mirror principle? *Linguistic Review* 16.1–42.

Alsina, Alex, and Sam A. Mchombo. 1993. Object asymmetries and the Chichewa applicative construction. *Theoretical aspects of Bantu grammar*, ed. by Sam A. Mchombo, 17–45. Stanford: CSLI.

Baker, Mark. 1988. *Incorporation: a theory of grammatical function changing*. Chicago: University of Chicago.

Dembetembe, N. C. 1987. *A linguistic study of the verb in Korekore*. Harare: University of Zimbabwe.

Downing, Laura J. 1999. Prosodic stem ≠ prosodic word in Bantu. *Studies on the phonological word*, ed. by T. Alan Hall and Ursula Kleinhenz, 73–98. Amsterdam: Benjamins.

Good, Jeff. 2005. Reconstructing morpheme order in Bantu: the case of causativization and applicativization. *Diachronica* 22.3–57.

Guthrie, Malcolm. 1970. *Comparative Bantu: an introduction to the comparative linguistics and prehistory of the Bantu languages*. Vol. 3. Farnborough: Gregg.

—— 1971. *Comparative Bantu: an introduction to the comparative linguistics and prehistory of the Bantu languages*. Vol. 2. Farnborough: Gregg.

Horton, A. E. 1949. *A grammar of Luvale*. Johannesburg: Witwatersrand Press.

Hulstaert, G. 1965. *Grammaire du lɔmɔngɔ*. Deuxième partie: *Morphologie*. Annales du Musée Royale de l'Afrique Centrale, Série IN-8°, Sciences Humaines, No. 57. Tervuren: Musée Royale de l'Afrique Centrale.

---

[19] It is noteworthy in this regard that, while Bantu verbal suffixes are typically treated as derivational, one of the cases of deponency discussed here, pseudo-passives, involves a similar (the same?) morphosyntactic category as Latin deponency.

Hyman, Larry M. 1993. Conceptual issues in the comparative study of the Bantu verb stem. *Topics in African linguistics*, ed. by Salikoko S. Mufwene and Lioba Moshi, 3–34. Amsterdam/Phildelphia: Benjamins.

—— 1994. Cyclic phonology and morphology in Cibemba. *Perspectives in phonology*, ed. by Jennifer Cole and Kisseberth Charles, 81–112. Stanford: CSLI.

—— 2003a. Segmental phonology. In Nurse and Philippson (2003), 42–58.

—— 2003b. Sound change, misanalysis, and analogy in the Bantu causative. *Journal of African Languages and Linguistics* 24.55–90.

—— 2003c. Suffix ordering in Bantu: a morphocentric approach. *Yearbook of Morphology 2002*, ed. by Geert Booij and Jaap van Marle, 245–81. Dordrecht: Kluwer.

Hyman, Larry M., and Sam A. Mchombo. 1992. Morphotactic constraints in the Chichewa verb stem. *Proceedings of the eighteenth meeting of the Berkeley Linguistics Society, general session and parassession*, ed. by Laura Buszard-Welcher, Lionel Wee, and William Weigel, 350–63. Berkeley: Berkeley Linguistics Society.

Kiparsky, Paul. 2005. Blocking and periphrasis in inflectional paradigms. *Yearbook of Morphology 2004*, ed. by Geert Booij and Jaap van Marle, 113–35. Dordrecht: Kluwer.

Maganga, Clement, and Thilo Schadeberg. 1992. *Kinyamwezi: grammar, texts, vocabulary*. Köln: Rüdiger Köppe.

Maren, Lutz. 2003. The dynamics of Bantu applied verbs: an analysis at the syntax-pragmatics interface. *Actes du 3e congrès mondial de linguistique africaine Lomé 2000*, ed. by Kézié K. Lébikaza, 207–21. Köln: Rüdiger Köppe.

Meeussen, A. E. 1967. *Bantu grammatical reconstructions. Africana Linguistica* 3. 79–121 (=Annales du Musée Royal de l'Afrique Centrale, no. 61). Tervuren: Musée Royal de l'Afrique Centrale.

Meinhof, Carl. 1932. *Introduction to the phonology of the Bantu languages*, trans. N. J. van Warmelo. Berlin: Dietrich Reimer. First published 1910.

Ngunga, Armindo. 2000. *Lexical phonology and morphology of Ciyao*. Stanford: CSLI.

Nurse, Derek, and Gérard Philippson (eds.). 2003. *The Bantu languages*. London: Routledge.

Peterson, David. 1999. Discourse-functional, historical, and typological aspects of applicative constructions. Berkeley: UC Berkeley Ph.D. Dissertation.

Sadler, Louisa, and Andrew Spencer. 2001. Syntax as an exponent of morphological features. *Yearbook of Morphology 2000*, ed. by Geert Booij and Jaap van Marle, 71–96. Dordrecht: Kluwer.

Schadeberg, Thilo C. 2003. *Historical linguistics*. In Nurse and Philippson (2003), 143–63.

Schumann, C. 1899. Grundriss einer Grammatik der Kondesprache. *Mitteilungen des Orientalische Seminars zu Berlin* 2.1–86.

Stump, Gregory T. 2001. Morphological and syntactic paradigms: arguments for a theory of paradigm linkage. *Yearbook of Morphology 2001*, ed. by Geert Booij and Jaap van Marle, 147–80. Dordrecht: Kluwer.

# 10

# Spanish Pseudoplurals:
# Phonological Cues in the Acquisition
# of a Syntax-Morphology Mismatch*

## RICARDO BERMÚDEZ-OTERO

## 1. Introduction

IN ITS BROADEST SENSE, THE TERM DEPONENCY denotes a mismatch between the morphological shape and the syntactic behaviour of a word (Baerman this volume). Latin deponent verbs provide the eponymous and canonical example of this phenomenon: in (1), for instance, the verb *sequuntur* has a passive inflectional marker but is syntactically active—and indeed transitive.

(1) Nempe     patr-em         sequ-untur              līber-ī.
    of_course father-ACC.SG  follow-3PL.PRS.IND.PASS  child-NOM.PL
    'Of course the children follow the father.'

                                    Livy, *Ab urbe condita*, IV, 4, 11

Every case of deponency, in this extended sense, poses a learnability question: what evidence alerts the child to the fact that a particular word does not carry the syntactic features normally associated with its morphological make-up? In (1) the problem is actually rather mild, as the appropriate syntactic structure

* This paper develops and expands aspects of the analysis of Spanish nominal classes presented in Bermúdez-Otero (2007), and has greatly benefited from James Harris's and Iggy Roca's detailed criticism of that article; however, neither of them endorses the proposals made here. Early versions of this work were presented at the conference on 'Deponency and Morphological Mismatches' (British Academy, London, 17 January 2006), at the Linguistics and English Language seminar of the University of Manchester (7 February 2006), and at a meeting of the Cambridge University Linguistic Society (27 April 2006); I am very grateful to the audiences on all three occasions for their stimulating questions. I also thank Sonia Colina for her comments.

*Proceedings of the British Academy* **145**, 231–269. © The British Academy 2007.

can easily be inferred from local semantic and syntactic cues: the presence of a patient argument marked with accusative case (*patrem*) shows that *sequuntur*, though morphologically passive, must be syntactically active.

In contrast, present-day Spanish exhibits an instance of deponency in which the learnability problem appears much tougher. Spanish has a handful of nouns whose singular and plural forms are homophonous, both ending in /s/:[1] e.g. *Carlos* 'Charles.SG/PL', *virus* 'virus.SG/PL' (cf. *niño* 'boy.SG' ≠ *niños* 'boy.PL'; *mes* 'month.SG' ≠ *meses* 'month.PL'). For many speakers of the language these nouns fall into two sharply different morphological classes. In nouns like *virus*, the homophony between the singular and plural forms results from phonological neutralization: the stem /biɾus-/ is ATHEMATIC, i.e. it lacks one of the nominal stem formatives /-o/, /-a/, /-{e, ∅}/, or /-e/;[2] in consequence, the addition of the inflectional marker /-s/ in the plural creates a phonotactically illegal /ss/ sequence, which is repaired by degemination.

(2)   Nouns with an athematic stem ending in /s/[3]

|  | singular | plural |
|---|---|---|
| UR | [word [stem biɾus]] | [word [stem biɾus]s] |
| SR | [bíɾus] | [bíɾus] |

In nouns like *Carlos*, in contrast, it is not the phonology that renders the plural form homophonous with the singular; rather, the syntactic number opposition is neutralized in the morphology. More specifically, the singular form of such nouns behaves idiosyncratically in that it takes the plural suffix /-s/ whilst remaining semantically and syntactically singular. In this sense, nouns like *Carlos* are deponent: I shall henceforth refer to them as PSEUDOPLURAL nouns.

---

[1] In many dialects this final /s/ is subject to regular phonological processes of lenition, typically yielding [h]; this fact is irrelevant to the discussion below.
[2] Spanish nouns and adjectives fall into several inflectional classes. Each of the major or core classes is characterized by the presence of a particular stem formative, also known as the 'theme vowel': thus, the formative /-o/ is the marker of *o*-stems; the formative /-a/ is the marker of *a*-stems; and the formatives /-{e,∅}/ and /-e/ are the markers of *e*-stems, /-{e,∅}/ appearing in ordinary *e*-stems (Class III in Harris 1999; see §3.4 below), and /-e/ in the less numerous '*e*-only stems' (Class IV in Harris 1999). Athematic nouns like *virus*, lacking a stem formative altogether, are in the minority; partially assimilated loanwords or 'xenonyms' (Harris 1992: 66, 1999: 57) are athematic, but this class also contains nouns that conform fully with Spanish phonotactics (§3.4). See (30) for examples, and Bermúdez-Otero (2007) for discussion and references.
[3] I use hollow brackets to mark morphological constituents and the phonological domains associated with them; solid brackets enclose phonetic transcriptions and/or prosodic categories. In transcriptions I use IPA symbols, but I mark primary stress with the acute ['], mark secondary stress with the grave ['], and omit certain details such as the dentality diacritic [̪]. The symbol σ denotes a syllable, σw an unstressed syllable, σ́ a primarily stressed syllable, σ̃ a heavy syllable, and ω a prosodic word. Other abbreviations include UR for 'underlying representation' and SR for 'surface representation'.

(3)    Pseudoplural nouns

|  | singular | plural |
|---|---|---|
| UR | $[_{word} [_{stem} \text{karl-o}]s]$ | $[_{word} [_{stem} \text{karl-o}]s]$ |
| SR | [kárlos] | [kárlos] |

The main challenge for Spanish learners is to acquire the distinction between athematic nouns like *virus* and pseudoplural nouns like *Carl-o-s*, for there is absolutely no phonological or syntactic difference between the two classes. The opposition emerges only under stem-based derivation, i.e. in the presence of derivational suffixes that subcategorize for stems (as opposed to roots or words); in Spanish these include most evaluative suffixes, like diminutive *-it-o* (feminine *-it-a*) or augmentative *-ot-e* (feminine *-ot-a*). In this environment the /s/ of *virus* occurs inside the derivational suffix because it is part of the stem: e.g. *virus-ot-e* (4a). In contrast, the /s/ of *Carl-o-s* disappears because, being an inflectional (plural) marker, it lies outside the stem: e.g. *Carl-ot-e* (4b).

(4)    Augmentatives

| | a.  with an athematic base | b.  with a pseudoplural base |
|---|---|---|
| UR | $[_{word} [_{stem} [_{stem} \text{birus}]\text{ot-}\{e,\emptyset\}]]$ | $[_{word} [_{stem} [_{stem} \text{karl-o}]\text{ot-}\{e,\emptyset\}]]$ |
| SR | [birusóte] | [karlóte] |
| | 'virus.AUG.SG' | 'Charles.AUG.SG' |

However, most evaluative derivatives of athematic or pseudoplural bases have vanishingly low token frequencies and are therefore extremely unlikely to be robustly represented in the learner's primary linguistic data. This creates an obvious learnability puzzle: in the absence of any direct syntactic, morphological, or phonological cues, Spanish speakers producing the forms in (4) have managed to acquire a contrast between pseudoplural nouns and non-pseudoplural nouns with athematic stems in /s/. The existence of a learnability deficit in this area of Spanish grammar is independently confirmed by the observation that not all idiolects display the distinction shown in (4): e.g. although the most frequent diminutive form of *virus* is indeed *virus-it-o*, several other variants are attested (see §3.2 below for details). Nonetheless, the fact remains that a substantial proportion of Spanish learners do acquire a contrast between pseudoplural nouns and athematic nouns in /s/ even though the opposition is underdetermined in their trigger experience.

How is this possible? This paper suggests that learners of Spanish use a variety of indirect cues to estimate the probability that the final /s/ in a singular noun with a homophonous plural is part of the stem or is a pseudoplural affix. Some of these indirect cues are morphological. For example, the final /s/ is unlikely to be parsed as an inflectional affix if it is immediately preceded by any segment other than /o/, /a/, or /e/, for in that case the stem could not be a member of any of the three major classes to which the vast majority of

Spanish nouns belong: viz. *o*-stems, *a*-stems, and *e*-stems (see n. 2). On morphological grounds, therefore, learners prefer to parse singular *virus* as a non-
pseudoplural form with an athematic stem in /s/, i.e. [$_{word}$ [$_{stem}$ birus]], rather
than as a pseudoplural form with an athematic stem in /u/, i.e. [$_{word}$ [$_{stem}$ biru]s],
because the syntax-morphology mismatch incurred by the pseudoplural
parse affords no morphological advantages: in either case, the stem remains
a member of the marginal athematic class. Crucially, however, learners also
make extensive use of phonological cues. Among singular nouns with a
closed ultima, for example, antepenultimate stress is supermarked (Roca
2005), occurring by and large only in partially assimilated loans ('xenonyms':
see n. 2). This leads learners to parse proparoxytonic nouns like *Sócrat-e-s*
'Socrates.SG/PL' as pseudoplural rather than athematic (cf. diminutive
*Socrat-it-o*, not *\*Socrates-it-o*), since otherwise they would be metrically
deviant (Bermúdez-Otero 2007: §2.3.2).

The way in which Spanish learners deal with nouns like *Sócrat-e-s* indicates
that, in language acquisition, the phonological properties of a word can cause
it to receive a morphological parse that fails to match its syntactic features. This
result has important implications for our understanding of deponency and,
more generally, for the theory of the syntax-morphology interface. As we shall
see in section 5 below, the syntax-morphology mismatches found in the
languages of the world turn out to have a rather diverse ætiology. This raises
the question whether the formal mechanisms used to model instances of
semantically or pragmatically induced deponency will cast any light on syntax-
morphology mismatches driven by phonological factors. More generally, the
finding that phonological constraints on morphological categories can dra-
matically disrupt syntax-morphology correspondence lends new urgency to
the task of ascertaining the universal limits to possible syntax-morphology
mismatches.

The argument will proceed as follows. In section 2 I present the evidence
for distinguishing between pseudoplural nouns and non-pseudoplural nouns
with athematic stems in /s/; a key step in the argument is the demonstration
that Spanish evaluative suffixes such as diminutive *-it-o* and augmentative
*-ot-e* attach to stems, rather than to roots or to words, and can therefore be
used to establish whether a final /s/ belongs to the stem or to an inflectional
suffix. Regrettably, the distinction between athematic and pseudoplural
nouns has hitherto not been properly understood. In consequence, section 3
is devoted to clearing up certain misconceptions concerning athematic stems
in /s/: notably, I argue against the view that diminutive forms like *virus-it-o* are
ungrammatical even for those native speakers who produce them spontaneously. Having settled the relevant descriptive issues, in section 4 I chart the
acquisition path that leads Spanish learners to the contrast between pseudoplural nouns and non-deponent nouns with athematic stems in /s/. The paper

concludes in section 5 with a survey of the general implications of our findings.

## 2. Pseudoplural Nouns vs Non-Pseudoplural Nouns with Athematic Stems in /s/

Nouns like *Carl-o-s* and *virus* share the property that their singular form is superficially homophonous with the plural. This is shown by their behaviour under agreement. In (5a), for example, *Carl-o-s* bears the plural marker /-s/ according to our analysis, but it must nonetheless be specified as singular in the syntax since the copula *es* and the predicative adjective *buen-o*, which are required to agree with it in number, are both unambiguously singular.[4]

(5)  a.  Carl-o-s          es                    buen-o
         Charles-SF-PL    be.3SG.PRS.IND    good-SF[SG]
         'Charles is good'

     b.  Aquí   hay                    much-o-s       Carl-o-s
         here   there_be.PRS.IND    many-SF-PL    Charles-SF-PL
         'Here there are many Charleses'

     c.  Est-e          virus   es                    muy    peligros-o
         This-SF[SG]    virus   be.3SG.PRS.IND    very    dangerous-SF[SG]
         'This virus is very dangerous'

     d.  Est-o-s        virus   son                   muy    peligros-o-s
         This-SF-PL    virus   be.3PL.PRS.IND    very    dangerous-SF-PL
         'These viruses are very dangerous'

The main descriptive challenge posed by these nouns is to ascertain the morphological affiliation of the final /s/ in the singular form. Logically, two possibilities suggest themselves:

(6)  a.  The final /s/ of the singular may be part of the stem. In that case, the homophony between the singular and plural forms can be explained by positing a phonological process of degemination applying to the underlying /ss/ sequence in the plural: see (2) above. This process is well motivated as Spanish does not tolerate geminates.

     b.  Alternatively, the final /s/ of the singular form may lie outside the stem. In that case, this final /s/ will be phonologically identical with the plural marker /-s/ and will occupy the same morphological slot. We can therefore assume that it *is* indeed the plural marker, and that the singular form in

---

[4] For our purposes it does not matter whether number agreement takes place in the 'narrow syntax' (cf. Bobaljik 2006). Similarly, it is not essential that we identify the precise features involved; see Corbett (2000) for a typological survey of the possible values of the category number, and Harbour (2006) for a proposed universal inventory of number features.

question is deponent. This automatically explains the homophony between singular and plural, since both consist of the noun stem followed by the plural marker /-s/: see (3) above.

I have formulated the choice in (6) in terms of whether or not the final /s/ of the singular form is affiliated to the *stem*. Implicit in this formulation is the traditional trichotomy of root, stem, and word (see e.g. Benveniste 1935). In brief, a ROOT is defined as an uninflectable lexical item: roots cannot be inflected without first undergoing root-to-stem conversion, which may be either overt (involving some operation on the phonological form of the root) or covert. In contrast, a STEM is a unit that can provide the base for an inflectional operation, i.e. it is an inflectable lexical item. Finally, WORDS are fully inflected, i.e. syntactically free. These traditional definitions are fairly robust and can easily be transposed into a variety of theoretical frameworks. For example, the constituents identified in a traditional parse of the noun *caudales* 'capital.PL' (7a) can be straightforwardly mapped onto nodes in a Distributed Morphology representation (7b); for the latter, see Oltra-Massuet (1999, 2000), Oltra-Massuet and Arregi (2005), and Harris (1999).[5]

(7)   a. [_word_ [_stem_ [_root_ kawd]al-e]s]

b.

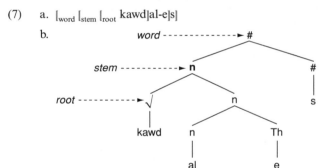

In this connection there is an important point to be made about the distribution and behaviour of stem formatives in Spanish. Unless it belongs to the marginal athematic class, every nominal or adjectival stem must end in one of the following theme vowels: /-o/, /-a/, /-{e,∅}/, or /-e/ (see n. 2). In this sense, theme vowels should properly be characterized as *stem formatives*.[6] Importantly, the

---

[5] The symbols in (7b) are to be interpreted as follows: √ is a categoryless root (Marantz 1997); n is a category-giving functional head creating a noun; Th is the theme vowel position adjoined to n (Oltra-Massuet 1999); # is the functional head containing number features. I should point out that, although the traditional parse in (7a) and the Distributed Morphology representation in (7b) are equivalent for our purposes, the theories behind them are of course not identical: notably, the traditional parse does not carry the assumption that words are built by head adjunction in the syntax.

[6] Whereas the term *theme vowel* is unhelpfully opaque in English, expressions such as *vocal temática* or *voyelle thématique* are entirely appropriate in the Romance languages, where the

requirement that a stem must end in a stem formative applies whether the stem provides the base for a derivational or for an inflectional operation. On the surface, however, this distribution is often obscured by the application of a phonological process which targets the stem-suffix juncture and deletes the final vowel of the stem if it is unstressed and immediately followed by another vowel. (8a) provides a rule-based statement of this process; for an optimality-theoretic implementation, see Bermúdez-Otero (2007: §2.1). The effects of stem-final vowel deletion are illustrated in (8b).

(8)    a.

$$V \rightarrow \varnothing \ / \underline{\bigsqcup}_{w}{}^{\sigma_w} {}_{stem}] \ ]_{suffix} \ V \qquad \text{(noniterative)}$$

       b.                   casitas

$\lfloor_{word} \lfloor_{stem} \lfloor_{stem}$ kas-**a**    ] -it-**a**   ]-s    ]    $\rightarrow$    [kasítas]

house-SF -DIM-SF -PL

'little houses'

See Bermúdez-Otero (2007) for more extensive discussion.

   Both of the options outlined in (6) are broached in the extant literature: for example, Contreras (1977) posits the rule of degemination assumed in (6a); similarly, Hooper and Terrell (1976) and Den Os and Kager (1986) adopt the pseudoplural analysis sketched in (6b). However, previous scholarship has not seriously addressed the possibility that Spanish has *both* nondeponent nouns with athematic stems in /s/ *and* pseudoplural nouns; in consequence, there has been a failure to develop morphological criteria for distinguishing between the two types of noun. What we need, then, is a morphological test for deciding whether or not the final /s/ of a singular noun is part of the stem. The obvious solution is to observe the behaviour of the noun under stem-based derivational suffixation: if the final /s/ is retained before the derivational suffix, it will be part of the stem; if it fails to appear before the derivational suffix, it will be an inflectional marker. Finding the criterial suffixes for our test is no trivial matter, for a suffixation operation can in principle belong to any of the following four types: root-to-stem, stem-to-stem, stem-to-word, and word-to-word (see e.g. Kiparsky 2003). Fortunately, Spanish evaluative suffixes like diminutive *-it-o* (feminine *-it-a*), augmentative *-ot-e* (feminine *-ot-a*), and augmentative *-ón-Ø* (feminine *-on-a*) can easily be shown to attach to stems rather than to roots or words.[7]

---

trichotomy of root, stem, and word is conveyed by terms such as *raíz,* **tema,** *palabra* (Spanish) or *racine,* **thème,** *mot* (French). Of course, having argued for the replacement of *theme vowel* by *stem formative,* I should also substitute the adjective *formativeless* for *athematic,* but one can only push terminological reform so far.

[7] In this respect the Spanish evaluative suffixes make a remarkable contrast with one of the Portuguese diminutive suffixes, namely /-ziɲ-u/ (feminine /-ziɲ-ɐ/), which is demonstrably word-based (Rainer 1996: §3; Bachrach and Wagner 2006, Bermúdez-Otero forthcoming: ch. 2).

First, the evaluative suffixes do not attach to uninflectable bases, and so cannot be root-based. Consider for example the *e*-stem noun *caud-al-Ø* 'capital', which we first encountered in its plural form in (7) above. As we saw there, the stem of this noun is formed through the addition of the derivational suffix /-al-{e,Ø}/ to the base /kawd-/, which can only be a root since it is not inflectable: cf. *\*caud-o(-s)*, *\*caud-a(-s)*, *\*caud-e(-s)*.[8] In consequence, the evaluative suffixes are able to attach to the stem [[kawd]al-{e,Ø}], but not to the root [kawd].

(9)   a.                       caudalito
         [$_{word}$ [$_{stem}$ [$_{stem}$ [$_{root}$ kawd]al-{e,Ø}]it-o]]    →    [kawðalíto]
                                'capital.DIM.SG'

      b.   *[$_{word}$ [$_{stem}$ [$_{root}$ kawd]it-o]]

The finding that evaluative suffixation cannot be root-based is confirmed by a slightly more intricate phonological argument (Bermúdez-Otero 2007: §1.2.1). Spanish has a phonological process whereby certain lexically specified vowels are realized as diphthongs under primary stress and as monophthongs elsewhere: cf. (10a) and (10b) below (for surveys of the literature on this phenomenon, see Cole 1995: §6.2 and Eddington 2004: §6.1). However, this process misapplies in the presence of the evaluative suffixes: e.g. in (10c) primary stress falls on the diminutive suffix, but the vowel of the base nonetheless surfaces as diphthongal. The overapplication of diphthongization requires the cyclic derivation in (10d): the stem undergoes diphthongization in the first cycle, and then stress moves rightwards to the diminutive suffix in the second cycle.[9] However, if the diminutive were root-based, then it could not possibly have the domain structure shown in (10d): roots are commonly assumed not to constitute cyclic domains (Kiparsky 1982a: 144–5, 1982b: 32–3; Inkelas 1990: §3.5.5; Bermúdez-Otero forthcoming); therefore, if the diminutive suffix attached itself directly to a root, then it would already be present in the first cycle, as shown in (10e).

(10)  a.   puerta       [pwért-a] 'door.SG'

      b.   portero      [poɾt-éɾ-o] 'doorman.SG'

      c.   puertecita   [pweɾt-eθít-a] 'door.DIM.SG'

      d.   *correct derivation*
             morphological structure [$_{stem}$ [$_{stem}$ p{we/o}ɾt-a]eθit-a]
             domain structure              [[p{we/o}ɾt-a]eθit-a]
             first cycle                   pwérta
             second cycle                  pweɾteθíta

---

[8] There is a learnèd noun *caud-a* (< Latin *cauda* 'tail'), meaning 'train of an episcopal robe of state', which is synchronically and etymologically unrelated to *caud-al-Ø* (< Latin *capitālis*).
[9] A full analysis of *puert-ecit-a* would have to account for the selection of the augmented allomorph of the diminutive suffix. The details are not relevant here.

e. *incorrect derivation*
  morphological structure $[_{stem} [_{root} p\{we/o\}rt]e\theta it\text{-}a]$
  domain structure $[p\{we/o\}rt\text{-}e\theta it\text{-}a]$
  first cycle $*porte\theta íta$

The evaluative suffixes cannot be word-based either. This is shown, first, by the fact that they cause stem-final vowel deletion, as shown in (8) above. In this respect, diminutive and augmentative forms contrast with denumeral partitives with the suffix *-av-o* (feminine *-av-a*), which attaches to fully inflected bases, i.e. to words: (11a) shows *-av-o* occurring outside the plural marker *-s*, whilst (11b) shows that *-av-o* does not trigger stem-final vowel deletion (Pensado Ruiz 1999: 4461–2; Bermúdez-Otero 2007: §2.2).

(11) a.  doscientosavo
  $[_{word} [_{word} dos\text{-}\theta jent\text{-}o\text{-}s] \text{-}ab\text{-}o]$  → $[dos\theta jentosá\beta o]$
  two-hundred-SF-**PL**-PARTITIVE-SF
  '200th'

  cf. doscientos '200'

b.  onceavo
  $[_{word} [_{word} on\theta\text{-}e] \text{-}ab\text{-}o]$  → $[on\theta eá\beta o]$
  eleven-SF-PARTITIVE-SF
  '11th'

  cf. once '11'

Relatedly, evaluative derivatives constitute single prosodic words. This opposes them to deadjectival adverbs formed with the word-based suffix *-ment-e*. In the latter, the base and the suffix surface as separate prosodic words. This complex prosodic structure permits stress clashes (12a) and non-initial lapses (12b), which are never found in evaluative forms.

(12) a.  común  $[_{\omega}ko.mún]$  'common.M/F'
  comúnmente  $[_{\omega'}[_{\omega}ko.mùn][_{\omega}mén.te]]$  'commonly'
  cf.
  camión  $[_{\omega}ka.mjón]$  'lorry'
  camioncito  $[_{\omega}kà.mjon.\theta í.to]$, $*[_{\omega'}[_{\omega}ka.mjòn][_{\omega}\theta í.to]]$  'lorry.DIM'
b.  penúltima  $[_{\omega}pe.núl.ti.ma]$  'penultimate.F'
  penúltimamente  $[_{\omega'}[_{\omega}pe.nùl.ti.ma][_{\omega}mén.te]]$  'penultimately'

If the evaluative suffixes are neither root-based, as shown in (9) and (10), nor word-based, as shown in (11) and (12), then they can only be stem-based—*quod erat demonstrandum*. As suggested above, therefore, we can use the evaluative suffixes to test the morphological affiliation of the final /s/ in singular nouns with homophonous plural forms: if the final /s/ appears before the suffix in evaluative derivatives, the noun is athematic and the /s/ is part of its stem; if the final /s/ does not appear before the suffix in evaluative derivatives, the noun is pseudoplural and the /s/ is a plural marker, lying outside the stem.

The application of this morphological test confirms that nouns of both classes coexist in the mental lexicon of many Spanish speakers. In (13a), for example, I present a sample of evaluative forms from my own Northern Peninsular idiolect. All of these forms are found in both Peninsular and Latin American dialects. Their occurrence in spontaneous language use is documented in Bermúdez-Otero (2007: §2.3.1); see (13b) to (13f) for additional examples.[10] In certain cases there are competing variants, but the forms given in (13) are clearly the most frequent: see §3.2 for further details and discussion.

(13) a.

| noun type | singular | plural | evaluative derivative | | gloss |
|---|---|---|---|---|---|
| athematic | *virus* | *virus* | *virus-it-o* | DIM | 'virus' |
| | *brindis* | *brindis* | *brindis-it-o* | DIM | 'toast' |
| pseudoplural | *Carl-o-s* | *Carl-o-s* | *Carl-ot-e* | AUG | 'Charles' |
| | *Sócrat-e-s* | *Sócrat-e-s* | *Socrat-it-o* | DIM | 'Socrates' |
| | *crisi-s* | *crisi-s* | *cris-ecit-a* | DIM | 'crisis' |

   b.   *virus-it-o* [birusíto]

Un **virusito** de estos grásticos me vendrían a mí bien para cerrarme el estómago un par de días
'I could do with one of these little gastric viruses to shut my stomach for a couple of days.'
<http://foro.adelgazar.net/phpBB2//viewtopic.php?p=180423&highlight
=&sid=ff253f606309db852f6b97c2d1a12ccc>

   c.   *brindis-it-o* [brindisíto]

Péguense un **brindisito** por mí, sí? Que lo disfruten!
'Drink my health, will you? Enjoy!'
<http://foros.grippo.com.ar/mensajes/Forum1/HTML/004975.html>

   d.   *Carl-ot-e* [karlóte]

Más bien debería llamarlo '**Carlote**' pues el joven Carlos, que cumplía veintitrés años, medía dos metros y calzaba cincuenta.
'I should rather call him 'Big Charles', for young Charles, who became twenty-three that day, was two metres tall and wore size-fifty shoes.'
<http://www4.loscuentos.net/cuentos/link/214/214888/print/>

   e.   *Socrat-it-o* [sokratíto]

Susana, Sebastián, Valentina y **Socratito** participan el fallecimiento de su querido amigo.

---

[10] The Internet pages quoted in (13) were all accessed on 17 September 2006.

'Susan, Sebastian, Valentina and Little Socrates announce the death of their beloved friend.'
<http://cableydiario.com/index.php/diarios/2006/09/16/
necrologicas/index.html>

f.   *cris-ecit-a* [kɾiseθíta]

[A]l igual que a nuestras Cortes autonómicas las denominan por estos lares las cortitas, nuestra crisis autonómica la llamarán la **crisecita**.

'Just as people hereabout call the parliament of our autonomous region the little parliament, they will call the crisis of our autonomous region the little crisis.'

Ramón Saura, *El País*, 1 August 1985

# 3. Apparent Problems

## 3.1. Obstacles to knowledge

As we saw in section 2, the literature on the morphological structure of Spanish nouns contains analyses that roughly match the categories 'non-deponent athematic stem in /s/' and 'pseudoplural' as defined above. However, previous scholarship has failed to recognize that both classes are needed and actually coexist in the mental lexicon of Spanish speakers. Generative linguists, in particular, have consistently misanalysed athematic nouns such as *virus* and *brindis*, parsing the final /s/ of the singular form as being outside the stem (e.g. Harris 1983, 1985, 1991, 1992, 1999). As a result, this work incorrectly conflates the athematic and pseudoplural classes. For recent instances of this error, see Bonet (2007), Lloret and Mascaró (2005), Oltra-Massuet and Arregi (2005), Roca and Felíu (2003), and Roca (2005).

The chief obstacle in the way to a proper understanding of the structure of nouns like *virus* and *Carl-o-s* has lain in inaccurate reports of their behaviour under evaluative suffixation. In turn, these flaws in the empirical record have largely followed from the limitations of data-gathering methods such as introspection, form elicitation, and judgement elicitation. Ordinarily, these techniques can be relied upon to produce valid information about wide areas of grammar, but they prove inadequate for probing items of linguistic knowledge such as the contrast between athematic and pseudoplural nouns in Spanish, for here learners are forced to rely opportunistically on indirect, partially conflicting language-particular cues to overcome an underdetermination effect in their trigger experience (§4); tools such as introspection and elicitation are too blunt to access the resulting knowledge. It is only recently that it has become possible to overcome these obstacles by automatically searching the massive volume of data available on the Internet (cf. Rainer 2003). This new source of information proves crucial to evaluating the

grammatical status of forms such as *virus-it-o* and *brindis-it-o*, which occur
with vastly greater frequency than competing variants. Smaller, purpose-
built corpora such as the *Corpus de referencia del español actual* (CREA) fail
to capture the relevant quantitative patterns: see (26) below and cf. also
Eddington (2002: 409–10).

In section 3.2 below I discuss the implications of the Internet data.
Subsequent sections (§3.3 to §3.5) deal with other descriptive issues that bear
on our understanding of nouns with athematic stems in /s/.

### 3.2. The grammaticality of *virus-it-o* and *brindis-it-o*

Evaluative derivatives such as *virus-it-o* and *brindis-it-o* are essential to my
argument because they show that nouns like *virus* and *brindis* cannot be
analysed as pseudoplural, despite frequent claims to the contrary (see §3.1). In
section 2 I noted that these forms are in competition with other variants, but
the Internet data show that this variation is quantitatively structured: crucially, the frequency of *virus-it-o* and *brindis-it-o* sharply outstrips that of their
competitors. In this section I shall take the diminutive of *virus* as a test case;
for information about *brindis*, see Bermúdez-Otero (2007: fn. 28).

The diminutive of *virus* occurs in the five variants shown in (14).
Frequencies are estimated on the basis of the number of Google hits on
23 July 2006; in each case this corresponds to the number of webpages identified by Google as being in Spanish and containing one or more tokens of
the relevant form. These data are relatively noisy: webpages are sometimes
duplicated, and Google occasionally misidentifies the language of a webpage
(a fortiori, it cannot discriminate between native and non-native writers).
Nonetheless, frequency asymmetries are so large that reliable conclusions can
be drawn despite the noise. Where the plural differs from the singular (e.g.
singular *virus-it-o* vs plural *virus-it-o-s*, singular *vir-it-o* vs plural *vir-it-o-s*),
the figures refer to the singular only. In general it is not possible to ascertain
the geographical provenance of the data, but I have not come across any
evidence of bias in the dialectal distribution of variants.

(14)  *Variation in the diminutive of* virus

    a.  *virus-it-o* [birusíto]

        1,060 Google hits. The data are relatively clean, with few instances in which
        the form is not the diminutive of *virus*; cf (14c). Speakers producing this
        form parse the base noun as having a nondeponent athematic stem ending
        in /s/.

            Me imagino . . . pero te cuento que yo en MAC en los más de 9 años
            que llevo en la informática y usando MAC solo agarré un **virusito**
            inofensivo que vino metido en un CD de una revista que compré
            mucho que se llamaba MacFormat.

'I can imagine . . . but let me tell you that, as for me, with a Mac, in over nine years in IT using a Mac, I only got a harmless little virus that came in a CD with a magazine I used to buy a lot, which was called *MacFormat*.'

<http://foros.softonic.com/showthread.phtml?t=13939>

b.   *vir<it>us* [birítus]

96 Google hits. Relatively clean data. This form is derived by means of a comparatively rare type of diminutive infixation; the diminutive infix usually subcategorizes for bases with unstressed /o/ or /a/ in the nucleus of the final syllable (see §3.3 below). It is not possible to determine whether speakers producing this form treat the base as pseudoplural or just as athematic.

Bueno a mi parecer yo conzco muchos q por hacer un **viritus** (lease virus pequeño) o abrir un hotmail ya se creen hackers.

'Well, in my opinion, I know many people who, just because they've made a wee virus (read, a little virus) or they've got into a Hotmail account, they think they're hackers.'

<http://somos.lamerma.com.ve/mermachat/index.htm?TID=67&PN
=1&TPN=10> (cached by Google on 9 August 2005)

c.   *vir-it-o* [biríto]

Approximately 40 genuine Google hits out of a total of 454. Very noisy data: most hits are morphologically unrelated to *virus*, but correspond to the personal name *Virito*. Speakers producing this diminutive of *virus* parse the singular form of the base noun as pseudoplural, i.e. [$_{word}$ [$_{stem}$ biru]s]. No Google hits for a similar variant with the augmented allomorph of the diminutive suffix, i.e. \**vir-ecit-o*; cf. (14d).

A veces son problemas de software, que se corrompen por apagones indebidos, a veces problemas de memoria y a veces algún **virito** pescado en internet.

'Sometimes the problem is software, which gets corrupted through an improper shutdown; sometimes the problem is memory; and sometimes it is some little virus caught on the Internet.'

<http://www.yoreparo.com/foros/reparacion_de_computadoras/
23017.html>

d.   *virus-cit-o* [birusθíto]

13 Google hits. Clean data. Speakers producing this form parse the base noun as having a non-deponent athematic stem ending in /s/. This variant differs from (14a) only in the choice of the allomorph of the diminutive suffix.

Quizas Tomas haya estornudado sobre la pantalla sin tapar la boca, asi infectandole con un **viruscito**.

'Perhaps Thomas has coughed all over the screen without putting his hand over his mouth, thus infecting it with a little virus.'

<http://ndialectica.blogspot.com/2003_02_01
_ndialectica_archive.html>

e.  ∅ (defectiveness)

Elicitation tasks and linguistic introspection sometimes yield the report that *virus* does not have a diminutive form: e.g. 'in many of these cases derivation is normally avoided' (Méndez-Dosuna and Pensado 1990: 101). This is likely to be true for at least some speakers, but the inherent unreliability of elicitation tasks makes it difficult to estimate the real proportion: see section 4 for indirect evidence that the extent of defectiveness is in fact rather limited.

The quantitative evidence in (14) is conclusive. *Virus-it-o* occurs at least 11 times more frequently than its most frequent competitor (viz. *vir<it>us*).[11] Diminutive forms unambiguously implying a non-deponent parse of *virus* (viz. *virus-it-o* and *virus-cit-o*) are approximately 27 times more frequent than *vir-it-o*, the only diminutive form unambiguously implying a pseudoplural parse. Among those speakers for whom *virus* does have a diminutive form, an athematic parse with a stem in /s/ is somewhere between 8 and 27 times more likely than a pseudoplural parse.[12] This finding roundly refutes the claim that, for all speakers, the final /s/ of singular *virus* lies outside the stem; cf. section 3.1 above.

The Internet data also enable us to draw firm conclusions regarding the grammatical status of evaluative derivatives such as *virus-it-o* and *brindis-it-o*. Iggy Roca (personal communication, 29 March 2006) asserts that, for most speakers, *virus* does not have a diminutive form. If so, one could argue that ∅ is the core variant in (14), and that *virus-it-o* is at best marginal, along with *vir<it>us*, *vir-it-o*, and *virus-cit-o*. Can this claim be reconciled with the evidence of over 1,000 tokens of singular *virus-it-o* in spontaneous language use across the Spanish-speaking world? The obvious way to advance Roca's argument would be to appeal to the distinction between competence and performance (Chomsky 1965). One could thus suggest that the form *virus-it-o* is in fact an artificial creation, constructed by means of extragrammatical problem-solving strategies such as metalinguistic reasoning or ad hoc pattern-matching, and perhaps intended for special rhetorical effect. Roca certainly countenances this possibility, for in a different connection he speaks of 'online performance trial outputs' as opposed to 'finished I-language products' (Roca 2005: fn. 32). Relatedly, Méndez-Dosuna and Pensado (1990: 100–1) describe some of the diminutive forms produced by their informants in an

---

[11] The actual figure should be higher than 11 because (14) gives the number of Google hits for *vir<it>us* in both the singular and the plural, whereas the hit count for *virus-it-o* excludes 288 hits for plural *virus-it-o-s*.

[12] The lower figure, i.e. 8, corresponds to a scenario in which every speaker producing *vir<it>us* parses *virus* as pseudoplural. The higher figure, i.e. 27, corresponds to a scenario in which every speaker producing *vir<it>us* parses *virus* as having an athematic stem in /s/.

elicitation task as 'aberrant'. If we take this line, therefore, *virus-it-o* would be ungrammatical even for those speakers who produce it spontaneously.

However, there are powerful arguments against treating *virus-it-o* either as an artificial creation or as a speech error. First, the evidence in (14) reflects spontaneous language use; it is therefore free of the suspicion that attaches to data obtained by means of forced elicitation. In addition, most of the tokens originate in message boards and weblogs, which are characterized by their informality and low degree of linguistic monitoring; the evaluative derivatives that occur in such texts are therefore unlike the lexical innovations of poets or scientists. Moreover, the diminutive data match the evidence of other evaluative suffixes: thus, alongside *virus-it-o* we encounter the augmentatives *virus-ot-e* and *virus-ón-Ø*.

(15)   a.   *virus-ot-e* [birusóte]

hola, estoy convencido de que tengo algun **virusote** malo por el disco duro
'Hello. I'm convinced I've got a big bad virus on my hard drive.'
<http://foros.zonavirus.com/image-vp59534.html>
(accessed on 17 September 2006)

       b.   *virus-ón-Ø* [birusón]

algun boludon le hara doble click y ahi entro el **viruson** a la PC.
'Some big idiot will double-click on it, and there goes the big virus into the PC.'
<http://www.foroescorts.com.ar/archive/inf-virus-1888.htm>
(accessed on 17 September 2006)

Secondly, the figures in (14) reveal that *virus-it-o* sits at the top of an abrupt acceptability cline. It is improbable that the judgements of informants relying on extragrammatical problem-solving strategies would match this gradation. For example, such informants might favour *Carl<it>-o-s* 'Charles.DIM.SG/PL' as an analogical model, since it occurs extremely frequently and is not subject to variation.[13] However, this strategy would favour infixal *vir<it>us*, which, as we saw above, is more than 11 times less frequent than *virus-it-o*. In this light, the speakers whose usage is recorded on the Internet appear more likely to be guided in the main by their tacit knowledge of the morphological structure of *virus* than by metalinguistic reasoning or ad hoc pattern-matching.

Thirdly, the variability that affects the diminutive of *virus* arises from an underdetermination effect in language acquisition: as we have seen, the information contained in the inflectional paradigm of *virus* does not uniquely determine the morphological affiliation of the final /s/. This situation can

---

[13] On the structure of *Carl<it>-o-s*, see §3.3 below. On 23 July 2006 *Carlitos* scored over a million hits in Google.

resolve itself in either of two ways (see §4 below). On the one hand, the learner may fail to commit herself to a particular parse below the word node; in that case, she will not be able to apply stem-based suffixation to *virus*, which will consequently lack a (suffixal) diminutive. On the other hand, the learner may settle on a parse for the final /s/ by relying on the indirect morphological and phonological cues to which I referred in section 1; in that case, the learner will acquire a grammar that generates one of the diminutive forms listed in (14a) to (14d). Given our limited knowledge of language acquisition, neither scenario can be rejected a priori, and the empirical evidence indicates that both are instantiated in practice. Therefore, if one wished to dismiss *virus-it-o* as the outcome of extragrammatical phenomena, one would have to accord an arbitrary and unwarranted privilege to the first scenario over the second. In fact, section 4 below provides some quantitative data suggesting that defectiveness is a rare outcome.

I conclude that the evidence reported in (14) should be taken at face value. For native speakers who produce *virus-it-o* spontaneously, this form is grammatical. Spanish speakers are between 8 and 27 times less likely to parse *virus* as a pseudoplural noun than as having an athematic stem ending in /s/. Therefore, previous scholarship was in error when it failed to recognize the existence of athematic stems in /s/ and their opposition to pseudoplurals.

## 3.3. Diminutive infixation

It is easy to use augmentative suffixes such as *-ot-e* (feminine *-o-ta*) and *-ón-Ø* (feminine *-on-a*) for isolating noun stems, as shown in section 2. In contrast, the diminutive presents additional complications, which however, when properly understood, turn to the advantage of our analysis. The initial difficulty arises over the fact that, in certain cases, diminutive formation is unambiguously infixal (Jaeggli 1980; Lázaro Mora 1999: §71.6; Méndez-Dosuna and Pensado 1990).

(16)  a.  singular                                     plural

          [aθúkaɾ]                                     [aθúkaɾes]
          azúcar-Ø                                     azúcar-e-s
          sugar-SF[SG]                                 sugar-SF-PL

      b.  diminutive singular (suffixal)               diminutive plural (suffixal)

          [aθukaɾ(θ)íto]                               [aθukaɾ(θ)ítos]
          azucar-(c)it-o                               azucar-(c)it-o-s
          sugar-DIM-SF[SG]                             sugar-DIM-SF-PL

      c.  diminutive singular (infixal)                diminutive plural (infixal)

          [aθukítaɾ]                                   [aθukítaɾes]
          azuqu<it>ar-Ø                                azuqu<ít>ar-e-s
          sugar<DIM>-SF[SG]                            sugar<DIM>-SF-PL

In the noun *azúcar-Ø* 'sugar', for example, the status of the string /aɾ/ is not in doubt: it cannot be some sort of exotic stem formative but must simply be part of the root, for the plural form *azúcar-e-s* shows the stem to be /aθukaɾ-{e,Ø}-/, with the formative /-{e,Ø}/ alternating predictably between [-Ø] in the singular and [-e-] in the plural (see §3.4 below). The diminutive variant *azucar-(c)it-o* follows the expected pattern for stem-based suffixation: the stem formative of the base disappears before the diminutive suffix, and the latter in turn determines the stem class of the derived form (for a masculine stem, the *o*-class). In *azuqu<it>ar-Ø*, in contrast, the diminutive morpheme /-it-/ appears inside the root and must therefore be an infix. From its infixal position, /-it-/ does not interfere with the selection of the stem formative of the derivative, which remains an ordinary *e*-stem like the base: cf. the infixal plural *azuqu<it>ar-e-s* with the suffixal plural *azucar-(c)it-o-s*.

Clearly, an infix is of no use for distinguishing between pseudoplural nouns and nouns with athematic stems in /s/. Fortunately, however, infixal and suffixal derivatives are easy to tell apart and, indeed, the evaluative forms adduced in (4) and (13) are all unequivocally suffixal. In the case of *virus-it-o*, the base *virus* appears whole on the left of the diminutive suffix, which, in addition, imposes a different stem class on the derivative; the same is true of *brindis-it-o*. In the case of *Carl-ot-e*, *Socrat-it-o*, and *cris-ecit-a*, suffixation results in the loss of the pseudoplural ending: as an inflection, the /-s/ cannot occur on the left of a stem-based suffix, and the suffix in turn blocks its appearance on the right. Crucially, forms like *Carl-ot-e-s*, *Socrat-it-o-s*, and *cris-ecit-a-s* do exist, but for most speakers these are not pseudoplural singulars; they are the genuinely plural counterparts of singular *Carl-ot-e*, *Socrat-it-o*, and *cris-ecit-a* (though see n. 14). Moreover, the evaluative suffixes in *Carl-ot-e*, *Socrat-it-o*, and *cris-ecit-a* again impose a different stem class on the derivative: e.g. *e*-stem *Sócrat-e-s* changes into *o*-stem *Socrat-it-o*. In this respect, the diminutive morpheme in *Socrat-it-o* behaves entirely like the suffix in *azucar-(c)it-o* (16b) and not at all like the infix in *azuqu<it>ar-Ø* (16c). Therefore, the existence of diminutive infixation in no way challenges our conclusions concerning the opposition between pseudoplural nouns and athematic nouns with stems in /s/.

In fact, recognizing the existence of diminutive infixation is essential to understanding what would otherwise be an intractable puzzle (Bermúdez-Otero 2007: §2.3.1). For most Spanish speakers, the paradigms of SÓCRATES and CARLOS are as follows:[14]

---

[14] There are some speakers for whom *Socratitos* can be a singular form. Compare the following example with (13e):

(17)                                          'Socrates'              'Charles'

   a.   singular                    Sócrat-e-s              Carl-o-s
         plural                       Sócrat-e-s              Carl-o-s

   b.   diminutive singular         Socrat-it-o             Carl<it>-o-s
         diminutive plural           Socrat-it-o-s           Carl<it>-o-s

   c.   augmentative singular       Socrat-ot-e             Carl-ot-e
         augmentative plural         Socrat-ot-e-s           Carl-ot-e-s

Both *Sócrat-e-s* and *Carl-o-s* are pseudoplural nouns, but they behave subtly differently under evaluative derivation. In the evaluative derivatives of *Sócrat-e-s* we see all the expected effects of stem-based suffixation: the pseudoplurality of the base is lost, and the stem class of the derivative is determined by the evaluative suffix (*o*-stem in the case of the diminutive, *e*-stem in the case of the augmentative). The augmentative of *Carl-o-s* follows the same pattern: the pseudoplural /-s/ of the base is absent in the singular *Carl-ot-e*, and the derived stem switches to the *e*-class. The surprise comes in the diminutive of *Carl-o-s*, which retains the pseudoplural /-s/ of the base in its singular form: thus *Carl<it>-o-s* can be both a pseudoplural singular or a genuine plural; cf. (5a,b) and (18).

(18)  a.   Carl<it>-o-s            es                  buen-o
         Charles<DIM>-SF-PL      be.3SG.PRS.IND      good-SF[SG]
         'Charley / little Charles is good.'

      b.   Aquí    hay                 much-o-s       Carl<it>-o-s
         here    there_be.PRS.IND    many-SF-PL     Charles<DIM>-SF-PL
         'Here there are many Charleys / little Charleses.'

This intriguing pattern can be explained by making two simple assumptions, extensively discussed in Bermúdez-Otero (2007: §2.3.1). First, diminutive /-it-/ can either be suffixed or infixed, but augmentative /-ot-/ can only be suffixed. Secondly, the diminutive infix subcategorizes for bases in which the nucleus of the final syllable consists of unstressed /o/ or /a/. This subcategorization requirement can be explained diachronically: the diminutive infix arose by reanalysis from the diminutive suffix, which selects the stem formative /-o/ in masculine forms and /-a/ in feminine forms; the morphological selection properties of the suffix were simply reanalysed as phonological

---

Querido **Socratitos**, a ver si coincidimos por el ciberespacio de nuevo.
'Dear Little Socrates, let's see if we meet again in cyberspace.'
     <http://www.ludopatia.org/forum/forum_posts.asp?TID=862&PN=2>
                     (accessed on 18 September 2006)

However, such speakers are in a minority. On 18 September 2006 there were 43 Google hits for singular *Socratito*, and only 5 for singular *Socratitos*. These figures provide only a rough indication of relative frequency, as both include cases in which the same token appears in multiple copies of a webpage.

selection properties in the infix. Thus, /sókɾat-e-s/ cannot take the diminutive infix, for, being an *e*-stem, it does not contain an unstressed /o/ or /a/ in the final syllable; accordingly, it takes the diminutive suffix, which attaches to the stem /sókɾat-{e,∅}-/, losing the pseudoplural /-s/. In contrast, /káɾl-o-s/ fulfils the phonological selection requirements of the diminutive infix /-it-/, which is inserted to the left of the stem formative /-o/ without disrupting the adjacency of the stem and the pseudoplural /-s/: [kaɾl<ít>-o-s]. Finally, both augmentatives are suffixal, and hence lose the pseudoplurality of the base.

Against this background, the infixal diminutive [biɾ<ít>us], which we encountered in (14b), appears problematic, since it violates the requirement that /-it-/ should be infixed immediately to the left of a final syllable nucleus consisting of unstressed /o/ or /a/. In this respect, we should observe that the form is unacceptable for many speakers, and is indeed more than 11 times rarer that the suffixal variant *virus-it-o* (see n. 11). I suspect that speakers who produce [biɾ<ít>us] take advantage of the fact that the diminutive infix /-it-/ is aligned with the left edge of the nucleus of the final syllable of the base, in contrast with the diminutive suffix /-it-o/, which aligns itself with the right edge of the base. Thus, by exceptionally relaxing the selectional requirements of the infix, these speakers are able to generate a diminutive form for /biɾus/ even if they do not know whether the right edge of the stem falls before or after the final /s/. If this suggestion is on the right track, the occurrence of [biɾ<ít>us] is another symptom of the underdetermination effect that besets nouns with homophonous singular and plural forms ending in /s/.

### 3.4. On *\*vírus-e-s*

Before turning to the explanatory task of showing how learners respond to this underdetermination effect, it remains still to clear up two descriptive problems that have occasionally hampered the analysis of nouns like *virus*.

Consider the paradigms in (19). The singular forms illustrate the full range of consonants permitted word-finally in Spanish, excluding xenonyms (see n. 2). These legal word-final codas are all monosegmental: viz. /d, θ, s, n, l, ɾ/ (see e.g. Harris 1999: 60).

| (19) | a. | singular | | b. | plural | | |
|---|---|---|---|---|---|---|---|
| | | pared-∅ | [pa.ɾéð] | | pared-e-s | [pa.ɾé.ðes] | 'wall' |
| | | cruz-∅ | [kɾuθ] | | cruc-e-s | [kɾú.θes] | 'cross' |
| | | iris-∅ | [í.ɾis] | | íris-e-s | [í.ɾi.ses] | 'iris'† |
| | | certamen-∅ | [θeɾ.tá.men] | | certámen-e-s | [θeɾ.tá.me.nes] | 'contest' |
| | | ángel-∅ | [áŋ.xel] | | ángel-e-s | [áŋ.xe.les] | 'angel' |
| | | mujer-∅ | [mu.xéɾ] | | mujer-e-s | [mu.xé.ɾes] | 'woman' |

† For some speakers this noun does not belong in the *e*-class, but is rather an athematic stem ending in /s/: singular *iris*, plural *iris*, diminutive singular *iris-it-o*. See Bermúdez-Otero (2007: fn. 26).

It is sometimes suggested that the [e] which appears in the plural forms before the inflectional marker [-s] is inserted by a phonological process that avoids illegal coda clusters. If this view were correct, then one might expect the plural of *virus* to be *[bí.ru.ses], with an epenthetic [e] breaking up the illegal word-final cluster in /birus-s/. Since epenthesis does not in fact apply, this might be taken as an argument for treating *virus* as pseudoplural rather than as having an athematic stem ending in /s/. However, the premise of this argument is false. Spanish does not use vowel epenthesis to repair illegal word-final strings (Bermúdez-Otero 2007: §1.2.2; Bonet 2007; Colina 2003a, 2003b; Harris 1999). When fully nativized, for example, English /stɒp/ becomes [es.tó], not *[es.tó.pe].

The behaviour of the nouns in (19) must be explained in terms of their morphological structure. They are all ordinary members of the *e*-class and, as such, their stems all end with the formative /-{e,∅}/. The allomorphy of this stem formative is controlled by phonological factors in the singular form, but by morphological factors in the plural (Bermúdez-Otero 2007: §1.2.2). In the singular, the phonology selects the null allomorph [-∅] after permissible word-final sequences, and the non-null allomorph [-e] elsewhere. In the plural, however, a morphological process pre-empts phonological selection:[15]

(20)      $\qquad$ SF
$$-\{e,\varnothing\} \rightarrow \text{-e} / \underline{\quad}_{\text{stem}}] \text{-s}_{\text{word}}]$$

In this sense, phonotactics do play a role in causing the null formative [-∅] to appear in the singular forms in (19a). However, the appearance of the non-null formative [-e-] in the plurals in (19b) has nothing whatever to do with phonotactics, at least synchronically.

This assertion is confirmed by two arguments. First, [-e-] fails to appear in plural forms when the stem is not a member of the *e*-class. This can be observed in xenonyms such as the noun *clip* [klip] 'clip'. For the native speaker, the fact that this word ends in a consonant other than [ð, θ, s, n, l, ɾ] marks it as phonotactically deviant and excludes it from the core vocabulary. The noun is thereby disqualified from membership of the *e*-class, and so it is assigned to the marginal athematic class, even though this compounds the phonotactic problem. Athematic stems have no stem formative, and so the

---

[15] Observe that allomorphy rule (20) is triggered by the morph /-s/, not by the syntactic feature [+pl] (or its equivalent; see n. 4). Accordingly, the rule does apply to the singular form of an *e*-stem pseudoplural noun like *Sócrat-e-s*, which contains the morph /-s/ but not the feature [+pl].

addition of /-s/ in the plural turns a deviant monosegmental coda into a deviant coda cluster: [klip-s], not *[klip-e-s].

Conversely, [-e-] appears in the plural form of *e*-stems even when it is not required to attain phonotactic well-formedness. In my idiolect, for example, there is a contrast between the *e*-stem adjective /indú-{e,∅}-/ 'Hindu' and the athematic noun /menú/ 'menu'. The contrast manifests itself in the plural, where the former has an [-e-] but the latter does not:

(21)                *e-stem*                          *athematic stem*

        singular    hindú-∅      [in.dú]             menú      [me.nú]
        plural      hindú-e-s    [in.dú.es]          menú-s    [me.nús]

The [-e-] in *hindú-e-s* is phonotactically superfluous, as [ús] is a legal word-final sequence: cf. *autobús-∅* [awtoβús] 'bus', *Jesús-∅* [xesús] 'Jesus', etc.

In conclusion, parsing the final /s/ of *virus* as part of the stem does not predict the ungrammatical plural *\*vírus-e-s* because Spanish does not apply vowel epenthesis to illegal word-final clusters.

### 3.5.  On *\*virus-al-∅*

Harris (1992) adduces data like (22) in support of the claim that the final /s/ of *virus* is not part of the stem.

(22)   vir-al-∅       [biɾál]      'viral'     cf. *virus-al-∅
       vír-ic-o       [bíɾiko]     'viral'     cf. *virús-ic-o

However, these forms yield to a different analysis (Bermúdez-Otero 2007: §2.3.1). The lexical item VIRUS has two root allomorphs: (23a). The first, [root biɾ-], is bound, occurring only in root-to-stem constructions with overt derivational suffixes: e.g. (23c), surfacing as (22). The second, [root biɾus-], is homophonous with an athematic stem, (23b), which provides the base for stem-based constructions such as the evaluative derivatives in (23d).

(23)   VIRUS

        a.   root allomorphs        [root biɾ-]
                                    [root biɾus-]

        b.   stem                   [stem [root biɾus]]

        c.   root-based derivatives  [stem [root biɾ]al-{e,∅}]
                                    [stem [root biɾ]ik-o]

        d.   stem-based derivatives [stem [stem [root biɾus]]it-o]
                                    [stem [stem [root biɾus]]ot-{e,∅}]

This situation is not at all unusual. For example, the lexical item DRAMA 'drama' has two root allomorphs too: (24a). The first, [root dramat-], is again bound and occurs only in root-to-stem constructions with overt derivational suffixes: (24c). The second, [$_{root}$ dram-], supplies the base for an *a*-class masculine stem, (24b), which is in turn the base of stem-based evaluative derivatives such as the *e*-class augmentative in (24d).

(24)   DRAMA

    a.   root allomorphs        [$_{root}$ dramat-]
                                  [$_{root}$ dram-]
    b.   stem                     [$_{stem}$ [$_{root}$ dram]a]
    c.   root-based derivative    [$_{stem}$ [$_{root}$ dramat]ik-o] 'dramatic'
    d.   stem-based derivative   [$_{stem}$ [$_{stem}$ [$_{root}$ dram]a]on-{e,Ø}] → [dramón]
                                                          'drama.AUG'

Two arguments confirm that the derivational suffixes which appear in (22), /-al-{e,Ø}/ and /-ik-o/, can attach to roots (cf. §2). First, we have seen plenty of evidence that they occur with uninflectable bases: cf. (7) and (9), (23c), (24c). Secondly, they do not cause diphthongization to overapply. This shows that their base does not constitute a separate cyclic domain, which is precisely how roots are supposed to behave: cf. (10) and (25).

(25)   a.   *root-based derivation*: portal 'gate'

        morphological structure   [$_{stem}$ [$_{root}$ p{we/o}rt]al-{e,Ø}]
        domain structure          [p{we/o}rt-al-{e,Ø}]
        first cycle                portál

    b.   *stem-based derivation*: puertecita 'door.DIM'

        morphological structure   [$_{stem}$ [$_{stem}$ [$_{root}$ p{we/o}rt]a]eθit-a]
        domain structure          [[p{we/o}rt-a]eθit-a]
        first cycle                pwérta
        second cycle           pwerteθíta

I conclude that derivatives such as *vir-al-Ø* and *vír-ic-o* tell us nothing about the stem of *virus* because they are based on a bound root allomorph.


# 4. Acquiring the Contrast Between
# Athematic Stems in /s/ and Pseudoplurals

Our descriptive work is done: now, at last, we have a precise grasp of the facts to be explained. Most Spanish speakers tacitly know that *Carl-o-s* is a deponent noun whose final /-s/ lies outside the stem not only in the plural but also in the singular form. They also tacitly know that *virus* is a non-deponent noun with an athematic stem ending in /s/ and subject to phonological degemination in the plural. However, they cannot have acquired their knowledge of this morphological contrast by inspection of the inflectional paradigms of the two nouns, since these simply show that both nouns have homophonous singular and plural forms ending in /s/. The only direct morphological cue to the distinction comes from suffixal evaluative derivatives: e.g. *Carl-ot-e* vs *virus-ot-e*. Only suffixal evaluative derivatives are of use: neither root-based constructions (e.g. *vir-al-Ø*, *vír-ic-o*) nor evaluative forms derived by infixation (e.g. *Carl<it>-o-s*, *vir<it>us*) can determine the location of the right edge of the stem in *Carl-o-s* and *virus*. We, as linguists, can learn about the contrast by diligently searching for the crucial data on the Internet; but children acquiring Spanish natively cannot. Yet the criterial forms have such low token frequency that we must assume them to be largely unavailable to learners of Spanish. Therein lies the learnability puzzle.

To appreciate just how infrequently the crucial forms occur, consider the figures in (26). In (26a) I give the number of Google hits scored by each datum in (4) and (13) on 23 July 2006.[16] (26b) gives the number of tokens of the same forms in the corpora CREA and CORDE, which together contain 387,488,848 words.

| (26) | a. *Google hits* | b. *CREA+CORDE* |
|---|---|---|
| virus-it-o | 1,060 | 0 |
| virus-ot-e | 56 | 0 |
| brindis-it-o | 62 | 1 |
| Carl-ot-e | 549 | 0 |
| Socrat-it-o | 13 | 0 |
| cris-ecit-a | 0 (5 irrelevant hits) | 1 |

This evidence confirms that Spanish learners have a negligible chance of hearing suffixal evaluative forms such as *Socrat-it-o* or *cris-ecit-a* in spontaneous discourse. Those who eventually produce such forms must therefore be supposed to have relied on other cues for the knowledge that *Sócrat-e-s* and *crisi-s* are pseudoplural nouns.

Before proceeding to search for those cues, however, we should ask why the forms in (26) occur so infrequently. It might be suggested that their rarity is in fact a symptom of defectiveness: for most speakers, the base nouns would simply lack suffixal evaluative forms (cf. §3.2 above). However, this is not true; the forms in (26) are infrequent mainly because the base nouns occur only rarely in pragmatic circumstances favouring the use of evaluative derivation. To establish this point, let us again take *virus* as a test case. If the low frequency of *virus-it-o* were caused by defectiveness, then we would expect non-defective nouns with similar meanings to occur much more

---

[16] The five irrelevant Google hits for <Crisecita> correspond to tokens of the diminutive of *Cris* 'Chris', which is in turn the hypocoristic of *Cristina* 'Christine'. For the one token of *cris-ecit-a* 'crisis.DIM' in CREA, see (13f) above. Additionally, Iggy Roca (personal communication, 24 March 2006) reports hearing a speaker on a Spanish radio channel produce the augmentative *cris-ón-Ø* 'fully on line and with utter spontaneity'. This datum supports our conclusion that the base *crisi-s* is a pseudoplural noun with an athematic stem in /i/.

frequently in the diminutive. The facts prove otherwise: although deriving the diminutives of nouns such as *o*-stem *organism-o* 'organism' and *e*-stem *germen-Ø* 'germ' is morphologically unproblematic, forms like *organism-it-o* and *germen-cit-o* are not proportionally more frequent than *virus-it-o*.

(27)

|     |              |                  | *Google hits*† | *% of diminutives* |
|-----|--------------|------------------|---------------:|-------------------:|
| a.  | virus        | 'virus.SG'       | 16,300,000     |                    |
|     | virus-it-o   | 'virus.DIM.SG'   | 1,060          | 0.0065             |
| b.  | germen-Ø     | 'germ.SG'        | 1,180,000      |                    |
|     | germen-cit-o | 'germ.DIM.SG'    | 112            | 0.0095             |
| c.  | organism-o   | 'organism.SG'    | 19,500,000     |                    |
|     | organism-it-o| 'organism.DIM.SG'| 17            | 0.000087           |

† Google seems to automatically round up the number of hits when it reaches the tens of thousands.

The evidence in (27) strongly suggests that the frequency of a diminutive form depends mainly on the pragmatic connotations of the base, rather than on its morphological structure. Anecdotal observation supports this conclusion: *virus-it-o* has a comparatively healthy number of tokens on the Internet because contributors to message boards concerned with information technology often have cause to use the noun *virus* in situations of heightened emotion; in the same way, the poor showing of *cris-ecit-a* is explained by adverse pragmatic conditions. However, I do not wish to deny that some speakers avoid constructing suffixal evaluative derivatives like those in (26): as we saw in section 3.3, the occurrence of unexpected infixal forms such as *vir<it>us* (14b) suggests that this is sometimes the case.

Indeed, of all the possible outcomes of the learnability problem posed by nouns with homophonous singular and plural forms ending in /s/, the easiest to explain is ineffability, i.e. the situation where adult speakers are unable to generate suffixal evaluative derivatives. Consider, for example, a child who has been exposed to both the singular and plural forms of *virus* early in life. Since in the general course of language acquisition inflection is acquired before derivation, we are compelled to assume that, at some developmental stage, the child will store the singular and plural forms of *virus* in her protolexicon in a format resembling (28a). The representation in (28a) encodes the child's knowledge that *virus* can be either a singular masculine noun or a plural masculine noun, but it does not provide any information concerning the structure of either form below the word node. We can therefore call (28a) the 'undecomposed parse'. To progress beyond (28a) the child must choose between two decomposed parses: the non-pseudoplural parse in (28b) and the pseudoplural parse in (28c).[17] But

---

[17] The representations in (28b,c) can easily be transposed into a Distributed Morphology format by observing the equivalences noted in (7). I leave this exercise to the interested reader.

at this point, as we have seen, the child comes up against an underdetermination effect: the inflectional paradigm of *virus* cannot determine the morphological affiliation of the final /s/. Therefore, unless the child resorts to other indirect sources of information, she will remain stuck at (28a).

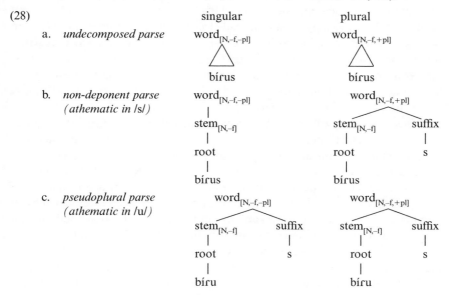

(28)                                    singular                        plural

    a.   *undecomposed parse*

    b.   *non-deponent parse*
          *(athematic in /s/)*

    c.   *pseudoplural parse*
          *(athematic in /u/)*

A speaker whose lexical representation of *virus* looks like (28a) will be unable to apply evaluative suffixation to this noun. As we saw in section 2, evaluative suffixes subcategorize for stems rather than for words, and demand to be aligned with the right edge of the stem. In (28a), however, there is no stem node and, a fortiori, no right edge of a stem. In conclusion, a lexical entry like (28a) fails to provide a suitable input for stem-based suffixation (see further §5.1 for some technical considerations).

Nonetheless, *virus* is robustly attested in the diminutive: see again (14) and (27). This indicates that most learners do eventually overcome the underdetermination of the choice between (28b) and (28c). However, the variation reported in (14) also suggests that learners achieve this result by means that are not fully deterministic, but rather probabilistic. Therefore, our account of the learning path should have two properties. First, it should explain the most frequent outcome: namely, the knowledge of mature native speakers for whom *virus* and *brindis* are non-deponent nouns with athematic stems in /s/, whereas *Carl-o-s*, *Sócrat-e-s*, and *crisi-s* are pseudoplural; see (13). Secondly, it should have a certain degree of in-built flexibility, so that minority outcomes are not ruled out in principle.

My proposal is that learners choose between parses like (28b) and (28c) by relying on a number of indirect cues. These consist of parsing preferences grounded on morphological and phonological properties of the Spanish lexicon. These parsing preferences are violable and partially conflicting, so that the outcome of their interaction depends on their relative weights. As we shall see below, the weighting that leads to the majority outcome in (13) can be at least partially explained by lexical statistics: the rarer a particular structure in the lexicon, the stronger the preference to avoid it. This approach possesses the required flexibility: variation in the size and composition of the lexicon across individuals and across developmental stages may significantly affect the weight of parsing preferences.

These parsing preferences should not be mistaken for optimality-theoretic constraints. First, I am not necessarily claiming that they are components of the grammar of Spanish; readers who take the grammar and the parser to be separate cognitive modules (cf. Neeleman and van de Koot 2004) may choose to regard these preferences as a description of the way in which properties of the Spanish lexicon guide the learners' parsing choices. Secondly, their relative weights can be expressed as a ranking, but I shall argue that they are not arranged in a strict dominance hierarchy in the sense of Prince and Smolensky (1993: §1.1): indeed, we shall encounter instances in which two low-weighted preferences are able to gang up together and defeat a high-weighted preference.[18] Thirdly, I am assuming that the relative weighting of parsing preferences is largely a function of lexical frequency; thus it differs from the ranking of constraints in an optimality-theoretic grammar, which can have a rather tenuous connection with lexical frequency, at least in some learning models. I note, however, that there are theories of grammar in which it would be natural to conceive of the parsing preferences I shall posit below as grammatical constraints. The maximum entropy model of phonotactic learning described in Hayes and Wilson (2006) is a case in point: in this model, constraints are not innate, but are selected by means of a broadly inductive procedure; the weight of a constraint is closely attuned to the frequency with which it is violated in the learner's trigger experience;[19] and weights interact additively, rather than through a strict dominance hierarchy.

The first parsing preference that I shall consider is the following:

(29)   *Avoid pseudoplurals*

Prefer parses in which singular nouns do not contain $_{stem}]s_{word}]$.

---

[18] Admittedly, versions of Optimality Theory incorporating local constraint conjunction (Smolensky 1993) can replicate this effect by means of rankings of the format A&B » C » A, B.
[19] More precisely, constraints are weighted in such a way that the *expected* number of violations of each constraint equals the *observed* number of violations: see Hayes and Wilson (2006: §3.2) for details.

Preference (29) needs little justification. The only function of /-s/ in Spanish nouns is to mark plural number; it has no other inflectional or derivational role, and it is not involved in any kind of syncretism. In this light, (29) simply expresses the fact that, by default, learners assume forms not to be deponent.

Next I shall consider a parsing preference grounded on another morphological property of the Spanish lexicon. Spanish nouns fall into exactly four stem classes: *o*-stems, *a*-stems, *e*-stems, and athematic stems (Bermúdez-Otero 2007). The *e*-stems comprise two subclasses: ordinary *e*-stems with the stem formative /-{e,Ø}/, and *e*-only stems with the stem formative /-e/. Because of allomorphy rule (20), however, ordinary *e*-stems and *e*-only stems differ only in the singular; the plural ends in /-e-s/ in both subclasses.

(30)

|   |   |   |   | singular | plural |   |
|---|---|---|---|---|---|---|
| a. | *o*-stem | | | grúp-o | grúp-**o-s** | 'group' |
| b. | *a*-stem | | | més-a | més-**a-s** | 'table' |
| c. | *e*-stem | ordinary *e*-stem | | luθ-Ø | lúθ-**e-s** | 'light' |
|    |          |                   | | mónt-e | mónt-**e-s** | 'hill' |
|    |          | *e*-only stem | | krúθ-e | krúθ-**e-s** | 'crossing' |
| d. | athematic stem | | | menú | menú-s | 'menu' |

The athematic class is very small, containing only a tiny fraction of Spanish nouns. Some of these nouns are phonologically well-formed. One such instance is *menú* (plural *menú-s*): its segmental and prosodic structure is no bar to membership of the core inflectional classes, as shown by the *e*-stem *hindú-Ø* (plural *hindú-e-s*); see section 3.4. However, phonologically deviant forms are consistently assigned to the athematic class: recall our discussion of *clip* in section 3.4. In this sense, the athematic class is marginal both numerically and structurally. Accordingly, we can assume that learners of Spanish observe the following parsing preference:

(31)  *Avoid athematic stems*

   Prefer parses in which nouns are not members of the athematic class.

So far we have not established the relative weight of preferences (29) and (31), but we can already achieve a crucial result: *virus* must be parsed as a non-deponent noun with an athematic stem ending in /s/. Recall that, for this noun, the learner faces a choice between structures (28b) and (28c). However, both parses put *virus* in the athematic class: (28b) makes it an athematic stem in /s/, and (28c) makes it an athematic stem in /u/. Accordingly, *Avoid athematic stems* does not discriminate between the two possibilities. The choice is left to *Avoid pseudoplurals*, which favours the non-pseudoplural analysis in (28b). At this point, therefore, we can legitimately claim to have explained, in the technical sense of Chomsky (1965: 25), why most Spanish speakers prefer diminutive *virus-it-o* to *vir-it-o*: see (14a,c).

The case of *Carl-o-s* is more complex. This noun could be parsed either as a non-pseudoplural athematic stem in /s/, as in (32a), or as a pseudoplural *o*-stem, as in (32b).

(32)                                'Charles.sg'              'Charles.pl'

   a.  *non-pseudoplural athematic*  $[_{word} [_{stem}$ kárlos]]   $[_{word} [_{stem}$ kárlos]s]  ✗

   b.  *pseudoplural o-stem*      $[_{word} [_{stem}$ kárlo]s]     $[_{word} [_{stem}$ kárlo]s]  ✓

In this case, the two preferences we have considered so far conflict: *Avoid pseudoplurals* favours (32a); *Avoid athematic stems* favours (32b). We therefore would obtain the right result, namely (32b), if we gave greater weight to the avoidance of athematic stems than to the avoidance of pseudoplurals. However, since we have no independent means of estimating the weight of preference (29), this would be a circular argument—descriptive, but not explanatory.

Fortunately, it is possible to break the circle, for there is another parsing preference which, though relatively low-weighted, favours treating *Carl-o-s* as a pseudoplural *o*-stem. This preference is grounded on phonological facts. In brief, the position of primary stress in Spanish singular nouns with a closed final syllable follows a markedness cline: final stress is unmarked, penultimate stress is marked, and antepenultimate stress is supermarked (see e.g. Roca 2005). This markedness cline corresponds directly to a scale of type frequency. The figures in Table 1 are based on an electronic list containing 91,000 words from all syntactic categories, including inflected forms (Alfonso Morales-Front, personal communication, 26 August 2006).

The cognitive effects of this markedness cline have been amply demonstrated in psycholinguistic experiments: for example, Waltermire (2004: 185) reports that 'the weight of the final syllable is consistently the most powerful factor in the placement of stress for nonce words'. Crucially, however, the domain of this metrical generalization excludes the plural marker /-s/; in other words, the presence of a final consonant affects the stress profile of a

**Table 1.**  Type frequency of stress patterns in Spanish words with a closed ultima

| antepenultimate stress (supermarked) | penultimate stress (marked) | final stress (unmarked) |
|---|---|---|
| 0.05% | 2.03% | 97.80% |
| e.g. [ré.xi.men] | e.g. [θer.tá.men] | e.g. [al.ma.θén] |
| *régimen* | *certamen* | *almacén* |
| 'diet, régime' | 'contest' | 'store' |

Source: Núñez-Cedeño and Morales-Front 1999: 211.

noun only if the final consonant is part of the stem.[20] We are therefore justified in deducing the following two parsing preferences:

(33) *Avoid óσ̄ stems*

For a paroxytonic noun with a final syllable closed by /s/, prefer a parse in which the final /s/ lies outside the stem.

(34) *Avoid óσσ̄ stems*

For a proparoxytonic noun with a final syllable closed by /s/, prefer a parse in which the final /s/ lies outside the stem.

Given the type frequencies shown in Table 1, we can confidently predict that (34) will have greater weight than (33). This will be independently confirmed in (39a) below.

Let us now focus on *Avoid óσ̄ stems*. Paroxytonic nouns with closed final syllables like *ángel-Ø* [áŋ.xel] 'angel' and *germen-Ø* [xér.men] 'germ' are a minority in the Spanish lexicon, but a sizable minority. Moreover, their membership of the *e*-class places them squarely within the core vocabulary: recall that phonologically deviant loanwords ('xenonyms') are excluded from this class and forced to join the athematic set. We therefore predict that *Avoid óσ̄ stems* will be rather weak. This is confirmed by the behaviour of *virus*: the parsing bias against pseudoplural nouns favours structure (28b), whereas the avoidance of paroxytonic stems with closed final syllables favours (28c), and it is (28b) that most speakers select. Thus, *Avoid óσ̄ stems* proves weaker than *Avoid pseudoplurals*.

---

[20] The plural marker /-s/ does not affect the position of stress. One can capture this fact by assuming that Spanish has the following extrametricality rule (or its equivalent in terms of ranked alignment constraints):

(i)  $C \rightarrow <C> / _{\text{stem}} (\ldots) \_\_ _{\text{word}}$

Rule (i) says that a word-final consonant becomes extrametrical if it belongs to an inflectional marker.

This statement has the advantage of applying both to nouns and to verbs. In verbs, stress is morphologically determined in the majority of tenses: in the imperfective, for example, the stem formative is accented even if this gives rise to a metrical structure which is unattested in non-verbs (e.g. *am-a-ba-is* [a.má.bajs] 'love.2PL.PST.IPFV.IND'; cf. *convoy* [kom.bój] 'convoy', not *[kóm.boj]). In the present indicative and present subjunctive, however, stress alternates between the root and the stem formative in response to syllable structure (see e.g. Bermúdez-Otero 2007: n. 21; cf. Oltra-Massuet and Arregi 2005). However, although the default stress pattern for words with a closed ultima is oxytonic as shown in Table 1, closed final syllables do not attract stress in the present tenses: e.g. *am-a-s* [á.mas] 'love.2SG.PRS.IND'. This shows that the final consonant, supplied by the person and number marker, is extrametrical.

A cyclic account of the facts would be inappropriate because all the inflectional suffixes of a verb are included in its innermost cyclic domain together with the verb stem (Harris 1995: 879). Notably, verbal inflection markers do not cause diphthongization to overapply: e.g. *encuentr-a-s* [eŋ.kwén.tras] 'find.2SG.PRS.IND', but *encontr-á-is* [eŋ.kon.trájs] 'find.2PL.PRS.IND'; cf. (10) and (25).

We can now return to *Carl-o-s*. It now emerges that there are two independent parsing preferences militating against the non-deponent athematic
parse in (32a): *Avoid athematic stems* and *Avoid óō stems*. The two combined
prevail against *Avoid pseudoplurals*, which favours (32a). Thus, *Avoid pseudoplurals* is strong enough to defeat *Avoid óō stems* by itself, but it yields to the
combined forces of *Avoid athematic stems* and *Avoid óō stems*. This kind of
'ganging-up' effect should not surprise us: since we are not dealing with
optimality-theoretic constraints but rather with parsing biases emerging
from lexical statistics, we should expect them to interact additively.

In fact, an example we have not so far considered provides another interesting instance of an additive interaction: it is the masculine noun *Atlas* [áᵗ.las]
'Atlas.SG/PL'.[21] This noun has two conceivable parses: as a non-deponent
athematic stem in /s/, or as a pseudoplural *a*-stem. Given what we know so far,
we would expect the preferred parse to be pseudoplural, like *Carl-o-s*. Yet
this is not what the evidence shows. As it turns out, *Atlas* has two attested
diminutives: infixal *Atl<it>as* [aᵗ.lí.tas] and suffixal *Atlas-it-o* [aᵗ.la.sí.to].

(35)   a.   *Atl<it>as*

           estoy muy seguro que el monterrey tiene muchos mas aficionados que tu
           **atlitas**, clarooooooo no tanto como las chivas pero si tiene mas que el atlas
           'I am quite sure that Monterrey have many more fans than your little Atlas,
           of course not as many as Chivas, but they definitely have more than Atlas.'
                       <http://skyscrapercity.com/archive/index.php/t-277410.html>
                                                           (accessed on 22 May 2006)

       b.   *Atlas-it-o*

           jajajajajaj te afe'ctó bastante ese SI de **atlasito** XDDDD jajajajaja pero
           bueno me alegro por ti
           'Ha ha ha ha ha, that YES from little Atlas affected you rather deeply,
           XDDDD ha ha ha ha ha, but, well, I'm happy for you.'
                       <http://miarroba.com/foros/ver.php?foroid=174926&temaid=2146952>
                                                           (accessed on 27 July 2006)

Like all infixal diminutives, *Atl<it>as* tells us nothing about the morphological affiliation of the final /s/, but *Atlas-it-o* can only be derived from the
athematic stem /atlas-/. Why does *Atlas* not behave like *Carl-o-s*? The answer is
that, whilst both nouns are masculine, *Carl-o-s* belongs in the *o*-class, whereas
*Atlas*, if parsed as a pseudoplural noun, would belong in the *a*-class. Accord-

---

[21] Like its English cognate, Spanish *Atlas* can be either a proper noun or a common noun: the
proper noun refers to the Greek deity, or to something or someone named after him; the common noun denotes a collection of maps. Both tokens in (35) are instances of the proper noun:
(35a) is taken from an Internet discussion of the relative merits of Atlas and Chivas, two
Mexican football teams based in the city of Guadalajara; (35b) comes from an Internet forum
on Japanese manga and animé in which one of the contributors role-plays as a character called
Atlas.

ingly, parsing *Atlas* as pseudoplural would lead to a conflict between masculine gender and membership in the *a*-class: as is well known, *a* is the default
class for feminine stems, whereas the default class for non-feminine stems
is *o*. On this basis, we may assume the existence of the following parsing
preference:

(36)   *Avoid masculine* a-*stems*
       Prefer parses in which nouns are not simultaneously masculine and *a*-stem.

What we see in the case of *Atlas*, then, is *Avoid pseudoplurals* and *Avoid
masculine* a-*stems* ganging up together against *Avoid athematic stems*.

We can now proceed to discuss *Avoid* óσō *stems*. The way in which Spanish
speakers treat proparoxytonic stems with closed final syllables indicates that
this parsing preference is extremely strong. First, items of this sort are numerically very rare: see Table 1. Secondly, virtually all of them are assigned to the
athematic class: a xenonym like *Benetton* [bé.ne.ton] 'Benetton', for example,
is predictably assigned the plural *Benetton-s* [bé.ne.tons] (Bermúdez-Otero
2007: §2.3.2). This indicates that native speakers see these nouns as phonologically deviant and incapable of entering the core vocabulary as members of the
*e*-class. There is only one potential exception in common use: the noun *régi-
men* [ré.xi.men] 'diet, régime', which has a learnèd plural *regímen-e-s*
[re.xí.me.nes] where stress shifts to the right in order to keep within the final
three-syllable window. Nonetheless, it is not at all unusual even for this noun
to move into the athematic class: thus, *pace* Roca (2005: fn. 32), the plural
*régimen-s* [ré.xi.mens] is not an 'on-line performance trial output' but a manifestation of morphophonological knowledge on the part of native speakers
(see also §3.2 above).

(37)   *régimen-s*
       Debería hacernos pensar que los **regimens** autoritarios acorralados (Irán y
       Siria) quieren ganar tiempo y harán todo lo posible para crear confusion en
       Occidente hacia la moralidad de un enfrentamiento.
       'It should make us think that the besieged authoritarian régimes (Iran and
       Syria) want to gain time and will do everything possible to create confusion in
       the West as regards the morality of a conflict.'
       <http://www.infomedio.org/2006/02/16/echando-lena-al-fuego>
       (accessed on 27 July 2006)

Finally, the judgement of deviancy attached to óσō stems is so strong that
Spanish speakers sometimes impose antepenultimate stress upon loanwords
with closed final syllables as a marker of exoticism and un-Spanishness: thus,
Dutch *Amsterdám* becomes Spanish *Ámsterdam* (cf. Roca 2005: 368).

Given this evidence, we should expect that *Avoid* óσō *stems* weighs heavier
than *Avoid pseudoplurals*. This is indeed what we find:

(38)        singular                    plural                      diminutive singular

a.    [$_{word}$ [$_{stem}$ sókrat-e]s]    [$_{word}$ [$_{stem}$ sókrat-e]s]    [sokrat-ít-o]
                                                                    'Socrates'

b.    [$_{word}$ [$_{stem}$ análisi]s]     [$_{word}$ [$_{stem}$ análisi]s]     [analis-ít-o]
                                                                    'analysis'

In the case of *e*-stem *Sócrat-e-s*, the pseudoplural parse is favoured by both *Avoid όσό stems* and *Avoid athematic stems*. However, *análisi-s* remains athematic whether the final /s/ is placed inside or outside the stem; hence, the fact that the noun is parsed as pseudoplural shows that *Avoid όσό stems* alone suffices to defeat *Avoid pseudoplurals*. This case is highly significant: it illustrates a phonologically grounded preference single-handedly triggering a syntax-morphology mismatch. The implications of this finding are discussed in section 5.2 below.

In sum, we have so far motivated the relative weights shown in (39). In these diagrams, higher preferences are stronger and can defeat lower preferences. The ampersand denotes the additive combination of two preferences involved in a ganging-up effect.

(39)    a.

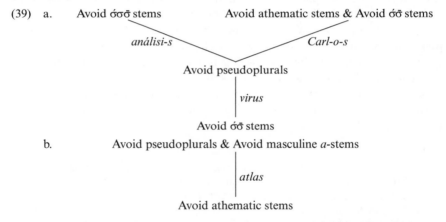

    b.        Avoid pseudoplurals & Avoid masculine *a*-stems

                              |

                           *atlas*

              Avoid athematic stems

There is only one group of nouns for which the weighted parsing preferences in (39) cannot account: paroxytonic pseudoplural athematic nouns like *crisi-s* (diminutive *cris-ecita*, augmentative *cris-on-a*/*cris-ón-Ø*: see n. 16). These should behave like *virus* and *brindis*, which are nondeponent athematic stems in /s/. I suspect that native speakers perceive a close morphological relationship between *crisi-s* and proparoxytonic items in the scientific, technical, or learnèd vocabulary like *análisi-s* 'analysis', *hipótesi-s* 'hypothesis', *parálisi-s* 'paralysis', *síntesi-s* 'synthesis', and so forth. Some speakers may even isolate a recurrent empty element /-{e/i}si-s/—a kind of *cranberry* morph. If that is the case, then the pseudoplural parse will be imposed by highly weighted *Avoid όσō stems* through its effects on the parsing of the proparoxytones.

In conclusion, the acquisition of the contrast between nouns with athematic stems in /s/ and pseudoplural nouns in Spanish raises a stark instance of Plato's Problem (Chomsky 1986). The key to its solution, however, is to be sought not so much in Universal Grammar as in language-particular parsing preferences motivated by morphological and phonological properties of the Spanish lexicon. The basis of these parsing preferences and of their weighting is ultimately statistical, but our account in no way replaces 'structure' with 'statistics': it is only in the context of a grammatical system distinguishing between autonomous syntactic, morphological, and phonological levels of representation and incorporating the trichotomy of root, stem, and word that the problem can be meaningfully formulated, let alone solved.

# 5. Implications for the Syntax-Morphology Interface

Our findings have general implications for two important phenomena at the syntax-morphology interface: defectiveness (morphological ineffability) and deponency.

## 5.1. Ineffability

To account for the fact that some Spanish speakers avoid constructing suffixal evaluative derivatives of nouns like *Carl-o-s* and *virus*, I have proposed that the underdetermination of the choice between pseudoplural and non-pseudoplural parses can literally deprive the learner of a suitable input for stem-based suffixation. This explanation opens up a promising avenue for research into defectiveness and, more widely, into the general problem of ineffability. It suggests that at least some instances of ineffability are caused by learnability deficits: speakers need to make a crucial syntactic, morphological, or phonological choice in order to generate the intended expression, but the choice cannot be made because it is permanently underdetermined in the trigger experience of learners. A case that appears to fit this pattern is the diminutive of German nouns whose last syllable contains an unstressed full vowel: e.g. *Monat* 'month' (Féry and Fanselow 2003, cited in an unpublished manuscript by Marc van Oostendorp). German speakers seem not to know which vowel should carry the umlaut triggered by the diminutive suffix, and so some avoid the construction altogether:

(40)    *Underdetermination of the diminutive of* Monat *'month'*

        ?Monatchen, ?Mönatchen, ?Monätchen, , ?Mönätchen, ?∅.

I should point out, however, that the implementation of this insight about ineffability is not without technical difficulties. Notably, an excessively powerful theory of Universal Grammar is likely to make the learner's mind up for her. In phonology, for example, most optimality-theoretic approaches to acquisition assume strong ranking biases, so that it is possible in certain circumstances for the relative ranking of two constraints to be determined in the absence of all experience; relatedly, failing to rank two crucially interacting constraints in Optimality Theory results in optionality, not ineffability. In Spanish, however, the technical implementation of our proposal is straightforward, provided that the stem-based character of evaluative suffixes is expressed as a categorical subcategorization requirement rather than as a violable constraint (Bye forthcoming). In that case, undecomposed lexical entries like those in (28a) will fail to feed stem-based suffixation; the relevant evaluative derivatives become ineffable simply because they lack a suitable input.

### 5.2. Deponency

The main implications of our results concern the issue of deponency. In this connection, Corbett (this volume) seeks to catalogue the possible departures from ideal agglutination in inflectional morphology. His typological survey suggests that it is actually not possible to draw a sharp demarcation between deponency and other phenomena such as syncretism, defectiveness, and suppletion (see also Matthews this volume, Spencer this volume). This is shown, among other things, by the existence of several instances of syntax-morphology mismatches that diverge to a greater or lesser degree from the canonical pattern of deponency illustrated by Latin verbs like SEQUĪ 'follow': see (1). Canonical deponency is defined by the following three properties (Baerman this volume, Stump this volume):[22]

(41)  a.  *Mismatch of form and function*
          *Sequuntur* 'they follow' is passive in form but active in function.

      b.  *Concurring defectiveness*
          The paradigm of SEQUĪ has no truly passive form meaning 'they are followed'.

      c.  *Lexical exceptionality*
          The deponency of SEQUĪ is unpredictable and lexically stipulated.

However, Bobaljik (this volume) exhibits a case of deponency, the spurious antipassive of Chukchi, which involves neither concurring defectiveness nor lexical exceptionality. Spanish pseudoplural nouns lie somewhere in between:

---

[22] In (41) I follow Stump's wording.

they are lexically exceptional, and indeed constitute a minute proportion of the Spanish vocabulary, but they fail to exhibit concurring defectiveness insofar as the same morphologically plural form can behave syntactically as singular or as plural; see (5a,b) and (18).

As regards the causes of deponency, the main conclusion of my examination of Spanish pseudoplurals is that, during language acquisition, the phonological properties of a word can cause it to receive a morphological parse that fails to match its syntactic features. Whether a learner parses a particular segment as belonging to the stem or to an inflectional marker may depend upon such morphosyntactically irrelevant properties as the weight of syllables and the arrangement of feet within prosodic words. The noun *análisi-s* provides a clear instance of this phenomenon: Spanish learners treat it as pseudoplural for no other reason than to avoid a proparoxytonic singular with a closed ultima; see (39a). If this is true, then we should expect at least some instances of deponency to have arisen diachronically through processes of reanalysis that were phonologically motivated. This prediction is strikingly confirmed by Good (this volume): in the Bantu language Ganda, for instance, all verbs with roots ending in /s/ have been reanalysed as having the morphological structure of causatives regardless of their syntactic properties, even if intransitive (see Hyman 2003). These instances of phonologically induced deponency contrast with cases whose ultimate causes are to be sought in semantics, pragmatics, and/or general cognition. In Latin, for example, membership in the class of deponent verbs appears to be partially—though by no means completely—governed by lexical semantics (Xu et al. this volume). Similarly, the spurious antipassive of Chukchi is motivated by a constraint against the morphological expression of certain combinations of subject and object in which the object outranks the subject in the person hierarchy (Bobaljik this volume).

The diverse ætiology of deponency poses a significant challenge to the theory of grammar, for it is unlikely that the mechanisms proposed to deal with semantically or pragmatically triggered deponency will adequately deal with all the cases where the motivation is essentially phonological. In Bobaljik's analysis of the spurious antipassive of Chukchi, for example, the syntax carries the main burden of explanation: the appearance of non-active, intransitive agreement morphology on the verb in the relevant environment is argued to fall out automatically from the syntactic structure of the clause, given a simple morphological operation of deletion which removes the features of the object in a disallowed subject-object combination within the T domain. In contrast, Spencer's (2000) analysis places the burden of explanation on the morphology itself, invoking rules of referral (Stump 1993). Be that as it may, it is not immediately clear that the use of either feature deletion operations or rules of referral will particularly illuminate any aspect of the behaviour of Spanish pseudoplural nouns. One's response to this state of affairs may be simply to assert, with Bobaljik (this volume), that the term 'extended deponency' does not denote a natural class of phenomena and that it would therefore be wrong to look for a unified theory of deponency. However, the way in which Spanish pseudoplural nouns show phonological constraints riding roughshod over the requirements of syntax-morphology correspondence must surely give us pause and cause us to ask just what limits there are to syntax-morphology mismatches in the languages of the world (Corbett this volume, Matthews this volume, Spencer this volume).

On a more positive note, however, my analysis of Spanish pseudoplural nouns suggests that morphological categories such as *stem* and *morphological word* possess a considerable degree of autonomy (see Aronoff 1994). Although the definitions of *stem* and *morphological word* in section 2 make reference to syntax, the evidence of Spanish pseudoplurals shows that both categories can define domains for phonological constraints and, moreover, that the satisfaction of these phonological requirements may be attained through rather dramatic mismatches between syntax and morphology. In many other cases, however, the combinatorial demands of syntax cause stems and words to violate phonotactic requirements. Ultimately, then, it is because morphological categories are subject to simultaneous and contradictory pressures from syntax and phonology that they are reducible to neither.

# References

Aronoff, Mark. 1994. *Morphology by itself*. Cambridge, Mass.: MIT Press.

Bachrach, Asaf, and Michael Wagner. 2006. Syntactically driven cyclicity vs. output-output correspondence: the case of adjunction in diminutive morphology. Handout of paper presented at the 29th GLOW Colloquium, Barcelona, 6 April 2006. Available at <http://glow.uvt.nl/GLOW2006/BachrachWagner173.pdf> (accessed 3 January 2007).

Baerman, Matthew. This volume. Morphological typology of deponency.

Benveniste, Émile. 1935. *Origines de la formation des noms en indo-européen*. Paris: Librairie Adrien-Maisonneuve.

Bermúdez-Otero, Ricardo. 2007. Morphological structure and phonological domains in Spanish denominal derivation. *Optimality-theoretic studies in Spanish phonology*, ed. by Fernando Martínez-Gil and Sonia Colina, 278–311. Amsterdam: John Benjamins.

—— forthcoming *Stratal Optimality Theory*. Oxford: Oxford University Press.

Bobaljik, Jonathan David. 2006. Where's ϕ? Agreement as a postsyntactic operation. Storrs: University of Connecticut, ms. <http://bobaljik.uconn.edu/papers/Phi.pdf> (accessed 3 January 2007).

—— This volume. The limits of deponency: a Chukotko-centric perspective.

Bonet, Eulàlia. 2007. Gender allomorphy and epenthesis in Spanish. *Optimality-theoretic studies in Spanish phonology*, ed. by Fernando Martínez-Gil and Sonia Colina, 312–38. Amsterdam: John Benjamins.

Bye, Patrick. forthcoming. Allomorphy—selection, not optimization. *Freedom of analysis*, ed. by Martin Krämer, Patrik Bye, and Sylvia Blaho. Available at <http://www.hum.uit.no/a/bye/Papers/allomorphy_book.pdf> (accessed 3 January 2007).

Chomsky, Noam. 1965. *Aspects of the theory of syntax*. Cambridge, Mass.: The MIT Press.

—— 1986. *Knowledge of language: its nature, origin, and use*. Westport, Conn.: Praeger.

Cole, Jennifer. 1995. The cycle in phonology. *The handbook of phonological theory*, ed. by John A. Goldsmith, 70–113. Oxford: Blackwell.

Colina, Sonia. 2003a. The status of word-final [e] in Spanish. *Southwest Journal of Linguistics* 22(1).87–107.

—— 2003b. Diminutives in Spanish: a morphophonological account. *Southwest Journal of Linguistics* 22(2).45–88.

Contreras, Heles. 1977. Spanish epenthesis and stress. *University of Washington Working Papers in Linguistics* 3.9–33.

Corbett, Greville. 2000. *Number*. Cambridge: Cambridge University Press.

—— This volume. Deponency, syncretism, and what lies between.

CORDE = Real Academia Española. Corpus diacrónico del español. <http://www.rae.es> (accessed 3 January 2007).

CREA = Real Academia Española. Corpus de referencia del español actual. <http://www.rae.es> (accessed 3 January 2007).

Den Os, Els, and René Kager. 1986. Extrametricality and stress in Spanish and Italian. *Lingua* 69.23–48.

Eddington, David. 2002. Spanish diminutive formation without rules or constraints. *Linguistics* 40.395–419.

—— 2004. *Spanish phonology and morphology: experimental and quantitative perspectives*. Amsterdam: John Benjamins.

Féry, Caroline, and Gisbert Fanselow. 2003. Ineffability in grammar. *Linguistische Berichte*, Sonderheft 11.288–310.

Good, Jeff. This volume. Slouching towards deponency: a family of mismatches in the Bantu verb stem.

Harbour, Daniel. 2006. *Morphosemantic number: from Kiowa noun classes to UG number features*. Dordrecht: Kluwer.

Harris, James W. 1983. *Syllable structure and stress in Spanish: a nonlinear analysis*. Cambridge, Mass.: MIT Press.

—— 1985. Spanish word markers. *Current issues in Hispanic phonology and morphology*, ed. by Frank H. Nuessel, 34–54. Bloomington: Indiana University Linguistics Club.

—— 1991. The exponence of gender in Spanish. *Linguistic Inquiry* 22.27–62.

—— 1992. The form classes of Spanish substantives. *Yearbook of Morphology 1991*, ed. by Geert Booij and Jaap van Marle, 65–88. Dordrecht: Kluwer.

—— 1995. Projection and edge marking in the computation of stress in Spanish. *The handbook of phonological theory*, ed. by John A. Goldsmith, 867–87. Oxford: Blackwell.

Harris, James W. 1999. Nasal depalatalization no, morphological wellformedness sí: the structure of Spanish word classes. *MIT Working Papers in Linguistics* 33.47–82.

Hayes, Bruce, and Colin Wilson. 2006. A maximum entropy model of phonotactics and phonotactic learning. Los Angeles: University of California, ms. Available from the Rutgers Optimality Archive, ROA 858, <http://roa.rutgers.edu> (accessed 3 January 2007).

Hooper, Joan Bybee, and Tracy Terrell. 1976. Stress assignment in Spanish: a natural generative analysis. *Glossa* 10.64–110.

Hyman, Larry M. 2003. Sound change, misanalysis, and analogy in the Bantu causative. *Journal of African Languages and Linguistics* 24.55–90.

Inkelas, Sharon. 1990. *Prosodic constituency in the lexicon*. New York: Garland.

Jaeggli, Osvaldo. 1980. Spanish diminutives. *Contemporary studies in Romance languages*, ed. by Frank H. Nuessel, 142–58. Bloomington: Indiana University Linguistics Club.

Kiparsky, Paul. 1982a. From cyclic phonology to lexical phonology. *The structure of phonological representations*, ed. by Harry van der Hulst and Norval Smith, Vol. 1, 131–75. Dordrecht: Foris.

—— 1982b. Lexical morphology and phonology. *Linguistics in the morning calm: selected papers from SICOL-1981*, ed. by I.-S. Yang, 3–91. Seoul: Hanshin.

—— 2003. Finnish noun inflection. *Generative approaches to Finnic and Saami linguistics: case, features and constraints*, ed. by D. Nelson and S. Manninen, 109–61. Stanford, CA: CSLI Publications.

Lázaro Mora, Fernando. 1999. La derivación apreciativa. *Gramática descriptiva de la lengua española*, ed. by Ignacio Bosque and Violeta Demonte, 4645–82. Madrid: Espasa Calpe.

Lloret, Maria-Rosa, and Joan Mascaró. 2005. Depalatalization in Spanish revised. Barcelona: Universitat de Barcelona and Universitat Autònoma de Barcelona, ms. Available at ROA 708–0105, Rutgers Optimality Archive, <http://roa.rutgers.edu> (accessed 3 January 2007).

Marantz, Alec. 1997. No escape from syntax: don't try morphological analysis in the privacy of your own lexicon. *University of Pennsylvania Working Papers in Linguistics* 4(2).201–25.

Matthews, Peter. This volume. How safe are our analyses?

Méndez-Dosuna, Julián, and Carmen Pensado. 1990. How unnatural is Spanish *Víctor → Vict-ít-or*? Infixed diminutives in Spanish. *Naturalists at Krems: papers from the Workshop on Natural Phonology and Natural Morphology (Krems, 1–7 July 1988)*, ed. by Julián Méndez-Dosuna and Carmen Pensado, 89–106. Salamanca: Ediciones Universidad de Salamanca.

Neeleman, Ad, and Hans van de Koot. 2004. The grammatical code. London: University College London, ms. Available at <http://www.phon.ucl.ac.uk/home/hans/grammatical_code.pdf>.

Núñez-Cedeño, Rafael A., and Alfonso Morales-Front. 1999. *Fonología generativa contemporánea de la lengua española*. Washington, DC: Georgetown University Press.

Oltra-Massuet, Isabel. 1999. On the constituent structure of Catalan verbs. *MIT Working Papers in Linguistics* 33.279–322.

Oltra-Massuet, Isabel. 2000. On the notion of theme vowel: a new approach to Catalan verbal morphology. *MIT Occasional Papers in Linguistics* 19.

Oltra-Massuet, Isabel, and Karlos Arregi. 2005. Stress-by-structure in Spanish. *Linguistic Inquiry* 36.43–84.

Pensado Ruíz, Carmen. 1997. On the Spanish depalatalization of /ɲ/ and /ʎ/ in rhymes. *Issues in the phonology and morphology of the major Iberian languages*, ed. by Fernando Martínez-Gil and Alfonso Morales-Front, 595–618. Washington, DC: Georgetown University Press.

Prince, Alan, and Paul Smolensky. 1993. Optimality Theory: constraint interaction in generative grammar. New Brunswick: Rutgers University; Boulder: University of Colorado; ms. Published with revisions 2004. Oxford: Blackwell.

Rainer, Franz. 1996. Inflection inside derivation: evidence from Spanish and Portuguese. *Yearbook of Morphology 1995*, ed. by Geert Booij and Jaap van Marle, 83–91. Dordrecht: Kluwer.

—— 2003. Studying restrictions on patterns of word-formation by means of the Internet. *Rivista di Linguistica* 15(1).131–39.

Roca, Iggy. 2005. Saturation of parameter settings in Spanish stress. *Phonology* 22.345–94.

Roca, Iggy, and Elena Felíu. 2003. Morphology in truncation: the role of the Spanish desinence. *Yearbook of Morphology 2002*, ed. by Geert Booij and Jaap van Marle, 187–243. Dordrecht: Kluwer.

Smolensky, Paul. 1993. Harmony, markedness, and phonological activity. Paper presented at Rutgers Optimality Workshop 1, Rutgers University, New Brunswick, New Jersey, October 1993. Handout available from the Rutgers Optimality Archive, ROA 87, <http://roa.rutgers.edu> (accessed 3 January 2007).

Spencer, Andrew. 2000. Agreement morphology in Chukotkan. *Morphological analysis in comparison*, ed. by Wolfgang U. Dressler, Oskar E. Pfeiffer, and Markus A. Pochtrager, 191–222. Amsterdam: John Benjamins.

—— This volume. Extending deponency: implications for morphological mismatches.

Stump, Gregory T. 1993. On rules of referral. *Language* 69.449–79.

—— This volume. A non-canonical pattern of deponency and its implications.

Waltermire, Mark. 2004. The effect of syllable weight on the determination of spoken stress in Spanish. *Laboratory approaches to Spanish phonology*, ed. by Timothy L. Face, 171–91. Berlin: Mouton de Gruyter.

Xu, Zheng, Mark Aronoff, and Frank Anshen. This volume. Deponency in Latin.

# 11

# Pseudo-Argument Affixes in Iwaidja and Ilgar: A Case of Deponent Subject and Object Agreement*

NICHOLAS EVANS

## 1. Introduction

DEPONENCY, IN THE EXTENDED SENSE in which it is used in this volume, is the *mismatch between the expected and actual function of a morphological form or paradigm*. In this paper I describe a particular type of deponency found in several languages of the Iwaidjan family (Northern Australia) that involves pseudo-argument affixes on the verb. These appear at first glance to be subject or object pronominal prefixes, with forms and positional possibilities appropriate to well-behaved members of the subject/object/tense prefixal paradigm. However, they do not in fact mark arguments at all (at least synchronically), and instead have various non-argument functions. These range from derivation-like alterations of the basic verb meaning to a semantically empty conjugation-like marker, which effectively functions as part of a

* I would like to thank the workshop organizers, Grev Corbett, Matthew Baerman, Dunstan Brown, and Andrew Hippisley for their kind invitation to attend and present this material in such a stimulating environment; Ruth Singer and Bruce Birch for discussing the Mawng and Iwaidja material with me and (in the case of Birch) for following up some queries about Iwaidja with additional field questions, and Anna Thornton for pointing out the parallels with Italian 'expletive-style objects' and furnishing a number of nice examples of these. I would also like to record my appreciation to the institutions that have supported my fieldwork on Ilgar and Iwaidja, namely the Australian Research Council (projects: *Analysing Aboriginal Languages* and *Reciprocals Across Languages*) and the Volkswagen Foundation through its DoBeS program (project: *Yiwarruj, yinyman, radbihi lda mali: Iwaidja and other endangered languages of the Cobourg Peninsula (Australia) in their cultural context*). Most importantly, I would like to thank the many speakers of Ilgar and Iwaidja who have taught me about their languages, particularly †Charlie Wardaga, Joy Williams Malwagag, David (Cookie) Minyumak, Goldie Blyth, Khaki Marrala, and Tim Mamitba.

*Proceedings of the British Academy* **145**, 271–296. © The British Academy 2007.

discontinuous lexical stem with the verb root. We have here, then, a case of deponent argument agreement by means of verbal prefixes: either the argument which this morphology leads you to expect does not exist at all, or it is something else. Both synchronically and diachronically, there is a continuum strung out from canonical argument uses to clear cases of deponent pseudo-arguments. A main goal of this paper will be to map out the various points along this spectrum, firstly because it can assist us in sharpening our definitions and our descriptive treatment of languages with the phenomenon, and second because it can help us to establish how pseudo-argument agreement can evolve by the gradual lexicalization of agreement affixes on the basis of prototypical features of arguments used with particular senses of the verb.

I will focus on two closely related languages, Iwaidja (Iw) and Ilgar/Garig (Ilg).[1] These languages share around eighty per cent vocabulary, and would be considered sister dialects by many criteria, but a series of changes to the prefix paradigms which has resulted in initial mutation in Iwaidja and the selection of different subsets of an original five-gender system by the two languages (Ilgar basically retaining the old masculine and feminine, and Iwaidja jettisoning these but retaining the old 'miscellaneous' gender), has produced sufficient formal differences that non-bilingual speakers claim the two varieties are not mutually comprehensible. Iwaidja still has around one hundred and fifty speakers, and is still being transmitted to children in some families, whereas the last speaker of Ilgar passed away in 2003.

Iwaidja and Ilgar are in turn rather closely related to Mawng (plus the extinct and barely known Manangkari), which adjoined them to the east along the Arnhem Land coast and on Goulburn Island; this whole grouping (known as Iwaidjic) are about as closely related as the Romance languages. Mawng (Capell and Hinch 1970)—with around two hundred speakers—retains the proto-Iwaidjic five-gender system (Evans 1998), and because of its conservatism is helpful in understanding the phenomenon to be discussed in this paper. Singer (2006, 2007) contains a detailed description of related structures in Mawng; see Evans (2000) for a general survey of the family.

Several other languages—Wurrugu, Marrku, and Amurdak—have also been classified traditionally as members of the Iwaidjan group. However, their relationship to the Iwaidjic languages is much more distant, the level of

[1] Throughout this paper I will use 'Ilgar' to cover two almost identical varieties, Ilgar and Garig—the former traditionally spoken on the islands to the east of Croker Island, and the latter on the mainland around Port Essington. My own work has primarily been on Ilgar, though I have also gone through the extant materials on Garig and, with only one exception to be mentioned below, both exhibit identical behaviour with respect to deponent argument agreement.

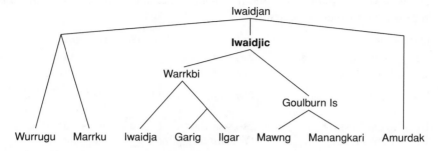

**Figure 1.**   The Iwaidjan language family

description is basic at best, and they do not show obvious evidence of pseudo-argument marking, so they will not be discussed here.

The genetic relations between all these languages are summarized in Figure 1.

# 2. Introductory Remarks: Standard Use of Argument Agreement

Iwaidja and Ilgar are head-marking languages whose verbs employ suffixes for tense/aspect/mood marking, and prefixes for subject, object, direction, and some tense/mood categories (basically irrealis/future vs unmarked, with distinct imperative forms as well for a few person values). In this article we are exclusively concerned with the prefixing system of the verbal morphology.

Abstracting away from those morphological elements that are irrelevant to the argument, the verb structure in Iwaidja and Ilgar is basically as in (1); I use the pipe sign (|) to indicate that two or more inflectional categories have a range of formal realizations, with respect to both order and fusion, according to the precise combination of values involved.

(1)    Intransitives:    Subject(|Future)              — V
         Transitives:     Subject|Object(|Future)    — V

(2) and (3) illustrate intransitive verbs in Ilgar and Iwaidja respectively. Note that 3rd person singular forms, in Iwaidja, undergo initial mutation, caused by the (underlying) 3rd singular prefix conventionally represented as K-, which hardens any following nasals and glides to the corresponding stop but does not itself surface as a segment. Note also that it is possible, and

indeed normal, to omit free NP arguments, since the requisite information is supplied by the verbal prefixes.[2]

| (2a) | *nga-wani* | (2b) | *ang-bani* | (2c) | *yi-wani* |
|---|---|---|---|---|---|
| Ilg | 1SG.S-sit(NPST) | | 2SG.S-sit(NPST) | | 3SG.S-sit(NPST) |
| | 'I am sitting.' | | 'You are sitting.' | | 'He is sitting.' |

| (3a) | *nga-wani* | (3b) | *ang-bani* | (3c) | *bani* |
|---|---|---|---|---|---|
| | | | | | *K-wani* |
| Iw | 1SG.S-sit(NPST) | | 2SG.S-sit(NPST) | | 3SG.S-sit(NPST) |
| | 'I am sitting.' | | 'You are sitting.' | | 'He is sitting.' |

(4) and (5) illustrate transitive verbs.

| (4a) | *a-yun-dalkun* | (4b) | *ngan-bu-ldalkun* | (4c) | *ngan-b-ana-ldalkun* |
|---|---|---|---|---|---|
| Ilg | 1SG.A-3F.SG. | | 1SG.OBJ-3PL. | | 1SG.OBJ-3PL. |
| | OBJ-cut(NPST) | | A-cut(NPST) | | A-FUT-cut(NPST) |
| | 'I am cutting them.' | | 'They are cutting me.' | | 'They will cut me.' |

| (5a) | *a-yun-dalkun* | (5b) | *ngan-bu-ldalkun* | (5c) | *ngan-d-a-ldalkun* |
|---|---|---|---|---|---|
| Iw | 1SG.A-3PL.OBJ- | | 1SG.OBJ-3 | | 1SG.OBJ-3A-FUT- |
| | cut(NPST) | | A³-cut(NPST) | | cut(NPST) |
| | 'I am cutting them.' | | '(S)he/they are | | '(S)he/they will |
| | | | cutting me.' | | cut me.' |

Syntactically, free NPs can be freely omitted, as illustrated here, and the order of major constituents when they do occur is quite free, apart from in a few specialized constructions such as reciprocals where a number of postverbal elements must occur in fixed order. Outside the pronominal agreement system it is difficult to find tests which unambiguously identify grammatical relations: there is no affixation for case, no infinitives or other forms giving evidence of control or deletion, and no evidence for syntactic pivots in complex sentences, since relative clauses are simply formed as headless relatives off any argument, and the equivalents of complement and adverbial clauses are simply fully inflected verbs strung together as appropriate.

There are, however, several regular patterns of transitive alternation which can be most simply characterized in terms of argument alternations: passives and mediopassives, which involve the substitution of an intransitive for a transitive prefix frame and the concomitant promotion of object to subject, and causatives, which involve the substitution of a transitive for an

---

[2] The following practical orthography is used (note that there is no phonemic voicing contrast): j= /c/, ng= /ŋ/, rn = /ɳ/, ny = /ɲ/, rt = /ʈ/, rl= /ɭ,/ rd = /ɽ/, ld = /ʎ/, r = /ɻ/, rr = /r/, h = /ɰ/. K represents a hardening morphophoneme surfacing in various ways (Iwaidja only), and :: represents prosodic lengthening to show duration (see example (29)).

[3] In Iwaidja some combinations do not distinguish third singular from third plural (historically, they have generalized the plural form); these will be glossed simply as '3'.

intransitive prefix frame, the demotion of intransitive subject to object, and the introduction of the causer as a transitive subject. The reciprocal construction, as well, can most simply be characterized in terms of subject and object slots: reciprocal constructions normally take the form 'A-B-V and B.in.turn' (where A is subject, and B is object). Though this originated as a truncated biclausal construction (A Ved B, and then B in turn . . .) it has been grammaticalized in all the Iwaidjan languages to the status of a single clause, as shown by the placement of certain postverbal elements (such as theme NPs of ditransitives) after the 'B.in.turn' component (Evans et al. in prep.). It is convenient to characterize all these alternations in terms of the grammatical relations of subject and object, but this is by no means the only viable analysis, and it is not difficult to get Role and Reference Grammar-style analyses in terms of direct projection of macro-roles like actor and undergoer on to the relevant prefixal slots. In this paper, however, I shall follow the more conventional path of referring to subject and object roles, for simplicity of exposition.[4]

### 2.1. Morphological realization of subject and object prefixes

Since part of our argument turns on identifying deponent subject and object prefixes, it is worth saying a little more about the morphology of this system. Intransitives are straightforward, as illustrated in (2) and (3) above: the subject pronominal prefix is followed, where applicable, by the future prefix. (Things get slightly more complex when the 3-way directional contrast—neutral, towards, and away—gets factored in, since there are a number of portmanteau and suppletive forms. We need not consider these here.)

Transitives are more complicated, because of the existence of competing ordering principles and a number of less than transparent forms for certain combinations. Where both subject and object are third person, the object is ordered before the subject, with the future prefix between them if present (6c, 7c).

(6a)  *yi-nga-ldalkun*

Ilg   3M.SG.OBJ-3F.SG.A-cut(NPST)
      'She is cutting him/it.'

(6b)  *yi-ni-ldalkun*

      3M.SG.OBJ.3F.SG.A-cut(NPST)
      'He is cutting him/it.'

---

[4] As the reader will realize as the paper unfolds, the existence of deponent argument agreement creates problems for the identification of subjects and objects with certain verbs, precisely because of the lack of independent tests (outside the prefixing system) for these argument roles. However, alternative analyses (e.g. in terms of macro-roles) will face exactly the same sorts of problems—the phenomena here would simply become cases of e.g. 'deponent undergoer agreement' rather than 'deponent object agreement'.

(6c)   *y-ana-nga-ldalkun*
       3M.SG.OBJ-FUT-3F.SG.A-cut(NPST)
       'She will cut it.'

(7a)   *ka-ldalkun*                         (7b)   *ri-ldalkun*

Iw     *K-nga-ldalkun*                             *K-i-ldalkun*
       3C.SG.OBJ-3F.SG.A-cut(NPST)                 3C.SG.OBJ-3M.SG.A-cut(NPST)
       'She is cutting him/it.'                    'He is cutting him/it.'

(7c)   *banangaldalkun*

       *K-wana-nga-ldalkun*
       3C.SG.OBJ-FUT-3F.SG.A-cut(NPST)
       'She will cut it.'

Where one argument is a speech act participant (henceforth SAP, i.e. 1st or 2nd), and the other is not (3rd person), the SAP occurs first. The future marker always follows the first pronominal prefix, but may precede or follow the second prefix according to the form involved ((4), (5), (8), (9)).

(8a)   *a-ny-jalkun*       (8b)   *ngan-nga-ldalkun*     (8c)   *ngan-bana-nga-ldalkun*

Ilg    1SG.A-3F.SG.              1SG.OBJ-3F.SG.                 1SG.OBJ-FUT-3F.SG.
          OBJ-cut(NPST)             A-cut(NPST)                    A-cut(NPST)
       'I am cutting her.'        'She is cutting me.'          'She will cut me.'

(9a)   *aralkun*           (9b)   *abanaldalkun*

Iw     *a-K-ldalkun*              *a-K-mana-ldalkun*
       1SG.A-3C.SG.               1SG.A-3C.SG.
          OBJ-cut(NPST)             OBJ-FUT-cut(NPST)
       'I am cutting him/her.'    'I will cut him/her.'

Where both subject and object are SAPs, a portmanteau is employed, as is common in many languages (cf Heath 1991, 1998) and it is not possible to identify an ordering.

   Turning to the forms of the prefixes, no single account can be given that works across the whole paradigm. Some exponents add -$(V)n$ to the S-form (intransitive form) or A-form to give the corresponding O-form, e.g. *nga-* '1SG.S' > *ngan-* '1SG.OBJ', *a-* '3PL.S' > *an-* '3PL.OBJ', *ku-* '2SG.A' > *kun-* '2SG.OBJ', *kurr-* '2PL.S/A' > *kurrun-* '2PL.OBJ'. For some there is a suppletive relationship between A and S/OBJ forms, e.g. Ilg *ni-* '3SG.M.A' but *i-* '3SG.M.S/OBJ', *nga-* '3SG.F.A' but *iny-* '3SG.F.S/OBJ', Ilgar and Iwaidja *bu-* ~ *wu-* '3PL.A' vs *a-* '3PL.S' vs *an-* '3PL.OBJ'. As the above forms indicate, some person/number/gender combinations distinguish all three core functions (A, S, and OBJ), some oppose S/OBJ to A, and some oppose A/S to OBJ. The net effect of all these irregularities is that attempts to give regular rules for the formation of the prefix combinations only go a fraction of the way to accounting for the forms by regular rule, and a word-and-paradigm approach is the most appropriate model to follow.

Of the two languages we are focusing on here, Ilgar is both more transparent and closer to the proto-Iwaidjic system (though Mawng is closer still). Iwaidja has innovated by:

(i)   generalizing the 'miscellaneous' gender prefix *aK-* to cover most third person singular values, then undergoing morphophonological changes that eliminate the initial *a-* everywhere except before monosyllabic roots (of which there are only a handful), and realizing K- as the hardening of following consonantal segments (nasals and semivowels to corresponding stops, and lateral flap *ld* to retroflex glide *r*) and as *w* before *a*

(ii)  losing the masculine and feminine prefixes almost everywhere (replaced by the generalized *aK-* ) except for the specific combination 3SG>3SG: cf *ri-* '3M>3SG' and *ka-* (< *K-nga-* ) '3F > 3SG'.

(iii) generalizing the 3PL.A form to 3A in all but the 3SG>3SG combinations. Thus the form *nganbu-* ~ *ngandu-*, which in Ilgar is restricted to 3PL.A>1SG combinations (and can be segmented as *nga-n-bu* [1SG-OBJ-3PL.A]) has been generalized in Iwaidja to cover all combinations of 3rd person acting on 1SG, i.e. 'he, she or they > me'; similar remarks apply to all other 3rd person A forms except where 3SG > 3SG.

## 2.2. Diachronic background

Looking further back in time (see Evans 1998 for fuller arguments), proto-Iwaidjic had a productive five–gender system, still preserved in Mawng: masculine (m), feminine (f), vegetable (v), neuter (n), and miscellaneous (mis). This original system is shown in the central two columns of Table 1. (The alternate forms *iny-/nga-* and *yi-/ni-* represent suppletive pairs, with the former used for OBJ and S, and the latter for A).

The vegetable class includes trees, plants (and parts thereof), as well as bush and wood; the neuter class includes places, country, cultural manifestations (ceremonies, languages, etc.—all linked to place), and water—indeed, Singer (2007) labels this the 'land and liquids' gender in Mawng.

Iwaidja and Ilgar have each simplified this system in different ways: the Ilgar system is shown on the left, and the Iwaidja system on the right.

In Ilgar/Garig the miscellaneous gender is lost completely, the masculine is generalized as the default, and only the masculine and feminine are possible with all verbs. In Iwaidja, by contrast, the miscellaneous gender has been generalized as the default 'common' gender (abbreviated as 'C'). The

278                                  *Nicholas Evans*

**Table 1.** Collapse of proto Iwaidjic gender systems in Iwaidja and Ilgar

| Ilgar 3SG S/OBJ UNRESTRIC | Ilgar 3SG S/OBJ RESTRIC | Proto-Iwaidjic and Mawng | Iwaidja 3SG S/OBJ RESTRIC | Iwaidja UNRESTRIC |
|---|---|---|---|---|
| F  *iny-* | | F  *iny-/nga-* | F  *iny-/nga-* | |
| M  *yi-* | | M  *yi-/ni-* | M  *yi-/ni-* | |
| | V  *ma(n)-* | V  *ma(n)-* | V  *ma(n)-* | C  *-(u)K* |
| | N  *ang-* | N  *ang-* | N  *ang-* | |
| | | MIS  *aK-* | | |

masculine and feminine only survive in the subject of 3SG>3SG combinations.

In both languages, the vegetable and neuter prefixes, for both object and intransitive subject, survive in restricted contexts, and morphologically behave exactly like the other gender prefixes in terms of their behaviour within prefixal combinations, such as their positioning with respect to other argument prefixes and the prefixing marking future/irrealis. A subset of these give the primary situations where deponent argument agreement occurs (to be discussed in §3). To continue our preliminaries, however, and before passing to deponent agreement, we need to examine some other cases where their use can be treated as genuine gender agreement, albeit with a restricted set of verbs: their choice contrasts with that of the productive gender markers, and can be motivated by the semantics of the appropriate referent (§2.3). With yet other verbs, they can likewise be treated as a type of gender agreement, but where the verb is not attested with any other agreement marker (§2.4).[5]

### 2.3. Restricted gender contrasts in third person OBJ and S

In both Iwaidja and Ilgar, a restricted set of verbs permits some of the ancestral gender contrasts. Note that, since in Iwaidja and Ilgar this type of gender agreement is only found on verbs (not within the NP on modifiers, for example), there is no independent method of determining the semantics of these genders, meaning that we are using gender in a rather archaicizing sense from a language-internal perspective, though in Mawng gender can be deter-

---

[5] This paper concentrates on describing the phenomenon from an Ilgar/Iwaidja perspective, and risks giving the impression that the breakdown of the proto-Iwaidjic gender system was an essential causal factor in the development of pseudo-argument agreement. In fact, however, even in Mawng, with its productive system of five genders, we find the phenomenon is widespread. The reader is referred to Evans (2004) and particularly Singer (2007) for a detailed treatment of the Mawng facts.

mined in a more straightforward manner through agreement within the NP as manifested on determiners and adjectives.

First consider an Iwaidja example, the verb *ngijbungku* which normally means 'name OBJ, call OBJ by name, call name of OBJ'. This verb can be used with a neuter O prefix to mean 'call the name of (a country or place)', as in (10). This example can be viewed as a restricted type of gender agreement with the object 'country'; that 'country' is the object is shown by the fact that the verb exhibits partial right-reduplication caused by the fact that its object is plural. (Note, though, that since this is a non-human referent, plurality is not shown in the relevant pronominal prefix).

(10)    *Jumung    janad kunak    k-ardbirrun*                    *wardyad*

Iw  3SG.OBL    3SG    country    3SG>3SG.C-throw(NPST)    stone

    *amu-ngijbungku-ku*                                *kunak.*
    3PL>3SG.C-name-ITERATIVE(NPST)        country

    'The custodian of the country throws stones and calls out the name of the sites.'

Other examples of this sort of agreement are:

**(a)** the Iwaidja and Ilgar verb *wurrun*, which means 'know, recognize' when used with a human object (in the masculine, feminine or plural as appropriate), but which means 'know (a fact, or language)' when used with neuter agreement; recall that the semantic domain of the neuter includes all cultural manifestations associated with place, including languages and systems of knowledge.

**(b)** the Iwaidja and Ilgar verb *artudban* 'abandon, leave', which when used with neuter agreement means 'leave a place'—used with standard masculine, feminine, common or plural agreement it would mean e.g. 'leave (a person)'.

**(c)** the Iwaidja and Garig verb *lda* 'eat', which when used with neuter agreement means 'drink'; recall that 'water' belongs to the 'neuter' class.

The reason for the caveat 'restricted type of gender agreement' given above is that not all verbs with neuter objects will display such agreement—it is restricted to just some verbs. It may also happen that a given verb will display such agreement with one gender, but not another. The verb *ayan* 'see', for example, may (though need not) employ neuter agreement in the context of looking at the ground or a place (e.g. Ilgar *angbayan malalkuj* [3PL>3SG.N-see.NPST island] 'they are looking around the islands' (again, since the object is non-human, its plural status is not signalled by the pronominal agreement system). But we have no examples of it being used with vegetable agreement when looking at a tree or plant, for example. Likewise there are no examples of *artudban* or *lda* being employed with vegetable agreement, in contexts like leaving a tree behind, or chewing grass.

Let us turn now to two Ilgar examples in slightly more detail, one with *ldi* 'stand, be (of vertical object)' and one with *wildimbin* 'dry, dry up'.

*Ldi* can be used, with masculine prefix *yi-*, of any masculine subject, but also of typical 'vegetable class' entities like trees, plants, e.g. *yildi kujali* 'there is a tree'. However, this verb may also take the vegetable prefix *ma-* when its subject is a tree, bush, or shrub, as in (11). It may also take the neuter prefix (in its allomorph *an-*) in the fixed expression illustrated in (12), when talking about old customs or practices.

(11)    *ma-ldi*              *raka*      *arlirr*
  Ilg    3SG.V.S-stand(NPST)    DEM        tree
         'There is a tree there.'

(12)    *wularrud*   *an-di*
  Ilg    before      3SG.N.S-stand
         'as it was in the old days'

*Wildimbin*, used with a human subject, means 'dry oneself, get dry' (13). But it may be used of a piece of landscape to mean 'get dry, dry up', in which case it takes a neuter prefix (14). This can be regarded as neuter agreement with its intransitive subject, a noun denoting part of the landscape.[6]

(13)    *nga-wildimbi-ny*
  Ilg    1SG.S-get.dry-PST
         'I dried myself, got dry.'

(14)    *raka*      *kabal*        *ang-bildimbi-ny*
  Ilg    DEM        floodplain     3SG.N.S-dry-PSTS
         'The floodplain has dried up.'

In some cases the selection of restricted gender prefixes is accompanied by a certain amount of semantic specialization. Consider the verb *wun* 'hit' in Iwaidja. With a 'common gender' object prefix—or with a first, second, or third plural object—it simply means 'hit' (15). With a vegetable object prefix it means 'hit, chop (tree, vegetation, log)' (16), while with a neuter object prefix it means 'dig a hole in ground (e.g. for burying, or cooking), make an impression on the ground (e.g. by leaving tracks)' (17).

---

[6] A rather similar example, again from Ilgar, is the verb *ldaharryu* 'to have or be a hole'; this may take the neuter prefix when referring to a well or other water-bearing 'hole' in the landscape, as in *ardbarak andaharryu* 'there is a well (there)' (*ardbarak* = 'well').

(15a) *ka-wun*                                    (15b) *ri-wun*
      K-nga-wun                                         K-ni-wun
      3SG.C.OBJ-3F.A-hit(NPST)                          3SG.C.OBJ-3M.A-hit(NPST)
      'She hits him/her/it.'                            'He/it hits him/her/it.'

(16)  *Barduwa lda yawaran riwung wuka abiny*
      barduwa   lda   ya-K-ara-n        K-ni-wu-ng                wuka   aK-mi-ny
      finished  and   away-3SG.S-go-PST  3SG.C.OBJ-3M.A-hit-PST   LOC    3SG.S-do-PST

      *mambuwung maldajarnarri barduwa.*
      man-bu-wu-ng                    ma[-]ldajarnarri              barduwa
      3SG.C.OBJ-3PL.A-hit-PST         [3v.s-]⁷writhe.making.track   finished
      'Then he got inside (the hollow log) and started writhing around like a snake.'

(17)  *Kuwi!*   *Kurrurtayanjing*       *ruka*   *warang*        *angkuwun.*
      *Kuwi!*   *Kurr-uK-rtaya-njing*   *ruka*   *w-ara-ng*      *ang-ku-wu-n*
      come      2PL.A-3SG.C.OBJ-see-IMP  there   3SG.C.S-go-PST  3SG.N.OBJ-3A-hit-PST
      'Come and have a look at these tracks!'
      (lit. 'come and have a look where it has gone, impacting on the ground')

This verb can also occur with what is etymologically the feminine object prefix, though so far this is the only verb attested which occurs with this prefix. In this combination it has the meaning 'rub firestick', apparently based on a sexual metaphor involving 'male' and 'female' parts of the firedrill.

(18)  *Janad*   *iny-ju-wun*                    *kijbu.*
      3SG       3SG.F.OBJ-3A-hit(NPST)          firestick
      'S/he is rubbing the firestick.'

## 2.4. Metaphoric coercion with particular objects

In all the above cases we do not need to modify our characterization of verb-meaning when the neuter or vegetable prefix is used—we are simply specifying that a particular sort of object is involved. On the other hand, there are some verbs where the verbal meaning is metaphorically coerced when a vegetable or neuter object is involved. Consider the verb *mang* 'grasp': when used with neuter object agreement this means 'understand' (i.e. 'grasp an idea or thoughts'),[8] extending the notion of 'grasping' to 'understanding' just as in English, but in this case only when a neuter object prefix is present.

As a second illustration, consider the verb—*unma* 'count'.[9] When used with a neuter object, it means 'tell' (19). Though semantically comparable pairs

---

⁷ The segmentability of this word is arguable—see discussion in §3.2 below.

⁸ With a further extension possible when the word *kuwa* 'true' is added after the predicate: *ang-ku-mang kuwa* (Iw) or *a-ni-mang kuwa* (Ilg), lit. 'he-N-holds/grasps true', means 'he believes it', i.e. 'he holds it (as) true'.

⁹ This verb may also be used intransitively, with the meaning 'try'.

in European languages like *zählen/erzählen, contare/raccontare* and so forth suggest this is a sort of derivational relationship, the Iwaidja version could still be treated as a sort of gender agreement, with the object NP *yiwarruj* 'story' in (19) motivating the choice of neuter.

(19)          *Kayirrk  barda     ang-man-unma*                      *nuwung*
       Iw     now        here      1SG.A>3SG.N.OBJ-FUT-tell(NPST)   2SG.OBL

              *badba    yiwarruj  artbung.*
              other     story     different
              'Now I'm going to tell you a different story.'

**2.5. Restricted-gender verbs**

Verbs in the last section occur with a contrasting set of argument prefixes, ranging over several genders. Some verbs, however, are only attested with a vegetable or neuter prefix. Usually this prefix is in the object slot (more rarely, in the S slot), though there are a couple of meteorological and tidal verbs with both A and OBJ fixed, and some 'experiencer object' verbs with A fixed (Evans 2004). However, since the gender can be motivated on semantic grounds, we assume this is a genuine argument with selectional restrictions.

Some examples are the Iwaidja verbs *ldijbun* (neuter OBJ) 'collect water' (20), *marrun* (vegetable OBJ), 'eat (food)' (21), Ilgar *yawun* (neuter OBJ) 'dig (ground)' (22), and *urrun* (vegetable OBJ) 'burn off (bush)' (23a,b).

(20)     *ang-bu-ldijbun*
     Iw   3SG.N.OBJ-3A-collect.water(NPST)
          'He/she/they collect water.'

(21)     *mam-bu-marrun*
     Iw   3SG.V.OB-3A-eat(NPST)
          'He/she/they eat (food).'

(22)     *ang-bu-yawun*
     Ilg  3SG.N.OBJ-3PL.A-dig(NPST)
          'They are digging (the ground).'

(23a)    *ma-n-urrun*                        (23b)  *ma-ng-urrun*
     Ilg  3SG.V.OBJ-3SG.M.A-make.fire(NPST)        3SG.V.OBJ-3SG.F.A-make.fire
          'He's burning off (the bush).'            (NPST)
                                                    'She's burning off
                                                    (the bush).'

A further example is Ilgar *murrung* 'make fire signal by burning grass'.

Some restricted-gender verbs participate in argument-structure alterna-tions: used with a vegetable-gender (intransitive) subject they have a mediopassive/stative reading, while used transitively with a vegetable-gender object they have active/causative reading. An example is the verb *ma . . . irrkurang* 'close', which must always have a vegetable-gender absolutive argument, but which may either be used intransitively (24a) or transitively (24b); similar patterns are found with its antonym *ma . . . adbungku* 'be open (intr. with vegetable subject); open (tr. with vegetable object)'. Such alternations parallel the intransitive / causative alternations found with many verbs without any gender restrictions, such as *malkba* 'come out (v.i.); take out (v.t.)'.

(24a)  *store*    *m-irrkura-ng*
Iw           3SG.V.S-close-PST
        'The shop is closed.'

(24b)  *store*    *ma-n-irrkura-ng*
           3SG.V.OBJ-3SG.M.A-close-PST
           'He has closed the store.'

(25a)  *yi-malkba-ny*
Ilg    3SG.S-come.out-PST
        'He/it came out.'

(25b)  *yi-ni-malkba-ny*
        3SG.M.OBJ-3SG.M.A-take.out-PST
        'He took him/it out.'

To the extent that the motivation for gender choice becomes unclear (or that it is hard to gloss the root) such cases shade into a 'conjugational' type of pseudo-argument use (see below). An example is (26)—can we rationalize the choice of F.A as referring to 'sea' or 'tide', and of V.O as referring to the shoreline, or perhaps the seaweed, in which case we could treat it as a very restricted type of subject and object agreement (as suggested by the first gloss given under the example), or should we simply treat it as a verb with two deponent prefixes (as suggested by the second gloss)? Without independent attestation of the verb root it is difficult to prove exactly what are the individual contributions of the root and the affixes, so I analyse examples like this as belonging to the conjugational type.

(26)     *Ma-na-nga-yambu-ng*                          *kuburr.*
Iw    3SG.V.PBJ-FUT-3SG.F.A-tide.exceed-NPST    tomorrow
                         be.king.tide
         'It will be a king tide tomorrow.'

In fact, a general problem with all restricted-gender verbs is to show, in a non-circular way, that the gender is motivated by the subject/object, since, as seen above, the languages do not provide other evidence for agreement with these genders outside the system under consideration.

# 3. Pseudo-Argument Uses of Agreement

All examples so far can be assimilated to more or less standard uses of agreement, sometimes with slight idiomaticity or coercion of verb meaning by the nature of its absolutive argument. In other words, in all cases discussed so far, we can plausibly postulate an argument which is represented by the relevant pronominal prefix, and whose ontological characteristics are those we would expect from the relevant gender. We now pass to pseudo-argument uses of the same prefixes, in which there is no evidence that there is a corresponding argument of the verb. In some cases, the existence of contrasting pairs of verbs differing just in the presence of a required agreement pattern makes it possible to identify a semantic contribution made by the pseudo-argument (e.g. 'with respect to a place'); I shall term these 'derivational uses'. In other cases, the verb root is only attested with the relevant pseudo-argument, and the lack of any contrast makes it impossible to identify a semantic contribution by the prefix: I shall term such cases 'conjugational' since the choice of prefix is automatically selected for by the verb root, without any detectable semantic contribution.[10] Table 2 summarizes the spectrum along which the various types of argument use are strung out.

We now pass to a more detailed discussion of the derivational and conjugational uses. I consider both the derivational and conjugational uses to be deponent, in the sense that each uses a form whose expected function is argument agreement for another function—derivational in the first case, conjugational in the second.

Derivational type: Here deponent-agreeing verbs form pairs with corresponding ordinary verbs whose argument prefixes behave canonically. The deponent prefix occupies one of the argument prefix positions, and adds a specifiable meaning (e.g. 'with respect to place, country'), but there is no evidence for an argument of appropriate gender being present.

Replacive type: Here the ordinary verb is transitive; its object slot is filled in the deponent verb by a pseudo-object use of the vegetable or neuter prefix. The 'displaced' original object, however, does not stop being the syntactic object: it may appear as a cardinal free pronoun[11] directly after the verb, and it may trigger the iterative reduplication found with plural objects. Consider the two regular Ilgar transitive verbs *ldakinun* 'ask' and *ldangan* 'send, cause, allow'. Each of these has a corresponding deponent-object verb where the object slot is filled by a neuter prefix, and in each case the added meaning is

---

[10] Obviously such analytic decisions are always provisional, particularly given our incomplete knowledge of the languages concerned: the discovery of the same verb with a different affix could shift our analysis of a given case from conjugational to derivational. Likewise, a more explicit understanding of the semantic contributions made by pseudo-argument prefixes might allow us to state the meaning of the verb root, in 'conjugational' uses, by subtracting the semantics contributed by the pseudo-argument prefix.

[11] There are three free pronoun series in Ilgar and Iwaidja: a cardinal series, used for subject, object, and possessive functions, an oblique series, used for indirect objects and beneficiaries, and a contrastive subject series. The possibility of being represented by a cardinal pronoun is a good test for distinguishing object from indirect object status.

**Table 2.**  Cline of uses of *ma-* and *ang-* prefixes in Iwaidja and Ilgar

| Type | Subtype | Characteristics | Section |
|---|---|---|---|
| True argument use | | Prefix indexes a bona fide syntactic argument, in terms of which the overall meaning can be clearly formulated, and which can be detected by such tests as argument structure alternations (§2.5) or use of iterative reduplication for multiple objects | |
| | Canonical | Semantic effects of gender agreement are completely compositional | §2.3 |
| | Idiomatic coercion of meaning | Metaphorical or other semantic extension coerced by meaning of object associated with gender marked by prefix | §2.4 |
| | Restricted gender | Verb is only attested with one gender value for S or O (in one case both A an O) | §2.5 |
| Derivational | | Prefix adds some semantic specification (e.g. 'with respect to a place') without any evidence that it has argument properties. There is always an agnate verb without a pseudo-argument | |
| | Replacive | Agnate verb is transitive; pseudo-argument affix fills the object slot and the displaced object is realized by a free pronoun | §3 |
| | Additive | Agnate verb is intransitive; pseudo-argument affix fills the object slot without any syntactic argument being added | §3 |
| Conjugational | | No agnate verb without a pseudo-argument, so it is impossible to identify the separate semantic or syntactic contribution of the root and affix. These verbs behave as if the the deponent agreement prefix is an arbitrary conjugation marker | §4 |

'with respect to country': *ang . . . ldakinun* (N.OBJ) 'ask (owner of clan estate) about where to go, inquire as to where one should go', *ang . . . ldan-gan* (N.OBJ) '(clan owner) give (person asking) permission to be on his country, lit. 'send (person asking) to (clan) country'.

Example (27), involving the first of these verbs, shows how a cardinal free pronoun can be employed to represent the person asked, even though the prefixal object slot has been filled with a neuter prefix.

(27)  *ang-bu-ldakinu-ng*                  *nuyi / ngabi*

Ilg   3SG.N.OBJ-3PL.A-ask-PST           you    me

'They asked you/me where to go.'

Example (28), involving the second of them, shows how the number of the displaced object may also be indexed by iterative reduplication of the root, which is normally reserved for marking plurality of absolutive arguments (cf. (10) above for a reduplication where it is the number of the neuter object argument that is represented).

(28)        *anildangakan*                          *raka*

    Ilg     *ang-ni-ldanga-ka-n*                    *raka*
            3SG.N.OBJ-3SG.M.A-send-ITER-NPST        DEM
            'He gives those several permission to be on his country.'

Additive type: Here the verb root is normally intransitive. The addition of a pseudo-object prefix is accompanied by addition of a specified meaning (e.g. 'w.r.t. ground'), but without any syntactic consequences such as the addition of a further argument. An example is the intransitive Iwaidja verb *naka* 'go (dual)': when a neuter object prefix is added the resultant verb *ang . . . naka* means 'search the ground (dual) as when going for yams to dig up'.[12]

# 4. Conjugational Types

Here the verb root cannot occur without the relevant vegetable or neuter prefix, which thus forms a sort of prefixal conjugation. There is no 'syntactically active' argument corresponding to the morphological slot. Although it may be possible to find some weak semantic motivation for the presence of prefix, the verb does not co-occur with any external NP, which gives plausibility to postulating an argument with semantics appropriate to the deponent prefix.

Consider the verb *ang . . . marrajba* 'walk, go for a walk', found in both Ilgar and Iwaidja, which takes a neuter object prefix (29). It is not implausible to relate this to the fact that walking occurs on ground or tracks, so that the meaning 'with respect to a place', found in some derivational uses (§3) may be postulated, and perhaps this verb once had an argument structure that reflected this more directly, e.g. 'walk a path' or 'pace the ground'. Synchronically, however, such arguments do not appear,

---

[12] There is one example, in Ilgar, where it appears that a true object (albeit collocationally restricted) has been added along with the pronominal prefix. This involves the verb *min*, an intransitive verb meaning 'say; do'. If this verb is used with a transitive prefix combination including a vegetable object marker, plus the fixed object NP *raka mali* 'that idea, those thoughts', this means 'to agree, to be of like mind', as in

(F1)    *Ngabi*    *nga-waharl*    *a-ny-bana-mi-n*                    *raka*    *mali.*
        1SG        1SG-head        1SG.A-3SG.V.OBJ-FUT-say-NPST       that      idea
        'I agree with that, I am of like mind with that idea.'

nor is there any corresponding verb without the deponent object prefix which would allow us to state the meaning of the root independently of this particular combination—this is the crucial difference from the derivational types discussed in section 3.

(29)  *barda*      *jarr-ung-marrajba*                    *jarr-ara*
     and.then    away:1PL.A-3SG.N.OBJ-walk(NPST)      away:1PL.S-go(NPST)

     *ngarr-ara-::*        *ngarr-ung-marrajba*       *ngarru-rtaya-n*
     1EXCL.PL.S-go-CONT    1EXCL.PL.A-3SG.N.            1EXCL.PL>3SG.
                      OBJ-walk(NPST)              C-see-NPST

     *w-arndi*
     3SG.C.S-be.high(NPST)

'And then we go on walking, we walk along and see it up there.'
(Pym and Larrimore 1979: 221)

Just as with other uses of the vegetable and neuter prefixes, the 'conjugational' deponent morpheme may or may not directly adjoin the root—this depends on the particular subject/object combination involved. In (29), for example, the particular subject/object combination (first person acting on third) means that the deponent object morpheme, which counts as third person, is placed last in the sequence *ngarr-ung* (or 'away' form *jarrung*) and hence adjoins the root. If this were put into the future it would be separated from the root by the prefix -*mana*: *ngarrungmanamarrajba* 'we will walk' (the deponent object prefix and root are in bold). And if the subject is third person, then the usual ordering rules (§2.1 above) place the object before the subject: 'he/she/they walk' is thus **angku**marrajba, where *ang* is the exponent of the third person neuter object slot in this combination,[13] and its future form is **angk**anamarrajba. These are all general positional properties of object prefixes, as outlined in section 2, and I simply mention them here to stress that the different syntactic status of pseudo-argument prefixes, in respect to regular argument prefixes, does not lead to any difference in how they are realized morphologically.

There are a large number of conjugational uses of deponent object prefixes. Some examples with neuter objects are *ang . . . muldirran* 'reverse, go back' (Ilg), *ang . . . urtbulang* 'pour out on ground' (Ilg, Iw), *ang . . . maranga* 'go round in a circle' (Iw), *ang . . . ldaharrun* 'tell lies' (Ilg, Iw). In all of these cases there is no candidate syntactic object.

---

[13] The *ku* in *angku* is an allomorph of the regular 3plA prefix *bu*: a rule of 'peripheral dissimilation' in pronominal prefixes means that peripherals (*b*, *k*, *ng* and *m*, i.e. non coronals) dissimilate in place before peripheral initial roots (like *marrajba*)—ironically in this case by assimilating in place to the preceding nasal.

There are also a large number of meteorological expressions of this type, many involving conjugationally specified prefixes for both subject and object. Some examples from Ilgar are *manildijarrngani* 'sheet lightning lighting up sky' (*mani-* '3SG.M>3SG.V'), *mangundularniny* '(there be) a thundercrack' (*mang(a)-* '3SG.F>3SG.V') and *mangildadbarrjin* '(there be) a rainbow extending down to the ground or sea' (*mang(a)-*, again '3SG.F>3SG.V'); see also the 'high tide' example in section 2.5 above. All these examples, of course, have a somewhat different status owing to both the subject and the object prefix being fixed.

In the case of vegetable prefixes with conjugational *ma* verbs, the situation is somewhat different, since all relevant verbs allow an NP to occur with them which can plausibly be regarded as the syntactic object of the verb— either of the restricted-gender type (e.g. *ma . . . adbungku* 'open' and *ma . . . irrkurang* 'close', discussed above, and *ma . . . arrun* 'eat' and *ma . . . wirlmanbun* 'smoke, suck'), or of a replacive type, as with *ma . . . wur-rurtban* 'lead on a rope', where the vegetable object prefix is presumably motivated by the plant status of 'rope' (woven from bark) while the displaced object is the animal being led.

The reader will have noticed that in all of the above examples it is a deponent object prefix that is involved (with additional specification of transitive subject for some of the meteorological expressions). In fact it is difficult to find clear examples of intransitive deponent argument affixes used conjugationally, because it is then hard to establish that the relevant initial sequence (*m(a)* . . . for the vegetable gender, *ang* . . . for the neuter) is in fact a prefix rather than simply part of the root of an invariant word. This is because, unlike with the transitives, we do not have a whole paradigm of forms that we can use to establish the free combinability of the pseudo-argument prefix. If there is a transitivity alternation (as in the 'open' and 'close' verbs discussed in §2.5) then I have analysed it as a 'restricted-gender' verb, though by arguing that this is not in fact a matter of gender such cases could be reassigned to the conjugational type. If there are corresponding verbs without one of these prefixes (as in the example *angbildimbiny* 'dry up (of land)' discussed in §2), this will either be a case of gender agreement, or conceivably of derivational use (though I have no examples).

Nonetheless, there are some prima facie cases of intransitive conjugational uses. One is the Ilgar word *maldarradban* '(tree) rub boughs together; sound thereof', which appears to be a verb conjugationally required to contain a vegetable intransitive subject. A second is the Iwaidja verb *malda-jarnarri* 'writhing snake track, writhe leaving track in grass', which was exemplified in (16). This looks like a verb with a conjugationally specified vegetable prefix *ma-*, but since it does not occur with any other prefix we cannot eliminate the possibility that it is (at least synchronically) simply an uninflecting nominal word that happens to begin with *ma-*. A third example is the Iwaidja word *angmarranguldin* '(place, time, wind, or weather) hold special memories, invoke special feelings', which appears to contain a conjugation-ally specified neuter prefix.[14] Again, the absence of any other form with which the root recombines means we cannot eliminate the alternative analysis that it is simply an uninflecting nominal word (possibly deverbal in origin) which happens to begin with the sequence *ang-*.[15]

A theoretically possible test, which would clinch the prefixal status of *ma-* and *ang-* in such cases is to see whether they are capable of taking the relevant future form (e.g. *angmanamarranguldin*). For Ilgar, unfortunately, it is too late to gather new data on this, and for Iwaidja we have not succeeded in confirming the availability of future forms with these verbs, but it is too early to say whether this is a categorical impossibility or simply reflects our failure so far to set up an appropriate context. For the moment, then, we need to express some reservations about whether there is any deponent intransitive subject agreement.

## 5. Conclusion; Pseudo-Arguments and the Typology of Deponency

As indicated on the Deponency Project data-base, pseudo-arguments of the type discussed here can clearly be fitted into a typology of extended depo-nency: the *formal subsystem involved* is that of *verbal agreement affixes*, the *expected function* of the affixal material is the *encoding of subject and/or object arguments of the verb*, while its *actual function* is either to *add some derivational*

---

[14] Although this verb is often translated into English using expressions like 'I remember', the Iwaidja structure contains no overt expression—either in the verbal agreement system, or in a free pronoun—corresponding to the 'rememberer'. Consider the following two examples given to me by Joy Williams (in February 2006) to illustrate its use: *ardaka angmarranguldin maldun arurdan* [lit. 'hey, *ang-marranguldin*, the wind has come up'] which she translated freely as 'the wind changed and it makes me remember', and *ardaka angmarranguldin jumung, ngabi jawirna* [lit. 'hey, *angmarranguldin* to her, my friend'], which she translated as 'I remember my friend, when she was here with me'. These examples suggest that *angmarranguldin* is best translated as '(something about the current environment or atmosphere) evoke memories', with the identity of the rememberer being filled in pragmatically (and normally interpreted as first person).

[15] In this and other examples there are various phonotactic and other phonological characteristics which point to the verbal analysis, including the fact that the post-*ma* or post-*ang* element begins with one of a circumscribed set of phonemes which may begin bound roots, that most end with a nasal (e.g. *-n*) characteristic of inflected verbs, and that stress is appropriately placed (e.g. primary stress on the putative root-initial in *àngmárrangùldin*). However, since these would all also be true of deverbal nouns they do not constitute decisive evidence.

*meaning to the verb,* or merely *to function as a sort of conjugational marker required by some verbs.*

## 5.1. Review of the cline from regular argument coding to deponent argument agreement

As we have seen, the forms surveyed in this paper may, with some verbs, mark regular argument functions. The regular argument agreement functions of the vegetable and neuter prefixes remain clearly productive in Mawng, which still has a fully-functioning five-gender system. In Iwaidja and Ilgar, by contrast, there are just a few verbs for which it is possible to contrast the use of the vegetable and/or neuter prefixes with prefixes indicating other genders (masculine and feminine in Ilgar, common in Iwaidja). These prefixes simply reflect properties of the relevant argument, e.g. that it is a plant or tree for the vegetable class, or is a place, water, or place-linked cultural phenomenon in the case of the neuter (§2.3). For this small number of verbs it is possible to analyse these prefixes as archaic residues of a once-productive five-gender system.

With other verbs one can still identify a basic agreement function, but with one of two types of deviation. First (§2.4), there may be some semantic specialization, attributable to semantic coercion (such as metaphor) arising from properties of the gender-specified argument—for example, taking 'grasp' in the metaphorical sense familiar from English 'grasp an idea' when it has a neuter object. Second (§2.5), there may be every appearance, from the semantics of the verb, its argument, and of the gender involved, that the affix represents a genuine argument, but the absence of any structural contrast with another gender value combined with the same verb makes this impossible to prove. Though I take both these deviations to fall within the 'regular range' of agreement phenomena as they occur cross-linguistically, they sow the seeds for the particular pathway that led to the development of deponent argument agreement.

The further detachment of these affixes from agreement functions, in the case of other verbs, appears to have been promoted by two developments.

Firstly, a suite of subtle lexical shifts appears to have favoured a more holophrastic interpretation of the combination of verb stem plus agreement affix. These semantic shifts would originally have been analysable as coercion of the verb stem's meaning to accommodate the semantic modifications necessitated by the involvement of arguments stereotypically associated with particular genders—a semantic shift rather similar to that found with certain types of noun-incorporation (and, significantly, primarily associated with arguments in absolutive roles). We can infer from the high frequency of such phrasal argument-gender + verb combinations in Mawng, which still has a productive five-gender system, that this development was not contingent on the simplification or loss of the gender system, though it is not outrageous to suggest that the larger the number of verbs for which such phrasal interpretations became normal the less 'agreement-like' the functioning of these affixes would have become.

The second development, then, is one we can observe in Ilgar and Iwaidja: the system of gender agreement was weakened and (in Iwaidja) almost lost entirely, with different genders winning out in the two languages: masculine and feminine in Ilgar, and 'miscellaneous' in Iwaidja. This decline of agreement occurred throughout the system: gender agreement in demonstratives (productive and normal in Mawng) has been lost in both Ilgar and Iwaidja; gender agreement in adjectives barely hangs on in Ilgar (now restricted to masculine vs feminine) and disappears completely in Iwaidja, and gender agreement on verbs becomes restricted in both Ilgar and Iwaidja. Once the vegetable and neuter argument affixes on verbs were no longer embedded in an integrated system of gender agreement functioning both within NPs and between NP arguments and verbs, one option would have been to jettison them entirely (as happened—with a couple of exceptions— with the masculine and feminine in Iwaidja, and across the board with the miscellaneous in Ilgar), so that they simply vanished from the verbal morphology. But the vegetable and neuter affixes were rehired rather than fired—or at least were handed a radically revised job description, in the form of the derivational and conjugational functions outlined in sections 3 and 4.

It is interesting to ask how far our treatment would be different if the argument-like uses described in section 2 were to vanish from these languages—not an implausible outcome, given the small number of verbs involved in these more argument-like uses. We could no longer say that they ever have an argument-coding function, and in this sense their 'expected function' would no longer be that of encoding arguments at all. However, it would still be the case that they occur in the argument slots of the subject/object paradigms of these languages, and exhibit positional and formal features in common with other argument-coding affixes. In that sense they would still be a type of deponent agreement, though a less clear case. Should the languages then undergo a further formal or positional dissociation between the (originally) vegetable and neuter prefixes and the affixes coding other person and number values—something which would not be outrageous, given that different morpheme orderings are involved with speech act participants—there would then no longer be any reason to consider them part of the agreement system at all, and they would simply become discontinuous elements of the verb stem, with a derivational or conjugational function.

**5.2. Other languages with comparable phenomena**

The Iwaidjan languages are not alone in attesting deponent agreement.

To begin with their immediate region, a very similar phenomenon is found in another non-Pama-Nyungan language, Gaagudju (Harvey 2002: 339–49), spoken just to the south of the Iwaidjan languages though only distantly related to them. Gaagudju has a very similar phenomenon which Harvey labels 'lexicalised cross-reference patterns', by which particular verbs have gender-specific direct object prefixes. In some cases it is possible to motivate the choice by cognate-object or stereotypical body-part nouns which may combine with the verb, e.g. the vegetable[16] -gender *mabalaabala* 'corroboree, song' in the case of the verb *barlabu* which obligatorily takes a vegetable object, and the vegetable-gender *magaarnamu* 'throat' with the verbs *bagarra* 'choke' and its synonyn *molgarra*, both of which have deponent vegetable-gender objects. But in other cases no such nominal can be found. Examples of other verbs with deponent vegetable-gender prefixes are *barlabu* 'sing' (deponent vegetable object prefix), *woreenjngu* 'whistle' and *barnarrega* 'slide, slip'. Deponent neuter object prefixes are found with *balabu* 'talk', *galamarrwa* 'be jealous', *gardaba* 'look for' (deponent neuter object prefix), *gabanjma* 'go first', *gabalarrbu* 'shine (of sun and moon), *gardamala* 'rub oneself', *djarrobarroma* 'smoke' and *mawaala* 'breed, give birth to, lay'. Many of these verbs can then add an indirect object clitic to index the person who is the goal of communication. There are also three intransitive verbs with lexically specified gender: *gardawidji* 'break (intr.)' (neuter), *gabarrnggi* 'become daylight' (neuter) and *marlanmagi* 'become night' (vegetable); Harvey points out that the latter two are typically subjectless verbs cross-linguistically.

Further afield, a wide range of other languages appear to exhibit similar phenomena. A full typological survey would be rewarding, but for the moment I just mention a few examples to illustrate the geographical spread of deponent argument agreement. Beginning with Northern Asia, the Yeniseian language Ket (Vajda 2001, 2003, MS) employs fixed forms in subject/object agreement positions as a component of stem creation, though the phenomenon in Ket is rendered more complex by the interaction of what I have been calling deponent argument agreement with the large array of different argument-agreement positions (probably originally reflecting a large set of distinct argument arrays associated with different thematic role sets). Moving to North America, rather similar phenomena are found in a number

---

[16] Harvey employs a Roman numbering system to identify genders, but the semantic content is essentially similar to that I have been using for Iwaidja and Ilgar: his III = vegetable, and his IV = neuter.

of Athabaskan languages,[17] e.g. Tolowa Athabaskan (Givón and Bommelyn 2000), and may in some cases be a diachronic source for the 'discontinuous stems' for which Athabaskan languages are notorious.

In Africa, Ewe employs a 'redundant object' marker with some verbs— '"Redundant" because unlike other objects it has not been possible to establish that it operates as a complement in clause structure; "Object" because in all respects it is phonologically identical with the third person singular object of the pronoun' (Ansre 1966: 71).

And in the Papuan language Nimboran (Anceaux 1965: 186, 202, 218; see also Inkelas (1993) and Baerman (2005)) there is 'spurious masculine object marking', tangled up with certain forms of the directional-locational suffixes, with a number of verbs, including 'dream', 'bring', and the iterative forms of 'hear' and 'laugh' (interestingly, several of these involve ø-roots). This 'spurious masculine object marking' is a further specific case of the 'pseudo-argument agreement' discussed in the present paper.

The extended deponency website refers to a number of other languages with the phenomenon: these include Amele, Basque, Belhare, Cree, Kiowa, and Tiwi; Takelma (Sapir 1922) could be added. The lack of terminological integration across descriptive traditions has impeded recognition of parallel phenomena cross-linguistically, and it is likely that deponent argument agreement is much commoner than we thought.

In closing, it is worth mentioning three other related phenomena and the sometimes tricky issue of how to delineate them from pseudo-argument agreement.

To begin with, there are obvious parallels with dummy subjects and so-called expletive objects in such familiar English examples as *it is raining*, *beat it!* and, in Australian English, *he carked it* (= he died). The most obvious difference, of course, is that here the phenomenon is syntactic rather than morphological, but aside from this there are many parallels, in particular the lack of any referential or anaphoric potential for the *it* pronoun (*\*Beat what? \*He carked what?*).

Secondly, there are even closer similarities to expletive-style feminine object clitics in languages like Italian, which again have no referential or anaphorical possibilities. These always co-occur with the reflexive clitic *se*, and form a tight semantic grouping referring to rather negative emotions or behaviours. Illustrative examples are *rider-se-la* [laugh-REFL-3SG.F.OBJ] 'be secretly happy at someone else's misfortune, feel Schadenfreude', *prender-sela* 'take offence' (homophonous with the compositional interpretation

---

[17] It has sometimes been proposed, not implausibly, that Athabaskan languages (more specifically, the Na-Dene family) are related to Yeniseian at some deep level (see e.g. Vajda 2005). This is irrelevant to the present argument.

'take it [fem.] for him/herself'), *cavarsela* 'get off/out of a situation, rid oneself (of something)'. Some examples involve conjunction of two such verbs—e.g. *se la suona e se la canta* [REFL 3F.OBJ sounds and REFL 3F.OBJ sings] '(s)he makes up his/her own song (without reference to reality)'—and in at least one there is an object complement which agrees in gender with the expletive object: *se la vede brutta* [REFL 3F.OBJ sees ugly(F)] '(s)he is in a dangerous situation'. Apart from the fact that we are dealing here with an object clitic rather than an affix, the differences between this and the types of deponent argument agreement described in the body of this paper are minimal, and suggest it may be profitable to widen the definition so that it does not necessarily involve strictly bound morphology.

Finally, and as briefly mentioned in section 5.1, there are clear analogies between pseudo-argument agreement and certain types of lexicalized incorporation. If we pass from Iwaidja and Ilgar to the polysynthetic Gunwinyguan languages a couple of hundred kilometres to the south, many verbs with deponent absolutive agreement are rendered with incorporated objects of a broadly generic kind, as in Bininj Gun-wok (Evans 2003) where verbs like *bolk-nan* [place-see] 'look at country', *dulk-di* [tree-stand] 'there be a tree' and *bo-ngun* [liquid-eat] 'drink' are the translation equivalents of Iwaidja *ang . . . ayan* [3SG.N.OBJ . . . see], Ilgar *ma . . . ldi* [3SG.V.S . . . stand] and Iwaidja and Garig[18] *ang . . . lda* [3SG.N.OBJ . . . eat] respectively. Apart from the fact that we are dealing in the one case with pronominal gender agreement, and in the other with noun incorporation,[19] the main difference is the size and semantics of the choice-set: with gender in the Iwaidja family, we are dealing with a five-way contrast, while with incorporated nouns in Bininj Gun-wok there is a choice of some fifty-seven generic terms (Evans 2003: 333). This makes the semantic contribution of the deponent argument prefixes rather less precise than is the case with incorporated nominals, although the gender system gets some semantic mileage from the existence of polysemically linked foci (e.g. for the neuter the three foci of place, water, and place-based cultural phenomena such as ideas and ceremonies). In both cases, though, we have the gradual semantic melding of the contributions of the predicate-denoting element (the stem) and the morphological means of denoting one of the arguments (either by incorporated nominal, or by gender agreement prefix).

Unlike some other types of deponency, which still remain puzzling in terms of their motivation and the evolutionary pathways that engender them,

---

[18] Ilgar has a different form for this verb, one of the few dialectal differences between Ilgar and Garig.
[19] Though many commentators have pointed out the functional parallels between incorporated nouns and pronominal affixes, including Mithun (1984), Baker (1995), and Evans (1997).

deponent argument agreement is reasonably comprehensible. It originates from the fact that—in contradistinction to our idealized logic-based models in which the ontology of predicates and their arguments are completely orthogonal—there is often a correlation in the real world between event-types and the entities that are stereotypically involved in them. From this it is not a long step to the use of entity-denoting expressions (including bound agreement morphology) as shorthand for semantically modifying the expressions for the events themselves, and perhaps eventually being absorbed into a discontinuous event-denoting expression in which their original role in agreeing with particular arguments is no longer discernible.

# References

Anceaux, J. 1965. The Nimboran language. *Verhandelingen van Koninklijke Instituut voor Taal-, Land- en Volkenkunde* 44.

Ansre, Gilbert. 1966. The grammatical units of Ewe. Ph.D. thesis. University of London.

Baerman, Matthew. 2005. The Surrey deponency databases. *Surrey Morphology Group, CMC, University of Surrey*, http://www.smg.ac.uk/deponency/Deponency_home.htm (accessed 15 July 2006).

Baker, Mark. 1995. *The polysynthesis parameter*. Oxford: OUP.

Capell, Arthur, and Heather E. Hinch. 1970. *Maung grammar, texts and vocabulary*. The Hague: Mouton.

Evans, Nicholas. 1997. Role or cast? Noun incorporation and complex predicates in Mayali. *Complex predicates*, ed. by Alex Alsina, Joan Bresnan, and Peter Sells, 397–430. Stanford: CSLI Publications.

—— 1998. Iwaidja mutation and its origins. *Case, typology and grammar: In honour of Barry J. Blake*, ed. by J. J. Song and A. Sierwierska, 115–150. Amsterdam: John Benjamins.

—— 2000. Iwaidjan, a very un-Australian language family. *Linguistic Typology* 4.2:91–142.

—— 2003. *Bininj Gun-wok. A pan-dialectal grammar of Mayali, Kunwinjku and Kune*, (2 vols.). Canberra: Pacific Linguistics.

—— 2004. Experiencer objects in Iwaidjan languages. *Non-nominative subjects, Volume 1*, ed. by Bhaskararao Peri and Subbarao Karumuri Venkata, 169–192. Amsterdam; Philadelphia: John Benjamins Publishing Company.

Evans, Nicholas, Ruth Singer, and Bruce Birch. In prep. The Iwaidja/Mawng reciprocal construction and its origins.

Givón, T., and Loren Bommelyn. 2000. The evolution of de-transitive voice in Tolowa Athabaskan. *Studies in Language* 24.1:41–76.

Harvey, Mark. 2002. *A grammar of Gaagudju*. Berlin: Mouton de Gruyter.

Heath Jeffrey. 1991. Pragmatic disguise in pronominal-affix paradigms. *Paradigms: The economy of inflection*, ed. by Franz Plank, 75–89. Berlin: Mouton de Gruyter.

—— 1998. Pragmatic skewing in 1 <-> 2 pronominal combinations in Native American languages. *International Journal of American Linguistics* 64.2:83–104.

Inkelas, Sharon. 1993. Nimboran position class morphology. *Natural Language and Linguistic Theory* 11.4:559–624.

Mithun, Marianne. 1984. The evolution of noun incorporation. *Language* 60.847–94.

Pym, Noreen (with Bonnie Larrimore). 1979. *Papers on Iwaidja phonology and grammar*, Series A, Vol. 2. Darwin: SIL-AAB.

Sapir, Edward. 1922. The Takelma language of south-western Oregon. *Handbook of American Indian languages* [vol. 2], ed. by Franz Boas, 1-296. Washington, DC: Government Printing Office.

Singer, Ruth. 2006. Lexicalized agreement in Mawng. Paper presented at Conference on Rara and Rarissima, Leipzig, April 2006.

—— 2007. Agreement in Mawng. University of Melbourne, Department of Linguistics and Applied Linguistics: Ph.D. Thesis.

Vajda, Edward. MS. Čto takoe <<rolevoj jazyk>> i počemu ketskij jazyk takovym ne javlajetsja.

—— 2001. The role of position class in Ket verb morphophonology. *Word* 52.3:369–436.

—— 2003. Ket verb structure in typological perspective. *Sprachtypologie und Universalienforschung* 56, 1/2.55–92.

—— 2005. *Yeniseic and Na-Dene*. Handout for presentation at MPI-Leipzig, December 2005.

# 12

# How Safe Are Our Analyses?

P. H. MATTHEWS

## 1. Why There is a Problem

THE TERM 'DEPONENT' REFERS TRADITIONALLY TO AN ANOMALY in the inflection of verbs, throughout or in part of a paradigm. Its origin lies in ancient analyses of Latin, to which we will return in a moment. But, in a modern account, words such as Latin *morior* 'I am dying' or *revertor* 'I am turning back' are deponent in that they had endings, such as -*or*, which were typically passive; their syntax, nevertheless, was active. Being deponent is defined here as a property of, in the first instance, individual word forms. The present form *revertor* 'I am turning back' was thus a deponent form of one verb; although other forms of the same lexeme, such as *reverti* 'I turned back, have turned back', were both active in syntax and had the normal active endings. But a verb such as MORIOR 'die' had no forms that were not deponent. Therefore it can be described, in turn, as a 'deponent' lexeme.

Being deponent is by definition an anomaly; in which an inflection has exceptionally something other than its normal role. It is therefore natural to look for a typology in which it is compared, as one kind of anomaly, to others. The paradigm of, for example, Latin FERO 'carry' was anomalous in another way, in being based, exceptionally, on three phonologically distinct stems. Compare the present *fer-o* 'I am carrying' with the perfect *tul-i* 'I carried, have carried' and the participle *la-t-us* 'carried'. The paradigm of AIO 'say' was anomalous, in turn, in that it was atypically incomplete. Thus, on the one hand, it included frequent forms such as the presents *aio* 'I say', *ait* 'he says', or in the plural *aiunt* 'they say'. On the other hand, there is no evidence that AIO had, for example, a corresponding present '*aimus*', with the meaning 'we say'. For these verbs too the pattern of exponence was in a broad sense irregular. But they and the deponents illustrate irregularities of three distinct types, each departing differently from the more simple pattern of verbs such as AMO 'like' or 'love', or REGO 'rule', which were not deponent, which showed no suppletion, and whose paradigms were not, in the traditional term, defective.

None of this, in substance, is now seen as controversial. In presenting it I take for granted one view of inflectional morphology in general, which Stump (2001) has called 'inferential-realizational'. Other specialists might prefer to draw equivalent distinctions in alternative terms. But no one will deny that verbs like MORIOR, FERO, and AIO are unusual each in their own way. It is therefore natural to see such properties not simply as peculiarities of Latin, but as instances in Latin of anomalies that might be found in any language. In the sense that FERO 'carry' is suppletive, so too is GO in English or ALLER 'go' in French. As AIO is defective so, it might be argued, is the modal OUGHT in English, since unlike most verbs it has no past form such as *oughted*. But 'deponent' is a term still mainly used in the description of Latin and of other older Indo-European languages. Therefore our first aim would be to define this type of anomaly more generally. In that light we may inquire which other languages might 'have deponents'; what other properties such languages may have in common; under what constraints, if any, patterns of deponency are possible; and so on.

Such is the project, as I understand it, that inspires this volume. But typologies in linguistics are notoriously not of facts, or of phenomena that can be observed directly. Both the terms they distinguish and the way they are applied rest on the analyses that linguists make of individual languages. The arguments that support these are sophisticated and not always made clear; and, in principle, they are always open to revision. The statement, in particular, that a form *x* 'is deponent', or exactly what it means to say this, is less straightforward than it may at first seem.

Let us return, for a preliminary illustration, to the example of MORIOR. As a lexeme it is an abstraction; as, in alternative terms, would be a 'die' morpheme. So too are the morphosyntactic categories of words such as *morior*, or the inflectional morphemes with which, in an alternative treatment, *mor-* would combine. To most linguists, all this may again appear uncontroversial. But on what grounds is such a form, as in the traditional account, an 'active'? Traditionally, to be precise, it is described as active 'in meaning'. The anomaly is that, despite its meaning, it is passive 'in form'. But, for a start, it is intransitive. Dying, that is, is not something that one individual 'does to' another individual. Nor does its meaning imply agency. Dying is something that simply 'happens to' whoever or whatever dies. The verb is therefore of a type that many linguists would now class as 'unaccusative'. But is an unaccusative more like an active such as *caedo* 'I am killing', or a passive such as *caedor* 'I am being killed'? One might argue, at first sight, that being killed and dying both imply a 'patient': an individual that 'undergoes' a process. As a verb whose subject is an 'undergoer', *caedor* has the inflectional ending -*r*, in contrast to *caedo*. Is there any anomaly, in that light, if a form like *morior* ends similarly?

There are counter-arguments, of course. While MORIOR 'die' is in this way like, for example, NASCOR 'be born', most other verbs described as deponent, as can be seen from the survey by Aronoff and his colleagues reported in this volume, were not semantically of this class. There were also other verbs in Latin that did not imply an agent, such as CRESCO 'grow larger', but whose inflections were like those of CAEDO 'kill'. But the case is still, in the end, debatable. It could be argued on the one hand that the syntax of other deponents, such as SEQUOR 'follow', was unproblematically both active and transitive. 'Following', that is, is often voluntary and, like transitives which were not deponent, such as CAEDO 'kill', a transitive deponent often took an object in the accusative. But, on the other hand, it might be claimed as crucial that verbs such as MORIOR 'die' or NASCOR 'be born' do not.

## 2. Deponents as Seen in Antiquity

It may be helpful too to remember how the term 'deponent' was first used. Its sense is literally that of 'putting down' (*de* 'down' plus a participial stem in *-ent-*); and one explanation is that these were verbs which 'laid aside' the role in syntax usual for ones with their endings. Compare, for example, the older Latin dictionary of Lewis and Short (1879: s.v. *depono*). But in ancient grammars a deponent was not 'active' on one level and then 'passive' on another. All three terms were part of the same classification. Verbs which were 'active', such as *caedo* 'I kill, am killing', were of one type. 'Passives', such as *caedor* 'I am being killed', were of another. 'Deponents', such as *morior* 'I am dying' or *sequor* 'I am following', formed another type, which was implicitly neither active nor passive.

To understand this classification, we have first to understand the form of grammar of which it was part. A sentence or an utterance (Latin 'oratio') could be divided into, among other things, a sequence of words: thus, for example, *Caesar moritur* 'The emperor is dying' into *Caesar* 'the emperor' and *moritur* 'is dying'. These units were, accordingly 'parts of an utterance' (in the Latin term 'partes orationis'); and by definition were the smallest segments of a vocal signal which, in addition, had a meaning. An ancient grammar was then, at its heart, a classification of 'parts of an utterance'. In *Caesar moritur* the first part was a noun, and nouns had in detail an array of 'accidentia' or contingent properties, in the standard account six. One was number; and, on this dimension, *Caesar* was classed as a singular. On other dimensions it was classed similarly as, for example, masculine or as simple as opposed to compound.

A verb, such as *moritur* 'is dying', was another part of an utterance, or in the modern term a 'part of speech', whose contingent properties were, as most grammarians described them, seven. Some too are familiar: *caedo* 'I am killing', for example, was on one dimension a first person and on another it was singular. But there was no precise equivalent of what we now call 'voice'. *Caedo* was again, on one dimension, 'active'. This was, in the term used by Donatus and most other grammarians, its 'genus'. Actives were identified, however, by two criteria. Firstly, they have an ending in -*o* ('in -o desinunt'); and, secondly, 'by the addition of -*r*, they turn themselves into passives' ('accepta r littera faciunt ex se passiua'). *Caedo*, that is, → *caedo-r*. The passive type, as represented by a verb like *caedor* 'I am being killed', was identified as the opposite. They were verbs, that is, which end in -*r* and, 'if it is removed, turn back to actives' ('ea dempta redeunt in actiua'). *Caedor*, conversely, → *caedo*.

Three other 'genera' could then be distinguished. First there were verbs such as *curro* 'I am running' which, like *caedo* 'I am killing', had an ending in -*o*; but, if an -*r* is added, the forms are 'not in the language' ('sed accepta r littera latina non sunt'). These were therefore not, in the ancient classification, 'active'; but, in a term that is still familiar from older dictionaries, 'neuter'. In Latin this was simply the word for 'neither'. As a neuter noun belonged to a 'genus' (now translated 'gender') which was 'neither' masculine nor feminine, so a verb such as *curro* belonged to one that was, implicitly, neither active nor passive.

As *curro*, however, had no corresponding form '*curro-r*', so a 'deponent', such as *morior* 'I am dying' or *sequor* 'I am following', had no corresponding '*morio*' or '*sequo*'. Like passives, therefore, the deponents have an ending in -*r*; but 'if it is removed', they are in turn 'not in the language' ('sed ea dempta latina non sunt'). A deponent was thus identified as the converse of a 'neuter'. Finally, a fifth 'genus', as the grammarians perceived it, was represented by verbs which; 'like a deponent', had an ending in -*r* ('in r desinunt, ut deponentia'). But, as Donatus put it, they 'fall into two patterns' ('in duas formas cadunt'), 'of an agent and an undergoer' ('agentis et patientis'). *Criminor*, for example, could mean 'I am accusing'; and, on the evidence of at least some uses, 'I am being accused'. Their 'genus' was accordingly distinguished, in another term used also of a 'gender' of nouns, as 'common' (Latin 'commune').

The grammar from which these formulations have been cited dates from the fourth century (Donatus, *Ars minor*, ed. Holtz 1981: 592f.), and is one of a series, all from the late Roman empire, shown by Barwick (1922) to be closely related. Some varying schemes are mentioned in another of this period by Charisius (ed. Barwick 1964: 210–14). But the problem that the ancient grammarians faced was in substance the same that we would face if we were to approach the language for the first time. We can distinguish verbs, that is, by their endings. But their meaning, or in Latin their 'significatio', is found to match inflections only in part. *Loquor* 'I am speaking' was another that ended in *-or*, but, like killing, speaking is an activity performed by an agent. Equally, one might say, *cresco* 'I am growing larger' is a verb in *-o*; but, like dying or being born, getting larger is something that merely happens to the entity that 'undergoes' the process.

One solution, if Charisius does not mislead us, was to distinguish classes primarily by meanings. Thus, in the simplest account, one 'genus' was again of actives: these have the meaning of 'doing something' or refer, alternatively, to 'a motion of a body or a mind'. Another was of passives, whose meanings were complementary. A third type was of, in the Latin term, 'habitatiua', for which the examples cited include both *crescit* 'is growing larger', with an ending we would now call 'active', and the 'deponents', as the standard account describes them, *nascitur* 'it is being born' and *oritur* 'it is rising'. The term is from the Latin 'habitus', which we may translate as 'state of being'; and, according to Charisius, these were verbs defined as 'signifying something which in itself comes into being or is' ('quae per se quid fieri aut esse significant', ed. Barwick, 212). As such they were alike, then, in their meanings; but were formally heterogeneous. But the usual approach was, evidently, to take form as the primary criterion. Of the types distinguished by Donatus and others, the actives and passives were, in the broadest terms, semantically homogeneous. As Priscian was to put it more than a century later, an active 'always', with some qualifications, 'signifies an action'; and, in the traditional criterion, has a corresponding passive. A passive likewise 'always', with the corresponding qualifications, 'signifies something undergone' ('semper passionem significat'); again, in the traditional criterion, it has a corresponding active. In Priscian's account these are the leading 'species' of verbs ending in *-o* and in *-or* respectively. But he points out that, in contrast to them, neuters and deponents both have a variety of different 'significations' (Priscian, ed. Hertz, in Keil 1855: 373f.). There was variation, as we have seen, among semantic types like those of *curro* 'I am running' and of *cresco* 'I am growing larger'. But such verbs were alike, once more, in that there were no verbs such as '*curror*' or '*crescor*'. There was likewise variation among the types of, for example, *sequor* 'I am following' and of *morior* 'I am dying'. But these were alike, again, in that there were no verbs such as '*sequo*' or '*morio*'.

## 3. How Ancient Treatments Might be Interpreted

Such accounts may at first seem naive, or at best primitive. The ancient grammarians drew no clear distinction, on the lines we are now taking for granted, between lexemes and specific words or word forms. A verb such as *caedo* 'I am killing' or *caedor* 'I am being killed' was simply one 'part of an utterance', as were *curro* 'I am running', *morior* 'I am dying', and so on. They had likewise no distinct sense of a morphosyntactic category, in the sense that has been clarified (or at least I like to think it has been clarified) since the 1970s. A verb such as *morior* was accordingly a 'part of an utterance' classed as deponent, just as it was classed as first singular or indicative. The distinctions implied in modern treatments of this topic are precisely modern.

Let us try, however, to reformulate what Priscian, in particular, was saying. On the one hand, there were lexemes such as CAEDO 'kill' or, in the grammarians' standard illustration, LEGO 'read', whose paradigms contrasted forms that were morphosyntactically active with others that were morphosyntactically passive. These were the only verbs, if Priscian's formulation can be transposed into a modern context, 'that have a complete and balanced inflection' ('perfectam habentia declinationem et aequalem', ed. Hertz 373); and, of their nature, they tended to refer to processes initiated by an agent and undergone by a 'patient'. On the other hand, there were many lexemes, covering a wide range of meanings, whose paradigms had no such contrast. Most then had inflections like those which, in a 'complete and balanced' paradigm, were those of the active. That was the pattern of, again, verbs such as CURRO 'run' or CRESCO 'grow larger', whose forms were the ancient 'neuters'. But in a real sense the deponents too were 'neuters'. They too, that is, were neither active nor passive; but realized verbs whose paradigms included no such contrast. The only difference is that, in most cases, verbs that did not distinguish voice had forms like those of the unmarked actives. *Curro* 'I am running' was thus formally, though not morphosyntactically, like *caedo* 'I am killing'. But, as an exception, verbs like MORIOR 'die' or SEQUOR 'follow' had instead the endings that were elsewhere those of the marked passive. Forms such as *morior* 'I am dying' or *sequor* 'I am following' were thus formally, but again not morphosyntactically, like *caedor* 'I am being killed'.

Where would this leave the notion of deponency in general? It is presented in this volume as a form of 'mismatch': as a case where forms of words relate to a grammatical category in a pattern not, in Corbett's term, 'canonical'. But what is 'non-canonical', in this interpretation, is the appearance of a marked form when an opposition is neutralized. Thus, to repeat, words such as *caedo* were distinctively active and words such as *caedor* were distinctively passive. But a word like *curro* was not specifically active; any more than, for example, in a word like *speed* in English, the second consonant is distinctively 'voiceless'. In Prague school terms, the morphosyntactic opposition of voice was neutralized—that is, simply, there was no distinction— throughout this paradigm. But oppositions like this, as perceived by Jakobson especially, are between a marked term and an unmarked: in this case, between features that are morphosyntactically '[+ passive]' versus '[− passive]'. Now in phonology, the form appearing in a 'position of neutralization' would lack the 'mark', as Trubetzkoy described it, that is distinctive elsewhere. Thus the [p] of *speed* is not 'marked' phonetically by a feature '[+ voice]'. In morphology, categories are realized by inflections: [+ passive], for example, by forms in, for example, *-r*. This is similarly a mark, then, of the opposition: and, where the opposition is neutralized, we expect a form without it, as in *curro*. The anomaly in *morior* or *sequor* is that this mark is present, not in forms that are specifically 'active', but where the feature [± passive] is not relevant.

For the description of Latin this may not make that much difference. We are merely looking at the same facts from a different viewpoint. But for the cross-linguistic definition of deponency, it is perhaps more of a problem. A 'mismatch', that is, could in principle be found in paradigms where there is no neutralization, and in words whose morphosyntax is, in Prague school terms, unmarked. Suppose, for the sake of argument, that plurals in language L are normally marked by a suffix *-x*. But then, in a few irregular paradigms, the plural is instead marked by a suffix *-y* and *-x* marks instead, exceptionally, the singular. There is no neutralization: for either inflectional class there is a singular on the one hand and a plural on the other. But there is nevertheless a mismatch, in the exceptional case, between the number 'singular' and an affix *-x* that generally marks it opposite. Therefore singulars marked by *-x* would be 'deponent', under the cross-linguistic definition generally accepted in this volume. But is the same then appropriate for both that case, where in short there is a contrast with a mismatch, and a case like that of Latin, where, although an affix appears, there is in one analysis no contrast?

One reaction is, of course, that that analysis of Latin is wrong. The right treatment is again the one traditional in the modern period. But it is not clear how such judgements of what is right and what is wrong are justified.

## 4. Which Treatment Might be Better?

The facile answer is that we are dealing with an issue of theory. We are looking, again, at the same facts; but with different assumptions about the nature of language in general. The problem then lies in the conflict between these; one of which we must see as mistaken.

The issue is thus, more precisely, of criteria. In either analysis words are assigned a place in a paradigm, defined by categories such as person, tense, and so on. These categories are 'morphosyntactic': they 'play a role', if I may go back to my own original formulation, 'both in the morphological structure of the Word ... and in its external relations within the syntax' (Matthews 1972: 162). But either role can be described more simply, or with what we might claim to be greater insight, at the expense of the other.

The crucial insight is, in one view, into the nature of oppositions. In morphology, as in phonology, they may be constant or they may be neutralized, as proposed in the case of [± passive], in specific circumstances. This term is used again as Trubetzkoy intended in the 1930s; not, therefore, in the different sense which has been usual, in the tradition of generative phonology, since the 1960s. The insight, that is, is that words like *morior* were neither active nor passive; not that, while such words were active, or were [− passive], at an underlying level, the realization of this feature at a lower level then became identical to that of words which were [+ passive], such as *caedor*. The description is simpler, we might argue, if a category is not seen as entering into the description of words, or of the paradigms of lexemes, where it is not relevant.

The opposite insight is that actives, 'neuters' and deponents are united by their syntax. A passive such as *caeditur* 'is killed' is distinguished from an active such as *caedit* 'kills', in its potential relation to, in the traditional sense, an 'agent' rather than an object. Hence the category [± passive]. But all verbs bear a similar relation to a subject in the nominative. Therefore we have no grounds to establish further morphosyntactic differences between a transitive verb with active inflections, such as *caedit*, and an intransitive verb with similar inflections, such as *currit* 'runs'. Latin was straightforwardly a language of the type now called 'accusative', in which, in Dixon's terms, the 'S' of an intransitive is identified, both by its case and by the inflections of the verb, with the 'A' of a transitive (Dixon 1994: 9). Hence the anomaly, once more, in forms such as *sequitur* 'is following' or *moritur* 'is dying', whose syntax is like those of 'actives' and 'neuters', but whose inflections are not.

Is it right, then, to describe a language primarily in terms of paradigmatic relations among sets of features? This viewpoint might be said to have its origin in European structuralism, as carried to an extreme by Jakobson. Or is it right, instead, to think of sentences as represented syntagmatically at different levels, with rules by which such representations are related? This view was formulated clearly by American structuralists, Chomsky in this respect included, in the 1950s. If the issue were one of 'theory', these are the questions that a general theory of language might be expected to answer; and although, in either analysis, the deponents in Latin are anomalous, how precisely we define 'deponency' in general, as one type of 'non-canonical' pattern of exponence, seems to depend on the answer given. But on what grounds is one 'theory', or one way of looking at a language, to be judged right and the other rejected?

## 5. One Lexeme or Two?

Problems like this have long been familiar to typologists. As many linguists see it, we require not just a full and accurate investigation of specific languages, but descriptions that allow direct comparisons, often at high levels of abstraction, of the 'phenomena'—as it is so tempting to perceive them—that concern us. Ideally, that is, we would like all languages to be described in terms of the same 'theory', from a common viewpoint, and by common criteria. 'Phenomena' such as deponency can then be identified by reference to this theory, not as facts in any crude sense.

In another view such talk is no more than unhelpful posturing. For the moment, however, our problems may concern not just distinctions among morphosyntactic categories, such as voice in Latin, but the identity, also, of the lexical units to which paradigms belong.

Let us return, for a preliminary illustration, to the ancient 'common genus'. A form such as *criminor* was again, in our terms, either an active, with the meaning 'I accuse', or a passive, with the meaning 'I am accused'. Thus, in a modern account, we might establish a lexeme, CRIMINOR 'accuse', whose paradigm would include both actives with the endings of a passive, which would in modern treatments be deponent, and homonymous passives, which would not be deponent. One complication, however, is that being deponent is in this sense partly variable. We are, as always, at the mercy of our corpus of texts; but compare, for this root, the imperfect subjunctive *criminaret* '[he, she] should accuse' in Plautus, *Pseudolus* 493. There is also later evidence of a non-deponent passive participle, *criminatus* '[which is] accused'. An alternative, therefore, might be to assign the same root to two different lexemes. One we can again call 'CRIMINOR', and this would be throughout deponent. Like MORIOR 'die' or SEQUOR 'follow', it would include forms such as *criminor*; which, as a deponent, would have only an 'active' meaning 'I am accusing'. But there would then be variation between CRIMINOR and a collateral lexeme 'CRIMINOR'. Compare, with the term 'collateral', its separate entry in the older Latin dictionary of Lewis and Short (1879: s.vv.). The paradigm of CRIMINOR would straightforwardly include forms such *crimino* 'I am accusing', on the assumption that they too were in use. The corresponding passives would, again straightforwardly, be forms such as *criminor* 'I am accused'.

Was there variation and homonymy within the paradigm of one lexeme, or between those of two different lexemes? Was the 'deponency', accordingly, in just one part of a paradigm, which was morphosyntactically active? Or was it in the paradigm of one lexeme as a whole, whose root was also that of another lexeme alongside it? A partly similar question might be raised, in principle, for the forms reported from Tsez, for 'child' and 'children', discussed by Corbett in this volume. In ancient terms, these would have constituted a 'common number': *xex-bi*, though it has the ending of an absolutive plural, is used in reference to one child or to more than one child; so is *xex-z-as*, with the ending of a 'genitive 1' plural; and so on. Such patterns are, as Corbett says, unusual. But the status in Latin of the 'common genus' of verbs does seem to be similar. Ignore, for the sake of argument, the evidence of collateral variants: of forms such as *crimino* for the deponent *criminor*, and so on. Then throughout what is traditionally the 'present' paradigm of CRIMINOR 'accuse', the inflections which in general are those of the passive are ambiguously exponents either of the passive or the unmarked active. Similarly, throughout the paradigm of XEX 'child' in Tsez, those that usually distinguish the marked plurals serve too as exponents of the unmarked singulars.

Or could these forms belong to different paradigms? The case in Latin is part of a wider pattern; but if, still for the sake of argument, we could discount collateral variations, it would be possible in principle to distinguish lexemes with inherently an 'active' or a 'passive' meaning. We might thus establish one verb, call it 'CRIMINOR$_1$', with the meaning 'bring an accusation against'. This would be, lexically, a deponent. But we could then establish another, 'CRIMINOR$_2$', with the meaning 'be accused', whose paradigm would be passive. Similarly, in Tsez, a lexeme 'XEX$_1$' might mean 'one child' and a different though semantically related lexeme, 'XEX$_2$', would mean 'children'. By virtue of its meaning XEX$_1$ would be compatible only with a morphosyntactic feature [− plural]; and would, as a lexeme, be straightforwardly deponent. The separate XEX$_2$ has a meaning by which it would be compatible only with [+ plural]. No issue of syncretism, or of identical exponents within paradigms, arises.

Such analyses are possible, to repeat, in principle. If we reject them, it is presumably because two lexemes should not have identical roots unless there is clear evidence of homonymy. If taken to an extreme, however, this would exclude conversions between, for example, parts of speech in English; let alone of zero-derivation of a transitive verb from an intransitive, and other conversions proposed similarly.

# 6. Where is There Suppletion?

As homonymy must be allowed for, so must suppletion. But here too the identity of lexemes may not always be straightforward.

Take, for a classic example, the relation between Latin FACIO 'to make, build, construct' and FIO 'to take place, occur, arise . . . develop'. The translations are cited from their entries in the *Oxford Latin Dictionary* (Glare, ed. 1982); and, implicitly, these are two different lexemes. But in that view both verbs are apparently defective. In the case of FIO, we would expect forms based on stems both of the perfect and (again as it is traditionally called) the 'present', not on the 'present' stem only. There is no reason, that is, why we should not expect them, except that in relevant constructions what we find instead are periphrastic passive forms of FACIO. Forms whose meaning might be represented by a gloss like 'to have come to be' are accordingly 'supplied', in the traditional explanation, by ones which can be glossed as causatives by 'to have been made to be'. In the case of FACIO, we would expect forms in the passive based on the present stem, as well as actives: thus familiar howlers, for those of us who learned Latin in the schoolroom, such as *faciebatur* 'was being made', corresponding to the active *faciebat* 'was making'. Instead, however, these forms were supplied by forms of FIO, whose inflections were active: thus not *faciebatur*, which would have the gloss 'was being made to be', but *fiebat* or 'was coming to be'. What is meant, however, by saying that one lexeme 'supplies' forms of another? In the older dictionary of Lewis and Short we find, not surprisingly, a different solution. There is implicitly a single lexeme, which we can represent as FACIO. A form such as *facio* (active) is one member of its paradigm. One like *fio* is another; and, despite its ending, is then seen as passive. Under 'forms' the entry for this lexeme reads: '. . . in *pass.;* fio, factus, fieri'. In an entry headed 'fio', we find merely a cross-reference: 'v. facio *init.*' (Lewis and Short 1879: s.vv.).

A third alternative would be to establish FACIO and FIO as two lexemes which were both suppletive. Forms such as *fio* would thus be ambiguously either active forms of FIO or the passive forms of FACIO; and, in the latter case, as in the solution implied by Lewis and Short, we would again identify a mismatch between 'active' endings, such as the first singular *-o*, and the meaning or the morphosyntactic property that the words would have within that paradigm. Therefore they too would count as 'deponent' in the sense that is general in this volume. Combinations such as *factus sum* (literally 'made I-am') would on the one hand form, as in all other accounts, a periphrastic perfect passive paradigm of FACIO. But they would also, on the other hand, supply the perfect active paradigm of FIO, and as such they too would count as deponent. Neither verb, in this analysis, would be defective; as both are in the analysis implicit in the *Oxford Latin Dictionary*. Nor would FACIO be defective in the account implied by Lewis and Short; but forms such as *fio* would be morphosyntactically passive, and therefore again, in our cross-linguistic definition, they would be 'deponent'.

Which treatment, then, is to be judged 'right'? The principle that linguists tend to cleave to is the one implied by the Saussurean doctrine of 'linguistic signs': or, in Bloomfield's formulation in the 1920s, of 'linguistic forms' as 'sames of form and meaning'. In the beginning this was central to the structuralist conception of a 'langue' or language system (commentary and references in Matthews 2001: ch. 2). As a principle of analysis, however, it is so familiar that it scarcely needs to be spelled out. We will be forced, of course, to recognize some cases of suppletion, as of homonymy. But the operative word is 'forced'. In the case, for example, of Latin FERO 'carry', the meanings are regular across all three stems: *fer-* in the 'present', perfect *tul-*, and participle *la-t-*. These are stems, moreover, corresponding to what are called traditionally the 'principal parts' of verbs individually, to which are referred irregularities of other kinds distinguishing the same parts of their paradigms. The argument, then, against the identity of FACIO and FIO would be that, on the one hand, the roots (*f*)*ac-* and (*f*)*i-* are not systematically alike: they are not 'sames' formally, as Saussurean 'signifiers'. On the other hand, each has a range of meanings which, though covered by schematic glosses such as 'make to be' and 'come to be', must in part at least be detailed separately. Under 'meanings' I include, as an ancient grammarian and as Bloomfield would presumably have done, their syntax. Neither, therefore, are they strictly 'sames' at the level of what is 'signified'. Different forms and different meanings, even though the meanings are related, imply different units. Nor would the suppletion of *fac-* by *fi-* be paralleled by any irregularity, as in the case of FERO 'carry', in corresponding parts of other paradigms.

Therefore FACIO 'make' would be one verb and FIO 'take place' or 'become' would be different. Nevertheless their meanings correspond in many uses; and it is in that light that we might in turn reject the last and the more complex of our three alternatives, on the grounds that it implies a series of ambiguities, between, for example, *fio* as an active of FIO and the same form as a passive of FACIO, that cannot otherwise be justified. But are we right now to impose such strict restrictions on suppletion? A structuralist analysis begins, as Bloomfield saw it, with forms rather than with meanings; and, where the root is constant, the meaning of a lexeme may reasonably include extensions natural to one part of its paradigm. If FACIO had a present passive with the stem *fac-*, we might not be surprised if it it had more generally the sense of 'to become', not just 'be made'. Need the explanation be different if its passives are like *fio* instead?

*Fio*, however, would not only be suppletive in its stem. A further argument might imply that deponency, as a form of mismatch in the role of 'signifiers', is itself to be avoided. Identity of form and meaning would, again, be our ideal. Just then as we reject suppletive stems, unless they are in some way forced upon us, so we will prefer to establish sign-like links between inflections, such as *-o* in *fio*, and the morphosyntactic categories corresponding to them. If FIO and FACIO are separate lexemes, *-o* and other endings of the active will form 'sames of form and meaning' wherever, in whatever paradigm, they are found. If *fio* and the like were seen as passives, they would fail to.

The principle, more generally, would be to avoid what Corbett terms a 'non-canonical' pattern of exponence—any that would deviate, we might say, from the structuralist ideal of 'one form and one meaning'—wherever possible. For most linguists, however, the foundations of linguistics are no longer as Saussure or Bloomfield saw them. We may need to consider, therefore, how far such a principle remains valid.

# 7. What Typologies Should Rest On

This last example might be dismissed, in Latin at least, as a one-off. Cases such as that of XEX 'child' as reported in Tsez, or of the 'common genus' of verbs in Latin, are again unusual; and in the latter case it makes sense that, alongside forms like *criminor*, with an active as well as a passive meaning, forms that were actives in both form and meaning, on the lines of *crimino*, should also be attested. But a more pervasive problem, which could clearly be explored at some length, is that of the middle voice, as it is called, in Ancient Greek or Sanskrit. The case of Sanskrit is examined by Stump in this volume, and it would be impertinent to comment on it, since the language is not within my field of expertise. But it is tempting, again, to ask if we are always dealing with forms of a single lexeme. Take, as one example, the Greek active *óllumi* 'I destroy' or 'I kill'. The corresponding middle *óllumai* meant 'I perish' or 'I die'; and, in dictionaries such as that originally of Liddell and Scott, these are implicitly forms of the same verb (revised edition by Stuart Jones 1940). But it is one of many verbs whose entries are divided systematically into a sense A for one voice and a sense B for the other. Nor are its stems and inflections entirely regular. An alternative, in principle, would be to establish A and B as senses of two different, though related, lexemes. Forms such as *óllumai* would be reclassed in that light as deponents: with, for example, ones like *boúlomai* 'I want (to)' (= *voulomai* as transcribed by Lavidas and Papangeli, this volume).

Enough has been said, however, to illustrate the familiar point with which we started: that typologies are of descriptions, not directly of facts or 'phenomena'. The problem, as it is natural to see it, is how projects like the one we are engaged on can ensure that grammars of quite different languages can be compared reliably. One answer, therefore, is that we have to agree on one set of criteria, which all analyses will ideally apply. We should hope that specialists in individual languages will, where necessary, have the decency to bow to our authority, and do as we prescribe. If not, we shall have to compensate for their recalcitrance by mastering the facts ourselves, and supplying our own reanalyses wherever they are needed.

On what basis, however, can we agree? A further temptation is to see this once more as an issue of theory. A theory of language will, it is often said, constrain the structure of an individual grammar. It could accordingly entail that FACIO and FIO, for example, could not but be separate lexemes; or, alternatively, that they could not but be one lexeme. In principle, it might be possible to formulate a 'theory' that would force such choices as this. But the problem then is how we choose between alternative proposals. What is it that a theory is intended to explain, and which one theory can be said to explain in a more successful or a more illuminating way than others? Have we any reason indeed to propose a 'theory', other than the belief that, somehow, our criteria must find some higher justification?

The fashionable answer is that a linguistic theory is a theory of 'Universal Grammar'. The capitals are meant to signal that this term is used as it has been used by Chomsky: the object, that is, will be to discover what each individual must inherit genetically, if we are to explain how knowledge of their language is internalized. Knowledge of a language includes, for example, that of its morphology. Therefore, so the argument might run, it cannot be formed in the minds of speakers unless there are specific constraints on the ways in which morphology can develop. That then is what a theory of morphology is about; and just as, say, a speaker's acquisition of the syntax of English is explained in part by constraints on, for example, 'Binding', so that of the morphology of, for example, Latin is explained in part by similar constraints on how lexemes are identified, and how they and other abstract units can be realized. But it is not obvious, in reality, that such a theory has an object. Let us accept, still for the sake of argument, that a Universal Grammar exists. We agree then that it will explain in part the acquisition of a particular language. But no one would, of course, claim that it explains all of it. It is therefore reasonable to ask why knowledge of the structure of paradigms, or the rules by which forms fill specific places in them, should be thought to be within its scope. The argument for principles like those of Binding has been that specific rules for sentences would be unlearnable, unless such structures are genetically inherited. There seems no reason, however, to see morphology as similarly unlearnable. What is it, once more, that a 'theory' of morphology would be expected to explain?

There is perhaps a weaker answer. We assume again that 'Universal Grammar' exists, and that syntax, at least, falls within the scope of such a theory. We therefore take it, as a working hypothesis, that there might in addition be a 'Universal Morphology', even though we have no direct evidence of any mystery that needs to be explained. But without this we again cannot say that one 'theory' might be right and others wrong. Do typologies need then to be founded in this way at all?

In themselves, at least, they are intuitively straightforward. Take, for an example that in practice no one will dispute, the way we talk about the paradigms of nouns in Latin. Case, as is well known, can be established as one category in syntax, independently of number; number, in turn, independently of case. The problem in morphology is that endings by which they are realized cannot be divided systematically into two separate suffixes. In the genitive plural, for example, *-um* or *-rum* is different as a whole from, on the one hand, other plural endings and, on the other hand, those of the genitive singular. Therefore the exponents of these categories are of a type traditionally called 'fused' or 'cumulative'; which again we can in practice easily identify in other languages.

The example is chosen because it is, of course, so very familiar. At first sight, the typology is once more of descriptions: of the forms of statement that a linguist can make. In a word like *puellarum* 'of girls', we could instead, in principle, establish separate allomorphs of genitive and plural: thus, for example, *puella-r-um*. In the last resort, one might be no more than a zero: thus, for example, *puella-Ø-rum*. We could alternatively see *-(r)um* as the allomorph of one minimal syntactic unit, which would be distinguished lexically, by the features 'genitive' and 'plural', from other minimal units which were lexically 'accusative' and 'plural', 'genitive' and 'singular', and so on. Harris perhaps came close to this in his analysis of morphemes into 'morphemic components' (1951: 306–9). In practice, however, we can agree that the traditional description is right. Now compare, for another simple illustration, the dative plural and the ablative plural. Their endings are identical: thus, in the same paradigm, *puellis* 'to girls' and, for example, '[by] girls'. Now we could, in principle, describe them as grammatically identical: a morphosyntactic distinction which holds in the singular, between in this paradigm *puellae* 'to girl' and the ablative *puella*, would simply not hold, as a distinction of syntax or of meaning, in the plural. In practice, however, everyone agrees that dative plurals are one category and ablative plurals are another. Therefore everyone agrees that there is syncretism.

Hence the temptation to proceed as if typologies were directly of facts. A further 'fact', as it is therefore tempting to see it, is that lexemes such as MORIOR 'die' or SEQUOR 'follow' were deponent. But there is obviously another way of looking at such a typology. To agree that *-rum* in *puellarum* realizes genitive and plural is to agree, we might say, on the solution to a problem. To agree that *puellis* is either dative plural or ablative plural is to agree on the solution to another. Their nature is, however, different and the range of possible solutions will accordingly be different in turn. The problem solved, however trivially, by treating *-rum* as cumulative, is in that sense, as a problem, of a different type from that solved, again trivially, by describing *-is* as an exponent of both cases. In the case of MORIOR or SEQUOR we are dealing with a problem that historically has proved more difficult, and the solution general in the modern period is not quite the one originally arrived at. But if we are perhaps less certain as to how exactly forms of such verbs should be analysed, we can agree that, as a problem, it is of a third type, which in turn will lend itself to different solutions, different from the others. If typologies are ideally of 'facts', the 'fact' that we are faced with a specific kind of problem would, in cases like these, or the others we have touched on, be less controversial than the 'fact', as it is tempting at first to see it, represented by any one particular solution to it.

This line of argument is not original; but is inspired especially by Bazell's inaugural lecture (1958), on linguistic typology in general. Unfortunately, it was one of the scholars from whom Bazell rightly differed (5f.) who was to lead a revival of interest in typologies in the 1960s. The work of Greenberg coincided further with the account by Chomsky of linguistic theory as a theory of Universal Grammar, and it is therefore hard to think back to the time when Bazell's lecture was delivered. But a typical objection to typologies lay in 'the demand', whenever they were mooted, 'for neutral descriptions based on agreed criteria, identical from linguist to linguist and from the description of one language to that of all others'. The demand is 'surely', he said, 'preposterous' (Bazell 1958: 4). But different languages, of the types traditionally called 'agglutinating' or 'inflecting', did raise what were plainly different problems; and 'an approach in terms of problems rather than of solutions renders us independent of the kind of analysis' (11) adopted in particular cases. Our concern in this volume is with a typology of a much more detailed kind. But a similar approach is surely worth considering.

# 8. Deponents as Exceptions

It is still a little hard, however, to see how a general concept of deponency might fit into it. The endings of, for example, *morior* or *sequor* form part of one problem, which is identified only in the context of the 'genera' of verbs, to use again the ancient term, more widely. A similar problem would be found in, for example, Ancient Greek and would involve again forms such as *boúlomai* 'I want (to)'. Given this problem in the case of Latin, that of, for example, *criminor*, with the meaning 'I accuse', would be part of or an extension of it. The traditional term 'deponent' could then have a use beyond this family, if similar problems can be identified. But this would not warrant any application where the problems are different. The relation, for example, of forms such as *facio* and *fio* is problematic in a very different way: as to how, in brief, we are to interpret evidence of near complementarity in meaning. To talk of *fio* as potentially 'deponent' would cast no light whatever on it.

However deponency might be identified, it remains presumably no more than an anomaly. By this I do not simply mean that it is not 'canonical': what is non-canonical in the sense of Corbett's contribution to this volume can be typical or normal in some individual languages. But deponents would by definition be exceptions to a regular pattern, in whatever language would be said to have them.

For many linguists an ideal structure is again the one implied by Bloomfield, in which words are divided into minimal signs. In his terminology these were morphemes each linked to a unit of meaning called a 'sememe'. It is an ideal not always realized. Therefore an account might be in general 'inferential-realizational'; not, in Stump's terms once more, 'lexical' and 'incremental'. Take, however, the structure in Latin of the active imperatives. We are concerned with two morphosyntactic oppositions: between, on the one hand, singular and plural; and, on the other, a lingering distinction between presents and what are described traditionally as 'futures'. This can again be presented as part of a paradigm. But the singular forms were, in the present, the bare stem; in the future, the stem suffixed by *-to*: schematically, Stem + *to*. The plural forms then had a further suffix *-te*: in the present, therefore, Stem + *te*; in the future, Stem + *to* + *te*. The pattern is of a type that is typical in, for example, Turkish; and, in whatever 'theoretical' or other framework it is described, would fit the Bloomfieldian ideal perfectly.

The example is one discussed, I think, by Jakobson, though I have failed to trace a reference. The point, however, is that while this pattern would be canonical from one general viewpoint, it is not at all canonical as part of the structure of Latin. The problems typical of this type of language are the ones which lead us to establish cumulative exponents; those where one solution is in terms of what I call 'extended exponence'; and so on. The term 'extended exponence' would refer, I repeat, to a solution to a problem, which does not strictly have to be addressed in that way. But it is a problem that we might say is canonical in the analysis of verbs in Latin: though, unlike the one posed by the active imperatives, this solution 'deviates' from the Bloomfieldian ideal. In passing, therefore, I have never seen convincing reasons to describe all languages in the same way. It is not simply that we need no general 'theory'. It is unilluminating, on the one hand, to fit the inflections of Latin to the Procrustean bed of early structuralism. Hill's sketch in the 1950s, in comparison with his account of English, may perhaps stand as a warning (1958: Appendix B). But what is canonical in Latin is not so already in, for example, English. That is, again, the problems are different. It may be unilluminating to describe either language as if they were the same.

This may be repugnant to the way most linguists see their discipline. Logically, however, other things that might be non-canonical in a general sense could nevertheless be typical in some instances. Take, for example suppletion. It is tempting to perceive it as in general an anomaly, as in cases such as those of Latin FERO 'carry', English GO, and so on. In principle, however, a distinction that we could describe as morphosyntactic might be realized in general by stems that were formally different. It might, for example, be of aspect; and semantically too regular to ascribe to the 'Aktionsart' of related lexemes. But if that were now the answer to our problem, suppletion would be typical of this system.

This may be a mere flight of imagination. But other non-canonical patterns cannot but be anomalous. One is that of Latin AIO 'say', as a verb whose paradigm was defective. The problem, that is, is not simply that it included fewer forms than others. It is that forms were not used where they could be reasonably expected, by analogy with those we do find, in the constructions that the verb does enter into. A deponent verb, in modern treatments, is again defined by contrast with the normal pattern, in which an ending such as Latin -*or* would realize an active. That is the basis for the cross-linguistic definition generally assumed by the contributors to this volume: as a case where morphosyntactic properties are realized, exceptionally, by forms that usually realize their opposites. But in any alternative definition it might still be, of its nature, an exception to whatever would be normal. The language might be one in which exceptions, this included, would be common. But as exceptions they could never be regular in it, as a 'non-canonical' pattern such as cumulative exponence, for example, can be.

# References

Barwick, Karl. 1922. *Remmius Palaemon und die römische Ars grammatica*. Leipzig: Dieterich.

—— (ed.). 1964. *Flauii Sosipatri Charisii Artis grammaticae libri V*, 2nd edn. Leipzig: Teubner.

Bazell, Charles E. 1958. *Linguistic typology*. London: School of Oriental and African Studies.

Dixon, Robert M. W. 1994. *Ergativity*. Cambridge: Cambridge University Press.

Glare, P. G. W. (ed.). 1962. *Oxford Latin dictionary*. Oxford: Clarendon Press..

Harris, Zellig S. 1951. *Methods in structural linguistics*. Chicago: University of Chicago Press.

Hill, Archibald A. 1958. *Introduction to linguistic structures: from sound to sentence in English*. New York: Harcourt, Brace.

Holtz, Louise. 1981. *Donat et la tradition de l'enseignement grammatical*. Paris: CNRS.

Keil, Heinrich. (ed.). 1855. *Grammatici latini*, vol. 2. Leipzig: Teubner.

Lewis, Carlton T., and Charles Short. 1879. *A Latin dictionary, founded on Andrews' edition of Freund's Latin Dictionary*. Oxford: Clarendon Press.

Liddell, Henry George and Robert Scott. 1940. *A Greek-English Lexicon*, new edn by H. Stuart Jones. Oxford: Clarendon Press.

Matthews, P. H. 1972. *Inflectional morphology*. Cambridge: Cambridge University Press.

Matthews, P. H. 2001. *A short history of structural linguistics*. Cambridge: Cambridge University Press.

Stump, Gregory T. 2001. *Inflectional morphology: a theory of paradigm structure*. Cambridge: Cambridge University Press.

# Subject Index

accusative case, 3n3, 28, 31–4, 39, 49, 63, 65, 97–102, 104n8, 105, 107, 109, 111–15, 118–20, 175, 187, 191, 192n19, 232, 235, 235n4, 265, 299, 304, 311

agreement, 4, 14, 17, 23, 28, 36–7, 39n9, 48, 55, 57, 59–64, 84, 177, 178n3, 180–3, 185, 187–91, 193–8, 271–95

analogy, 209, 222–3, 225, 229, 245, 314

anti-periphrasis, 28

applicative,180, 204–5, 208–16, 219, 221–2, 227–8

argument structure, 5, 8, 61–2, 91, 120, 178n5, 187–8, 195, 195n22, 203, 207, 217, 285, 286

athematic, 232–4, 235–41, 242–4, 246–7, 250–1, 252–63

canonical deponency, 31–5, 47, 71–4, 85–7, 90, 184, 231, 264

case, 28, 32, 37, 40, 49, 55–6, 58, 60–2, 65, 74, 91, 101, 111, 115, 119, 121, 164–6, 177–9, 181, 183n11, 188, 192–3, 274, 304, 311–12

causative, 7, 83n10, 84, 118, 138–9, 142, 203–6, 208–12, 215–23, 227–8, 265, 274, 283, 307

computational / computable, 147, 172

conjugation class, 6, 8, 16, 68, 83–4, 91, 128, 142, 148–9, 151–4, 157, 178n3, 197, 283, 285–6, 288–90

contrariness of form and meaning, 71–3, 85–7

conversational implicature, 82–3, 90

corpus, 100n5, 242, 253, 305

DATR, 147–9, 151

deadjectival, 51, 63, 66, 128, 137–9, 142, 239

declarative, 147, 171

default, 8, 53, 67, 74, 84, 145–51, 154, 156–61, 163–8, 170–2, 257, 259n20, 261, 277

defectiveness, 2n2, 14, 16, 27, 29, 30, 33, 46–8, 62, 64–7, 71–2, 74, 86–7, 146, 150, 162–4, 167, 171, 244, 246, 253, 263–5

denominal, 84, 90, 128, 137–9, 142

derivational, 50–1, 66, 83, 130, 203–4, 228–9, 233, 237–40, 242, 244–5, 247–8, 251–4, 257, 263–4, 271, 282, 284–9, 291, 306

diachrony, 51, 68, 97–121, 223–4, 248, 265, 272, 277, 293

exceptional / exceptionality, 5, 6, 23, 35, 39n10, 41, 47–9, 66–7, 72, 87, 97, 120, 147, 158, 164, 165, 181n7, 190, 194, 249, 265, 297, 313–14

exponent / exponence, 4, 17, 24–5, 56, 71–2, 86, 211, 214, 222–3, 297, 305, 312–13

formal / formally, 2, 4, 30, 146, 147, 150, 151, 152, 156, 157, 164, 166, 167, 172, 188, 191n17, 193, 218, 223, 234

form-deponent, 73–4, 87–8, 94

gap, morphological/paradigmatic, 14, 28, 150, 159, 206, 217, 222–4

generalized referral, 34

Google, 242–3, 248, 253–4

heteroclisis, 14, 16, 27, 28, 31, 45, 47, 49, 64, 65, 67, 146, 164, 168, 170–2

homophony, accidental, 223

imperfective deponent, 160–1

ineffability, 254, 263–4

inference / inferred, 149, 232

infix, 243, 247–9, 253–4, 260

innovation, historical 51, 79, 109, 117, 219, 226, 277

intransitive(s), 3n3, 6–8, 10–13, 33, 93, 101, 109, 115, 133, 134–5, 171n5, 179–80, 181, 183n11, 185–8, 193, 194–5, 196–7, 204, 206, 217, 219, 222, 227, 275, 280, 281n9, 283, 285–6, 288–9, 292, 306

learnability, 231–3, 254
lexeme(s), 3, 10, 12, 24, 25, 27–31, 34–5, 38,
    47–9, 50, 53, 55, 64, 66–7, 72–3, 80, 84,
    128, 140–2, 165–6, 168, 169, 171, 297–8,
    302, 305–7, 309, 310, 314
lexical entry, 121n18, 149, 152–4, 157–8, 161,
    164, 166, 169, 170, 255, 264
lexical semantics, 182n9
lexicalize(d) / lexicalization, 206, 209, 210–11,
    217, 227, 292
lexical-paradigmatic deponency, 10
long-distance effects, 213


meaningless formatives, 211, 214–16
middle / middle/passive, 2n2, 3n3, 74–91,
    99–106, 109–16, 118–23, 274, 309
mirror principle, 212
mismatch, vii, 1, 2, 3, 4, 5, 7, 14, 45–69, 85,
    145, 150, 160, 167, 175, 177, 181, 182,
    195n22, 206, 211–13, 227, 228, 231, 234,
    264, 266, 302, 303, 308
morphophonology, 51, 207, 211, 213, 214,
    215–16, 219, 222, 225, 226, 228


Network Morphology, 22, 34, 147–72
non-canonical transitive, 143
non-compositional, 210
number, 5, 12, 60, 65
numeral, 14, 63


overdifferentiation, 27, 28, 30, 39
override, 74, 145–7, 150, 158, 159, 163, 170,
    171, 172


palatalization, 208–9, 213–15, 220, 221
paradigmatic deponency, 7–10
periphrasis, 1n1, 4, 12–13, 25, 30, 54, 84, 85,
    88, 307
phonotactics, 232, 250–1, 256, 266, 289n15
physical affectedness, 128, 132–7, 143
polarity, 14–16
possessive adjective, 51–3, 61, 67
property-deponent, 71–4, 87–91, 94
pseudo-causative, 205–6 186, 211, 216–23
pseudo-passive, 205–6, 223–7


reciprocal, 81–2, 99, 104n8, 118, 119, 217,
    274–5

reflexive, 3, 81–2, 90–2, 99, 104, 118, 119,
    194, 293
root, deponent, 128, 137, 139–41


semantic drift, 224
semantic scope, 212–3
semi-deponent, 10–13, 34, 64, 137, 141,
    145–7, 150, 151, 160–1, 171
stative, 5, 93, 104, 119, 183, 184, 191n7, 197,
    228n18, 282
stem, 5, 10, 11–15, 22–5, 27, 30, 33, 39,
    40–1, 60, 61, 76, 105n9, 118n12, 128,
    137, 141, 142, 146, 148–9, 151, 152–5,
    160, 164–9, 171, 203–28, 232–40, 242–4,
    246–53, 255–66, 272, 290–4, 297, 307–9,
    313–14
suppletion / suppletive, 12, 23, 25–6, 30, 39,
    41, 128, 164, 169–71, 264, 275–7, 298,
    306–9, 314
surname, 52–3, 64, 67
syntactico-semantic verb classes, 127–37,
    195n22


template, 180, 193, 195, 211–13, 216, 221,
    225
theme vowel, 148–55, 157, 159, 232n2, 236
transitive / transitivity, 6–13, 33, 48, 75, 92–3,
    97–113, 115–6, 118–20, 133n3, 134, 135,
    142–3, 177–81, 183–5, 187–98, 204–6,
    208–9, 211, 213–23, 227n17, 228, 231,
    273–5, 282–5, 286n12, 288, 299, 304


underdetermination, 241, 245, 249, 263,
    255


valency (verbs), 4, 7, 204, 207
variation, 2, 24n4, 90, 242, 245, 255–6, 301,
    305–6
voice, active, vii, 1–4, 7–10, 12–13, 29, 32, 33,
    48, 65, 71–2, 74–5, 80–3, 85, 89–90,
    100n4, 107n18, 118, 127, 138, 141, 142,
    145, 150, 156–8, 160, 163, 175, 176, 177,
    179–84, 186–8, 190–2, 196–7, 231–2, 264,
    283, 297, 298–314
voice, passive, vii, 1–5, 7–8, 12, 13, 9, 29, 32,
    72–4, 77, 79, 90–1, 99, 101, 105, 114–19,
    120–1, 127, 142–3, 146, 150, 184, 192,
    204, 226, 228, 264, 274, 297,309
voice, antipassive, 48, 64–5, 176–92, 194,
    195n21, 197

# Language Index

Amele, 293
Amurdak, 272, 273
Arabic, 14, 100n4
Archi, 39–41, 146, 147, 148, 160, 163–71, 171

Bantu, ix, 203–30
Basque, 178n5, 193–6, 197, 293
Belhare, 13n8, 293
Bemba, 213–14, 223n14
Bininj Gun-wok, 294

Chechen, 13n8
Chichewa, 203, 210, 211, 212
Chimwiini, 218–19
Chukchi/Chukchee, 48–9, 50, 64, 65, 176–98, 264, 265
Ciyao, 209, 213, 215n7, 216–17, 221
Cree, 293

Estonian, 62
Ewe, 293

Fijian, 5
French, 100n4, 192n19, 237n6, 298

Gaagudju, 292
Ganda, 219–23, 227n17, 265
Garig, see Ilgar
Georgian, 178n5
German, 46, 49, 63, 263
Gothic, 16–17
Greek, viii, 2n2, 29, 97–123, 145, 160, 182, 192, 197, 309, 312
Gujarati, 23
Gunwinyguan, 294

Hebrew, 14
Hindi-Urdu, 46, 51, 55–61, 67, 178n5, 192

Ika, 13n8
Ilgar/Garig, 271–95
Indo-Aryan, 58, 61, 62
Indo-European, viii, 51, 56, 118n12, 298
Italian, 293
Itelmen, 191–2
Iwaidja, ix, 271–95

Japanese, 54, 55, 64, 67

Kayardild, 58n3
Keres, 5
Ket, 292
Kinande, 205, 211, 216, 217
Kinyamwezi, 223–8
Kiowa, 293
Kolami, 28
Koryak, 177n2, 181n7

Lango, 5
Latin, vii, viii, 1–2, 3n3, 4, 5, 7, 10, 13, 14, 16, 18, 29, 33, 47–8, 65–6, 71–4, 85–6, 90–1, 97, 99n3, 100n4, 105n9, 117, 118n14, 127–43, 145, 146, 147, 148, 149, 150–63, 164, 171, 175, 177, 178, 182–5, 192, 193, 197, 228, 231, 238n8, 264, 265, 297–314
Luvale, 209–10

Maltese, 28
Manangkari, 272, 273
Marrku, 272, 273
Mawng, 272, 273, 277, 278–9, 290–1

Miraña, 23
Mongo, 213, 215
Muna, 92–4

Ngiyambaa, 6
Nimboran, 293
Nyakyusa, 214–16, 217n8

Pali, 79
Polish, 26
Portuguese, 237n7

Romani, 46, 60, 61, 62
Russian, 26, 27–8, 46, 50–3, 54, 55, 56, 61, 62–3, 64, 65, 66–7, 151

Sanskrit, viii, 61, 74–87, 87–91, 92, 93, 94, 103n7, 105n9, 195n22, 309
Serbian, 39, 41

Serbo-Croatian, 189–91
Shona, 208
Slovene, 33–4, 35
Sora, 91–2
Spanish, ix, 68, 229, 231–66

Takelma, 10–13, 293
Tiwi, 293
Tolowa Athabaskan, 293
Tsez, 17–18, 32, 35–8, 39, 41, 49, 65, 86n11, 306, 309
Tübatulabal, 14–15
Turkish, 313

Upper Sorbian, 61

Wurrugu, 272, 273

Yurok, 7–10, 191n18

# Author Index

Abasheikh, Mohammed, 218–19
Alexiadou, Artemis, 99n2, 119
Alsina, Alex, 205, 207, 212
Anagnostopoulou, Elena, 99n2, 119, 192n19
Anceaux, J., 293
Anshen, Frank, viii, xi, 127–43
Ansre, Gilbert, 293
Aronoff, Mark, viii, xi, 74, 105n9, 120,
    127–43, 151, 153, 266, 299
Arregi, Karlos, 236, 241, 259n20
Arya, Ravi Prakash, 77–82

Babiniotis, Giorgos, 107
Bachrach, Asaf, 237n7
Baerman, Matthew, viii, xi, 1–19, 22, 26, 28, 30,
    31, 34, 51n1, 99n3, 145, 146, 147, 150, 155,
    164, 175, 176, 184, 191n18, 231, 264, 293
Baker, Mark, 203, 207, 212, 294n19
Baldi, Philip, 117, 128
Barwick, Karl, 301
Bayer, Josef, 187
Bazell, Charles E., 312
Bennett, Charles, 127
Benveniste, Émile, 236
Berg, René van den, 93
Bermúdez-Otero, Ricardo, ix, xi, 229, 231–69
Bickel, Balthasar, 13n8
Biligiri, Hemmige Shriniwasarangachar, 92
Birkmann, Thomas, 17
Bittner, Maria, 188n14
Blevins, Juliette, 7, 9–10
Bloomfield, Maurice, 75, 80, 308, 313
Bobaljik, Jonathan David, viii, ix, 48,
    175–201, 235n4, 264, 265, 266
Boguslavskaja, Ol'ga, 61
Bok-Bennema, Reineke, 188
Bommelyn, Loren, 293
Bonet, Eulàlia, 192n19, 241, 250
Börjars, Kersti, 120
Boškovic, Željko, 189–90
Branigan, Phil, 177, 178n4, 184, 185, 188, 191
Brown, Dunstan, 22, 26, 31, 34, 51n1, 148,
    151, 155
Burrow, T., 75
Burzio, Luigi, 119n16

Bybee, Joan, see Hooper, Joan Bybee
Bye, Patrick, 264

Cahill, Lynn, 147
Capell, Arthur, 272
Chapman, Carol, 120
Chomsky, Noam, 119n16, 244, 257, 263, 304,
    310, 312
Chumakina, Marina, 40–1
Clairis, Christos, 107
Cohen, Marcel, 100n4
Cole, Jennifer, 238
Colina, Sonia, 250
Comrie, Bernard, 18, 22n1, 32, 35–8, 177,
    178n2, 181, 183, 185, 191n17, 192
Contreras, Heles, 237
Corbett, Greville G., viii, xi, 17, 21–43, 45,
    47, 49, 51, 61, 64, 68, 86n11, 99n3, 101n6,
    146–7, 148, 155, 176, 184, 196, 229,
    235n4, 264, 266, 302, 306, 309, 313

Debrunner, Albert, 105
Delbrück, Berthold, 94
Dembetembe, N. C., 208
Den Os, Els, 237
Dench, Alan, 58
Di Sciullo, Anna-Maria, 120
Dixon, Robert M. W., 304
Donaldson, Tamsin, 6
D'Ooge, Benj L., 184
Downing, Laura, J., 207
Draeger, Anton, 117
Duhoux, Yves, 118n12
Dunn, Michael, 178n4, 179, 180, 184, 197
Durie, Mark, 196

Eddington, David, 238, 242
Edgerton, Franklin, 75, 80
Embick, David, 29n7, 120, 127, 143, 192n20
Emeneau, Murray B., 28
Ernout, Alfred, 3n3, 150

Evans, Nicholas, ix, xi, 22, 31, 34, 58, 148, 271–96
Evans, Roger, 147–9
Everaert, Martin, 119n16

Fanselow, Gisbert, 263
Felíu, Elena, 241
Féry, Caroline, 263
Flobert, Pierre, 5, 128, 129n1, 140, 150
Frank, Paul, 13n8
Franks, Steven, 189n15
Fraser, Norman M., 22, 148

Gazdar, Gerald, 147–9
Givón, T., 293
Glare, P. G., 129, 307
Gonda, Jan, 118n12
Good, Jeff, ix, xii, 203–30, 265
Greenberg, 312
Greenough, J. B., 184
Grice, H. P., 82n9
Grimshaw, Jane, 120n18
Guthrie, Malcolm, 224

Hale, Ken, 177, 178n4, 188n4
Halle, Morris, 120n17, 177, 178n4
Harbour, Daniel, 235n4
Harris, James W., 232n2, 236, 241, 249, 250, 251, 259n20
Harris, Z. S., 311
Harvey, Mark, 292
Haspelmath, Martin, 28
Hayes, Bruce, 256
Heath, Jeffrey, 195n21, 276
Hertz, 301, 302
Hetzron, Robert, 14, 61
Hill, Archibald A., 313
Hinch, Heather E., 272
Hippisley, Andrew, viii, xii, 145–73
Hofmann, Johann Baptist, 3n3
Holton, David, 107
Holtz, Louise, 300
Hooper, Joan Bybee, 237
Hopper, Paul, 142
Horrocks, Geoffrey, 98n1, 105
Horton, A. E., 209–10
Howard, A. A., 184
Hualde, José Ignacio, 193, 194
Hulstaert, G., 213
Humbert, Jean, 100n4

Hyman, Larry, M., 205, 207, 209, 210, 212, 213–15, 219–23, 227n17, 265

Inkelas, Sharon, 238, 293

Jaeggli, Osvaldo, 246
Jakobson, Roman, 303, 304, 313
Jannaris, Antonius N., 98n1, 105
Jones, Stuart, 309
Joseph, Brian, 122
Joshi, K. L., 77–82

Kager, René, 237
Katre, Sumitra Mangesh, 82, 84, 90
Keil, Heinrich, 301
Kemmer, Suzanne, 2n2, 118
Kennedy, Benjamin, 150
Kibrik, Aleksandr E., 40, 61, 164
Kiparsky, Paul, 91, 104, 120, 127, 142, 143, 228, 237, 238
Kittredge, G. L., 184
Kodzasov, Sandro V., 40
Koot, Hans van de, 256
Koptjevskaja-Tamm, Maria, 60
Kozinsky, Issac S., 180
Kratzer, Angelika, 120
Kühner, Raphael, 3n3, 150

Laka, Itziar, 193, 194, 195
Larrimore, Bonnie, 287
Lavidas, Nikolaos, viii, xii, 97–126, 145, 309
Lázaro Mora, Fernando, 246
Levin, Beth, 128, 129, 130, 131n2, 132, 133
Lewis, Carlton T., 299, 305, 307
Liddell, Henry George, 309
Lieber, Rochelle, 120
Lloret, Maria-Rosa, 241

McCarthy, John, 23n3
Mchombo, Sam A., 205, 210
Mackridge, Peter, 107
MacWhinney, Brian, 190n16
Maganga, Clement, 217, 224–7
Manney, Linda, 119
Marantz, Alec, 120n17, 236n5
Marten, Lutz, 227

Mascaró, Joan, 241
Masica, Colin P., 61
Matras, Yaron, 60
Matthews, Peter, ix, xii, 22, 27, 34, 182n9,
    184, 193, 264, 266, 297–315
Mayser, Edwin, 105, 106
Meeussen, A. E., 204
Meillet, Antoine, 117
Meinhof, Carl, 214
Mel'cuk, Igor, 28
Méndez-Dosuna, Julián, 244, 246
Menn, Lise, 190n16
Miller, Wick R., 5
Mithun, Marianne, 294n19
Mohanan, Tara, 61
Morales-Front, Alfonso, 258


Nash, Léa, 188
Nedjalkov, Vladimir P., 178n5, 181, 183n11
Neeleman, Ad, 256
Ngunga, Armindo, 209, 215n7, 216, 217n8
Nichols, Johanna, 13n8, 203
Noonan, Michael, 5
Nordlinger, Rachel, 58n2
Núñez-Cedeño, Rafael A., 258n


Oltra-Massuet, Isabel, 236, 241, 259n20
Oostendorp, Marc van, 263
Ortiz de Urbina, Jon, 193, 194, 196


Palsule, Gajanan Balkrishna, 87n12
Panini, 82, 84, 90
Papangeli, Dimitra, viii, xii, 97–126, 145,
    309
Payne, John, 61
Pensado (Ruiz), Carmen, 239, 244, 246
Pesetsky, David, 99n2, 189n15, 205
Peterson, David, 205
Philippaki-Warburton, Irene, 107
Polinsky, Maria, 36, 37
Polkinghorne, John, 22n2
Prince, Alan, 256
Pym, Noreen, 287


Rainer, Franz, 237n7, 241
Ramamurti, G. V., 92
Reinhart, Tanya, 99n2, 119
Rezac, Milan, 193

Richards, Norvin, 188
Rivero, Maria-Luisa, 119
Robins, R. H., 7–8
Roca, Iggy, 234, 241, 244, 253n16, 258, 261


Sadler, Louisa, 29n7, 127, 143, 228
Sapir, Edward, 10–13, 293
Schadeberg, Thilo, 207, 208, 217, 224–7
Schumann, C., 214
Schütz, Albert J., 5
Schwyzer, Eduard, 105
Scott, R., 309
Šebková, Hana, 60
Seifart, Frank, 23
Short, Charles, 299, 305, 307
Siloni, Tal, 119
Singer, Ruth, 272, 277, 278n5
Skorik, Piotr Ja., 178n4, 180, 181n7, 184,
    196, 197
Smirniotopoulos, Jane, 122
Smolensky, Paul, 256
Snell, Rupert, 59
Speijer, J. S., 75n5
Spencer, Andrew, viii, xii, 23, 29n7, 45–70,
    127, 143, 177n2, 178n4, 180, 184, 185,
    228, 229, 264, 265, 266
Sportiche, Dominique, 119n16
Stewart, Thomas, 73n4
Stump, Gregory, viii, xii, 22, 29n7, 31, 71–95,
    100n4, 103n7, 105n9, 151, 195n22, 228,
    264, 265, 298, 309, 313
Suthar, Babubhai Kohyabhai, 23
Szantyr, Anton, 3n3


Ter Meulen, Alice, 119n15
Terrell, Tracy, 237
Theophanopoulou-Kontou, Dimitra, 98n1,
    120
Thomas, François, 3n3, 150
Thompson, Sandra, A., 142
Trubetzkoy, 303, 304
Tsimpli, Ianthi-Maria, 119


Uuspõld, Elen, 62


Vajda, Edward, 292, 293n17
Valmet, Aino, 62
Vendryes, Joseph, 100n4, 105n9

Ventcel', Tat'jana, 60
Vincent, Nigel, 120
Voegelin, Charles F., 14–16

Wagner, Michael, 237n7
Waltermire, Mark, 258
Wechsler, Stephen, 39n9
Weightman, Simon, 59
Wharram, Douglas, 188n14
Whitney, William Dwight, 82n8, 84
Williams, Edwin, 120
Williams, Joy, 289n14

Wilson, Colin, 256
Wurmbrand, Susi, 179, 187

Xu, Zheng, viii, xii, 127–43, 182n9, 265

Zaliznjak, Andrej A., 22n1
Zhukova, Alevtina N., 177n2
Zlatic, Larisa, 39n9
Žlnayová, Edita, 60
Zombolou, Katerina, 104n8, 107, 118